BURNING UP THE AIR

"They're oA Here!"

STEVE ELMAN & ALAN TOLZ

BURNING UP

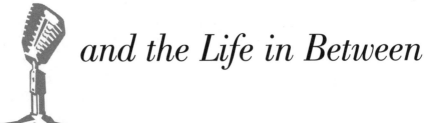

Jerry Williams,

Talk Radio,

and the Life in Between

THE AIR

COMMONWEALTH EDITIONS
Beverly, Massachusetts

Library of Congress Cataloging-in-Publication Data
Elman, Steve.
  Burning up the air : Jerry Williams, talk radio, and the life in between / Steve Elman and Alan Tolz.
    p. cm.
  Includes bibliographical references and index.
  ISBN-13: 978-1-933212-51-7 (alk. paper)
  ISBN-10: 1-933212-51-9 (alk. paper)
  1. Williams, Jerry, 1923– 2. Radio broadcasters—United States—Biography. I. Tolz, Alan. II. Title

  PN 1991.4.W53E46 2007
  791.4402'8092—dc22
  [B]   2007044964

Cover design by John Barnett / 4 Eyes Design
Interior design by Ann Twombly
Printed in the USA

Commonwealth Editions is an imprint of Memoirs Unlimited, Inc., 266 Cabot Street, Beverly, Massachusetts 01915. Visit us on the Web at www.commonwealtheditions.com.

To Joanne and Deborah

and every talk radio producer, everywhere

CONTENTS

Authors' Note

We decided early in the research phase of this book that we would not present it as a dispassionate biography. We wanted to take you through the eras of Jerry Williams's life as much as possible from his point of view. We also knew that a fair assessment called for us to hold Jerry's life at arm's length and step away from our protagonist from time to time to give you the unpolished truth about broadcasting realities as we see them.

This approach called for us to fantasize some conversations and to add speculative detail based on our own experience and the experience of others who know broadcasting well.

We have endeavored to support every fact in this book with research. In some cases, we have had to reconcile conflicting accounts of particular incidents using our knowledge of Jerry's personality and the realities of radio. In some cases, we have deduced what probably happened and written those passages accordingly.

When words appear in quotation marks, those statements are as Jerry himself said or recalled them on the air or in interviews, as one of our interviewees reported them, as we remember them, or as they can be inferred from accounts in interviews or Jerry's monologues. When words appear in indented passages, they are direct quotations from archive materials, original articles, or radio or television airchecks, with the exception of the Gag Busters scripts on pages 72–74, which we have slightly modified. When dialogue appears without quotation marks, it is our imagination of what may have been said in a particular situation.

And one more thing: throughout this book, we spell *mic* as we think it should be spelled—it's short for microphone, not somebody's nickname.

INTRODUCTION

Almost forty thousand hours, talking on the radio. It is barely comprehensible.

Let's be clear: talking on the radio is different from what most of us do during our working lives. Lots of us work more than forty thousand hours in our careers. Forty thousand hours on the time clock is just a twenty-year tally of fifty workweeks a year. But those hours include the coffee breaks, the bathroom time, the morning-after schmoozing, the staring out the window, the mind-in-neutral meetings.

We're talking about hours *on the air,* on the radio, as a talk show host, carrying the entire load, without a playlist of tunes to give you three or four or ten minutes to think about what you're going to say next. This is almost forty thousand hours without a place to rest.

Jerry Williams amassed more than 39,650 hours of talk radio in forty-seven years—from 1955, when he started doing a real talk show on WIBG in Philadelphia, to 2002, when he did his last shows on WROL in Boston. If you add in his television time, his days as a country music DJ, his comedy shows with Bud Smith, all the other hits and misses of his broadcast career, he probably spent more than 45,400 hours on the air. That's one of the biggest numbers in broadcast history.

What about the other guys—Larry King, for example? Let's get out the calculator. By 1994 (when he left radio behind) Larry—the iron man of broadcasting, by any measure—had logged a bit more than 37,600 radio hours in thirty-three years. Not all of that was talk, though; he did some music too. If we add his television work, we get more than 44,500 hours in broadcasting by the end of 2007. So make no mistake, this guy is no slouch—and he's "just gettin' stahted," as he said on that old CNN promo for his nightly interview show. He'll probably be adding at least 340 TV hours a year doing *Larry King*

Live until that title no longer applies. Bottom line: he'll pass Jerry Williams's grand total of 45,400 in May 2010.

How about Don Imus? The I-man started his radio career in 1968, ten years after Larry. In 1971 he started doing that heavy-lifting morning shift—at least four hours a day, sometimes six days a week. By the time CBS radio kicked him off the air in April 2007, he'd done his syndicated morning show for almost fourteen years and logged more than 42,000 hours on the radio—though he's been helped out, like so many others in morning radio, with side-kicks and regular characters. He passed Jerry Williams's talk total in February 2005, but he'll still have to work another three thousand hours to match Jerry's overall broadcast time.

Rush Limbaugh? Not even close. By the end of 2007, after twenty-three years of doing political talk on the radio, Rush had almost 18,000 hours under his belt. Just to match Jerry Williams's hours as a radio talker, he'll have to work his same three hours a day, five days a week, with a few weeks off for vacation, for at least another thirty years, until he's eighty-six.

And there are hundreds more who don't come close, people still working the front forty of their radio careers—Howard and Hannity, Liddy and Dr. Laura, and all those other names you know.

The stats are one part of the story, and by their measure Jerry Williams stands toe-to-toe with some of the biggest names in talk. But the numbers can't tell you what Jerry Williams's work means in the history of American broadcasting.

He was one of a handful of masters—no, not just masters, *originators*—of the craft of talk radio. In the Old Testament of talk radio, before the coming of Rush, he was one of the Major Prophets. Of all those great first talkers, only Bob Grant, who retired from WOR in New York early in 2006, lasted longer on the air than Jerry Williams. The next generation—Michael Jackson in LA, Gene Burns in San Francisco, and a handful of others—still keep the faith, doing what might now be called Classic Talk, the style Jerry Williams pioneered.

In the fifties, sixties, seventies, eighties, and well into the nineties, Jerry Williams was a force of nature, Someone to Be Reckoned With. For four decades every radio person in America who wanted to do this kind of broadcasting needed to come to terms with Jerry Williams's work—even if he or she didn't know his name or hadn't actually heard him.

He was out there, doing it, showing the way, proving it could draw listeners and make money, for five years before talk radio began to blossom, for ten years before it became common, for fifteen years before it became a "format." Other talk hosts could do things like him or they could do things differently, but he had defined such a huge area of talk radio turf, made it synonymous with his style, his manner, his method, that his way of doing talk became *the* way of doing talk. On the strength of his achievements alone, it wasn't possible to ignore him. And once you'd actually heard him—heard the ringing sonorities of that voice that made every minute of his best shows as thrilling as a ride on a roller coaster, heard the way he seized an issue by the throat and wouldn't let go—you knew that this was *it,* the way talk radio was supposed to be.

He talked on the radio for 39,652 hours: interviewing people, dueling with callers, delivering those incomparable monologues that were part commentary, part drama, part entertainment, all Jerry.

Here's what it's like when you're actually doing those hours, when you're a talk radio host on the air: you're balancing the listener on your shoulders as you walk a tightrope of words. You can't daydream or go blank or phone it in. You have to think ahead of your mouth all the time. The platforms at the ends of that tightrope—the commercials and the newscasts—give you places to relax momentarily. But you're still carrying all those listeners.

You have to give them a reason to stay with you, right after this word from our sponsors, immediately following the day's top stories. Just before the breaks, you have to be brilliant and tantalizing. During the breaks, you have to keep your energy up—and sometimes you have to do the breaks as well, putting on the salesman's blazer or the newsman's slouch hat, playing an entirely different role without betraying a shift in your persona. And just after the breaks, you have to return to your real radio self, fascinate immediately, hold on tight to that audience. Until the next break.

Paradoxically, most listeners aren't even paying close attention to what you're saying. Over decades of listening to radio and television, people have learned to filter, to use the flow of words as background and bring things up to the top of their minds only when they hear you say words that are important to them. That doesn't mean they ignore you. They expect you to keep the stream going, to continue a logical train of thought, to guide your guest from question to question, to be in complete control of that little corner of reality you've been allowed. If you waver, if you're unsure, if you break the flow—God help you, if you lose your place and there is unstructured silence, if the air goes dead—you suffer the worst of all possible fates. The listener tunes out, leaving you to pick up the shards of the illusion as well as you can. You are shouting into a void.

But when you do your work well, over and over, hour after hour, day after day, week after week, you get good numbers. Your work results in consistent listening, which translates into statistics the station's salespeople can sell to advertisers, which translates into money in your pocket. You are a success.

Jerry Williams was a success. Few others in broadcasting have ever matched what he did. He was a phenomenal, prodigious success in Boston in the late fifties and early sixties, from his first month on the air. He went to Chicago in the late sixties and was an even *bigger* success. He came back to Boston in the seventies, rebuilt his success with local listeners, and reached hundreds of thousands more in thirty-seven other states. After a five-year midlife crisis, wandering from city to city, he came back to Boston for a third run at success in the eighties and nineties, and he did it *again.* Of his 39,652 talk radio hours, almost two-thirds were spent leading the markets in which he worked.

Most people in radio can only dream of such achievements.

Alan Tolz and I were two of his producers—as if anyone could "produce" Jerry Williams. At best, we were very junior partners in the enterprise. We were lucky to get his ear when he hadn't made his mind up on an issue, to bring an exciting guest to his attention, to identify a topic that might become controversial. Usually, we were getters. Get that Vietnam Veterans against the War guy. Get that broad who wrote the sex book. Get the governor. Get the senator. Get Eisenhower, Kennedy, Johnson, Carter, Bush.

We were lucky to be with him for part of the ride. We remember looking through the glass, watching him perform, listening to him work, learning from his skills, shaking our heads again and again at what we were privileged to witness. Those hours in the control room shaped our careers, matured us as radio people. We owe Jerry Williams, big time. That's why we wrote this book.

And as we wrote it, as we talked to the others who knew him, as we dug through the clippings and the letters, the scrapbooks and the tapes, we heard something else, in the words of others and emerging from our own memories in Jerry's own voice. It was the same message, and it was a surprise: it was not how significant his work was, not how important he was, not how much he accomplished. Instead, it was how much more he could have done, how much greater he could have been, if only, if only, if only . . .

Steve Elman

Avec le talent, on fait ce qu'on veut.
Avec le génie, on fait ce qu'on peut.

If someone has talent, he does what he wants.
If someone has genius, he does what he can.

—Jean-Auguste-Dominique Ingres,
cited by Julien Green in his journal

1  THE MOMENT

When it started—*really* started, that is, when people were supposed to get excited and call in and talk on the air, on 1510, the new WMEX in Boston—it was Jerry, a microphone, and a telephone on the table.

Not a picture phone, or a cell phone, or a Slimline phone, or even a Princess phone. It was one of those heavy Bakelite jobs with a perforated metal plate on the bottom that showed off some of its dark guts. You could have killed somebody with one of those phones.

There were two pseudo-brass bells inside. They didn't work, of course, because nobody actually wanted to hear the phone ringing on the air. Instead, the tech staff stuck a light on the phone and connected the light to the bell contacts inside.

When a call came in, the light went on.

When the light went on, the fun began.

Then it was Jerry, the microphone, the telephone, and a voice out there in the dark.

In 1957 they didn't call it talk radio. They didn't even call Jerry a talkmaster or a talk show host then.

If you understand one thing about the history of American radio, you understand a lot about it: once radio passed through its amateur hour in the teens, the era of the inventors and the tinkerers, it became a commercial product—and, after that (maybe only begrudgingly), a public service. Almost as soon as ordinary folks understood what radio could do, a lot of businesspeople realized they could make money with it. The first real radio stations in the United States, unlike those in most other countries, were privately owned, and the reason their owners put them on the air was to sell things.

Jerry Williams in the WMEX studio, 70 Brookline Avenue, Boston, ca. 1958.

One of the best products to sell was the medium itself. That's why KDKA in Pittsburgh reported the election results on November 2, 1920, telling everyone who could hear the station that Harding had beaten Cox. The idea was to sell more radios for Westinghouse, which owned the station. What better way to prove the value of the new medium than by scooping the newspapers with the biggest story of the fall? People who had radios knew what had happened. People who didn't were left asking others what was going on. And you can bet the stores downtown couldn't handle the customers demanding Westinghouse radios the week after the election.

Twenty-five stations in 1921 led to six hundred stations in 1923, and thousands of stations in the blink of an eye after that. All those amateur radio hounds were left in the dust—the people who'd been tinkering with wireless equipment, doing their own amateur broadcasting in their garages or basements. Still, some of them loved the medium so much that they'd be technicians for real radio stations, set up the transmitters and such, for nearly nothing.

Through the twenties and thirties, radio got to be a very big deal. Nearly every owner heard the early motto of the industry: a radio station license is a license to print money. The only problem was the fact that you needed an almost endless supply of stuff to fill the air between the commercials, stuff that wouldn't cost you an arm and a leg.

At first, you had to keep it highbrow most of the time. Get the local music school to send over someone to sing a few classical songs in the studio, or a string quartet to saw away for a while. You could persuade the newspaper to provide a reporter to tell folks what was going on in town or how the local teams were doing. Area colleges could give you somebody to talk about ancient Egypt or the atom or Shakespeare. Somebody from a dress shop could advise ladies on current fashions. The auto dealers could provide people who had tips about how to buy a car. People from the local charities could talk about diseases or underprivileged kids or war orphans. Preachers were excellent—they could fill Sunday mornings. (Some of them would even pay *you* to be on the air.) Pretty soon, everyone in town who had a pet project or an idea to save the world wanted to come on and give a lecture—still, they didn't cost you anything, so why not?

You could get people from the agricultural extension to get up early and do "sunrise shows" with the commodity prices for the farmers. You could get local pols to read the funny papers on Sunday mornings. You could get commentators to "edit" the news. You could hire a local organist, or an organ-piano duo, who could provide the transitions between programs or play a "musical interlude" when you needed to fill the time. You could make a deal with a local ballroom or club to carry live broadcasts of their concerts or entertainment. And there was always some eager beaver out there in the waiting room who had an idea for a radio show.

You had to have your own announcers to hold all the pieces together, but anybody who had a reasonably clear voice would do; if he started to ask for too much money, you could replace him.

By the late twenties, you had a new source of stuff: network shows coming out of New York and Chicago and Hollywood, a lot of them produced by ad agencies that smartened the networks up about listeners' habits and preferences. These shows made your local station sound pretty good—during the day they kept the housewives company with soap operas; in the early evening they fascinated the kids with space adventures and westerns; and when families would sit down after dinner, they'd present the bands, the comics, the singers, the stars. The networks and agencies could make their money with national ads because they were on stations coast to coast.

Fast forward, through the sale of millions of radios, the big Art Deco boxes supplanting the hearth at the center of millions of homes, the triumph of the radio networks, the heyday of the great radio series and dramas, the comedy and variety shows, the big band broadcasts and live news remotes . . . to the fifties, the time of the Great TV Threat. The little glass picture was supposed to bury the big old box, or so the experts said.

But radio had an odd resilience: it was like Silly Putty. You tried to squeeze it into one little niche in life, and it popped out somewhere else. When TV came along, radio's innate advantages suddenly became obvious. You could take it with you. You could listen to it in your car. It was great company. It didn't ask you to look at it.

So, as the forties became the fifties, radio people discovered there was still plenty of profit to be made if you were smart.

A few of them had the same great idea: make the audience part of the program. Turn the people who were consuming the product into part of the product: reality radio. Talk about filling time on the cheap! They interviewed ordinary people who came to watch their shows, got them to come up onstage and make fools of themselves, surveyed men and women on the street.

Then they asked their listeners to call in with questions, with opinions, with problems. The telephone became part of the basic equipment of broadcasting.

Whenever Jerry Williams, born Gerald Jacoby in Brooklyn in 1923, a wiseass kid with plenty of smarts, heard radio shows that used the telephone, he was fascinated. But he also knew instinctively that there was something wrong.

For example, the way that John J. Anthony did his advice show on Mutual's "The Goodwill Hour." Anthony spoke to people on the phone, but because of the network's concern about things these ordinary people might say, the callers' voices weren't on the air. Anthony paraphrased what they said. "You say your husband doesn't love you any more? What makes you say that? Oh, I see. He's coming home later and later. Hmm. Doesn't seem to like your pot roast any more. Tell me more, dear. Oh, he's not listening to what you say? Well, never fear. *I'm* listening. Now, this is what I think you should do . . ." The big phony.

And there was that husband-and-wife team on KDKA, Ed and Wendy King. Big signal, KDKA. Even though it was in Pittsburgh, most of the country could pick it up on a good night. The Kings' show, *Party Line,* was just getting started back then. They took calls—again, you couldn't hear what the folks on the phone were saying. They asked people for stories about their pets, or about their kids, or about their vacations, and Ed and Wendy would repeat the stories and ask some questions and repeat the answers and then say something like "Isn't that nice." And every once in a while they would have a little puzzle or a contest on the air. It was like having your aunt and uncle over for coffee every night.

Jerry knew there was a better way, but to find out what actually worked on the air, he'd have to do his own telephone show regularly. And he didn't get the chance to try that until 1951, after winning decorations from years of service in the radio wars—that Oak Leaf Cluster you get when you lie to land your first job, the Purple Heart that comes with getting fired, the Silver Star for being Hot Young DJ of the Moment.

That first talk show ran from 12:15 to 1:00 every weekday afternoon on WKDN in Camden, New Jersey. Jerry called it *What's on Your Mind?* He had to listen to what the caller said, paraphrase it, make his *own* point, listen to the reply. He sounded like he was arguing with himself. But he learned a lot about how to make it work.

He tried talk again late in 1956, when *The Jerry Williams Show* aired on WIBG in Philadelphia. This time it was three hours a night, in the wee hours. Interviews with pols and personalities, talk about hot issues and showbiz, sometimes a record or two, and one-way phone calls again, all originating live from a restaurant downtown, where people sometimes paid attention and sometimes didn't. That was where he found the formula: the show had to be fast-paced. The audience had to feel that something exciting was always just about to happen. The host had to be outspoken. There had to be an edge to each interview, a challenge to each caller on the phone.

Jerry thought: if you take these phone calls and interviews, put them together with pointed commentary and short monologues on the state of the world, build them around a dynamic guy at the center, a guy who is street-smart and funny, a guy who represents the interests of the little guy in this big, hard world . . . that show could be a success. That guy could be a star.

The man who gave him his first chance to do all of that didn't know from talk radio. He was a veteran of the ad business, a hawker of schlock. Mac Richmond, one of the legendary whack jobs of broadcasting. Despite his craziness, his obsession with details, his office piled high with schmutz, Mac knew things about the business that no one could teach him. He had The Ear.

The Ear told him that Jerry Williams could solve the late-night problem at his Top-40 station in Boston—namely, what to put on the air when the rock 'n' roll kids went to bed. Mac had to have some public affairs—the FCC said so. Why not give a few hours to the kid from Brooklyn with the attitude? Give the older folks something to listen to. Keep it cheap. How bad can it be?

Jerry needed a job, so he was ripe for it. But he told Mac there was something new he wanted to try. He wanted to put the *voices* of his callers on the air, every night, as a regular part of the show. He had heard this new technology, audiotape, where you could delay the sound by a few seconds and your engineers could prevent the dirty words from getting out. It was a little tricky, but it could be done. Would Mac spring for the equipment? If he would, and the salary was right . . .

Mac said they could try it out using a wire recorder. Cheaper that way. Jerry gritted his teeth. Okay.

He moved to Boston to join the new WMEX.

September 2, 1957, 10:05 P.M. The wire recorder running up in the engineer's booth. The phone line installed with the special on-air number: CO2–1510. Jerry, snappy in his suitcoat and tie, hair Brylcreemed back, seated at a little table in a big studio facing a lot of empty chairs. That big black phone sitting in front of him.

That was the moment Jerry Williams put the pieces together.

2 HERITAGE

It wasn't "Jerry," and it wasn't "Williams." From the beginning, he was "Gerald" to his parents. Just as his brother was always "Herbert." No matter what the world might call him, his folks never wavered in their fidelity to his real name. Dignity and pride didn't have nicknames.

His father made that rule, and he stuck to it himself. He was "Samuel"—never "Sam," even to his friends—and "Mr. Jacoby" when you went into Jacoby's Kiddie Shop, the clothing store he and Jerry's mother, Frieda, ran near the corner of Nostrand and Church Avenues in Brooklyn.

That part of Brooklyn—Flatbush—was booming in the twenties, attracting all kinds of people looking to live in a nice residential neighborhood, get their kids started right. The apartments in Brooklyn were mostly in low-rise buildings, and there were even some nice little single-family homes, too. The schools in Brooklyn were good, especially that old high school that looked like an English Gothic church, Erasmus Hall, one of the best schools in the whole New York metropolitan area. If you were on the way up, Flatbush was a good stepping-stone.

Samuel's neighbors were bank tellers and stenographers, pressmen and sheet metal workers, clerks, nurses, salesmen, brokers, tailors, furriers, young doctors, and almost everything else. They came from other parts of New York, other parts of the United States, Italy, Ireland, Poland, Belgium, Austria, Norway, Persia, eastern Europe, and Russia. They were having kids by the carload.

Those kids needed clothes, and their folks didn't want to drag themselves and their squalling little girls and boys to one of the big Brooklyn stores or,

God forbid, into Manhattan to buy underwear or socks or a sailor suit or a dress for school. A kiddie shop was a growth property.

There was an entrepreneurial gene or something like it on both sides of Gerald's family. Frieda Post's family owned a dry goods store in lower Manhattan, and Samuel's folks (still using the old family name, Jacobowitz) had run an apartment building or rooming house uptown, right across from Mt. Sinai Hospital.

Samuel learned a lot in his early teens after his father died, when he had to help his mother, Sarah, deal with the building's tenants and the tradespeople. He learned even more while he was courting Frieda and working as a postal clerk at Grand Central Station in the teens and twenties. That was a plum job, government work, indoors, not much heavy lifting, waiting on folks at the window, weighing their packages, selling them stamps.

In a little while he had enough money, or at least the prospect of enough money, to ask Julius Post for his daughter's hand. They got married, and Samuel used the short version of his last name that had been adopted by his mother. Sarah gave them their own apartment in the family's building. Herbert, Gerald's older brother, was born in January 1919.

Then something happened. Perhaps Sarah Jacoby, Gerald's grandmother, was a victim of the Spanish flu and Samuel had to sell the family's apartment house. Maybe the flu took Julius Post and Frieda came into some of his money. Maybe Samuel put some of his own cash into stocks while the market was roaring and he made a killing before the crash. Whatever happened, Samuel and Frieda Jacoby came into enough money during the twenties to buy that kiddie clothing store in Flatbush and to move into an apartment just a short walk away.

Gerald Jacoby came into the picture on September 24, 1923.

Samuel was thirty and Frieda was twenty-six. For the next couple of years, while Gerald learned to walk and talk back and fight with his brother, and while Herbert started going to school, probably at P.S. 92, just a few blocks away, Frieda was mostly apartment-bound. Samuel worked like a mule to establish the store, and she worked with him when she could. For five or six years, as the twenties put money in Brooklynites' pockets, fathers and mothers put some of it in Samuel Jacoby's cash register every time their kids needed clothes. It looked as though they were on their way to good times.

By 1930 they could afford a nice apartment—one of the nicest on Martense Street, as a matter of fact, costing Samuel around eighty dollars a month, a lot of money back then. Samuel even bought a car, an Essex, one of the first cars marketed specifically to middle-class families, a closed car, designed to make

Gerald and Frieda Jacoby, ca. 1928.

driving more a pleasure and less an adventure. He'd take Frieda and the kids out for Sunday drives, light up one of his cigars, and feel like a success—until little Gerald started complaining and getting sick in the back seat. "Dad, *please*. The cigar. I'm *choking* here."

One of the first luxuries they had at home was a radio. Between 1920, when regular commercial broadcasting started to take off, and 1923, when there were six hundred stations on the air, the new medium seized the nation by the ears. The mid-twenties saw the rise of regular programs in every genre that would later be thought of as standard American broadcast fare—the sitcom, the soap opera, the kids' show, the variety show, the cop drama, the detective show, the comedy revue, breaking news, the roundtable discussion, the analysis of the issue of the day. Americans loved the idea of entertainment and information coming into their homes at the turn of a little knob. By the late twenties the country was radio-addicted.

Radio came along just in time, too. Just a couple of months after Gerald entered first grade at P.S. 92, the stock market crashed. People's perceptions of their circumstances changed from Success to Depression in what seemed like a heartbeat. They started saving every nickel they could—shows and movies and eating in restaurants became things for very special occasions. Mostly, they spent their evenings at home, listening to the big box in the living room.

Beginning in 1932, Samuel would stop everything on Sunday night at 9:30 so that he could hear Walter Winchell. He loved reading Winchell's column in the *Brooklyn Daily Mirror*. When the columnist got a radio show, it was a must in the Jacoby household. Winchell was clever, funny, sharp. He knew everything and everybody. Every week he brought his listeners the inside stories about the private lives of the stars and the politicians. He even delivered occasional offhand comments on the news, cutting the prime ministers and presidents down to size.

It also was important to hear what H. V. Kaltenborn had to say. Kaltenborn was a "commentator on the news" with a thin hard voice, but he knew a lot. He was a good, sober thinker, although Samuel didn't always agree with him.

On weeknights, whenever Samuel could get back from the store in time, the family started listening to the radio at 7:30. First, there was *Lowell Thomas and the News*—what a wonderful, rich voice that man had—and then there was Boake Carter, with his unusual name and English accent. He built a national reputation reporting on the kidnapping of the Lindbergh baby, and then the network had given him his own show. He wasn't just a commentator, like Kaltenborn—he was a provocateur, deliberately controversial. He spoke up for Johnny Q. Public, the name he invented for all those average Joes out there in radioland.

Usually the radio stayed on after Carter. The Jacobys loved the comedy and entertainment shows, so they heard *Amos 'n' Andy,* Rudy Vallee, Eddie Cantor, Fred Allen, Jack Benny, Burns and Allen. Not everyone knew that Cantor and Benny and Burns were Jewish, but that was fine. It was a matter of pride to see Jews doing well, becoming real stars in the radio business. Although they were entertainers, they had dignity.

Frieda thought that some radio shows were good for the children. She thought Uncle Don on WOR was good company for them. But when Herbert and Gerald actually got to choose for themselves, it was *Jack Armstrong, All-American Boy,* the Dodger games, and *Gang Busters.*

In 1932, during that summer between third and fourth grade, Gerald was eight years old and the country was slipping deeper into depression. That fall Franklin Roosevelt beat Al Smith. In March 1933 FDR was inaugurated for his first term. The Jacoby family heard him on the radio as he reassured citizens, "The only thing we have to fear is fear itself." A little more than a week later, the new president returned to the radio for the first of what came to be called the Fireside Chats. He spoke directly and calmly to people, not like an orator, but almost as a friend. He was intimate, persuasive, conversational. Gerald could almost see his face as he listened.

As the scope of Roosevelt's vision became clearer, some people who had supported him initially began to be nervous about the amount of power the new president was wielding and what they perceived as a leftist agenda in his policies. Father Charles Coughlin, the "Radio Priest" who broadcast from Chicago, turned against him right away, in the early summer of the first year. By 1935, when FDR was looking to be reelected, Louisiana's Governor Huey Long was making nationally broadcast speeches attacking Roosevelt's programs and setting himself up as a populist spokesman for the average American. Those voices came through the Jacoby radio alongside FDR's, and Samuel expressed his concern that some people weren't giving the new president a chance.

Gerald was just barely old enough to understand that something serious was going on. When his parents spoke about the disappointing sales at the family store, or the unemployed people they saw every day on the street selling pencils and apples, he felt a little stab of fear—could that happen to his family, too? It was hard to think about.

And he heard his father, along with many others in the Jewish community, worrying about what was happening in Germany. Of course, there had always been anti-Semitism there—there was plenty of anti-Semitism in New York, for heaven's sake, not to mention the things that Father Coughlin was saying about Jews on his radio program—but what Samuel heard about this National

Socialist Party shocked him. This man Hitler and his Nazis were taking over the country. By the middle of 1934, he was a virtual dictator and had turned the power of the German state against the Jews who were living there. He was building up Germany's armed forces. Samuel was afraid that there would be war in Europe. That couldn't be good for America.

That Nazi stuff was pretty scary, but the day-to-day matters of Gerald's life in the last four years of grammar school were much more pressing—his father was riding him about his grades, and he had to work in the store after school.

It was during these years that he began to love the Dodgers. All good Brooklynites cared about their baseball team, one of the great hard-luck stories in sports—every year fielding a promising squad with a few really exciting players, coming close to a pennant every once in a while, but always letting greatness slip through their hands somehow. During the mid-thirties the Dodgers were worse than usual, but there were shining moments that turned Gerald into a real fan.

In September 1934 they were playing one of their bitter crosstown rivals, the New York Giants, who had been dominant all season long and were in a hard race with the St. Louis Cardinals for the National League pennant. Brooklyn was statistically out of the running—all they could do was knock the Giants out of it. So it was a point of pride for the Dodgers when their boy Van Lingle Mungo took the mound on September 29. Mungo led the Bums to victory in Brooklyn that day and spoiled the Giants' party.

A year later, Mungo was even better. He was leading the National League in strikeouts and had a batting average in the .280s (not bad for a pitcher!) when he took the field for the last time that year—again on September 29. Gerald cheered as he struck out fifteen men in that one game, even though the Dodgers again had no chance of getting into the post-season.

Gerald loved Mungo and the other Dodgers, and he felt proud of his team for fighting hard even when only their honor was at stake. When he could, he'd walk or take the streetcar to Ebbets Field and hang around hoping for the tickets they gave away to kids—the Knot Hole Gang. Most of the time, he heard the games on the radio.

Something else happened during this phase of Gerald's boyhood, though he probably didn't hear about it at the time. Samuel might have mentioned it when he read about it in Walter Winchell's column, but it's not likely that anyone in the Jacoby family would have thought of it as anything more than a silly stunt.

It seems there was this young radio announcer in Washington, D.C., who was starting a new morning program. He thought it would be a swell idea to broadcast all night long the day before the new show was to begin—just for the publicity. The management of the station said it was okay with them, but the station's studios were closed during the off-hours, and this fella—Arthur Godfrey was his name—would have to broadcast live from the station's transmitter site, out in a swamp in rural Virginia. On January 19, 1934, management set Godfrey up with a turntable, a telephone, some records, and an engineer and wished him luck. He could have just filled the time with music and patter like so many other announcers did, but he was a natural promoter, a natural talker. He told his listeners that he was going to conduct a test to see how far away WJSV could be heard. He invited people to call him and make requests.

People from the D.C. area started phoning him right away—after all, request shows were nothing new on radio. After a couple of hours, however, Godfrey began holding the telephone up to the mic so that listeners could hear the voices of the people calling in. He began having conversations with them—what they did, where they were calling from, why they were up at that hour of the morning. That was so unusual that people began calling in from everywhere to hear themselves on the radio. Since WJSV had a strong night-time signal, Godfrey heard from Americans in all forty-eight states, and thanks to some lucky bounces, he got calls from a number of the Canadian provinces, Panama, and even South America.

At 4:30 A.M., Walter Winchell called. There was a party going on at Winchell's house, and the guests had stumbled on Godfrey's all-night show. Winchell thought this kid on the radio was pretty clever, and a week later Arthur Godfrey was mentioned in the Winchell column for the first time—which in 1934 was equivalent to having Oprah Winfrey and Larry King recommend your work on the same day. It wasn't too long before Arthur Godfrey was on the air in New York, and he then became a household name across the whole country.

Lost in the flurry of attention was the fact that that overnight publicity stunt was one of the first times—if not the very first time—that the voices of American radio listeners were heard live on the air via telephone. Even if Gerald did hear about it, he couldn't possibly know how significant that broadcast was.

As Godfrey got famous, Gerald Jacoby got to be a little more independent. His parents let him stay up later and go out on the streets by himself. He was a little, wiry kid, smaller than the other guys and getting into more scrapes because of his big mouth. He wore a round, white sailor's hat and an undershirt in the summer and got bundled up in a heavy coat in the winter. He sold magazines and papers to make a little money. Whenever he could, he went to the candy store near the family's shop—he ate the straight salted pretzels and drank the egg creams.

He watched his brother, Herbert, growing up, going out with girls, going to dances. He heard the new dance music on the radio—it had been "hot music" just a couple of years before, but when Benny Goodman hit it big in 1935, people started calling it swing. His father didn't seem to understand the excitement his son was feeling. The old man was always talking about responsibility. It seemed to Gerald that as soon as he was starting to have a little fun in life, his dad made him give up his after-school time to work in the family store.

And in fact, Samuel *didn't* understand. He was not naturally warm or open. He knew how to lay down the law when he needed to, but he expected his sons to learn from his example. And he had things to worry about. All around him, the habits he had depended on to keep his store prosperous had changed. People were mending clothes instead of purchasing things new and, when they did shop, buying the least expensive merchandise. Samuel had to stretch himself thin. He had to give credit. He had to buy cheaper cigars. He couldn't afford to give his kids the things they wanted. And even when he did—why, he got Gerald a yo-yo, and then the boy had it taken away in some sort of fight on the street.

Things at the store gradually went from flush to tough. That's one of the reasons Gerald was pressed into service as a kind of junior clerk. His mother showed him how to wait on people in the "me-do" department, especially mothers who came in with their toddlers. "Me-dos" were flannel underwear, like Dr. Dentons, only they had a split in the back instead of a flap. When the kid sat down, they opened up automatically. This was supposed to be a help in toilet training and good for the kid's self-esteem: "Look, mommy! Me do!" It was vaguely embarrassing for him, but the mothers who came in thought it was cute to have this young boy waiting on them.

Although he much preferred to be playing stickball or roller hockey or running around the streets of Flatbush, he actually learned a few things working in the store. The customers did a lot of the selling themselves. They wouldn't have been in there unless they needed something, after all. He'd show off the me-dos, and the mothers would say, "Isn't that a good idea!" All he had to do was be pleasant and courteous, which he learned from watching his father and mother interact with customers. So selling wasn't that hard—it was a kind of acting, really. Every once in a while, he would get someone to buy something she hadn't intended to buy, and that was almost fun.

Working in the store taught Gerald the difference between quality goods and junk. He also saw the difficulties his father faced, such as the people they knew coming into the store and asking for just a little more time to pay what they owed. On the other hand, he saw his father's self-reliance. Even though a lot of people were begging for jobs, losing their homes, even out on the street, Samuel Jacoby was paying his debts, making sure that his sons had a little pocket change when they really needed it, buying his wife the new clothes she wanted from time to time—all on his own initiative.

As Gerald progressed in grammar school, he was pushed to follow in his older brother's footsteps. But the shoes didn't fit. Gerald wanted to joke and show off, clown and cut up. He never was a serious student—mouthing off to his teachers, going to the principal's office, staying after school.

His folks probably would have been surprised to learn that anything in those grammar school classes actually stuck to his brain—but Gerald found history and civics interesting, when he was paying attention. Early American history, for example: a bunch of rebels fighting off the unfair rule of the British Crown. Setting up an idealistic system of government. Creating checks and balances so that no one in power could ever be a tyrant. Ben Franklin and James Madison and George Mason and Gouverneur Morris and all those other guys writing the Constitution and the Bill of Rights. Then the nineteenth century: Daniel Webster giving his great speeches in the Senate. Lincoln freeing the slaves and trying to keep the Union together. All those young soldiers fighting and dying in the Civil War. That guy John Peter Zenger, who fought for freedom of the press. The twentieth: Teddy Roosevelt busting the trusts. Those stories of regular guys fighting for what they thought was right touched him somehow.

One thing was good: he was a reader. The Tom Swift books caught his imagination and he started collecting them. There was lots of action and excitement there, and Tom had these great gadgets and gizmos. The funnies and the sports section got him looking at newspapers.

Somewhere along the line, Gerald began fantasizing about being an actor. What got him started wasn't what you'd expect, one of those grim grammar school kids' shows with parents squirming in their seats and grimacing through those off-key songs. It was Gilbert and Sullivan in rural Pennsylvania.

During the flush days in the twenties, Frieda and Samuel caught the fresh-air bug. Getting Out of the City became a rage as people got their own cars. More than that, mothers and fathers became concerned that city air was bad for their growing kids. Frieda and Samuel certainly responded to that, since they'd both been born and raised in Manhattan. So, sometime when Gerald was really little, they started sending Herbert to camp—Camp Towanda in Pennsylvania, a place mostly for Jewish kids—and it became a regular summer thing. This was no cheap camp. Other kids would say, "Oooh, a rich guy," when you said you were going there.

Towanda prided itself on a full program, for really young kids as well as older ones, so Frieda probably sent Gerald there pretty early in his life, in 1930 or 1931, soon after he'd started school. At first, Gerald hated going. He whined and acted out when Frieda took him down to Grand Central Station to put him on the train: "Don't send me away, Ma! I'll eat! I'll eat!" And Herbert didn't like having his kid brother around all the time, so he beat on him pretty regular once Samuel and Frieda weren't there to referee.

But some aspects of the camp were good. He learned to swim, and he discovered that he liked paddling around in the water. The camp offered a variety of cultural programs, including drama, and Gerald got interested in that, too. They did pretty ambitious stuff, putting on productions of musicals every week or two; the bigger kids took the leads and the little kids were in the chorus or carried spears. By the end of one summer, he actually got a part in a Gilbert and Sullivan operetta. The dressing up, the funny songs, the over-the-top characters—all that appealed to him. When he was performing, he found that he forgot about himself. He was someone else for a little while.

Gerald turned thirteen in 1936. It should have been the year of his bar mitzvah, but Judaism as a religion was never very important to either Gerald Jacoby or Jerry Williams, and it probably wasn't very important to his parents. Flatbush was not predominantly Jewish in character, and no more than a quarter of the people living in his immediate neighborhood were Jewish. Jews were civically prominent in Brooklyn at the time, but their devotion to their religion was not a criterion for respect or disrespect from their fellow Jews. Throughout his life, Jerry Williams did not choose to have seders in his home or attend temple on holy days. If Gerald Jacoby had a bar mitzvah, it was probably at Congregation Shaare Torah on Albemarle Street, but he probably learned his Hebrew badly, gave an undistinguished Torah reading, forgot about it fast, and never looked back.

Somehow, even though the Depression was getting worse, Samuel managed to get the family into their own home in the mid-thirties, a cute little bowfront row house. But Gerald was spending more and more time on the street. For him, life before high school was the Dodgers, and Sheepshead Bay, and Coney Island, and Nathan's hot dogs with mustard, those weak orange drinks they sold, chow mein samwitches, double-dipper ice cream cones so you could have two flavors side by side, hot evenings on the stoop, all that good stuff you did when you were a kid in Brooklyn. Gerald, like Pat Cooper, Roger Kahn, Larry King, Barbra Streisand, Woody Allen, and so many more, walked the tree-lined streets, jumped off the piers into the bay, did a lot of stuff that his parents never knew about, and finally went home.

The home that got stuck in his head wasn't that little bowfront—instead, when he thought back to his Brooklyn days, he recalled the big blocks from 201 to 221 Linden, buildings with six or seven stories and hundreds of families, where the Jacobys were living in the late 1930s and where they lived throughout his high school years. How did it happen that Samuel Jacoby, the guy paying the highest rent on Martense Street in 1930, a guy who was living in his own little house on Martense in 1936, was moving his family into a massive apartment building just a couple of years later?

Gerald's obviously gifted brother, Herbert, graduated from Erasmus Hall in June 1936 in a ceremony at Loew's Kings, one of the local movie palaces. He wanted to go to college, and his folks knew he deserved to go. Maybe Samuel felt that it was the family's responsibility to sacrifice so that at least one son could go on to college, to become a professional man. Maybe he looked over those new apartments on Linden, did the math, and decided that it wouldn't be too much of a hardship for the family to move there. It probably broke Frieda's heart to leave that house on Martense.

The end of 1936 came, and FDR beat Alf Landon and started his second term in 1937. Eighth grade at P.S. 92 was winding down, and Gerald figured his grades would be good enough to graduate. But what he really wanted was some pocket money, and he lucked into a job ushering at the Flatbush Theatre. The Flatbush did everything—there had been silent films there, vaudeville, music shows . . . it was a place everyone went, and it was exciting to see show business up close, sort of.

Then the word got around that the Paramount Theater in Manhattan, a big, classy first-run house, was looking for ushers. Gerald hustled over there and got one of the jobs. Since he had turned thirteen in September, he mighta stretched the truth about his age a little. But what a great job! Seeing those movies over and over, he got a feeling for the technique and the acting, the clothes and the style.

And it wasn't just movies. The Paramount booked Benny Goodman's band for a series of shows in March. That band was *hot*. There were going to be five shows on Saturdays and Sundays, four on weekdays, for at least for one week and maybe more. Every one of the Paramount's ushers would be needed, and the managers didn't seem to be too concerned that some of the shows would be taking place during the school day.

Gerald put his name down for every shift that was available. On Wednesday, March 3, more than four thousand people lined up outside the Paramount to plunk down their thirty-five cents to see Benny's band and *Maid of Salem*—a movie starring Claudette Colbert that was part of the show. Some of them got there at seven in the morning.

Samuel, Frieda, and Gerald
Jacoby, ca. 1937.

Goodman's thirteen men set up on the Paramount's hydraulic bandstand, down below the floor level in the orchestra pit, where no one in the audience could see them. The lights dimmed. Benny picked up his clarinet and counted off "Let's Dance." A stagehand pressed a button to start lifting the stage. The house exploded in shouts and cheers as the band rose up into the lights, smoothly swinging their way through that catchy tune that almost everybody already knew by heart.

The first time he saw that happen, Gerald stood there with his mouth open. It was amazing. In the next few days, he saw Benny play "Let's Dance" over and over and over, and never got tired of the magic of it, the showmanship of it, the precision of the music. He musta seen 'em do it a hundred times, maybe two hundred times. The band was held over for three weeks.

The crowd got crazy sometimes. They'd hoot and yell through the movie. "We want Benny! We want Benny!" The poor slobs who came in to watch Colbert musta wondered what the hell was going on. Sometimes they stood up in their seats, and a couple of times a few fans tried to rush the stage. That kept the ushers busy. Gerald and the others walked up and down the aisles: "Hey, you, oveh deh! Siddown!"

After that, it was even harder to concentrate on school, but somehow Gerald kept his grades up enough to get into Erasmus Hall in September 1937. It was supposed to be a new start in his life, a passport to the future, but it didn't feel that way. Things were simmering beneath the surface. He didn't want to be a straight arrow like his brother. He wanted to have some fun. He wanted to do something exciting—be a bandleader or a comedian or an actor. He was churning with ambition.

As Jerry Williams later put it, Gerald Jacoby was becoming a cantankerous pain in the ass. A star student he was not. A student of girls—you bet. And still a premier Dodger fan. He developed a sharp tongue, a sardonic smile, a sense of style in his clothes and his hair—and a well of anger inside.

During Gerald's first year in high school, Hitler annexed Austria and the Dodgers put lights in Ebbets Field. Every fan was looking forward to a schedule of weekday games that didn't force you to call in sick to work, so the game on June 15, 1938—the first one under the lights—was going to be a milestone in Brooklyn history. His mother promised him that if he did well at Erasmus Hall, she would pay for a ticket to get him into that game. He did well enough, and she came through with the fifty-five cents he needed. When he went through the gate that night, he was a witness to history—the first night game at Ebbets Field. But the lights were just half the story Jerry Williams liked to tell about that night.

The Cincinnati Reds' pitcher, Johnny Vander Meer, had great stuff. In his last game, four days earlier, he'd thrown a no-hitter against the Boston Bees. He started strong that night in Brooklyn, too, and as the innings wore on, he mowed those Dodger hitters down—Leo Durocher and Buddy Hassett, Babe Phelps and Ernie Koy. Seventh frame, no Dodgers on base. The eighth, another goose egg. The bleachers buzzed. Could it be that Vander Meer was going to do it again? When Harry Craft of the Reds caught that last fly ball, the fans roared. "D'ya know how many pitchis t'rown back-t'-back no-hittis? Not one, bruddeh, not one!"

That gave him something to talk about all summer, even when he went back to Erasmus Hall in September. But the anger inside him wouldn't go away. He skipped school. He chafed at his parents' rules. He gave them lip. His father was pissed at him most of the time. His mother understood that there was something paining him, but she couldn't reach it. When Orson Welles played his great Halloween radio prank on October 30, updating "War of the Worlds" and fooling most of the country into thinking that Martians had landed in New Jersey, it fit Gerald's mood precisely.

There were some days he felt he just couldn't take it. He wanted some real life, and he knew that real life wasn't in a classroom.

He admired Erasmus Hall's star football player, Sid Luckman, and palled with Sid's younger brother Dave. He lucked into Erasmus's all-male cheer-leading squad and got what mileage he could out of the reflected glory of the school's sports heroes. That got him a sweater with a letter on it, at least.

He got more reflected glory by being friends with Irving Weber. Irving was one of those guys who had it, had that *thing*. You wanted to be buddies with him or you wanted to beat him up, he was so cool. A great dancer, a guy who really made time with the girls. That architectural pompadour and alpaca sweater, those skin-tight pegged pants. Gerald got a kick out of calling the downstairs pay phone in the Webers' apartment building, using his newly deepened voice to ask for Oiving, and hearing Mr. Weber yell upstairs, "Oiving! A gangsteh's calling you!" Did he first start smoking seriously when he was hanging around with Irving? Maybe. It sure felt studly, walking along with Irving Weber, casually puffing on a Camel.

Then there was Freddie Fields—being friends with him almost put Gerald in show business, because Freddie's brother Shep led one of the nation's most popular big bands. True, that sweet "Shep Fields and His Rippling Rhythms" stuff was Mickey Mouse, a far cry from real swing, but Shep had connections, and every once in a while Freddie would get an extra ticket or two to a show. Gerald would sit there in the dark, envying the guy in the white jacket lead-ing the band. Why couldn't it be Gerald Jacoby and His Orchestra up there?

He and Freddie and Russell Weissman listened to records and ranked the bands. One day he was talking with Russell and they both were griping about how they needed money, couldn't get noticed by the best-looking girls, blah blah blah. Then the same thought occurred to both of them—they knew a bunch of guys who could play instruments, Russell had some musical ability, Jerry could sing a little bit, stock arrangements were pretty cheap—why didn't they start a band? Somehow they got a little money together, bought a white jacket, sold their musician friends on the idea, got the music, did the rehearsals, even played a few dances as "Jerry Russell and the Band." Since they couldn't agree on who was going to be the leader, they switched off being "Jerry Russell" from gig to gig. It was pretty funny, with one or the other of these sixteen-year-old kids up there in a white jacket, waving a baton around randomly while his bud-dies struggled through the tunes.

Spring and summer 1940: the Germans rolled over everybody. While they were deporting Jews and eating other countries for breakfast, Gerald heard something new on the radio. WOR gave an announcer named Henry Morgan a show—or was it a show? What the hell was it? Every weekday evening, the station put this guy on the air for fifteen minutes, just to talk. "Here's Morgan," he said, and then he blabbed on about anything he wanted. Sometimes he had a topic of the day. Sometimes it just seemed like he was making it up from minute one. He made fun of his sponsors, Adler Elevator Shoes. He talked to his engineer. He joked about the owners of the station. He told you whom he'd seen on the street that day, what he'd had for lunch, what he was planning to do on the weekend. He made it all funny somehow. He looked at life as though it was one big goof, as though most people were fools, as though he didn't care what happened. Gerald couldn't get enough of Morgan. He went to sleep thinking about what he would do if someone gave him the chance to be on the radio. And he wondered if those elevator shoes really did make you taller than she was—he could use something like that.

Then it was September, senior year. Showtime: graduation was looking a little iffy, college was a real question mark, and there was something even bigger to worry about—the government instituted the first peacetime draft in U.S. history. This means you, kid.

He just wanted to escape from it. He was already accomplished at skipping school to hang out at Coney, rehearse with the band, hole up in a movie theater all day. Now he started running away from home and spending the night God knows where. Sometimes he'd sleep in the basement of Beatrice Klotz's house on Avenue K—she had curves in all the right places, and she kind of liked him, so he thought he had a chance with her. Sometimes he went into the city, wandering around late at night and taking a room for a buck and a half in a fleabag hotel on Ninth Avenue in Manhattan. His ma got frantic. His dad shouted at him. He shouted back.

By the beginning of 1941, his grades were in the toilet and he stopped trying. Everybody else was planning for graduation, but he knew he wasn't going to make it. The school invited his parents in for a talk. If Gerald didn't straighten up, he was going to be discharged. Samuel and Frieda read him the riot act, but he just shrugged it off. On March 21, 1941, he got kicked out of Erasmus Hall.

At first he celebrated. Baseball season started in April, so he went to Ebbets Field. He went to Coney Island.

Finally, his father wouldn't stand for this idleness, and he insisted that Gerald help out in the store. So he dragged himself in in the morning and put in some regular hours. Some days he told the old man he felt lousy and couldn't work, but that was a lot harder than skipping school ever was. He hated working alongside his pa. Night and day, there was no escape.

When he could, he went to the movies. In June he saw Orson Welles's new picture, *Citizen Kane*. He'd never seen such amazing acting—Welles went from being a cocky rich kid to a bitter, desperate old man and made every change believable. He again thought about himself as an actor—a serious actor, somebody who'd do something profound and important.

Then graduation day came, and his friends got their diplomas. He still hung around with them, but it wasn't the same. They were moving on and he was stuck. Some of them were going to college. A lot of them talked about going into the Army. Everybody was afraid that the U.S. would be sucked into the war. The few smart guys figured they'd enlist while they could still have some say about what they were going to do or where they were going to be sent. Once they drafted you, they said, you were just a piece of meat, and they'd send you right up to the front lines.

The following months were a bitch. Samuel didn't need the stress in his store, much less stress coming from his own son. Frieda saw Gerald going nowhere. His eighteenth birthday was right around the corner, and he had no skills, no ambition, nothing except his interest in the Dodgers—who made it to the World Series that year but stumbled as usual.

During the late summer, when the pennant race was heating up, Frieda made a decision and presented it to Gerald as an ultimatum. He would have to go back to school—some kind of practical school, a school where they would teach him to type and give him business abilities that he could put to work in an office. She said they would pay for it somehow.

Gerald was furious, but he knew better than to fight his ma when she had decided on something. Secretly, he thought it might not be so bad. He'd be away from the store. A business school was likely to be filled with girls.

That fall he enrolled in—what was the name of that school, anyway? He never liked thinking about that short episode in his life. Instead of embarking on the road to fame, he was stuck behind a desk again. Yeah, there were girls all around him, but the drills and the monotony of it! Stars didn't type, he thought sourly. They had people to type for them. After a few weeks, he swallowed the resentment and gave it some effort.

One of the girls in the school was a German refugee, Ilse Weiss. She spoke pretty good English. A little older than he was. He flirted with her casually, the way he did with every cute girl, always on the make, trying out his lines and his jokes. One day he looked at her and something happened. It was hard to explain. He suddenly understood that she was carrying some sadness around back there, behind her smiles, and as soon as he saw the sadness he wanted to make it go away. She was a DP, a displaced person. He'd been kicked out of high school, but she had *real* troubles. Goddamn Nazis had stolen her country.

He wanted to protect her, soothe her. They went out, they got physical . . . in a few weeks, he wasn't a virgin any more. He told her he loved her.

But then Japan entered his life. He'd paid very little attention to the Japanese—they'd rolled over the Chinese, were taking over Indochina, had signed on to the Axis with Germany and Italy—still, whatever they did just didn't seem to have much effect on Gerald Jacoby. Until they decided to attack Pearl Harbor.

Life sped up. In one week, the Japanese bombed our base in Hawaii, we declared war on them, we declared war on Germany, the Germans and Italians declared war on us. The next month, the Germans came up with their Final Solution—kill all the Jews. By spring 1942, when he was supposed to be wrapping up his typing course, the Japanese had taken over Indonesia and they were marching up into Burma. It was nuts.

The only good things in life that year were Ilse and the Dodgers. He took her to ball games, tried to get her to understand what was going on. And incidentally, the Bums were having another killer season.

He and Ilse went to some of those September games, cheering and hoping and then getting the blues the same way that Dodger fans always got the blues in the fall. What the hell—there was always 1942. Durocher was managing full-time now, Dolph Camilli and Ducky Medwick and Pee Wee Reese were hitting, Whit Wyatt and Kirby Higbe were still pitching pretty well, Ilse and he were in love, maybe next year . . .

And then his draft notice came in the mail.

Lines. The Army was filled with lines.

Jerry and the other Brooklyn draftees got in the line at the Camp Upton processing center, just as they were told. Camp Upton, Long Island ("Long Guylind"). The place where the Army figured out what to do with you. He picked up forms, filled them out, talked to men in uniforms, filled out more forms, talked to more uniforms. Then, one uniform stopped as he was looking through Gerald's papers.

"Jacoby, what's this typing school? What'd they teach you?"

Was this guy kidding? "Well, it was typing, Corporal. Some shorthand, but I hated that crap. Business letters, office organization, typing."

"Lotta girls?"

"Yes, sir, Corporal."

"You the only man there?"

"No—a couple of other guys."

"You don't look like a fruit."

"No, Corporal."

"Well, Jacoby, how would you like to use that typing to kill a few Krauts? Or a few Nips?"

"I don't get it, Corporal."

"The Air Corps, Jacoby. Army Air Corps. The Army needs guys for the Air Corps, guys who can read, write, type. Guys who are smart. They have to learn about planes. You smart, Jacoby?"

"Sometimes too smart, Corporal."

"Wisecracks won't help you in this man's Army, Jacoby. Use your head to help us win this war. You're in the Air Corps."

They called it being sectioned off. He realized that the other guys were going on a different track. He would still have basic training, like anybody in the Army, but he had something on his forms that made him different. He didn't know it then, but typing school had just saved him from the infantry, where a lot of those poor bastards from Brooklyn would end up face down in the mud, in France or in Italy or on some Pacific island. He was lucky, damned lucky. After they dropped the bombs on Japan and he came back home, and he found out how many of those guys from Brooklyn had died, how many of them came back with their arms or legs shot off, he thanked God, or whoever was watching over him that day.

But he felt lucky even sooner, in fact the week after he got to Camp Upton, when he found out where he was going for basic training: Miami Beach.

There was a special kind of music in the words "Miami Beach." Before, during, and shortly after the war, especially for Americans in the Northeast, Florida was the Promised Land of Vacationworld, and Miami was its Jerusalem. People who could afford it went there every year for one glorious week, maybe two if they had a lot of money, in the middle of winter. When they came back, they talked about it like it was some kind of miracle. Instead of being stuck in the snow and ice, feeling that bitter hard wind in your face, banging on the radiator for heat once you got inside, fighting endlessly with the cold, it was soft, easy, beautiful. Instead of that armor—your coat, your gloves, your boots—you had the warmth of the sun, the way it was in June or July. The amazing fresh orange juice, the ripe grapefruit. Shorts and sunglasses and alligators. In the winter! If you were really adventurous, you could go on to Cuba, to gamble, dance, and . . .

Jerry had yearned for Miami ever since he first heard about it. And now, here he was, going to Miami Beach as the summer of 1942 was coming on. The Army had taken over hotels normally used by tourists there and turned them into barracks, so he got a chance to imagine what it would be like to be there on vacation.

Of course, basic training was the opposite of vacation. You might get a swim or two in, but most of the time the game was dawn-to-dark body work, running and jumping and sweating. The new recruits dropped like sash weights into their beds at the end of the day. Jerry could feel his muscles hardening under the regimen, and he knew that he probably had never looked better in his life.

Then he was a nomad for a few months. The Army shipped him to Fort Eustis, in Virginia. To Robins Air Force Base in Georgia. To someplace out in Ohio. More physical training and gun training and military rules. Getting ready to get shipped out, getting ready to fight, getting ready to kill, getting ready to die if you had to. By the way, getting to be pretty good at using that uniform to hit on girls. He wasn't afraid to talk about his status when he met a girl—gonna be a pilot, yep. Gonna go over there to drop those bombs. And what's *your* name, honey?

When he was at Fort Eustis, there was an Army WAC from D.C. he got to know well. Although he was only in the area a couple of months, he made time for the four hours of bus rides it took to get to her place on the weekend. After her, there were the girls in Macon, in Milledgeville, in Dayton . . . practice made perfect. And Ilse? Just a memory.

Finally, Jerry got on track to do the real Air Corps work they'd been promising him for more than six months. He got sent to Chillicothe, Missouri, for the academic part of his flight training, toward the end of 1942. Chillicothe was in the middle of nowhere. Two hours from Kansas City. Three hours from Des Moines. An hour and a half from St. Joseph, and when you got to St. Joe, you *still* hadn't gotten anywhere. There he was, in a dorm at Chillicothe Business School, a girls' business college. He'd come halfway across the country to spend the winter at a typing school, just like in Brooklyn.

Except that he was wearing a uniform now. And he was in pretty good shape. And he was an exotic flower . . . a handsome Jewish boy with a knowing smile, a prize from the Biggest City in the Country. When he and the other thirty-four trainees went to the dining hall for lunch and dinner, they were outnumbered by girls almost five to one. Each table had a faculty or Army chaperone, one or two guys, and nine or ten girls. You know, it was all right. And when the spring came, and the girls took off their coats . . .

Then, in May 1943, it was "graduation" time. They even took a picture of all the trainees in their uniforms, before they shipped them out to Texas, to Kelly Field in San Antonio, where it was already hot, hot as blazes, especially out there on the tarmac, where they first got their hands on real planes. It was in those planes that the differences between the trainees really began to show.

Flight training—shit, Jerry suddenly realized: they want us to *fly* these things! The classroom stuff continued, and then there were flight simulators on the ground to get the feel of the controls, and dozens of supervised runs in little PT-19s, Primary Trainers. Jerry got outfitted with his Air Corps gear— his leather helmet and his goggles. He and the other guys flew with their instructors, found out what all the instruments did, took the planes up and down in the air, touched the ground and rose again, came in for landings and practiced takeoffs. They flew tandems with instructors and then tandems with each other.

One day they got wings pinned on their uniforms. They were pilots now. Even Jerry felt macho. A *pilot*. A *man!* He remembered Richard Barthelmess, the cursed flier in that Howard Hawks potboiler *Only Angels Have Wings* from before the war. The guy who kept volunteering for the most dangerous stuff to chase away his personal demons. Jerry couldn't be that guy, but he could imagine himself playing that guy. He loved the trappings—and what they could do for him every time he went into a bar. He was still scared to death every time he got into the cockpit.

The Air Corps training officers could sense which of the guys had that lust to fly. It was something you couldn't bring out in a classroom or generate with a training film. Some guys had it in their blood. Other guys—well, they could be second men. Flight engineers. Guys who sat in the other cockpit seat, confirming the course, watching the instruments, along for the ride just in case the pilot conked out or got shot. They knew enough to get the plane out of the air, but they didn't have the fire in the gut, the need to fly. Jerry was one of the Other Guys.

That was all right with him. He really didn't want to be dropping bombs anyway.

There was an active scene around Kelly Field. The wartime expansion of operations there meant that they needed a lot of support personnel, so there were plenty of good jobs for women, and those Texas girls loved those pilots in more ways than one. The fliers even had a name for them, the "Kelly Katies." One of those gals was special, a Katie named Joanne McCoy. She had a magical combination of goyish good looks, personal fire, and sexpertise that pinned Jerry to the wall like a butterfly. She took him in hand. She gave him the ride of his life. She was the Real McCoy.

Of course, they didn't get along for long. Jerry kept looking around at the other talent, and Joanne wouldn't stand for that. When she headed back to Dallas to get on with her life, Jerry couldn't get her out of his head, and he pursued her there. Conveniently, the first-string student pilots were doing R&R air taxi service from Kelly to Dallas every weekend, with Jerry and some of the other second guys in the back cockpits. It was a fast, free ride, and he took every chance he could to get close to Joanne once again.

Those flights were incredible. The pilots loved showing how ballsy they were—and their balls were the big kind that Jerry and the other second men definitely did not have. These jockeys would get up in the air and fly their PT-19s in formation. Then they'd tighten up. They'd get closer and closer to the other planes . . . closer . . . closer . . . so close that you could see the other plane's pilot grinning back. They'd touch wings with the neighboring PT, and then zoom off, leaving the second guys white with terror every time.

He'd get out of the plane in Dallas, knees rubbery, glad to be alive, frothing to see Joanne McCoy, pumped up with adrenaline and lust, fear and testosterone.

Then there was a month of being treated like a steer in a boxcar. He and his Air Corps buddies were split up into units, shipped to the West Coast, herded onto a gigantic ship—five thousand guys on this tub, jammed in so tightly that you could barely breathe—and sent out to sea for three weeks. Finally, they hauled their stuff ashore in Calcutta. The hottest place he had ever been. Absolutely mobbed with people, choked with people, infested with people.

Then they were packed into trucks and transported a few miles away to Bengal Air Depot, near a town called Kharagpur—K-poor, the guys called it. They were settled into barracks and taught about life in India.

The barracks had loads of kids, and some older guys, too—depending on their roles, they were barrack-wallahs, mess-hall-wallahs, or some-other-kind-of-wallahs—to wait on the servicemen hand and foot. Jerry and the other guys were embarrassed at first—Jesus, they didn't need servants. They could take care of themselves. But the officers told them that things were different in India. They had to play their roles. They were white, they were like the Brits, they were superior. The wallahs were lower caste. Jerry discovered that there was a weird kind of formality. If a private dropped a rupee on the floor, he'd say, "I'll pick it up," but the barrack-wallah would already be scurrying around, saying, "Oh! sah'b, let me get it, please." They wouldn't allow you to reach down and pick up anything. Your head was never supposed to be lower than that of your barrack-wallah.

And yet, these people had an undeniable dignity. They worked hard, incredibly hard, hauling stuff around for the guys in uniform, using the simplest tools or their bare hands to do any kind of repair or maintenance, killing themselves for hours out there in that ferocious sun, overhauling the trucks and jeeps, carrying baskets of clothing around. And it seemed like each one of the kids and almost all of the men, except the men who had to do the heaviest and dirtiest work, came to the barracks every day in fresh white shirts and impeccably pressed pants. When the Army guys met the mothers and wives, these women always seemed to have immaculate top-to-bottom saris. How could they keep their clothes so clean in all this dust and grime?

After a while, Jerry came to enjoy the idea of personal service. What's more, he really liked the Indians, the sweet little kids who were his barrack-wallahs, their shy mothers, the sturdy fellas who did the heavy work, the tall, dignified village cops with their turbans. They were gentle and kind, and they seemed genuinely interested in doing what they could for you.

But the area around the base was a sort of oasis, and things were different out in the real India. For some months—since spring 1943 at least—all of Bengal province had been struggling with food shortages. Things went from bad to worse, and there was a genuine famine that summer. By the time Jerry got to Bengal Air Depot, the rumors on base were flying. Guys who'd been there a while said that the cost for everyday things to eat had skyrocketed. Something like ten thousand Bengalis were starving to death every day. And they said the Brits weren't doing very much to help. They'd seen mobs of Indians near the Calcutta docks, where food aid would come in on ships. The British soldiers would randomly throw bags of rice into the crowd, letting the Indians fight over them, just watching them punch and kick one another. Nearly every day, there was some kind of disturbance—sometimes a full-blown riot—over food. The American officers on the base warned their men to be careful in their R&R trips to the city.

Jerry and the other guys didn't take it that seriously. *They* had enough food. How could so many people be dying? But on his first exploratory trips around Calcutta, he noticed hundreds of vendors selling what seemed to be really valuable stuff—like star sapphires, what looked to him like high-quality gemstones, offering them for almost nothing, just so they could get money for food.

And then one evening, as he and three buddies were coming back from a day in town in one of the six-by-six Army trucks they used to get around, they heard something strange. They were coming down Chowringhee Road, Calcutta's vast main thoroughfare, a broad boulevard bordering a park. Off in the distance, there was a kind of rumbling or roaring. In a few minutes, as it got louder, they realized it was a crowd—a huge number of voices shouting and talking all at once: a blood-chilling kind of sound. Some Indians were running toward and past their truck, trying to tell them what was going on as they ran. It seemed that a mob had formed, looking to take revenge on the Brits. They had cans of petrol. They were grabbing any British soldiers they could find, dousing them with gasoline, and lighting them up.

Then Jerry actually saw the crowd. It was unreal—like the villagers coming after the monster in *Frankenstein,* but on a much bigger scale. *Nothing* but people, *masses* of people, with torches. Jerry and the others had to get through that crowd. They didn't know any other way back to the base. And then they all thought the same thing—how would these people know they weren't British? Someone said, "It's them or us." Jerry thanked God he wasn't driving. The guy behind the wheel put his foot on the gas and roared straight at the oncoming mob. They held on with all their strength. They didn't look back. They knew they were hitting people, hurting people, and they heard the rage all around them, the air saturated with shouts and screams. Somehow they got clear, but the driver didn't slow down. No one looked back. No one wanted to know how many people they'd hurt or how many they'd killed.

The next day, Jerry and some of the guys went back to Calcutta and returned to the base with the color drained out of their faces. They had seen the aftermath—the authorities had piled the human remains into pyramids three or four stories high along Chowringhee Road, preparing them to be set on fire. There were a dozen or so vultures on each pile, picking at the dead.

Was this what they had come over here for?

No. The war they'd been training for was up in the air. It wasn't as though anyone sat Jerry and the other new guys down and said, "Listen, men. You're now part of the Air Transport Command. You'll be flying the matériel needed by troops in China over the Himalayas so that they can keep fighting the Japs." Jerry figured that out from talking to the veteran pilots, and he saw it for himself when they began including him in the crews flying the planes to China.

They called it going Over the Hump. Loading up the cargo planes with stuff and then taking them up in the air over the highest mountains in the world. Dropping the stuff off in China. Turning around and going back. Over and over and over. Every month they were flying more than eight thousand tons of supplies to China. Sometimes they had even more dangerous missions over Burma, where the Japanese were in control. Jerry would look down over the vast, snow-white mountains, over green hills, over fields where little farmers were working the land, and he'd think about what would happen if his plane had engine trouble, or if someone said, "Our pilot's had a heart attack! Our copilot's been shot! It's up to you to fly this thing!"

He learned to swallow the fear. He focused on getting home, and what're we gonna do tonight, and where'll we get the beer. He learned one sentence in Hindi and used it every chance he got: "Aaj bibi maangta hai"—"I want a woman right now." He wrote cheery letters to his folks and sent pictures of himself, always grinning, with amusing captions. He clowned with the men in his unit—someone got a pith helmet that they were always passing around when they took pictures. He got used to sleeping outside on a rope bed, Indian style, to catch a little night air. He palled around and went to visit the local hookers with a guy named Lou, who made sergeant after a while. He adopted a local dog. He endured the resentment of enlisted men who thought the guys in the air had it soft—his crew even painted "Cowards" on the side of his plane in self-mockery. He named the pinup they painted on the plane "Joanne McCoy." He saw Gandhi when the Mahatma came to Calcutta, remarked on the reverence in the eyes of the thousands upon thousands upon thousands of people who came out to touch him or just get close enough to see him, and he felt some of that reverence himself.

Every once in a while, he'd get a serious, precise letter from his dad. He found out that Herbert had joined up—they made him an officer of course, a lieutenant, because of his college degree.

And one more thing. He kept running into microphones. If they needed some guy to call the men to attention at a gathering, or to introduce the emcee at a show, or to make the rounds at a hospital and cheer the guys up, he was ready. "Hey! I can handle that mic."

He put the fear aside. He focused on getting home. For the next two years, he ran those missions, did what he was told to do, and got away from it whenever he could. No one ever asked him to fly a plane. He never saw action the way the grunts did. He came through it alive.

By mid-1944 servicemen listening to Armed Forces Radio got the feeling that the tide was turning, at least in Europe. But it was harder for Jerry to feel the progress of the war in the Pacific. All the crews worked like dogs, and the flights over the mountains, once so breathtaking and frightening to him, became routine.

In Europe the commanders turned up the heat on Germany. A massive bombing of Berlin in February 1945 killed more than 20,000 people. A week later, Allied planes set Dresden on fire; most of the city was left in cinders and more than 100,000 people died. A month after that, the same tactics came to the Pacific: because the skies over Japan were now almost completely in Allied control, they could start carpet bombing of Tokyo. The planes incinerated twelve square miles of the capital and killed 80,000 people, but the Japanese military still refused to surrender. It seemed as though the Japanese general staff wanted the whole country to commit hara-kiri.

As supply missions slowed down in 1945, Jerry and his buddy, Sergeant Lou, got to Calcutta every chance they could. They goofed around in a haze of 3.2 beer, pulling one another around in rickshaws along Chowringhee

Private Gerald Jacoby at a vendor's stand,
Calcutta, ca. 1944.

Road, confounding the rickshaw-wallahs who were simultaneously embarrassed at these Army guys stepping out of their proper roles and terrified at the thought of damage to their livelihood. They raised hell. About a month later, in April, Roosevelt—the only president Jerry had known, really—died, and Harry Truman started running the show.

August: Fat Man and Little Boy dropped in on Hiroshima and Nagasaki. And that was that. In a few weeks, the brass shifted the transmission of the war machine into reverse.

After announcements and paperwork and waiting and make-work, Jerry boarded a troop ship in Calcutta—the same damn ship he'd ridden over on, packed exactly the same way, with another five thousand guys.

Another three weeks at sea, going in the opposite direction. The only thing different was this fainting thing. He'd never fainted before in his life, but one day early on, on his way down to KP duty to make coleslaw, he banged his head on the edge of an iron hatch. He got up, reached up, and there he was bleeding—the only service-related injury he'd sustained in two years. He felt a little woozy, so he went down to the infirmary. There were six medics down there, each of them with a different opinion. One guy: "I think he needs four stitches."

Another guy: "Awww, doesn't need 'ny stitches. He'll be awright."

Another guy: "I think y' oughta take 'im down t' surg'ry right away."

And while they were doing all this consulting, POW! Jerry passed out cold. Gone!

He came to a few minutes later, and they patched him up. But all the way back across the Pacific, he kept having the feeling that he was going to keel over. Every time he went down to the galley to chop up cabbage, he'd wobble and get dizzy and get sent back to his bunk. It was the only place he felt secure. So for about fifteen days out of the three weeks, he was mostly prone, and when he'd go to mess, he'd always get "You goofin' off from the coleslaw detail?" Finally, about a week away from home, the problem went away, and for the last five days, he was the coleslaw-wallah again.

When they arrived in San Pedro, California, the excitement on board was incredible. They were all waiting to get off the ship, and Jerry was one of the first guys in line, his pack on his back, all set to be the returning Veteran of World War Whatever It Was.

But there was one thing the crew had to do before they let their five thousand cattle go. Jerry looked over and saw the line of navy men, all carrying caskets. The boxes holding the guys whose luck ran out. The guys who would never see their old neighborhoods or their girlfriends or their folks or their families ever again. Bang. Jerry's lights went out again.

A few days later, he was on a train. A few more days, and he was back at Grand Central. An hour or so more, and he was in Brooklyn, his mother crying, his father shaking his hand. A few weeks later, what comes in the mail? A Good Behavior with an Oak Leaf Cluster, for hitting his head on the hatch. And for a year or so, he still had that funny feeling—that he was maybe going to pass out. Maybe should lie down for a while. It was 1945. They didn't have post-traumatic stress disorder then. After a while, you just snapped out of it. So that's what he did.

While he was waiting for the war to fade, he joined the 52-20 Club: he got twenty dollars a week unemployment compensation for fifty-two weeks—a gift from a grateful nation. At least it was something. But by the time 1946 came around, with Henry Morgan back on the radio with a new variety show, and commercial television stations beginning to sign on, and a sense dawning that the war years were actually over, he ran right into reality. For nearly three years, he'd been able to tamp down the fire inside. The Air Corps had given him some reason to be alive. What the hell was he going to do now?

3 ⚊ RADIO OR NOT

The war had been hell on day-to-day business in America, radio included. All the routines that station owners and network executives counted on—seasonal buying cycles, predictable listening patterns, stable personnel—had been affected by the war. Young staff people were drafted; some of them didn't come back. Rationing affected the consumer goods that drove a lot of the advertising revenue. Restrictions on gasoline made deliveries more expensive and kept people out of their cars, where they might be listening to their radios.

The long postponement of normalcy and the reined-in potential of a relatively unscathed America had the country ready to pop. When the guys in uniform returned, it meant that life could at last start getting back to normal—which for most people meant buying things, getting dolled up, going out, seeing shows, and making babies. All this activity meant lots of new revenue for the ad business, and for radio.

The social shift also meant a change in focus for programming. The guys who'd seen the world came back home with some attitude—let's get the country moving again. Who needs Ma Perkins and Mr. Keen, Tracer of Lost Persons? Let's have radio we can listen to in our cars, radio that'll wake us up with a smile, radio that'll keep us company. We've got things to do! We can't sit around the big old box in the living room after the sun goes down.

Television wasn't a factor yet in radio's changes, but it soon would be. The 1939 World's Fair predicted a TV in every home, but the war froze television manufacturing and production in its tracks. In March 1946 things began to move again, even though there were only nine commercial television stations on the air. TV makers began cranking out sets. NBC and CBS and DuMont were introducing regular TV programming schedules for a few hours each weekday. Successful radio station owners began investing their cash in new TV stations.

The onset of television accelerated the changes already under way in radio. The staginess of prewar radio dramas had given way to more intimate acting, snappier patter—radio shows that were more like movies. The old stentorian announcing style was sliding toward something more conversational. And, thanks to a couple of wartime strikes by the musicians' union that forced the big labels to pay royalties for jukebox and radio play, the few pioneering recorded-music hosts, like Martin Block, whose *Make Believe Ballroom* was one of Gerald's favorites in the late thirties, had become a platoon of easygoing disc jockeys.

Take Barry Gray, whose all-night show on WMCA in New York was a touchstone for listeners who wanted to hear the latest music. Barry had a relaxed, comfortable style. He was in touch with the musicians themselves, and he passed along tidbits he'd heard from them and about them—where they were touring, who was leaving their bands, who was joining up. There was one night in 1945—Jerry didn't hear the broadcast because he was in India at the time—when Barry got a call from Woody Herman himself, a guy with a modern big band who had just started recording for Columbia. The new tunes were coming out, and Herman was getting a great reception for his band—the Herman Herd, they liked to call it. That night in 1945, Woody called Gray to chat (and promote his band). Gray thought the conversation was so interesting that he decided to put it on the air—asking Woody questions and holding the phone up to the mic so that his listeners could hear the answers. People loved it, so Gray added more phone interviews. They constituted a few small digressions for a music show, but another moderate step toward talk radio.

The postwar Gerald Jacoby was a media hound, an appreciator of performance who was much more sophisticated than a lot of his peers. He heard the old-fashioned dramas and the new record spinners on the radio. He went into the city and saw plays and musicals whenever he could get cheap tickets. He went to the movies. He listened to new records and went out to see jazz groups and pop singers. Wherever he went, whatever he did, he got the same message: you belong up on the stage, behind the mic, in front of the camera. That led to a lot of grief with his folks. What kind of cockamamie life was show business? It was time for Gerald to be a mensch.

He had to show them he was serious. He couldn't dance. He wasn't much of a singer. He thought he was most qualified to act, but he had no experience, no training. Somehow he got into an amateur drama group led by an announcer from WHN, a guy named Bob Breyer.

Bob had one of these booming, throaty, jolly voices—if he'd come up a few years later, he could have slapped a grin on his sound and become a fast-talking Top-40 DJ. Bob was a pro. He warned Jerry, and all of his actors, about their regional accents. Pronounce those Rs, Jerry. Say "this" and "that," not "dis" and "dat." Gerald worked on his delivery, trying to sound like Bob, trying to get that big, room-filling noise coming up from his diaphragm. He actually could make a pretty loud sound, but he couldn't hit those low notes. And his voice was sort of adenoidal. He was never going to compete with the beautiful commercial and acting voices out there. He had what they called a "character voice," a high baritone.

The good news, Breyer said, was that voices like his tended to mature later and sustain themselves longer in life. If he used his "instrument" right and didn't strain it, he had just as much of a shot at a career as anyone else. Breyer coached: first thing, don't go too low; start in the mid-part of the voice. Know what your lowest comfortable note is, and don't try to go lower. Keep your throat relaxed. If it doesn't sound right, start a little higher. The key is to get all of the music of your speech into a place where the words don't sound screechy or growly.

They worked on plays as practice texts, and Breyer succeeded in getting practical experience for them by doing radio versions of the plays on WNYC, the radio station owned by the city of New York. That was the first time Gerald Jacoby got into a radio studio. He never was a lead, he never had any more than a few lines, and there was no money.

As the year went on, the end of his unemployment insurance loomed. Everybody asked Breyer about jobs in radio and TV, and his answer was always the same: "Are you reading *Broadcasting* yet?" So Jerry started reading *Broadcasting*.

It was a world of unfamiliar jargon to him, a new perspective on the insides of the box and the tube. Most of it was business: stations bought, sold, traded, started; salaries and strikes; equipment and signal strength; Sarnoff says this; Paley says that. There were no articles about how to get a job. There were always positions-available ads in the back, but everyone wanted to see experience. He noticed that people were starting new stations almost every day, capitalizing on the postwar ad boom. Then he realized that new stations needed warm bodies more than established ones did.

He tried to decipher the ads. He guessed that "Great opportunity for talent," "Dynamic growing market," and similar come-ons were codes for "new station." He chose a group of prospects and began writing letters. With the first line of that first résumé, he started lying about himself—that is, making himself into a more desirable candidate for employment. He knew that being

Jewish was a liability. "Gerald Jacoby" wasn't exactly "Chaim Rabinowitz," but it was ethnic enough to be suspicious. Besides, most people in broadcasting changed their names anyway, so he adopted a white-bread goyish American last name and became Jerry Williams.

Other than the phony name, he was honest at first—he described himself as eager, willing to work hard and learn. He made some transcriptions of his voice at WNYC and sent them out. God, they were awful. He still sounded like a tough-guy Noo Yawkeh, but at least he could show prospective employers that he had a brain and could read copy intelligibly.

One week he ran across an ad that felt right to him. A job in Bristol, Virginia, at a station that was just getting off the ground, WCYB. They weren't even on the air yet. They were going to devote most of their broadcast day to what had been called Hillbilly Music and then was becoming known as Country and Western. He looked it up on a map. There was Bristol, in the westernmost point of Virginia, sitting right on the border with Tennessee. North Carolina was a few miles to the east. West Virginia was a few miles to the north.

He wanted to get that job so badly he could taste it. They were offering forty bucks a week, twice as much as he was getting from the 52-20 Club. Out in the sticks, he could learn from his mistakes and no one important could hear him.

Since he was already lying about his name, he took the next step and started lying about his experience. Somehow he'd found out, maybe from a *Broadcasting* article, about the *Chicago Sun* purchasing a station in Hammond, Indiana, back in 1942. The call letters had been WHIP, but they were WJWC now. That ownership change fitted perfectly with his age and the start of his service in the Air Corps. So he told the folks at WCYB that he'd worked at WHIP, for the previous owners, before he went into the service. And he'd had some academic training, too—not anyplace they could check easily . . . a university's extension division would be a good fudge. He invented the Indiana University Extension School of Radio Technique and enrolled himself in it. And he was an experienced newsman, too.

The folks at WCYB bought it, or at least Jerry thought they did. They sent him a letter. We're interested. We'd like to talk to you on the phone. Jerry jumped. He got through to Fey Rogers, one of the owners. Rogers could tell that Jerry was green, but he also heard something in this kid's voice. When Jerry hung up the phone, he could hardly believe it. He'd gotten himself a job as a newscaster with WCYB.

He got off the train in December 1946. He was told the Blue Ridge Mountains were off to his right, but he couldn't see them. The Tennessee state line was a few hundred yards to his left, invisibly splitting the city in two. There was the town's signature hotel, the General Shelby—handsome, foursquare, red-brick, eight stories high, one of the biggest buildings along the tree-lined streets. He registered, his suitcase holding a couple of weeks' worth of new clothes his folks had bought him, some ties he'd picked out, shaving stuff, a second pair of shoes, not much else. As he carried it up to his room, he regretted that he couldn't afford to stay there any more than a few days before he'd have to find a furnished apartment. Staying briefly at the Shelby had a great advantage, though—WCYB had what could charitably be called its offices and studios in the basement of the building.

Once he'd unpacked, he went downstairs to introduce himself and look around his new place of employment. No matter what he was expecting, the station was a disappointment. It occupied a few tiny rooms without anything in the corridor to identify it as a radio station or even a business. It was a new operation, and its furniture and technical equipment were basic. There were a few new pieces of equipment, mostly in the studios, but everything else was cobbled together or secondhand.

He met Fey Rogers and Bob Smith, another one of the owners. In fifteen minutes he'd seen everything—the audio board, the turntables, a small room for live performers, the managers' offices, the Associated Press teletype, and a table with a typewriter where he'd be preparing his newscasts.

Rogers gave Jerry a pep talk. He was convinced that Bristol deserved a real radio station, not one of the semiprofessional operations in the area that embarrassed themselves with stretches of dead air and well-meaning but dull announcing. This station was going to be a calling card for the tri-city area (Bristol, Kingsport, and Johnson City). Of course, since Jerry was from the biggest market in the country, he knew what announcers were supposed to sound like and what they were supposed to do. Sure, Jerry said. He knew.

That day and in the week ahead, he saw a steady stream of groups auditioning to appear on the station's new program, *Farm and Fun Time*. Even though WCYB wasn't even on the air, the word had gotten out. Little string bands—fiddlers, banjo players, guitarists, semipro musicians who'd been playing dances regularly and folks who'd done nothing but pick together on the porch—tramped in and out of the studio all day long. They played a few tunes and got their auditions recorded on the station's electronic transcription turntable, which dug into record blanks and spilled piles of spiral shavings on the floor.

Within a few days, the station was on the air for the first time, with a choice dial position—690, on the left-hand side of the AM band, where it would be easy to tune in even on a cheap radio. By then, Jerry had rented a seven-dollar-a-week room.

Rogers had in mind that Jerry would be doing news through the day, splitting the newscasts with another newsman and then cohosting a summary of the day's events, the *Newspaper of the Air,* at 5:00 P.M. On the first day, with Rogers overseeing, Jerry pulled the text of an hourly "Five-Minute Summary, World News" off the Associated Press wire. He had never seen the text of a five-minute newscast before, and he was dumbfounded about how much copy there was. So, casually, cavalierly, he remarked to Rogers, "Wow, that looks like a lotta news for five minutes."

Rogers looked at him oddly and Jerry knew immediately that he had blown it. To a seasoned, schooled professional, it would have been obvious that you could read that copy in about four and a half minutes. Besides, would the Associated Press put "Five-Minute Summary" on top of something that took longer than that to read?

There was nothing to do but to come clean, sort of. Nah, he'd never been a newsman. Just spun records and that sort of thing. But he was ready to work. "You won't be sorry you hired me," he promised Rogers. "I'll do anything. I'll be here whenever you need me. You wait and see. Gimme a couple of months."

Rogers could have told him to pack his bags, but he didn't. He and Bob Smith saw something, or heard something, in this kid, and Jerry survived.

He made lots of mistakes at first, but then everyone made lots of mistakes—after all, it was a brand-new station. The difference between this operation and many others at the time was that management knew the sound that it wanted on the air and wouldn't accept second-best. They told everyone to shape up fast, and Jerry had to move just as quickly as the guys who actually had been on the radio before. In a way, those first few weeks were as tough on him as boot camp had been, but they had the same effect on his radio work that the physical training had had on his body.

In the morning and afternoon, he occasionally had to put together a five-minute newscast in fifty-five minutes, and he found out how hard that was to do. The Associated Press machine was spitting out state, national, and international stories, and he had to keep an eye on it right up to the minute before he went on the air. He dreaded the machine's bell—whenever it went off, something significant was moving across the wire, a news alert or a bulletin or some stupid thing that the AP local editor thought was worthy of a ding or two.

He had to learn the simple technical skills—turning on his microphone ("mic" to everyone in the business, thanks very much) with a switch on the little audio board, watching the needles on what they called the VU meter bounce back and forth as his voice got louder or softer, riding the volume of his mic with one of the knobs (pretty soon, just like the music announcers, he called them "pots," short for "potentiometers"), making sure he didn't go too far into the red zone, speaking without shuffling papers too much, watching that Brooklyn accent, finishing his cast with "Jerry Williams, WCYB news," just as the second hand swept across the twelve on the studio clock. And doing commercials. He discovered that he actually enjoyed reading those spots for the grocery stores and Home Furniture and Thrift Supply Company and the car dealerships. They called for a little zing in his delivery, and he liked schmalzing it up a bit.

He wasn't a newsman. That was plain. Rogers and Smith told Jerry that he could do anything, so long as he lived up to the station's standards. He talked to the station's music announcers and watched them work. It was pretty clear from the response of their listeners that music was the important thing for the WCYB audience. The music on the air was the reason local businesses bought advertising, and the music announcers created the personality of the station.

The music guys—and, in particular, one experienced DJ named Stuart George O'Dell—showed him the basics on the fly. They were working with 78s back then—big, heavy circles of brittle shellac or plastic, one tune to a side—spinning them on heavy, professional-grade tables with tough metal needles. They had three tables set up around the audio board, since you needed at least two to do a music show and sometimes you needed a third one for prerecorded commercials, which were also on disc.

The basic drill was simple, even though it took a lot of practice to do it smoothly: a DJ would slip a record out of its jacket and onto one of the turntables, listen off the air ("in the cue channel," they said) for the first note or beat, then stop the table and rotate the record back about one turn. Then he'd key his mic on, start his chatter on the last note of the finishing tune, whip the turntable pot down, maybe read a commercial, introduce the next song, start the second table spinning a fraction of a second before he wanted the cued-up tune to start, whip the turntable pot up, and key his mic off. Then he'd take out the next record. Over and over and over, the same routine of activities for an hour or two hours or however long the show lasted.

The music defined the station. Roy Acuff and Merle Travis sang country tunes, and after Jerry had been there a few months, there was a new song called "Never Again," by some guy named Hank Williams. ("Jerry Williams" had turned out to be a pretty good hillbilly name.) They played Eddy Arnold's "It's a Sin," and Roy Rogers and Gene Autry crooning cowboy ballads and western songs. An occasional string band tune for the old-timers. A spiritual or two: "Dust on the Bible" and "Standing in the Need of Prayer"—if a rabbi in Brooklyn could only hear him announcing *those* things! Every once in a while some Texas swing with Bob Wills. And Bill Monroe's Boys, of course, playing bluegrass, that intricate mix of fiddling, banjo, guitar, and singing that the locals really liked. But the one thing that truly gave life to the air was the guy talking. Each of the announcers, no matter what part of the country he actually was from, worked up an easy patter suggesting he'd been born in one of the hollers and had polished up his words a bit to be on the radio. They spoke the listener's language: "Well, howdy, friends and neighbors, ever'body ever'where. Hope you're feelin' good this afternoon, got the chickens fed, 'n' the pickles put up, but even if y' got more t' do, all 'f us here at dubya-see-why-bee want t' put some *fine* music on the radio t' make y' day a li'l better. Here's our ol' fren' Curly King—Curly 'n th' Tennessee Hilltoppers did a big dance last weekend in Blountville, and he's got another one comin' up in Parks Mill on Sat'day. Ever'body likes 'is one, an' it's good advice, too, 'Let a Smile Be Your Umbrella.'"

Nobody wanted to do the morning show. It wasn't like radio today, when a station lives or dies by what's on the air between six and eight. Jerry said he'd do anything, so they tapped him for that sunrise shift—signing the station on at 4:30 A.M. and playing records and doing the news until one of the station's better announcers came on at a reasonable hour. He was the only guy there in the morning, and almost every day one of the hotel guests or visitors would stumble down the stairs and wander into the studio where Jerry was—it seemed like every time this happened he was on the air—and they'd yell out, "Where's yer bathroom down hyere?"

At noon WCYB presented fifteen minutes of live performance with local musicians who'd made it through the audition process, and Jerry got announcing duty on this show as well. Before too long, *Farm and Fun Time* was generating fan mail, and the management expanded it to a full hour. Jerry got to know some of the first featured performers. Ralph and Carter Stanley were two young musicians just back from the war who had already worked up a little duo bluegrass act. He was fascinated with the way they presented themselves—they'd already perfected snappy hellos and tune intros for the dances they played, and they transferred the rehearsed material to *Farm and Fun Time*. When they were off the air, they spoke the same way, but not quite so fast, not quite so dynamically. Here were these country boys, in the middle of nowhere, and they already knew how to put on a show.

There were lots more players—their names tangling together over time as he tried to remember whom he'd actually seen and heard—the Blue Sky Boys, Jim and Jesse McReynolds, Flatt and Scruggs, A. C. Carter (the patriarch of the Carter family)—they were nobodies when Jerry started fill-in hosting on *Farm and Fun Time,* but as the years went by, he would hear one of those names from time to time and realize he'd been there for a little bit of music history. Forty years later, when he interviewed June Carter Cash on WRKO in Boston, he realized that WCYB had been just as important to these musicians as it had been to him.

He began injecting a little personality into his intros as he got the feel of the material. Pretty soon fans of *Farm and Fun Time* got to know his name, too. He discovered from the mail coming in that the station really got out there. Because of the oddities of AM, one thousand watts at 690 got them farther than five thousand or ten thousand or fifty thousand at the higher frequencies. By any measure, WCYB was a success and Jerry was part of it.

It didn't take long before he realized he had to have a car if he was to get anywhere in the area. He bought a beat-up jalopy on time. When the station decided to send *Farm and Fun Time* out on the road, he drove along with the Clinch Mountain Boys, usually carrying some of their instruments and boxes of photographs the boys'd had printed up. He had a few pictures of himself as well, done in one of Bristol's better photo studios.

They'd come into one of these little settlements—sometimes nothing more there than a crossroads and a little school, out in yonder land. They'd set up shop in a classroom or whatever hall they had, people would gather, Jerry would introduce himself and the boys, and the music would start. He liked the way eyes lit up when they heard his voice and recognized him as one of the WCYB radio hosts. The boys even worked out novelty items for Jerry to sing: a Merle Travis hit called "So Round, So Firm, So Fully Packed, That's My Gal," and an Eddy Arnold tune called "That's How Much I Love Ya." ("Now, if you were a horsefly, and I an old gray mare, I'd stand and let you bite me, and I'd never move a hair.") After the show, he'd sell autographed photos. The Stanleys got a dollar for their picture. Jerry got a quarter for his.

One afternoon, as he was poring through the local paper, he came across a notice: the Barter Theatre in Abingdon, Virginia, was holding open auditions for a new summer production. As he read on, he got more excited. The Barter had been named Virginia's state theater company in the previous year, and its director, Robert Porterfield, was sort of a local saint because of his idea to start a theater company in the depths of the Depression, accepting farm goods and produce as well as cash for admission. Jerry got a day off from the station and drove to Abingdon. He introduced himself, suggested he could help out with publicity on WCYB, and gradually talked himself into a small part in an upcoming production.

Somehow he found a way to shoehorn rehearsals, backstage work, and pitching advertising for Barter programs into his WCYB schedule. During performance weeks, sleep was incidental, but it was worth it when he got onstage. That feeling of stepping into a role, becoming another person, was magic—so was hearing that sound of so many hands clapping as the cast took their bows. He thought that nothing could beat the feeling he had when the curtain came down on a show. Acting. Acting. That was what he *really* wanted to do.

But the Barter only scratched the itch for a little while. Jerry didn't want to be in hillbilly country. Even though he loved driving through the hills and watching the scenery roll by, living in rural America had shown him that the city was in his soul. Months after he'd started there and even when the station had developed a reputation with local music fans, hotel guests were still walking into his studio thinking it was a men's room. He came to resent the seven bucks he was paying for his junky little room. And it was hard to find the kind of girls that were worth his time—if he was going to a bar, he always had to do it on the less classy Tennessee side of Bristol, because Virginia was still holding on to Prohibition.

He knew he had to go. He scoured *Broadcasting* for other start-up stations—preferably stations closer to New York, stations that might be in towns where there were other theater companies.

His next steps—really nothing more than stumbles—were stints near Pittsburgh, first at WEDO ("eight-ten on the dial") in McKeesport, Pennsylvania, and then at WLOA in Braddock, just a few miles away. *Broadcasting* gave Jerry the news about WEDO—new station, owned by a guy named Hershberg who had a furniture store in the area, first station established outside Pittsburgh proper. It looked good on paper, anyway. Jerry phoned, tried to get a line on what they were trying to do, whether they could use a good DJ. Not really—they had lined up all the jocks they needed. But, say, they needed a newsman. Did Jerry do news?

"Sure, I do news." Now that he knew which end of a teletype was up, he could do news. Why not?

So it was farewell to *Farm and Fun Time*, handshakes all around at CYB, and "Good luck, son." He packed his clothes and souvenirs into cheap suitcases, revved up his lousy Chevy, and hit the road. He rolled up Route 11 through Virginia and climbed into the Blue Ridge Mountains. At first, it was a new chapter in his life, taking a last look at the fall colors decorating those gorgeous mountain vistas, going back to the city. Then it was his car coughing and wheezing up the grades. Then it was overheating, breakdown, and dilemma by the side of the road. He was too far from Bristol to go back, and putting any more money into this car would have been pointless. Hitchhike the rest of the way? Sure, but he couldn't be weighed down with a lot of baggage. So he ditched the car and nearly everything else that he'd acquired in Bristol, got the necessary things into one suitcase, and stuck out his thumb.

When he got to McKeesport, he knew right away that it wasn't his kind of town. Pittsburgh's steel mills filled the air with soot. The newspaper headlines seemed obsessed with ore, smelting, strife and strikes in the coal mines, tension between the giant steel companies and the small operators. He knew almost nothing about this stuff, except for the little he'd picked up from miners and their wives who came out to see the Clinch Mountain Boys. He felt as if he were as far away from the East he knew as he was when he lived in Bristol.

But he had to make this job work—he needed money for another car, if nothing else. This time there was no getting off the news desk. It was hard, time-consuming work that demanded he become a quick study about who was who and what was important in the Pittsburgh area. It was pretty easy to be neutral about local politics, where he didn't know the players, but when it came to national and foreign issues, he felt different. He found himself wanting to comment on what was going on.

And WEDO's management wanted him to sweat the details. It was one thing to have heard of the Monongahela River and another to have to say the word nearly every day on the air. If he made one mistake in pronunciation, got one mayor's name wrong, somebody would be on the phone a minute after the newscast was over. "Hey, Jerry, *what* was that word you said? Don't you know the score *yet?*" He kept making mistakes, and by December 1947, they booted him out. Broadcasting veterans like to say that you aren't really in the business until you've been fired, so WEDO did him one favor anyway. A second, if you counted the money he saved from working there to buy his second used car.

He looked around the area for another chance, and got hired by a new station in Braddock, just a couple of miles away. WLOA was significantly less prestigious and less powerful—it was down at the crowded end of the AM dial, at 1550, where the transmitter really had to push out watts to get you heard. And it was even closer to the steel mills than WEDO was. He found that his shirts were grimy after he'd worn them outside for about a half an hour. Two weeks after going on the air in Braddock, he was out of a job again.

So much for Pittsburgh.

Three stations and two cars in two years had toughened him up. He still had doubts about his ability to find the right radio job, but he had no doubt about his ability to make a living on the air. He knew the ropes. He knew what he was good at. He resolved that there would be no more news. He would find a job that fit his real skills—DJ work, patter, personality. And he now had some ideas of his own about what worked and what didn't when you were programming a radio station. So he headed east, toward the territory he knew, and one day he found himself talking to Ogden Davies, the general manager of a new station going on the air in Allentown, Pennsylvania. He turned on the charm, made the most of his real credentials, and pumped up his imaginary ones. He sensed interest, kept talking, selling. He was ready to step up, he said. He had some great ideas for programming. If Davies hired him as program director, he'd be getting top-quality air talent at the same time.

It wasn't long before he had new business cards printed and started introducing himself all over town.

Allentown was a city with rural roots—in fact, it had one of the East's biggest and best county fairs, an event that went back generations and pumped significant money into the community. It also was far enough away from Philadelphia to make it more than a suburb, a community with its own character, its own economy, even a small Jewish community. At the same time, it was eastern Pennsylvania, a little more cosmopolitan than Pittsburgh, a little less working-class. And he was within earshot of Philly, one step closer to New York.

Davies and Jerry saw eye-to-eye on programming. This station should be mainstream radio, giving Allentown a modern, up-to-date sound. It was Jerry's job to develop an on-air schedule that would achieve management's goals. That inevitably meant asking and answering the basic questions that all radio people come to grips with eventually. How can we attract a large enough audience to sell them things? How can we attract (read: steal) other stations' listeners? How can we address the unspoken desire for instant radio gratification in every listener—"Give me what I want when I want it"—and make money doing it?

From the twenties to the forties, American radio had been an all-things-to-all-people medium. Nearly every station tried to reach the broadest audience possible, with "specialty programming" for ethnic groups and smaller chunks of the community relegated to parts of the day and the week when fewer people were available to listen.

The traditional thinking about programming structure was codified in the thirties and reflected the stereotypes of American life, no matter how true they actually were. Early-morning programming should appeal to nearly everyone, since nearly everyone was getting set to begin the day. After hubby left for work, the station should concentrate on housewives, since almost no one listened to the radio in the office (the sets were too big, for one thing). As the man of the house came home around five or six, the family would gather around the dinner table and it would be time to catch up on the day's news. There might be some kids' programs right after dinner, but most stations went for big-deal entertainment shows in the early evening. After the kiddies went to bed, things shifted to more adult fare—crime dramas, science fiction, strange tales of the unknown. And if the station was one of those bold operations that didn't sign off at midnight, there would be music programming for the insomniacs and the lonely during the wee hours.

After the war, as TV was growing fast, radio managers began to think seriously about formats designed to appeal to distinct parts of the listening audience. "Modern programming" took it for granted that some people weren't going to like your station—and that those who did like it would be more loyal to you as a result. The program directors would study their communities (or use seat-of-the-pants guesswork) to design something distinctive. The appeal still had to be broad, but now a station should have a "personality," something that listeners would find relatively consistent and dependable all the time.

As a new station in Allentown, WKAP had an ostensible disadvantage—NBC and CBS programs were already committed to older outlets there or in nearby markets. But Jerry had already seen how WCYB, a station with a narrow format, could be successful without a network, and in fact, for younger listeners, the network radio shows were becoming a mark of stodginess. So he set out to build a station on the most up-to-date thinking of the time. It would be built on disc jockey shows, of course.

Jerry knew what he and the other DJs had to do. Be casual, relaxed, fun, lively, direct. Keep the audience aware of the time, warn about the weather, drop some tidbits about the music. Inform and entertain. Convey in a subtle way that you know what's stylish and fun.

One of the more tedious of his tasks was deciding what music the jocks would actually play. The trade papers, such as *Billboard,* established the standards with their weekly reports on the best-selling records. If a record was on the charts, you played it. If not, well, you might play it . . . if the record company man came around and provided incentives (which might as well have been spelled in$entive$).

He wasn't going to do anything adventurous with WKAP's music format. The hits of the postwar years were sweet, uncomplicated, singable melodies with lyrics conveying warmth, wholesomeness, and occasionally a little bit of heartbreak. So WKAP listeners heard Perry Como languidly singing "Because." They heard Miss Peggy Lee's charmingly offensive ditty called

"Mañana," sung in the persona of a stereotypical lazy Mexican girl. ("I'll go to work mañana, but I gotta sleep tonight.") There were some black singers on the air occasionally—novelty performers like Louis Jordan ("Saturday Night Fish Fry"), sophisticates such as Nat King Cole (WKAP was playing his version of Mel Tormé's "Christmas Song" almost as soon as the station went on the air in 1947), and the famous quartets—the Ink Spots and the Mills Brothers. But none of that race music, thank you—Dinah Washington and Big Joe Turner were fine for those juke joint coin machines, but not for a clean family station. There were a few country tunes by singers who didn't sound too much like rednecks, people like Eddy Arnold.

The program director's duties extended well beyond the air. There was no point in having programming at all unless you had ads to pay for it. Jerry hit the street, his dark hair slicked back, in his best suit and tie, a twenty-five-year-old radio salesman going from business to business, introducing himself and WKAP. He explained how he was going to attract a young and vibrant audience, just exactly the kind of people that (your name here) would love to have buying your products, coming into your store, calling your appliance repair service, buying your engagement rings, putting money in your pocket. People will be coming into your place saying, "Jerry sent me," just you wait and see. All you need to do is buy a few ads—and the prices are very reasonable, dontcha think?

And when it couldn't hurt, he dropped a few phrases that let the prospective client know they shared a common heritage. "When I was growing up in Flatbush . . . My family's in the clothing business in Brooklyn . . . I wanted to get to you before you close for shabbas . . . You Jewish, too?" One of the first guys he got to know well was Archie Federman, who ran an all-purpose record shop—not just the full line of the brittle 78-rpm records lined up in their cardboard sleeves and bulky albums, but the record players, too, and the needles they ate up, plus a nice side business in jukeboxes. Archie was amused at first when Jerry came in. After a few moments, he decided he liked the kid. He gave him a few pointers about Allentown, since he was obviously starting out cold, with no sense of the likes and dislikes of the local people. But when it came to business, Archie said he wasn't ready to buy any ads. He'd think about it.

Then he listened to the afternoon record show. *Date with Jerry*, he called it—this kid had chutzpah; it was like he was advertising himself to the girls in town. But, Archie had to admit, he sounded good. He had an unusual voice—not exactly high, but higher than he expected, not like the big booming radio voices Archie had grown up with. When he spoke, he grabbed you. It was something about the way he paused between the words. He sounded *modern*, I guess you'd say. Then he heard Jerry pitch Lerner's Department Store in Northampton.

"Listen, folks, I know the clothing business pretty well, and I've *never* seen a *better* stock of styles—and at better prices—than I've seen at Lerner's in Northampton. When you go in, have a look at those winter dresses and coats. No one in the area can beat 'em. For beautiful material and great designs in women's clothes, it's Lerner's on Main Street in Northampton. And for that man in your life, you'll find some very sharp suits—lemme tell ya, I buy all *my* suits at Lerner's. And one more thing [here Jerry put in one of those pauses]—if you see Mr. Kauffman walking around the store, make sure you say hello and tell him Jerry Williams sent you."

Pretty soon, Archie's shop was on the air, too.

Archie was amazed when girls actually came in the store and said, "Jerry sent me." Cute girls, too. One of them actually said, "He's dreamy."

Archie said, "How do you know what he looks like?"

She said, "I can just tell."

By the spring of 1948, things seemed to be going pretty well. The station had been on the air for a few months, ad revenue was coming in, Jerry was making a little money for a change. It was time for another step up, something that said "Program Director" and "Man on the Move." Something that would make people say, "Who's that guy?" A car. A *real* car.

Just as Joanne McCoy represented some magical ideal of Woman for Jerry, his 1948 Hudson Hornet took pride of place before all his other cars—and he eventually owned a *lot* of cars. The Hornet was one of the first of the great streamlined vehicles, breaking away from the old-fashioned look of the boxy touring cars like Samuel Jacoby's Essex. Jerry fell hard for the Hornet. It was forward-looking, powerful, projecting thrust and drive. Almost like a torpedo. If it was a little suggestive, a little sexy, well, so much the better. Its design was so radical that few in town wanted to take a chance on it, and Jerry was able to get it for a pretty good price—eight hundred dollars, about two months' wages for him, which he spent without a qualm.

He had the car and he had the wardrobe to go with his title—Arnold Kauffman at Lerner's had given the clothes to him almost at wholesale. He had enough dough to show a girl a good time. He'd gotten out into Pennsylvania Dutch country and discovered that the food was all right. Hess Brothers restaurant. Those apple pies. Not bad, not bad at all.

He was enjoying life and getting to be a biggie. Not just with the listeners, either. The record guys were saying, "I gotta get t' Jerry Williams, because anything he plays gets t' be a hit. Gotta get those records on his show." Were they giving Jerry something on the side to put their platters on the air?

"Payola" wasn't a dirty word in 1947. It was just business. A lot of promotion men had extra cash to spread around and a lot of DJs were finding ways to supplement their income. Jerry had a new car . . .

One afternoon, while he was on the air, a young woman who wrote for the *Allentown Morning Call* and *Evening Chronicle* came to the station. She told the receptionist that she'd heard the show and wanted to see what Jerry looked like. Pretty soon she was in the studio, watching Jerry "in front of the console with ten dials and double that number of toggle switches, flashing colored lights and turn-tables," pressing him with questions about his background when there were records on the air.

He told her about Flatbush (leaving his ethnicity open to speculation), and the Dodgers, and then said he'd started his career by going to night broadcasting school in Hammond, Indiana, and at the same time working days at a station in the Chicago suburbs, sacrificing sleep for radio. He laid it on thick.

Then he gave her a little philosophy about programming. "Most of our programs are chosen for their overall appeal, but during the day we try to present things that housewives will like. When I do my Saturday show, I know that the kids are out of school, so I try to spin things they'll enjoy."

He also gave her a preview of his own Sunday evening monologue, inspired by Henry Morgan's WOR show. "Just now he is wrapped up in a new offering which will go on the air April 25 at 6:45 P.M.," she wrote in the published piece. "This will be 'Are You Kidding,' which Jerry says is a novelty and packed full of possibilities and promise."

He sent a copy of the story home to his ma and dad. See? One of these days, I'm gonna be a big star. His mother started a scrapbook for him.

Are You Kidding, the monologue show, was a stretch for him. He knew what it should feel like—smart, fast, witty, a little irreverent. Not quite as caustic or off-the-wall as *Here's Morgan*—he couldn't afford to thumb his nose directly at his sponsors or the station owners the way Morgan had. So he experimented: he started out the fifteen minutes with unusual stories from the newspapers, some observations drawn from columns that seemed particularly well written, examples of the follies of everyday life that he himself had observed—anything that would provide raw material for a free-form look at life. He prepared some routines, some jokes, some lines designed to get a laugh or two, but his ultimate goal was that loose, improvisatory quality that Morgan exemplified.

The experience was instructive. He learned that he couldn't do Morgan's shtick. His jokes weren't urbane enough; they kept sliding in the direction of dialect stories or Borscht-belt one-liners. His perspective wasn't distant enough; unlike Morgan, who had a disdain for almost everyone, he sympathized too much with the daily trials of regular folks. His background wasn't erudite enough; whenever he tried to do something a little brainy or to use a twenty-dollar word, he felt that his lack of education showed.

Jerry's last big idea to get the station noticed was a man-on-the-street show, right in the middle of town. He worked with a guy named Lou Steele. Handsome Lou. The two of them would buttonhole people on the street and ask them the Question of the Day. A little back-and-forth—Where d' you live? How many kids? What d' y' do for a living? How's business?—and pretty soon, you'd have a little knot of people around you, all wanting to be on the radio, all with an answer to the Question of the Day. The girls had a look at Handsome Lou, and Jerry got a little reflected attention, too. They threw in a couple of commercials for Kay Jewelers ("Don't forget, folks: It's okay to owe Kay to pay day!"), did some mildly amusing banter, and then kicked it back to the studio. Another thing for Allentonians to talk about. Another reason to listen to WKAP.

And another way to learn. The man-on-the-street thing was Jerry's first experience working with ordinary folks live on the air.

Despite the more-than-full-time job he had at WKAP, he was still trying to scratch that actor's itch. During the summer of 1947, he took his growing radio rep and his Barter Theatre credentials to a couple of theater companies in the area, and since any warm body (especially one with a little media clout) was welcome to help with their amateur productions, he was quickly embraced. He got some small parts in summer stock productions at the Hayloft Theater, and he parlayed that into more work, offstage and on, with other groups around town.

As the summer came to an end, Jerry saw his first Allentown Fair. It started on a Saturday, a week before Labor Day, and went on for more than a week. It was huge—animal shows, harness racing, a market for local farmers to sell their produce, 4-H displays, pie-eating contests, concerts featuring local stars, full-fledged evening shows with top-name performers. Lots and lots of food and drink. Hundreds of thousands of people came from everywhere in Lehigh County and well beyond. Some folks arrived at the fairgrounds when the gates opened and used it as an excuse to stay bombed for a week. Jerry and the station had a presence there, of course, and he did everything he could to get the word out about WKAP. He was dressed impeccably, and he loved having people see him drive up and park his Hornet in a VIP spot.

One evening he caught the eye of an attractive young woman who obviously was feeling no pain. Betty Tapley was this lady's name. She knew Jerry, of course—who didn't know *Date with Jerry*? Well, would he like a date with her? She was friendly. *Very* friendly. What began as one date at the fair became a hot little affair.

About a month later, as Jerry was driving back to his place from Betty's in the middle of the night, his schedule caught up with him. Radio, selling, schmoozing, acting, lovemaking, the long dark streets with almost no other cars, streetlights drifting by as he rode along Hamilton Street, his eyelids closing for a few seconds, then a few seconds more, then . . . WHAM! That horrible dead crunching metal sound. He woke up in the middle of an inter-section, a traffic light overhead blinking red and yellow, red and yellow, with the whole front end of his beautiful Hudson Hornet crumpled up, embedded in the side of another man's car. This other guy leaped out, distraught, wav-ing his arms, saying his wife was about to have a baby at Allentown Hospital and Jerry had to get his Hornet out of the way because he was going to drive there no matter what. He must have been planning to go there by force of will. Jerry got out and discovered that his own legs were like rubber. The two of them stared at the mess in the center of a major intersection in Allentown, the shock making them both a little nuts. Jerry tried to get hold of himself. The other guy was frantic. Finally, Jerry found some words. "Relax, man. Let a policeman come."

That was it for the Hornet. Insurance took care of the expense, and a local body shop tried to put it back on the road, but the front end never was right again. Jerry forgot about what happened to the other guy, what went on at the hospital, whether the wife and kid were all right. It was the death of his car that really pained him.

It would seem that he had Allentown by the tail. Good money, big rep, steady girl. Despite all that, by the end of 1948, Jerry had left WKAP. Why? Why ditch a day job as one of the area's leading program directors—and a prime DJ spot—for the midnight-to-4-A.M. shift on another Allen-town station?

Some scraps among Jerry's papers offer some clues, but they don't add up to a story. There's a December 1948 letter from Arnold Kauffman of Lerner's Department Store to Joseph Nassau, the GM of WAEB, that almost sounds as if Jerry wrote it. The letter says Jerry's looking for "betterment of his position in a new progressive set-up," which sounds like he's still at WKAP, but doing some fishing. Then there's an early fifties résumé that names WKAP's Ogden Davies as a reference.

Maybe things weren't so rosy at WKAP. Did Jerry get caught taking cash to play records at KAP, and did Davies want to keep it quiet? "Listen, Jerry, you know what you have to do. But if you want, use my name as a reference." In one of the great ironies of his life, if he'd just hung on at WKAP for a couple more years, he'd have been around for something big—the station debuted a show in 1952 called *Open Mic,* one of the first radio programs to put telephone callers' voices on the air with a delay system.

Soon Jerry knew that the decision he'd made had taken him in the wrong direction. Seven months later, the job at WAEB was done. He'd been through three communities and five radio stations in four years. He'd quit, flamed out, and been fired. His relationship with Betty Tapley was fun, but not serious. He was twenty-five. He still wanted to act. And he yearned to get back to New York.

He was still reading *Broadcasting.* He surely paid attention to the TV explosion of 1948 and 1949, and he probably saw the sales of sets booming all over the country. Almost every week in those two years, he would have read of another television station on the air in a major market—WCAU, Philadelphia; WBAL, Baltimore; WNAC, Boston; WJZ, New York; WXYZ, Detroit; KGO, San Francisco; KTTV, Los Angeles; and dozens more. The momentum was building for the new medium, and the lure may have been irresistible. There were open jobs at the new local stations and in the networks' TV departments, as they staffed up drama programs, soap operas, all kinds of things for the tube. So, if he went into television, he might have the chance to be an actor, a real actor, a full-time actor—failing that, he might at least be able to land a job hosting a game show, or doing staff announcing, or directing shows, or *something.*

One problem: he didn't know anything about how TV worked—the cameras, the video boards, the lights. It couldn't just be radio with pictures. In 1946 he'd been so eager to get going on a career in show business that he turned his back on the GI Bill education benefits available to him as a returning veteran. Now, he thought, the GI Bill might come in handy. He had to find some place that wouldn't require a high school diploma to teach him the nuts and bolts of television.

In the fall of 1949, he was back in the city, enrolled at the School of Radio and Television Technique. Not exactly Columbia or NYU. All the other guys there were veterans of the war who'd been going to school for the past four years—beauty school, plumbers' school, even chicken flicking school, where they learned to defeather the birds and got leftover plumage as a bonus for their own take-home pillows. These guys used their GI Bill benefits to keep postponing their growing up. Not Jerry. He was a real broadcaster already, a guy with experience. He just needed a few months of seasoning, to understand the jargon and get his hands on the equipment.

For someone who'd worked with audio boards, the basic concepts of television in 1950 weren't hard to grasp. He saw how lighting changed the appearance of people on camera. He found out how important it was for the talent to have the right color clothes for black-and-white TV, good makeup, good hair. He saw video cameras for the first time, and found out how cumbersome those old monsters were—the operators had to move slowly and carefully to avoid smearing the image. Framing up a good shot, choosing the right distance from the subject, cutting from camera to camera, keeping the boom mic out of the frame, using simple graphics on the title cards, cueing in music to enhance the power of a scene—all the individual elements of video production were pretty simple. Putting them together was another matter entirely. Unlike radio, which was essentially solo performance, TV was a group activity, and it was much harder for one person to put his or her stamp on a production. There had to be camera people, lighting people, sound people, a director in the booth and at least a couple of supporting engineers. If you were in front of the camera, you had to mesh with the others. You couldn't just improvise your way through. It was stiffer, more restrictive than radio.

Once he'd gotten familiar with the technical stuff, he put it in the back of his head. He figured he'd need to be able to tell when something was obviously wrong, but he had no intention of burying himself in a technical crew. He wanted to be in front of the cameras and let someone else worry about the lighting and sound. As soon as he thought he could handle himself in a TV studio, he got busy becoming an actor.

He plugged himself into the sources for casting calls, and began making the rounds of agents' offices with his head shot. He'd put a lot of thought into that photo, striking a dramatic, slightly menacing pose, arms folded, in a black turtleneck. He positioned his body at an angle and turned his face towards the camera so that his nose would look straight. Instead of a smile, the expression showed a little bit of disdain, with some vulnerability in his eyes. The message he wanted to send was: serious young actor, lean, masculine, not beefy, tough but sensitive. A darker Alan Ladd, maybe. Jerry Williams, twenty-six. Would prefer dramatic or romantic leads.

Of course, he never heard the snap judgments of the casting personnel and agents' secretaries. Charlie, here's a Cornel Wilde type with straight hair. Or maybe Dick Powell with softer features. A little Dan Duryea in the mouth. Okay-looking kid. Not a matinee idol, but good-enough-looking. Big dark eyebrows. They make him look mean. What is he, Armenian, Greek, Jewish? The eyes aren't big enough—they won't grab people, especially on TV. Could do character parts, though. Don't we have a street scene where we need a lot of bodies? Could use 'im there.

Instead of the leads he'd have killed for, or even the minor roles he coveted, he got crowd scenes and walk-bys, and precious few of those. He had to

Jerry Williams, budding television actor, ca. 1950.

relearn his Noo Yawk accent for his readings, since most of the casting people saw him as a dark or sinister character. He'd tell his folks: Watch *Famous Jury Trials* on DuMont this week. Or *Studio One* on CBS. Or *Philco Playhouse* on Sunday night. If they looked hard, they might see him for a fraction of a second. Ironically, he didn't see himself, except when the show's producers were nice enough to let him look at a kinescope. These were all live productions, where he had to provide his own wardrobe, make sure his hair was nicely cut, do his own makeup.

The day after he did a role, he couldn't rest. He had to keep making the rounds, over and over, one Yes for twenty No's. He got ten or fifteen tiny little parts that year, one every three or four weeks. And a couple of behind-the-scenes things, such as a quick turn assisting in the production of a DuMont drama called *Oh, Mother.* No money—that is, nothing to speak of. He was borrowing from his folks to meet the rent, picking up odd jobs for pocket money.

Late in the year, when he had some credentials under his belt, he went to an NBC casting call and finally got a real part—in a detective show, *Martin Kane, Private Eye,* starring William Gargan, a George Raft–type hard-boiled dick. Jerry was tapped to be a nameless Turkish bath attendant who was supposed to tell Kane that a guy he was looking for was in the next room. The role called for him to wear a T-shirt. Show off a little physique. Not bad. One line: "He's in there." His cue from Gargan would be, "Where is he?" In reply, Jerry was supposed to say his line and give his thumb a little jerk, or maybe point with his finger, depending on where the door would eventually be on the set.

For weeks Jerry rehearsed those three words. He lived the old story you've heard a hundred times—the tale of the young actor who worries his lines to death. He sweated every second he was going to get on the tube. "He's in there." What was the perfect way to say it, the way that was filled with dramatic intensity, the way that would capture viewers immediately? "Hey, who's *that* guy? He's *good!*"

He could do it like Kane's coconspirator, cocking an eyebrow and tossing a thumb over his shoulder: "He's in *there.*" No, wait. He could do it as though the guy Kane was looking for was his mortal enemy, with barely-concealed anger, through clenched teeth: "He's in there." No. Instead, he could stretch all the words out to prolong the time he'd get on screen: "Heeee's iiiiin theeeerrrre."

The day of the production comes. Jerry's perfect, in a spotless white T-shirt, erect. Gargan breezes into the scene, and the camera follows him. They shoot across Jerry's shoulder. They get the back of his head.

The camera watches Kane look at Jerry and growl, "Where is he?"

No one sees the bath attendant's face as he replies, tersely, with a little Noo Yawk accent: "He's in theh."

That was his big break. The rest of 1950 was one little job after another. Nothing to show for it except a few lines on his résumé and "He's in theh." But Jerry would have kept on going. Each visit to a TV set fed that little fire inside him, that lust to do more, that hunger for the inaudible applause out there in thousands of living rooms. He was convinced that if he just kept working his contacts and doing the calls, eventually he'd make it. Unfortunately, his folks didn't agree with him.

4 GETTING SERIOUS

Samuel Jacoby faced his son. "You're twenty-six years old. It's about time you did something with your life." Frieda looked across the table at him sadly.

Gerald was silent. He'd played this part too many times before. His dad didn't know anything about dreams. Just another year, maybe, and he'd be established. But he needed time.

"You know we love to see you on TV," Frieda said, her eyes begging him to be reasonable. "But it's not steady work. A man needs to have a job. When you find a nice girl and you want to get married, how can you support her with this acting?"

"The radio you did—it's steadier work, at least," Samuel said. One of the few times the old man gave him any credit, Gerald thought. "You could get a paycheck, and act when you got the chance."

Easy for him to say. His dad didn't know how hard radio was, how time-consuming. It ate up your life, with the selling and the organization and the other bullshit, and the tension on the air—he never smoked so much as when he was working in Allentown. If he went back to radio, he'd probably be kissing acting good-bye.

A couple of weeks later, there was something in *Broadcasting*. Experienced radio program director sought, Camden, New Jersey. Jerry didn't know exactly where Camden was, but he'd heard of it. Campbell's Soup had a big plant there. RCA Victor was there, with their recording studios and a TV factory. A job there would keep him pretty close to the city. So he sent one of his résumés and a letter to the *Broadcasting* box number, highlighting the program director credit from WKAP, the importance of his afternoon DJ show, his success selling to the local businesses in Allentown. He also included the usual creative credential enhancement—his phony academic training at Indiana University and his early days on WHIP in Hammond.

Some time passed, and he got a reply. Come to Camden for an interview. Where is it, anyway? Look at that, right across the Delaware River from Philadelphia.

He drove into town after a couple of hours on the road and discovered how tough and gritty it was. It didn't look like there was much reason for the Rittenhouses to cross the river. He found WKDN, on Mt. Ephraim Avenue, in a little nondescript one-story building at the base of a huge AM stick. He got a quick tour before he sat down with the owner. There were a couple of studios. A small newsroom. Some offices for the sales staff and the GM. Not much else.

Maybe it was the rough-around-the-edges feel of Camden in 1951. Maybe it was the fact that he really didn't care if he got the job. Maybe it was all the acting he'd been doing. Maybe it was the seventy-two-year-old man on the other side of the desk, the head of South Jersey Broadcasting, C. H. Ranulf Compton—Major Compton to you. All of the factors together added up to a feeling of superiority, a feeling that they needed him more than he needed them. Maybe that's why he aced the interview.

Jerry talked about his background—plenty of stories about Bristol and Allentown. Major Compton talked about his Purple Heart and his Legion of Honor. There was no reason for it, but something clicked between the young guy on the make and the old geezer.

"Jerry, howdja like t' be program director here?"

"By God, yes. Whaddya paying?"

"A hundred and twenty a week."

Pretty soon, he had a furnished apartment above a store on Haddon Avenue.

In early 1951 twenty-seven-year-old Jerry Williams was an announcer and the program director at WKDN, worrying a bit about his safety downtown at night. An eighteen-year-old Brooklyn kid named Larry Zeiger was finishing up his senior year at Lafayette High and trying to decide what to do with his life. William and Winifred O'Reilly were living not too far out on Long Island with their infant son, William Jr. Fourteen-year-old Thomas Magliozzi wasn't paying too much attention to his baby brother Raymond in Cambridge, Massachusetts. An eleven-year-old named David Brudnoy was getting curious about the world in Hutchinson, Minnesota. A little boy named John Donald Imus Jr. was living on a ranch in Prescott, Arizona. And at just about the same time, the Limbaughs of Cape Girardeau, Missouri, were welcoming an infant son to the family; the proud father gave the baby his own name and the name of his grandpa.

Not one of them—not Jerry Williams, Larry King, Bill O'Reilly, the Car Talk guys, David Brudnoy, Don Imus, or Rush Hudson Limbaugh III—had yet heard the phrase "talk radio," but something like it was already on the air in quite a few cities across America.

There were dozens of great radio interviewers all over the country in the late forties. These men and women were pure conversationalists, people with a broad range of knowledge, folks who could make even the dullest guest seem interesting. Almost every big town had a good one, and some of them were nationally known.

The year Jerry moved to Camden, Mary Margaret McBride could legitimately claim to be the nation's premiere radio interviewer. Less than two years earlier, when Jerry was doing his all-night show in Allentown, they celebrated her fifteenth year on the air in New York with an event in Yankee Stadium and damn near filled the place. Even Eleanor Roosevelt was there. McBride's show was planted in the middle of the day, among the soaps and housewife shows, so she was typed as a "woman interviewer," or worse, a "women's interviewer." On the surface her style was self-effacing, indirect, careful. She got some good stuff out of her guests, but she did it in a way that was "ladylike," you might say. Jerry had no interest in *that* kind of approach.

He preferred the work of a guy who had only a local reputation—Cal Ross, on WPEN in Philly. When Jerry got to Camden and could listen to him regularly, Ross captivated him, thrilled him with his ability to keep guests on the subject, to take on significant issues.

There was a guy in Boston, Sherman Feller, one of America's first true talk show hosts, remembered now mostly as that Boris Karloff–like PA announcer for the Red Sox ("Ladies and gen'lemen, boys and girrrrrrls . . ."). Sherm started during World War II, when the Federal Radio Commission mandated that a certain number of stations had to stay on the air twenty-four hours a day, just in case there was a need to broadcast emergency info. He was tapped by WEEI to hold the mic from midnight to 4:00 A.M. His show developed into *Club Midnight,* a sort of on-air after-hours cabaret. Sherm would play records, spotlight celebs passing through town, talk up musicals and plays, promote lounge singers and jazz bands. Sherm got to be Mr. Showbiz in Boston on the strength of that program.

Two other radio newcomers, Bob Elliott and Ray Goulding, didn't bother with celebrities; they were having too much fun talking to each other. Like Sherm, they'd started in Boston in the forties, when Ray was a DJ and Bob a newsman, on WHDH. They kept goofing around in the studio, doing skits and funny voices, making up ads for fictional sponsors, parodying old-time radio shows, deviating further and further from what they were supposed to be doing on the air.

A character named Jack Eigen came up with something else—or at least popularized it—and other announcers all over the country followed his lead. In 1947 his station paid for a telephone line to the lounge of Manhattan's Copacabana, where Jack introduced records that an engineer would spin back at home base. In between, he talked with the stars visiting the Copa after they'd finished working. And sometime around 1950 he started taking phone calls. None of the callers' voices ever made it on the air, of course. How could they make sure somebody wouldn't say a dirty word? It was one-way talk. "I'm at th' Copa. Wherah you?" Jack would say to folks on the phone. "Y' want talk t' Al Jolson? Y' do? Whadja wanna ask 'im?" A little pause, then: "So, y' wanna ask him whether he's gonna get married again." Then he'd turn to Jolson. "The caller wants t' know if y' gonna get married again." No one ever accused Jack of having a perfect radio voice, but he was an authentic Man of the Night, not just an observer. During Jerry's acting year, Eigen was his constant late-night companion.

One of the first guys to imitate Eigen was Steve Allison, a guy from Revere, Massachusetts, who started out doing a show on Boston's WVOM in mid-1948, first from a downtown restaurant and nightclub called Steuben's, and then from the Latin Quarter on Winchester Street. Again, this was a schmooze-with-the-stars kind of show, but Steve did some controversial topics, too.

An ex-Marine with a prosthetic leg had been working for about a year and a half in Wilmington, Delaware, when Jerry first heard him on WILM. Joe Pyne initially impressed him as a good interviewer. But then Joe took a ninety-degree turn to the right, making abrasive, sarcastic comments on the news and public personalities, and pummeling his unheard phone callers with one-liner insults: "Why don't you go gargle with razor blades?" or "Put your finger in your ear and go bowling." Jerry stopped listening after a while, but Joe got famous, anyway.

Another talker came to the Philadelphia area from Cincinnati in 1951, just a couple of months after Jerry arrived. He did a show on KYW, originating from a lounge or a dining room. He'd sit there with a live mic and talk to people as they came in—anybody who'd talk to him. He'd ask people what they did for a living, what they'd done that day, tell stories about himself. Somehow he made it interesting. Weird name. Jean Shepherd.

And of course, there was Barry Gray, the guy who put Woody Herman on the air in New York. His record show had gradually changed into a mostly conversation program. He wasn't talking just about music, either. He'd take on all kinds of topics, get into discussions of political issues and personalities. There would be one-way phone calls, too. Sometimes the callers would take issue with something Barry had said and he'd have to paraphrase what they'd said.

In many other markets, there were other people trying out talk with varying degrees of success. Listeners liked this stuff. It was engaging, interesting. Not like those old "panel discussions" or "forums of the air" on Saturday mornings, the obligatory public affairs programming. These newer shows put the host in the spotlight, taxed his or her ingenuity, kept the audience guessing. Once you got on the show's wavelength, it was like a continuing drama.

WKDN had a strong signal. You could hear it in Camden, all over Philadelphia, even in the southern part of New Jersey, including the state capital, Trenton. Major Compton had the notion that his station should position itself as the voice of South Jersey, since there were plenty of stations fighting for Philly business. The station had done pretty well on a limited budget. It had a cornerstone announcer named Doug Warren who served as morning man. There was a newsman, a funny guy named Harry Smith. ("Call me Bud, everyone else does.") They had a sports announcer and a kid to help him, since high school sports was one of KDN's keys to success in South Jersey. A couple of salesmen. A chief engineer. Some office staff. And a few people who would work for next to nothing just to be in broadcasting.

When Major Compton said, "Program director," he meant "Everything." It was WKAP again, only more so.

Jerry had his opening conversation with Doug Warren and saw that there'd be no point in messing with this gruff old character, who actually sounded pretty good, even if he was playing music that sounded pretty old and dated (Patti Page singing "The Tennessee Waltz" and Mario Lanza belting out "Be My LOOOOOVE!" Oh, well). To make the station more exciting, Jerry figured on beefing up the midday, and putting himself in the chair after Warren. His first great inspiration was a name for his new show—*A Word to the Wives*. He was going to shoot for women at home, the audience that everyone was targeting after 9:00 A.M. He planned to use some of that *Date with Jerry* charm that had worked so well in Allentown. He spun records (jazzier stuff than the station played in the mornings), did the weather, chatted and joked with Bud Smith after the newscasts, kept it lively and sharp.

One day he invited Bud in during the show to help him do a joke that called for a woman's voice. Bud did a great job—Jerry laughed out loud on the air. This led to more and more jokes, and Jerry realized that Bud was a real talent.

It was a waste to have him just doing news. Maybe they could do some crazy material, like those TV shows from Philly hosted by that madman named Ernie Kovacs.

They started doing bits on the air, much in the way that Bob and Ray had started. Jerry gravitated toward the role of straight man. Bud had a versatile set of pipes and was a pretty good mimic, so he could do character voices and all the women's voices. A whole world of fantasy opened up for them, and the initial feedback from listeners and senior management on their funny stuff was good. A little over-the-top for Camden, but what the hell?

In the first few months, he realized that the station needed some kind of spark at noon. People were taking a break at lunch, changing their routine. If there was something to get them tuning in at midday—the station had a noon newscast; what if there was something after that—a program that *talked about* the news?

As Jerry began to hear it in his head, it would be a kind of hybrid radio program. Highlight things in the news that were interesting each day. Throw in some commentary, provocative material, not old-time-radio stuffy. And, like Jack Eigen, take some phone calls. But what if the listeners could hear the callers' voices?

Jerry decided to call it *What's on Your Mind?* It was his idea, and he knew what he wanted it to sound like, so he would be the host of *this* show, too. The WKDN engineers were dubious, but Jerry was the PD. They rigged up a phone system and tested it out. It worked. The rest was up to Jerry.

"Give us a call, folks, and we'll put you right on the air. What's on your mind?" And people did call. Tentative at first, not sure that this guy answering the phone was the same one that was talking on the radio. He sounded so different in their ears. Jerry used his man-on-the-street style to draw them out. Where do you live? You married? What does your husband do? What kind of car d' you drive? Are the streets clean in your part of town? What can we do to make South Jersey better? Have any suggestions for the mayor? For the governor? He was really hearing the voice of the people.

It worked great! Until Major Compton heard about it.

"Jerry, are you crazy? Don't you know we can't do that? What if we get one of those Puerto Rican nationalists on the phone, like the guys who tried to kill Truman last year? What if some woman decides she's gonna say yoo-hoo to her neighbors—that's point-to-point, the Commission says that's a license violation. What if someone says 'Hell' or 'Damn'? We'd have to take the station off the air!"

Yes, sir, Major. So the callers' voices were verboten. Jerry did *What's on Your Mind?* the way Eigen and Barry Gray and Sherm Feller did their shows.

Harry "Bud" Smith and Jerry Williams (soon to be known as the Gag Busters), during a remote live radio telethon on WKDN, Camden, New Jersey, ca. 1952.

He listened to the question or comment, paraphrased it on the air, and then reacted to it.

It didn't take long before he realized that he would have to light a fire under people. He didn't have celebrities to attract attention to his show. He would have to shape the conversation, set the tone. Opinions on the air were tricky. Broadcasting was supposed to be neutral, and one of the areas the FCC looked at carefully was fairness. And Jerry knew he hardly had any credibility with his new audience—where would he get off delivering his views on the issues?

He realized that he could get opinions on the air if they were *other* people's opinions. So he brought newspapers into the studio and started talking about what was on the editorial pages in Camden, in Philly, in New York. He would react to what he read, just as an average person would if he were reading the paper to his wife or his buddy.

Over time, he found a persona and he began to build a rationale for the show. He decided to be the voice of the little guy. He wouldn't talk down to the audience the way old-time radio commentators had. He would be one of them. He showed his listeners that it was okay with him if they wanted to disagree with the newspaper columnists or editors, if they wanted to criticize the governor, take issue with the president.

On the other hand, he had little patience for callers' personal problems or eccentricities. If they were off the topic, he dismissed them quickly. He had even less patience if they defended the people in power who were wasting their tax dollars, or if they sympathized with the bigots or the charlatans.

Listeners began to look forward to hearing him argue with himself. "You mean t' tell me that you said that I was a Communist? Izzat what you said? You called me a—a what? Why, we can't even say that word on the radio, sir! Lemme talk to someone smart for a change! See ya later."

Jerry had a long workday, starting at about 8:30 in the morning, or a little bit later, just so long as he wasn't late for his hour with Bud beginning at 9:00. There was time between 10:00 and noon for mail and some prep, going through the newspapers, before *What's on Your Mind?* came up at 12:15. He might be able to get out for some appointments with prospective advertisers in the early afternoon. That might be enough for a normal PD, but Jerry gave himself another shift, the hour from 4:00 until 5:00 P.M., with his third for-mat innovation, a blend of old and new jazz styles called *Jazz Unlimited.*

Through *Jazz Unlimited,* Jerry got to know a sax player in the area named Charlie Ventura, a guy who'd worked with Gene Krupa's big band and had done pretty well with the bop craze in 1948 and 1949. "Cholly" had his own club, a roadhouse in the sticks he'd opened at the end of 1950 at a Jersey crossroads called Lindenwald. He was smart—the place was on White Horse Pike, a big beach route, and it was close to New Jersey's vintage amusement park at Clementon. People would stop by in the evening on their way back into Philly, knock back a couple of drinks, see the band, have some laughs. It was bringing in some reasonable dough. Jerry drove out and had a look at the place. Not bad.

It's a funny thing about the jazz crowd. The more you're in a club, the more you get to be family. The musicians start to recognize you, you make friends with other regulars, you buy someone a drink, he realizes that he's heard you on the air—pretty soon, when you come into a place, it's "Hey! Jerry's here! Mr. DJ! Jerry, man, how are ya?" He was seeing local talent—jazz, pseudo-jazz, straight singing, cocktail-lounge stuff—and getting to know who was good and who wasn't.

Within a few more months, Jerry had the notion of doing some live broad-casts of *Jazz Unlimited* on Saturdays. There was a joint called The Ren-dezvous in Philly that expressed interest, and pretty soon he was working six days a week. When The Rendezvous stopped being interested, he moved to a club in a black neighborhood that offered some real jazz—the Blue Note.

It wasn't long before Jerry heard from his old flame Betty Tapley. When she moved to Camden she could hardly miss him. He was on the air three times a day, five days a week (not to mention the live shows on Saturday). One day she looked him up at WKDN. "Hey, how are ya? Gimme a smooch. Let's get together later . . ." and pretty soon the affair was under way again. Betty was good that way—didn't hold a grudge about Jerry's sudden departure from Allentown, loved a good time, enjoyed music, appreciated his jokes, found him sexy. It was fun unwinding with her at the end of a long day, and he felt that she needed him, somehow.

How do you start a band? Why do you start a band? Ask some musicians how their group got together. They were hanging around, fooling around, felt a rapport, somebody knew somebody who could get them a gig. It just happened.

Maybe Cholly told Jerry that he needed an intermission act for his club and Jerry figured he could put something together. He'd heard Kay Justice, a good-looking girl, not bright, but a very good singer. A couple of guys she knew had musical ability and could handle vocal arrangements. Why not a Four Freshmen–style vocal quintet with Kay as lead singer? Jerry would be the front guy, the guy with connections, the guy with the white jacket.

They worked out backups behind her on "You've Changed," that old Billie Holiday vehicle, and some contemporary tunes. Nobody ever said Jerry could really sing, but he could hold his own with the simpler harmonies, and he had enough cash to spring for a tall snare drum and a cymbal so that he could provide some rhythm backup. "Cocktail drums," they called it, which he played standing up, so that he would look like part of the group and not the backup guy. When they auditioned, maybe Cholly thought the band was second-rate, but Kay was pretty, Jerry could promote the club on the radio, and everybody drank and talked during the intermission act's set anyway.

Late in 1951 the Jerry Williams Quintet started working at Charlie Ventura's Open House Club in Lindenwald and had a nice run there through the end of the year, relieving the local talent and a few comics. Early in 1952 Cholly told them they'd be doing intermission duty for Gene Krupa, Benny Goodman's drummer, who was out on his own with a bassless trio that included Cholly on saxes and Teddy Napoleon on piano. Ventura's club was a perfect place to shake down the repertoire before they went on tour.

Jerry was thrilled about meeting Krupa and working with him—he remembered the drummer's flying hair and heavy bass drum from the Goodman band. For several weeks he reveled in the chance to get to know him, sitting at the bar, hearing him tell stories about working with Benny—not a load of laughs, if y' know what I mean, Jer. Krupa wasn't a bad guy, even if he did slip out back to smoke some reefer from time to time. That was the scene, man, y' know?

One day early in 1952, on the way back to his apartment, he saw a newspaper he hadn't noticed before at the newsstand—the *Christian Beacon,* published by the Reverend Carl McIntire, that right-wing preacher in Collingswood. Jerry knew of him. McIntire was on the radio, too, Sunday nights on WCAM, a station that was owned by the city—WKDN's big competitor. McIntire was always thumping the Bible, blending sermonizing with politics: "America first, last, and always," and "FDR was a commie," and "You better watch out for those Catholics, because they want the pope to run our country." Jerry thought he was a nut. But he was drawing a thousand people for some of his Sunday services.

Week after week, the *Christian Beacon* provoked him. He saw the ads from the American Board of Missions to the Jews—a series that ran in regular rotation throughout the paper, urging readers not to be anti-Semitic, to recognize Jews as the Chosen People of the Bible . . . and then the kicker, about how it was everyone's responsibility as Christians to show them that Christ came to redeem them, too. To convert them.

And these guys were at war with other Protestants, too, especially those lefty Methodists. These modernists—sometimes the *Beacon* called them liberals—wanted to institute the welfare state, socialized medicine, so-called civil rights. They were putting the liberties of God's own country at risk. McIntire thought the National Council of Churches was too pink, so he started his own group, the American Council of Christian Churches, in which only pure-as-snow fundamentalists were welcome.

In the early spring of 1952, Jerry heard that the ACCC was going to hold their national convention in Philadelphia. That gave him a hook.

"Say, folks, didja hear that the Reverend Carl McIntire is bringing all of his American Council of Christian Churches friends to Philadelphia for their convention in April and May? Should be a big deal. You know about Reverend McIntire, dontcha? He's all over town, even on the other radio station here—can't say their call letters, but you know the one. Y' know what's really getting him going?"

Jerry took a little dramatic pause. He'd learned how to use space in dialogue when he was an actor, and he thought that a little silence on the air was a pretty effective way to get people's attention. "Get this. Reverend McIntire and his friends are wringing their hands about President Truman's idea to appoint a U.S. representative to the Vatican. They say that'd violate the First Amendment. Get the government too close to one religion. Favoritism for the Catholics. They want that separation of Church and State in the First Amendment." Another pause.

"Vatican City *is* a country, you know, Reverend. They got stamps and everything. What *is* it that Reverend McIntire is so concerned about?" Another little pause here. "Lemme see if I can tell ya. The pastor talks about it on his radio show. It's the Catholic conspiracy, the pope's plan to take over the world. They're comin' t' town. Watch out, you Catholics in South Philly! The lawns aren't very big over there, but there might be room enough for a burning cross, whadja think, huh? Well, what's on your mind? Let's take a call.

"Hello! Yes, this is Jerry Williams, on WKDN, eight hundred on your dial." He took in a few sentences from the caller. "Let me understand you, sir. What you're saying is that Pastor McIntire is correct? That there's a big Communist threat right here in our own country, and we ought to be concerned, is that right?" Another pause.

"Uh-huh. I see. Well, I'm not so sure about that. So what about those Catholics? You've heard about this papal representative business, right? President Truman wants to have diplomatic relations with the Vatican. Izzat okay with you?" Another pause. "So you think that Catholics have too much influence in America. What's wrong with Catholics, huh? Oh, they follow a false faith. Is that what Pastor McIntire says, or is it what you say? Ah, I see, you've heard Pastor McIntire say things like that." Another pause to listen. "And you don't like what *I'm* saying. I understand that. That's *very* clear, sir. You mean t' say that you think I'm anti-fundamentalist? No, I'm not! What else does Reverend McIntire say about the Catholics?" A pause. "He says they don't read the Bible? Well, that's not true, sir. Oh, I see. It's not the real Bible. They have their own Bible, it's not the right one."

Jerry took a breath.

"You know what Pastor McIntire has to say about the Jews, don't you?"

A long pause.

"Are you still there? You were so quiet, I thought you went away. You *do* know what he says about the Jews, don't you? He says the Jews are fine, the Christians ought to respect 'em. They gave us the Bible, he says. They're okay, the Jews—just as long as they come around to seeing things *his* way, that is. That's the kind of America you want? Is it? *Is* it? Well, thanks for calling."

This stuff was hot. The phone wouldn't stop ringing. *That* filled the hour nicely. So he picked up on it the next day, and the next . . . Without intending it consciously, he discovered that carrying over a topic from day to day, especially a topic like this one, built his audience. The people who listened yesterday would come back, and the people who tuned in today felt they'd missed something.

And the listeners talked about it. "That Jerry Williams—did you hear his show?" It didn't take long for Reverend McIntire to hear about Jerry.

One morning Jerry picked up the *Camden Courier-Post* on his way into the studio, as he always did, and there it was. Huge ad. Don't listen to Jerry

Williams! Anti-Christian, blah blah blah, outsider, blah blah blah, probably a pinko, blah blah blah. Signed, Bible Presbyterian Church, Carl McIntire, Pastor.

He grinned. You can't buy publicity like this. This'll be good for the show today, and *then* we'll have some fun.

And then it was McCarthy. Throughout the preceding couple of years, the papers and radio and TV were full of the fury of Joseph McCarthy, the charismatic Republican senator from Wisconsin. Early in 1950 Joe got a lot of attention when he claimed he had proof that Communists were infiltrating the U.S. government. "Are you now, or have you ever been, a member of the Communist Party?"

In 1952 McCarthy was up for reelection and a presidential race was under way. Normally, a Wisconsin senate contest wouldn't be national news, but Joe was a national figure who'd made a lot of people very uncomfortable, and folks wondered whether Wisconsin voters would ratify what he'd been doing or toss him out. Jerry started talking about McCarthy. Almost nobody had the guts to question what he was doing—few Democrats wanted to be nailed as commie sympathizers. There was one guy, though, not a senator—just a lowly Democratic rep from the upper Midwest, Joe's neck of the woods, who said he'd debate Joe on national TV. It was funny—they both had the same last name. Eugene McCarthy versus Joseph McCarthy, going toe-to-toe on the issues.

Jerry saw the debate. It made good material for *What's on Your Mind?* He commended Representative McCarthy of Minnesota for his courage. He lit into Joe. The senator was a demagogue, pure and simple. This hunt for commies was nothing more than a way to build himself up and tear the other party down. But it was worse than that. He was undermining the great principles of the Bill of Rights. Didn't Americans have the right to express their opinions? Didn't they have the right to meet with other people to talk about their beliefs? The voters of Wisconsin ought to throw this guy out of office. Callers got fried about it, but Jerry wouldn't back down.

One afternoon, a Greek American kid from the Boston area working on his degree at Swarthmore caught the show when Jerry was carrying on about Joe. Who *was* this tough guy on the radio? He'd never heard anything quite like it before. While everyone else was ducking and weaving on the subject of McCarthy and his accusations, Jerry Williams was unequivocally whacking the tar out of him. Michael Dukakis wasn't a big radio listener, and he heard Jerry only a few times while he was in school in Pennsylvania. But he remembered the name.

McCarthy wasn't the only political topic on the show. Jerry made no secret of his preferences in the presidential race. He was for Adlai Stevenson, the egghead Democrat, the guy who wanted to talk sense to the American people. The Republicans were running avuncular Ike, General Dwight Eisenhower, and Nixon, that weaselly little Red-baiter. Jerry had disliked him the first time he saw his picture in the paper, back when he was on the Un-American Activities Committee. Beady eyes. Hiding something.

Jerry got some good stuff to work with in September that year, when Ike hung Nixon out to dry on those corruption charges. The *New York Post* said Nixon had a secret expense fund. Ike wouldn't give him a big public defense, so Nixon went on TV to speak for himself. He whined about how poor he was, how his wife, Pat, had to wear a cloth coat, how he loved his dog and he wasn't going to get rid of it even though someone had given him poor little Checkers as a gift. Pathetic. Jerry loathed pathetic. The guy didn't even have a decent-sized dog.

When the dust settled in November, Ike and Nixon had won. Stevenson was humiliated. Jerry was philosophical, although it was the first time he'd voted for a loser. Oh, well—give the general a chance.

But McCarthy had won, too. In fact, the Republicans had won across the board. They'd be in control of the House and Senate, which would probably give McCarthy a committee chairmanship and an even bigger platform. Jerry didn't like that very much.

His status in Camden in November 1952 wasn't what it was during that golden-boy moment in Allentown, but he was getting a minor-league rep. He had a nice green DeSoto that he drove around town, sometimes with Betty. He moved to a better apartment out in Haddonfield—still on the main drag, but in a much nicer neighborhood. He had lots of musician friends, thanks to *Jazz Unlimited.*

The salespeople told him about a fella named Maxwell Richmond, who had a little ad shop in Philly, the M. Evans Richmond Agency. This Richmond liked the morning show, liked Jerry on the air. He had a strategy for one of his clients, a shop selling radios and TVs. It worked great on the Philadelphia stations. Would Jerry give it a try?

So he met Richmond—kind of a slob, but you could tell he was a hustler. He wanted to buy a series of quarter hours. His client would be the only sponsor. The idea was to build momentum, minute by minute. He described how Jerry would do it. Every time he keyed his mic, he'd be pushing people to call for a special deal, available just at the moment he was pitching it.

The special show was scheduled for the heart of the Christmas shopping season. As they got closer to the airdate, Richmond would call him up every couple of days. "Jerry, don't play 'I Saw Mommy Kissing Santa Claus' when you pitch the TVs. Not enough energy. Instead, play this one." Then it was another call, another tune Mac had heard that he wanted in his quarter hour. "No, change that first tune I toldja about. Play this one instead." Richmond was juggling the songs around right up until airtime.

So, finally, Jerry's got all the records stacked up, in the order Richmond wants. He kicks off the segment, a nice bright pace: " . . . brought to you by your friends at Muntz TV. Got a special holiday offer for you, folks! *A new-for-fifty-two* Muntz *nineteen-inch* television set! Delivered! In *one hour!* That's right, if you call POplar 5-0303 right *now.* A great Christmas gift for your hubby, only $93.95. That's POplar 5-0303. Okay, here's Guy Mitchell and 'Pittsburgh, Pennsylvania.'" Then Guy's singing along, and Jerry's cueing up the next record. "Jerry! Phone call! Maxwell Richmond."

And there's Richmond on the phone. "Not enough drive. Hit it harder. The big pitch is coming up." Jesus! The record was in its end groove. "Gotta go, Mac!"

"Guy Mitchell, at 800 on the dial, WKDN Camden, with Jerry Williams. Remember that Muntz TV set I toldja about, folks, that Christmas gift? That big beautiful *nineteen-inch* set is *only* $93.95—an incredible price from Mad Man Muntz. And, can you believe it, if you call *right now,* I mean right at this *very minute,* they're gonna put this set in a truck and bring it to your home in just *one hour.* No matter where you live, you'll have it by eleven A.M. *this morning!* This is a *nineteen-inch* set, folks! *Huge!* It's like having Jack Benny in y' living room, I'll tell ya. Imagine the looks on the kids' faces when they see it. *$93.95!* Call 'em now, *right now,* POplar 5-0303. A nineteen-inch Muntz TV, *brand new,* for *just* $93.95. POplar 5-0303. Got it? *Use* it! Now, Buddy Clark's 'Linda'!"

Buddy gets going, and Richmond is back on the horn. "Good job, Jerry, just speed it up. And remember, they've gotta call right now and we'll get the set t' them in just an hour!" Buddy's finishing up. "Okay, Mac, Okay!"

"Hey, don't forget, call *right now,* call POplar 5-0303, and let's call right now, because we're gonna get that Muntz television set t' you. Perfect for Christmas. It's a nineteen-inch set, *new-for-fifty-two,* and we're gonna get it to you, and it's only $93.95. Mad Man Muntz'll drive t' you in just one hour, and they'll set it up for you and you'll be watching *You Are There* tonight, folks, *tonight!* POplar 5-0303, *Muntz,* $93.95, nineteen inch, *right now,* deliver in one hour, what a great gift, POplar 5-0303, tell 'em Jerry Williams sentcha, and now Jo Stafford and 'You Belong to Me'!"

You know what? It worked. It actually worked. Mad Man Muntz moved those sets. M. Evans Richmond became a fan of Jerry Williams, bought more time, and Jerry saddled up as the pitchman, hawking more of this schlocky garbage over and over until he could do those ads in his sleep.

The musical career was going pretty well too, but it took its toll on Jerry's stamina. After five months or so working at Cholly Ventura's place, night after night, finishing up at 1:30 or 2:00, driving the half hour back to Haddonfield, and getting up again at 8:00 A.M. to work with Bud, Jerry began looking around for gigs closer to home.

The Jerry Williams Quintet with Kay Justice (usually billed as "Lovely" Kay Justice or sometimes "Gorgeous" Kay Justice) got work at some places in downtown Camden—the Rainbow Grille, the Five O'Clock Club, Andy's Log Cabin. There was a gig at a tiny walk-down bar in Philly called Lou's Moravian. They went south to a place called Nicholson's in Gloucester Heights. Over into Pottstown, northwest of Philly, to play the Veterans. Someone even got them a gig in Canada! They worked a one-nighter at Toronto's big deal nightclub, the Silver Rail.

Why did he get married? In retrospect, it made no sense. He was still flirting—when he and Bud Smith would go out, Bud was amazed at the way Jerry could attract women. But Betty had something, or maybe it was Betty's charms plus the tax advantages—since Jerry was starting to earn some significant money from his radio and musical activities. Late in 1952 they got hitched and started living together in Jerry's apartment in Haddonfield. With the dogs Jerry had begun to collect. Betty was okay with that—a couple of dogs, no big deal.

One evening after his gig with the quintet was done, Jerry went into Philly to have a look at something he'd been hearing on the air. Steve Allison, that guy who'd been on the air in Boston, had replaced Cal Ross on WPEN and they were giving him the star treatment. Jerry had to admit that he sounded good. He was smooth and polished. He handled his interviews well—not as well as Cal, of course. But what really caught Jerry's attention was the framework WPEN had built around Allison, and he had to see it for himself. Jerry went a little dizzy in a rush of pure envy—Allison had his own after-hours joint right there at the studios, with tables, chairs, and waitresses serving food and drink. Why wasn't it Jerry Williams up there at the little table with the snappy sport coat and tie, schmoozing with the stars? After the show, he introduced himself to Steve. Had to come over from Camden to say hello. Inside, he simmered. Philly, not Camden. On-air star, not program director. He wanted it, wanted it bad.

But it wasn't *What's on Your Mind* that got Jerry across the Delaware to Philly. It was the comedy stuff with Bud Smith.

By the end of 1952 Jerry and Bud had a rhythm. Each hour of the show was structured, sort of, with bits they'd written or worked out, more or less, some ad-lib time, music, and general craziness. Some jokes were sharp, some were groaners, and others—well, the others are best forgotten.

JERRY: This is the program that proves Two Can Live as Cheaply as One— providing one has lockjaw.

BUD: Yes, it's *A Word to the Wives*, with yours truly Harry Smith and his sincerely Jerry Williams, broadcasting on eight hundred kilocycles, thirty-eight motorcycles, and two bicycles.

JERRY: Here's our first news flash of the day: "Man found shot, stabbed, poisoned, and hung. The Camden regulars suspect foul play."

BUD: We're brought to you today by Sinko Soap. It doesn't float, it doesn't smell nice, it doesn't soften your skin, it doesn't break in two, it doesn't even get you clean. It just keeps you company in the bathtub. Jer, what've we got today?

JERRY: We'll have a visit with our travel agent, and a report about driving in America, and Adelaide Idlewild will be here, and if none of that works, I'll play the drums until we get an idea.

BUD: And now for our first tune of the day, "The Sun Shines Bright on My Old Kentucky Home Because There's a Great Big Hole in the Roof."

You never know who's listening. It could be a guy who owns another radio station. Ben Gimbel—that's right, the big department store guy—took a liking to the show. Somehow he communicated to Jerry that he might have a place for him on his station in Philly—WIP, right across the street from the store.

There were some conversations. Jerry and Bud went out and had a drink on it. The show was a lot of work, but it was a lot of fun, too. If they had all day to work on material, who knows what they could come up with?

BUD: Now, here's Jerry with a word from one of our regretful sponsors.

JERRY: It's the 1952 Ultim-8! The first self-steering, button-controlled, radar-directed automobile! All you do is make the payments! The clutch pedal is gone, so you drive shiftlessly! It's so advanced in performance that it's apt to be blocks ahead of itself! It's the car that lets you see where you're going and where you've been, even if you don't know whether you're coming or going! Compare any crate with the Ultim-8!

Bud was a go-along-to-get-along kind of guy. He never thought of himself as a comic, but working in Philly was the big time, and WIP was about as big as working in Philly got. If Jerry could make a good deal, he was willing to come along for the ride.

Jerry worked it out with Gimbel. They'd be on every weekday, 3:00 to 4:00 P.M. Since WIP was a Mutual Network station, Jerry wanted them to make the show available to the rest of the network. Gimbel okayed that, too. And Jerry got a little extra money for himself—he was the leader of the team, after all, and what Bud didn't know wouldn't hurt him.

The two of them said good-bye to Major Compton and started their new career in the big city across the Delaware. Bye-bye, *Jazz Unlimited.* Bye-bye, *What's on Your Mind?* Jerry was going to miss that noontime show.

> JERRY: Adelaide Idlewild has just dropped in, and as usual, we drop every-
>   thing to say hello to her. Adelaide, didn't you tell us you were going shop-
>   ping today?
> BUD (as IDLEWILD, in a Bob-and-Ray Mary McGoon voice): Oh, I went
>   shopping. I just had to come in and rest a bit.
> JERRY: You should have taken a break for lunch.
> BUD: I did that. I'm on a diet now—just had creamed soup, pork chops,
>   mashed potatoes, chocolate cake, and ice cream.
> JERRY: How does that help you reduce?
> BUD: Well, it ruins the appetite, for one thing.

The new comedy show needed a name—they couldn't use *Word to the Wives,* since that would only be confused with what they'd been doing on WKDN, and their new show was going to aim for more than just housewives. They hit on the idea of letting their listeners name the new show on WIP. To get some ink ("so that there won't be any favoritism"), they asked a group of local press types to be the judges. Ben Gimbel liked the promotion, and he put up a fifty-dollar bond as a prize. The winner was one Mrs. William Werner, who came up with *The Gag Busters,* which was a pretty good name, when you thought about it, perfect for what they were trying to do. So she got the bond, and Jerry and Bud got a few mentions in the paper out of it.

Nothing eats up time like comedy. Jokes are ephemeral, and you have to keep them coming. So it was a relief when someone suggested that Jerry and Bud do interviews with showbiz types coming through town. Interviews fill time very well. When the guests were willing, they worked with Jerry and Bud in skits or interacted with the Gag Busters characters they had created. Audrey Meadows did the show, and she told them they had real talent. That was a boost—she was working with Jackie Gleason, so she knew what she was talking about.

For a moment or two, Jerry and Bud were hot. A producer working for Channel 6, the *Inquirer's* TV station, gave the guys a tryout, and they proposed doing a Kovacs-style late-night show. Jerry's first star turn in video, *Madmen at Midnight*, flamed out after three weeks. "The only one who got mad was our producer," he told the press.

Every once in a while, Jerry would sneak in a political jibe.

BUD: Once again, here's our columnist of the air, Sid Ghastly, with news from Washington, Hollywood, and other little towns coast-to-coast.

JERRY (as SID GHASTLY, parodying Walter Winchell): Flash! The next trend on TV will be stripteasers. They'll be seen on a coast-to-coast unhookup . . . I hear that Senator McCarthy didn't catch a single fish on his summer vacation. How do you like that? Even the fish won't go for his line . . . A local playboy confided to me that he drinks nothing stronger than pop, but that doesn't cramp his style. There's nothing that his Pop won't drink . . . Localite Ed Shmendrick is thinking of running for governor next time out. If he wins, it'll certainly be a proud moment for his mother. Maybe he can even get her pardoned . . . When I look at the candidates for mayor over in Hammonton, I'm just glad that only one of them can be elected . . . Kirk Douglas socks his way through the new private eye saga, *Defective Story*, and by the time it's over both he *and* the audience are punchy . . . It was so cold in Washington the other day that some of the senators had their hands in their own pockets . . . And today's editorial comment: Remember, don't settle for a cheap used car—it's hard to drive a bargain.

They had conferences with Ben Gimbel every time they did something outrageous. There was big old Ben, down at the end of his huge office, behind an enormous carved oak desk. (When he wasn't afraid of losing his job, Jerry usually thought: Someday I'm gonna have a desk like that.) He had a huge, hoarse, powerful voice. "What the hell'd you guys do this afternoon? Hah come y' said unkind things about Hammonton, New Jersey?"

Jerry knew better than to say what he was thinking: you couldn't say anything *kind* about Hammonton, New Jersey.

"Hah come y' did that?"

"Sorry, Ben. It won't happen again, Ben." Until the next time.

Actually, Ben knew the score. He was a businessman. As long as the boys brought in the advertisers, they had a job. Not a bad guy, once you got to know him.

The (slightly) lightened daily workload on the radio side meant that Jerry could give a little more time to the quintet. Halfway through 1953, his agent, Nat

Segall, landed an intermission gig for them at Chubby's, one of the best rooms in Philly. Kay and the boys filled the space between the headliners' sets—what the showbiz types called "the lull"—for almost a year. They worked with Kay Starr, who was still milking her 1952 hit, "Wheel of Fortune," and other minor stars of the time. They spelled comics, too. Don Rickles was at Chubby's fairly frequently, and he and Jerry got to know each other pretty well. It wasn't exactly glamorous work. One night, Don, already working his trademark rapid-fire insults, told a lady with a big hat walking by the little stage to take off the chapeau. When she ignored him, he threw a shot at her back: "Hey, where y' goin'? Ladies' room? Lissen, do me a favor, do a half-gainer off the bowl, and destroy y'self!" It got a laugh, but she didn't like it very much. She came back with some wet toilet paper and threw it onto the stage at Rickles. It was still there when Don finished and the quintet came on, so guess who had to pick it up?

Still, Chubby's was about as high as you could rise in Philly unless you had a hit record, and it was good money. Nat had gotten them nearly five hundred dollars a week to start, and he gradually upped the money to the point where everybody in the group was taking home a hundred dollars (less Nat's cut) every Sunday.

The only thing about the job that really bothered Jerry was Chubby Stafford himself. Every Sunday night, while other members of the group waited around for him to fulfill his leader's responsibilities, he went into the office to get paid. Chubby would stare at him and say, "Who're *you?*"

"Mr. Stafford, I'm Jerry Williams. I have the group here. Nat Segall booked us. We're playing the lull. We're in the *show.*" Chubby behaved like he'd never seen Jerry before. "We have a *contract.* Hell, I'm the guy who picked up the toilet paper on the stage tonight. My group's out there waiting for their money." Eventually, Chubby would come across with the bread, but it was always a struggle.

Financially, Jerry was finally doing more than making ends meet. The money at WIP and the gig at Chubby's brought his income for 1953 up to around $15,000—in twenty-first-century money, that's more than a hundred grand. Not that he kept much of it.

He bought a new car on time, a nice one, and it cost him. A Jaguar XK-40 hardtop. Three thousand dollars, plus the interest. He'd get the Jag out on an old country road in South Jersey, where there were no cops around, and open it up. First, second, third—when he got that car into third, *see you later.* He'd blow carbon out the back, roaring along at 80, 90, 110 miles an hour. Nobody saw him—it was just him and the chickens.

He moved out of his apartment, too. He and Betty needed something bigger. He was a Philadelphia radio personality now. At the very least, he wanted a freestanding house, close enough to Philly to get to work without too much trouble, but also within striking distance of New York and his folks' retirement house in Lakewood, near the coast. It turned out that the only places he could afford were way out there in South Jersey. The agent finally showed them a little log cabin with heat, next to a pond. It was in a vacation community, in the middle of a cluster of artificial lakes where people rented places for the summer, took their boats out, fished, and swam—officially, the village was Taunton Lake, but everyone referred to the area as Medford because that was the nearest town of any size. Something about this place out in the sticks on the shores of Lake Pine spoke to Jerry, and he decided to rent it. Maybe it reminded him of camp. Probably it was cheap. Betty wasn't too crazy about being so far away from the city, but there were a few nearby neighbors, and she always had the dogs to keep her company.

The double-barreled career of Jerry Williams, Philadelphia entertainer and radio personality, was moving along well as he celebrated New Year's 1954, working with his group at Chubby's, of course. By that time, *The Gag Busters* had so much interest from advertisers that WIP had doubled the show's airtime—Jerry and Bud were on Monday through Saturday, 2:00 to 4:00 P.M. Bud would come out to see the quintet every once in a while, watch Jerry wear the white jacket and flirt with good-looking women whenever Betty wasn't around. In his spare time, he'd wonder which side of the career Jerry would ultimately choose, and, if the quintet really took off, where that would leave *him*. They didn't talk much personally—it was mostly business. Bud had the impression that Jerry had an agenda, something he was priming himself to do, and he had seen enough of Jerry's behavior to know that he wasn't particularly loyal, personally or professionally.

Probably it was Jerry's agent, Nat Segall, who had a lot to do with the transformation of the Jerry Williams Quintet into the Escorts in late 1953 and early 1954. Nat got them on Dick Clark's *Caravan of Music* radio show on WFIL. Then he pitched them to Dave Miller, who owned a Philadelphia record label called Essex Records.

Essex was a hot little label, since it had issued a tune in 1952 called "Rock the Joint" by a then-unknown group, Bill Haley and the Comets, and Haley's group had since become the first bona fide rock 'n' roll stars. The quintet certainly couldn't turn themselves into rock 'n' roll singers, but they might capitalize on the little bump close-harmony vocals were getting from the success of the Four Freshmen and other groups that were copying their style—for example, the Four Lads did "Istanbul" in 1953 and got a gold record out of it.

Portrait of Jerry Williams, ca. 1953.
PAUL GEORGE

Miller and his music director, a bass player named Joe Kuhn, heard Jerry's quintet and figured they had potential. Nat and Jerry were pleased with the prospect of recording, so they made a deal to cut a single. It was obvious to Miller that Kay was the star and that Jerry Williams's name couldn't move any more than a few discs in the Philly area, so Jerry's group became the Escorts.

Miller acquired a tune from a local songwriter named Milton Kellem called "If You Took Your Love from Me." Jerry and the group rehearsed the tune, tried it out at Chubby's, and they thought it would be as good as anything else to start their career in the studio. It wasn't much like jazz, but the record company guys seemed to know what they were doing. At the same session, they recorded one of the things they performed regularly, Sy Oliver's "Yes Indeed." Jerry's cocktail drums were augmented by a real drummer, which was just as well as far as he was concerned.

The record came out, Jerry and the group talked it up to everyone they knew, they sang "If You Took Your Love from Me" at Chubby's, and people started to buy the darn thing. Nat got them gigs at other clubs on their days off from Chubby's. They headlined at Florence O'Boyle's Cadillac Sho-Bar. They played on Arthur Godfrey's *Talent Scouts* show, simulcast on TV and radio, and won.

On the strength of the sales from the first single, Jerry registered the name of the group to cement his ownership of the band, and they contracted to record two more singles for Essex. Miller brought them a couple of jumpy, prerock things called "You Won't Be Satisfied" and "Oh Honey," and a couple of ballads—a Mercer Ellington tune called "Paradise Hill" and "What Good Am I without You." At their next session, in mid-1954, they cut them with a little band led by Joe Kuhn. Jerry was politely told he could leave his drums at home.

These singles did nothing, and the Escorts' career as recording stars came to an abrupt halt early in 1955. Sic transit gloria mundi. Dave Miller and Joe Kuhn didn't exactly need Jerry and Kay; they went on to found the 101 Strings and Somerset Records, a middle-of-the-road music empire that made them both very wealthy men.

The Four Aces released "Love Is a Many-Splendored Thing" that year, and *that* showed how close harmony could make you famous. But it hadn't worked for Jerry Williams and the Escorts.

Try filling twelve hours of comedy every week. It ain't funny after a while. And if your music career has gone into the toilet, and your marriage is on the rocks, too, you might have real trouble staying on the sunny side. By mid-1955 Jerry was closing in on ten years of scuffling. He'd been rich for a minute, poor longer than he'd been rich, and just making ends meet most of the time. He liked rich. He'd been management and talent in radio. He'd been actor, singer, local personality, bandleader, zany comedian, hillbilly host, jazz DJ, monologuist, and host of a talk show. He loved the spotlight whenever he was in it, but someone was always turning it off, and that left him alone with himself in the dark. By the time Samuel Jacoby was thirty-one he had his own store in Flatbush and was well on his way to being a success. Jerry smoldered inside. He wasn't anything, really.

And then Bud found out that he was getting the short end of the stick. Somehow he learned that WIP considered Jerry the senior partner in the Gag Busters, and he did a burn on that. Who was the funny guy, after all? Who did most of the gag voices? Who was holding things together during the day, cranking out scripts, finding goofy music, working with the station engineers and management while Jerry was trying to become a singing sensation? Just who did Jerry Williams think he was, anyway? The go-along guy blew up at him.

So Jerry said the hell with everything. He shook hands with the other Escorts, kissed Kay, wished them all good luck, gave away the white jacket and the drums. He broke up with Betty—or Betty broke up with him. He told Bud that he was right—Jerry knew that Bud was the guy with the gift for comedy, and he deserved to find a partner who cared; he wasn't going to leave him high and dry, but they should both look around for other things to do.

If he could just get some money together, he had an idea. He knew that Steve Allison was vulnerable—he was enough of a radio pro to sense where a show was going right and where it was going wrong. When you listened to that nightly gab show Steve did, it didn't have an edge. People could take it or leave it. There was room in this town for another show—something tougher.

Joe Pyne had shown Jerry that a bare-knuckles approach on the air could actually work. It got attention from listeners. But Jerry saw and heard that Joe's approach got old fast. Jerry knew a show should have staying power, continuity. There had to be a story—not like a drama, but something that kept people coming back for more. Like his battle with Carl McIntire.

And one more thing. He hated being at the mercy of management. Those guys could tell you to take a walk with a moment's notice. He liked the production-company model that so many people were using for TV. You got investors, you bought the time, you owned the show: entrepreneurial.

In his head he heard the way it should sound. He knew no one could do this new concept the way he could. He could just see himself up there at that little desk, holding court the way Allison did, but doing it right.

He talked it up to everyone he knew with money. Allen Summers, who had a public relations/ad agency, and Sam Hatoff, who was the Philly representative for a big charity called City of Hope, bought in. Jerry got a little loan from his father. He had a few bucks of his own.

Jerry identified WIBG as a good prospect for his venture, and they hammered out a deal. Jerry and his partners would rent the hours from 11:00 P.M. until 2:00 A.M., the same hours that Allison was doing his show on WPEN. IBG would provide the engineering staff. Jerry would sell most of the advertising and keep the proceeds, to be divvied up with his investors. IBG had the option to sell their own spots if they could and keep all the money they made from them. Jerry wanted to do his show from a restaurant, so it was up to him to make the deal with the venue. They'd split the cost of the phone lines connecting the show to the studio. IBG would lend the group equipment to do the program at the restaurant. Jerry would be responsible for hiring his own production staff.

There were a furious few weeks of work, including farewell handshakes for Bud Smith and Ben Gimbel. *The Jerry Williams Show* premiered on WIBG, Philadelphia, in the fall of 1955, with Jerry at a little table in the lounge of a restaurant in northeast Philadelphia. He had a mic and a telephone, a turntable, and an audio board.

What did the show sound like? There are just a few airchecks (that is, off-the-air recordings) of Jerry on IBG, and they're from early 1957, almost a year and a half in, when Jerry had worked out all the bugs. But it's safe to say that those first shows wouldn't have been much of a surprise to listeners who had heard Steve Allison, Joe Pyne, or Barry Gray. It was a restaurant show with one-way phone calls—probably not running as smoothly as the host or the listener would have liked. When the host needed a break, or the calls weren't coming in, listeners would hear a tune or two.

People who knew Funny Jerry or Housewife Jerry or DJ Jerry were probably surprised. This Nighttime Jerry had a powerful high baritone voice, and he knew how to use it. When he was serious, he didn't sound like any of the Gag Busters characters. He sounded like—well, he didn't sound like anyone else.

He distinguished himself from Allison by putting the hard stuff at the center. Allison was essentially an amusing guy who occasionally took time out for something significant. Jerry was a guy who wanted to talk about the issues most of the time and every once in a while would lighten things up with some showbiz. He'd be Don Rickles's punching bag one night, because he knew how to be a straight man. But a few nights later, the mayor of Philadelphia would be the guest, and Jerry would be doing the punching.

When you heard Jerry's show, you got caught up in the way he seized on a topic and turned it around and around. He'd build momentum on it through the three hours. He'd take a few calls and start arguing with himself about it. He'd come back to the same thing a couple of nights later and add some new element you hadn't thought of before. Listeners discovered that Jerry Williams was addictive. He got under your skin.

Philadelphia was in the middle of a reform movement—a group of well-meaning we-know-better types was proposing to make the city more "modern," clear out those old slums, encourage redevelopment, build interstate highways, get the suburbanites to come back into the city. Mayor Joe Clark wanted to fight the old days of the machine and give the city a facelift. Jerry was skeptical. What about the people who might be displaced by all these goodwill schemes? The ethnic communities of the city were strong and entrenched; they gave the city some of its distinctive character. What would happen to the Italian neighborhood, the enclaves of Irish and Polish? How about the areas where Eastern European and Russian Jews were living? What did the mayor propose to improve the lives of Philly's Negroes?

And speaking of that side of town . . .

In December 1955 a diminutive black woman named Rosa Parks refused to move to the back of a bus in Montgomery, Alabama. The way she was treated outraged other blacks, and they began boycotting the municipal bus system in Montgomery. There was a shiver throughout the country as white Americans and black Americans began taking sides on whether the blacks were right or wrong.

The movement hadn't caught fire in Philadelphia yet, but when Jerry read the news reports, he had no doubts—he'd thought segregation of the races in America was an injustice from the first time he'd understood it. Black callers and restaurant patrons got respect on his show. After all, they were little guys, too. One time a black woman called up and said she was so down that she wanted to kill herself. Jerry kept talking to her, telling her to come on in to the restaurant, meet him, say hello to folks, find out that life really was worth living. Damned if she didn't show up an hour or so later to thank him on the air.

There was an election just a year away, and Jerry loved talking about that stuff, national and local. Nixon was going to run with Ike again. Jerry kept asking why the general couldn't find anyone better on the Republican side, why he was settling for that creep with his ill-fitting suits, his ski nose, his mealy-mouthed Checkers speech. General Eisenhower was a great man, no doubt about it, but when you added it all up, Jerry thought Adlai Stevenson would have been a better president in 1952, and people ought to give him a chance to make things better in 1956.

After a few months, Jerry knew that he needed someone to handle the mechanics of the show so that he could concentrate on performing. While at

WIP, he'd met a nineteen-year-old kid named John Rosica, who'd caught the radio bug when he was a freshman at Villanova—like a few others around the country, the school was fostering new broadcast talent by letting the kids make their mistakes on its own radio station. When the school year was winding down in May 1955, Rosica made the rounds of the area stations looking for a summer job, and he got one at WIP. They made him "Assistant Music Director," whatever that meant, and that's how he met Jerry.

Radio spoiled him for school. He went back to Villanova as a sophomore, but by early 1956 his heart wasn't in it anymore. WIP was ready to offer him a job producing the area's premier all-night show, *The Milkman's Matinee*, with Gene Milner, but Jerry got wind of it. "I want you to come work for me. Thirty-five bucks a week."

Rosica was flattered, but he said, "Jerry, I got an offer from Milner. They're gonna pay me more than that."

Jerry shot back: "He's a no-talent." This established guy with a big rep, brush him aside as a no-talent—that was Jerry all over. "I know I can't pay you what IP can, but *this* show is gonna *do* something, John. It's going to be *big*. Listen. It's better to play a bit part on Broadway than to be a star in a little theater group."

Rosica couldn't get that line out of his head. He turned IP down and went to work for Jerry. The upsides: he was working in bars where he could drink even though he was underage; he got to meet some of the big names when they came into town; he observed Jerry's pickup technique with women when they hung out after hours; he was getting a decent salary—about $250 a week in modern money; he didn't have to work at the IBG studios, which were stuck in the middle of nowhere; and he got to study the radio skills of a real professional, a guy on his way to being a master. The downsides: he had to get out ahead of Allison's people and the other shows in town to get the guests Jerry wanted; he had to schlep all the equipment around; he had to be ready to turn on a dime when Jerry got an idea; and the hours were long—he was booking during the day, working the show at the Prime Rib until 2:00 A.M. and canoodling till the wee hours.

Jerry liked this kid, and he sure needed someone on the phone during the day to chase down the people he wanted to have on the show. Rosica proved he could handle the technical stuff, too—watching the levels, getting the mics right, spinning the discs—and that meant Jerry wouldn't have to worry about messing up his suit. Instead, Jerry could stay in character, the Star, Mr. Fashionably Dark and Handsome.

Rosica quickly became important in another way, as a one-man sounding board, the representative of all the people out there in the dark. One of the most frustrating things about working in these restaurants was that no one was really paying very much attention to you. Some people weren't paying *any* attention to you. You'd be sitting there, talking to somebody on the phone, trying to capture what they were saying, making your points, trying to get them over to your way of looking at the issue, hoping that it was coming across well, and some guy who was blotto would shove his mug up next to the mic and say, "Hey! Whatta ya doin?" or "You know where the bathroom is?" Or maybe you'd be talking to some beautiful girl—Tina Louise or Julie Newmar, some real knockout, and people would be coming up in the middle of your interview. "Oh, Julie, sign this napkin for me, please." "You were great in *Li'l Abner*, Miss Louise." And of course, the girl would be nice and sign the napkin or shake their hands, and the rhythm would be broken.

So Jerry started watching Rosica. If John liked a bit, that was good. If he thought an interview wasn't going over, that was bad. If his concentration drifted—damn! Jerry would wave his hand to get him back to business. He was paying Rosica to pay attention, not make eyes at some chick at the next table.

There were two other influences on Jerry that year.

He began to hear talk about a guy named Mike Wallace, doing a TV interview show. Jewish guy from the Boston area. After bouncing around as a news reporter and announcer and even doing a stint as an actor—why did this sound so familiar?—Wallace had started this show in New York, and DuMont had picked it up for syndication. Jerry tuned in and was impressed by what he saw. Wallace was a few years older than he was, but he had the same kind of looks—dark-haired, intense, serious. Big broad smile. No doubt: Mike looked good on TV. What was new, and what people were talking about, was Wallace's manner with his guests. Jerry thought he was building on the nononsense interview style that Ed Murrow had pioneered, but Wallace was more of a bulldog. He dug in with these newsmakers, and even with showbiz types, asking them one tough question after another, preventing them from sidestepping, bringing up embarrassing or inconvenient things they might have said or done in the past. He also was willing to take on topics others were scared of—like the idea that homosexuals might want to live their lives in the open, not be persecuted by the police and the pulpits. Mike Wallace. A guy to be reckoned with.

And Long John Nebel. This guy was on the radio in New York, on the overnights, with nutty offbeat topics—Unidentified Flying Objects, psychics, astrologers—well, actually, some of that stuff was kind of interesting. Maybe he could use it sometime. One night, coming back from WIBG, Jerry heard it:

hey, that was a caller's voice. It was *on the air*. Nebel and this woman were having a conversation on the telephone, and you could hear *both sides*.

He listened carefully. Was it live? It *sounded* live. He remembered how *Broadcasting* reported about an experimental recording technology the Nazis had developed. An American company was rolling it out for broadcasters in the United States now. Audio tape. A thin strip of plastic that captured the sound. The playback was supposed to be really good, not fragile and scratchy like disc transcription, or muddy like wire recording. Somebody famous was investing in this company. Right, Bing Crosby. Ampex, the company was. He listened to Nebel's show some more. *Broadcasting* had said that some stations were experimenting with this audio tape to record what was coming out of the studio and play it back a few seconds later on the air. Was this what Nebel was doing with his phone calls? How much did it cost? This was the missing piece his show needed. If you had this, what you could do with promotion! Call Jerry tonight! Your voice will be *on the air!*

As Philadelphia media personalities go, Jerry was a minor leaguer on the way up (again). The big-deal guys were music DJs and hosts riding the first wave of rock and roll, people like Bob Horn, who had a TV show on which kids danced while he played records—*Bob Horn's Bandstand* on WFIL. Bob got into some hot water that year. He was charged with driving while intoxicated and then accused of having sex with an underage girl. His station couldn't have that, so the guy who'd been doing fill-in for Bob, Dick Clark, was tapped as the new permanent host for the *Bandstand* show. Funny thing, though—even though Bob was gone, the sex business wouldn't go away. There were reports of a porno ring that was trapping these young girls into doing photo sessions. Somehow Steve Allison got dragged into the mess and he left WPEN under a cloud of suspicion. That left Jerry as Philadelphia's new Prince of Talk.

WIBG paid attention to the ad revenue Jerry was pulling in, and they realized that they could make more money by owning the show than they could from the rent Jerry's group was paying them. They made an offer to take Jerry and John Rosica on as staff. Jerry took it, presumably arranging for the station to buy out his partners, and WIBG moved the show to a classier venue, Lew Tendler's restaurant and lounge, downtown on Broad Street. Tendler's had dark wooden wall booths that hurt your back to sit in them, little white tiles on the floor, waiters with crisp towels on their arms. The stuff on the wall established a prizefighting theme, since Lew had been a bantamweight, a featherweight, a lightweight, and a welterweight. Because it was situated on Broad Street, a Philly main drag, right at the corner of Locust, it attracted the show crowd from the theaters and the clubs, night people winding down their night on the town, numbers runners—a nice mix for what Jerry wanted to do.

Late in 1956, partly on the strength of his radio show, Jerry got his first solo shot at TV—as the host of a weekly fake quiz and fashion show (*Pick Your Ideal!*) on Channel 3, WPTZ. Its fifteen minutes were bought and paid for by Ideal Clothing, and its one claim to fame was that Ernie Kovacs had once been its host. You'd send in a postcard to be a contestant, and if they picked your name, they'd call you up on the air, and then bring out two lovely models. Then Jerry would say, "Okay, one of these two gals is wearing an Ideal dress. One is wearing a New York fashionable top-of-the-line garment, and the other is a dollar-twenty-two pick-your-Ideal dress. Pick Your Ideal!" You'd make your guess and win the dress. The idea was that you couldn't tell the cheapie Ideal model from the one sold in the designer shop.

Ideal and the producers agreed that each show had to have a winner, so it was a complete setup. In one segment, maybe the model on the right would be wearing the Ideal dress. In the next one, it'd be the model on the left. If the contestant on the phone didn't hit it in either of those tries, the last one was a gimme, because both models were wearing Ideal dresses.

Across the street from Tendler's there was an after-hours place called the Harvey House. It had started out as one of a chain of restaurants catering to passengers on railroad trains, and it still had pretty good food in 1957. When Jerry's show was over at 2:00 A.M., the bars were closed. The Harvey House was one of the few places you could go to get a bite—it had good pancakes and waffles, good bacon and eggs. That breakfast food tasted surprisingly good after you'd been working hard for three hours. One night Jerry and Rosica were unwinding there and he noticed a dark-haired girl who would have suggested Jackie Kennedy to him if he'd known who Jackie Kennedy was in 1957. She looked familiar, this girl. Hadn't he seen her someplace before?

Pretty soon he was over near her table, using the ol' Jer charm. He'd gotten numbers a hundred times before. This was just another . . . but when he got close to this girl, something happened. All the time he was talking, he was getting crazy inside. Jerry could see she had innate style, a quality he loved, because he figured he had innate style, too. She was perfectly made up—discreet but enticing. Dressed beautifully. Cool and hot at the same time. Elegant, this girl. But sexy. Jesus, so *sexy!* And she brushed him off! This great girl, and he couldn't even get her name?

The chase started the next time he saw her. Hey, remember me? Come on over and join us. Got a radio show, you've probably heard it. No, she didn't think so. Well, come across the street to Tendler's tomorrow, see the show.

No, she couldn't. She had a job playing piano in a hotel lounge. Well, he'd like to come see her play. Where was she working? Oh, just one of the hotels around town.

This went on night after night for a couple of weeks. He was encouraged—at least she kept coming back, even after she was sure he'd be there. Small smile at first, then big smile. Oh, God, she's gorgeous when she smiles. Hi, how are you? Gradually the facts came out. He got her name, Teri. Funny last name—first time he heard it, he thought she might be Jewish—Yetzi or something like that. The spelling turned out to be "Iezzi." Ohhh. Italian name. He saw her play piano—hey, she was *good*. Some highbrow stuff in her repertoire, Chopin or something. She had a boyfriend, sort of. Med-school guy.

Finally a phone number. Finally a date. It turned out the med student had dumped her or something. His family didn't think Teri was good enough for him. Too bad for him! Jerry didn't need a second invite. It was the full-court press after that. Dates once a week, putting the moves on her . . .

Then this med student comes back into the picture. Anthony. Teri can't see Jerry. Wants to think about it. Jesus, what is there to think about? Pretty soon, Jerry's hanging out in her neighborhood, in Holmesburg, a quiet, little, almost-rural suburb. There's the little house she lives in with her folks and her little brother, Bill. Looks like an old farmhouse. There's Jerry, in his suit, standing in the vacant lot across the street, mooning. Whosa that? Her papa wants to know. He's a boy Teri knows. Hey, you! Go away!

Another day, Jerry's driving along Roosevelt Boulevard in the Jag, just going out to be near her, and he spots Teri in a convertible with another guy—this Anthony. He goes nuts! He turns around and he's driving along next to them, waving at them, trying to get them to stop. Eventually Anthony pulls over. Who *are* you, buddy? But Jerry's just looking at Teri. "I love you! I love you! I love you! You can't do this to me! I love you!"

You know the rest. Jerry Got the Girl. First, just going steady. Then, Jerry says, "Let's get married."

Teri: "Are you crazy?"

The family had never seen such a hurricane as this boy. He was well-dressed, he had a nice car, they could hear him on the radio. He was a big shot, maybe. Jerry kept wanting to take her folks, Giuseppe and Marianne, out to dinner, show them a night on the town. No, no, you come-a here, we eat. The restaurants, you never know what they put in the food. Jerry would go over and listen to the two of them argue in the kitchen.

Jerry took a shine to eleven-year-old Bill Iezzi, and Bill loved the treatment he got from Jerry, riding around in his hot car, going out to Taunton Lake to see Jerry's log-cabin bachelor pad, playing with Jerry's dogs, especially his favorite boxer, Clicquot. Jerry took Bill to the station, showed him around, introduced him as his future brother-in-law. Jerry was a cool guy.

"Let's get married." Teri heard it over and over again. How long had they known one another? Five months? No, Jerry, no.

Let's get married. His divorce was almost final. NO. He got her a ring with a rock. No, Jerry. Well, not yet.

He got her a bigger rock. Well . . . all right. When? Maybe in the fall. Let's see.

When it became clear that Teri and Jerry were serious, Marianne fretted and her brother, old Uncle Vince, Tio Vincenzo, frowned. This is a good Catholic family. What kind of husband would this boy be? He's divorced! He's Jewish! Madonna! You'll have to go to the priest.

So Jerry went down the street to St. Dominic's, met the pastor, went through the mixed-marriage instructions, signed the paper that said he promised to raise the kids Catholic. Teri just laughed and said, "Don't worry."

He called her T. He loved her. They made plans for a wedding in the fall. Teri began looking for an apartment they could afford.

Jerry made promises to her, his heart full. He told her that no matter what, she would never have to work. She could concentrate on her music, take students if she wanted to. He would get her a piano. He loved her.

He came up with a new signoff for the show. It had a kind of Edward R. Murrow flair, but there was a coded message at the end, just to show her that he knew she was listening.

"This is Jerry Williams. Good night, good luck, good morning. Good night, T."

5   BOSTON

Best city I've ever lived in? New York, when I was kid . . . Brooklyn. That was the best place I ever lived. Next best? Boston and Philly. If you have an eastern mentality, Boston and Philly are somewhat the same. But Boston is another kind of tradition . . . those legislators are in session all day long. All *year* long. They never go home. You wander up to the State House, see all those guys chompin' at each other. It's a great political city . . . There's a youthful vigor, and vim, and pep, and energy about Boston that no other city in America has . . . Lot of universities . . . that big, youthful population . . . There's a certain *je ne sais quoi* about that city . . . I mean, there's action, *action!*
   —*Jerry Williams, May 22, 1981, WNWS, Miami*

Teri never got the chance to find that apartment in Philly. Almost as soon as they'd decided on a wedding date, Top 40 came to town and threw Jerry off the air.

In the mid-fifties, Top-30 or Top-40 record shows were gimmicks. You'd often hear them on Saturday nights, when kids wanted to turn on the radio for dancing and party music, or on weekend afternoons, when a station needed something exciting. The songs on these shows weren't just what the DJ liked, or what his program director told him to play, or the ones the local pluggers had paid to get on the air, although all those elements still had a part in the mix.

The DJs and program directors built these shows by talking to local folks who owned record stores—and if they were advertisers on the show or on the station, so much the better. What's moving out of the racks, what's selling? Top 40 was directly in contact with the local scene. These songs were the ones people in your own town were willing to pay for.

By 1956 station program directors began thinking about Top 40 as a round-the-clock format. A lot of major markets had some of it on the air, and a distinctive sound was beginning to develop around the music. These new DJs' voices jumped out of the radio. They weren't trying to soothe you—they wanted to excite you. And a lot of stations were buying new jingle packages from the Production Advertising Merchandising Service (PAMS) in Dallas. PAMS created catchy little tunes to order, just a few seconds long, incorporating your call letters, a slogan, the spot on the dial, the DJ's name—anything you wanted, really.

The kids who were listening got the concept instantly. The point of Top 40 was buying records. The more rock 'n' roll you bought, the more likely it was that your local Top-40 station was going to be playing rock 'n' roll. There was something democratic about that, something streetwise, something innately American. The kids who made buying pop music into a hobby and listening to it into an obsession loved it. It almost made music into something important.

So the wave broke on the radio beach in Philadelphia in the summer of 1957. Storer Broadcasting was buying the station. It was going Top 40. No room for a talk show.

Jerry's producer, John Rosica, heard about it early on a Friday morning from Jack Mahoney, WIBG's general manager, and Jerry got the bad news a few minutes earlier. He felt bad for Rosica, but worse for himself. He had a fiancée who was ready to start nesting, in-laws who thought he was a radio star, a ton of premarital expenses that were going to hit any day now. He'd been pulling in more than ten grand a year, which was pretty good money for 1957, around $95,000 in today's dollars. Without money coming in, he would be in serious hot water.

When he told Teri, he was surprised at how well she took it. She knew something about the entertainment business. It blew hot and cold. But he'd better get something lined up fast so her parents didn't worry.

He called his local contacts—Philadelphia, Allentown, even Camden. Nothing. So he widened the circle. He called people he knew in the business in New York. Maybe someday, Jer, but not right now.

Somehow Mac Richmond heard about the situation. M. Evans Richmond, the schlockster of schlocksters, was now a radio station owner—in Boston.

"Sorry to hear about the show, dad," Mac said. (For some nutty reason, Mac called everyone "dad.") "But it could be for the best. I'm starting a Top-40 station up here, and there could be a nice place for you in it."

Mac had figured out that the Achilles' heel of Top 40 was late nights, especially during the week. The later at night it got, the smaller the audience of kids. Jerry's show was just the thing Mac needed on the air when he had to shift the orientation to adults.

They had some serious conversations, first on the phone and then in person. Jerry tried not to sound desperate: Mac knew how well his show had been doing. It was a format change, not his fault. He had some other offers, pretty good ones (some creative license there, as usual). If he relocated to Boston, he'd have a lot of expenses. What could Mac put on the table?

Mac pushed back. "You'll have your own studio, dad, a big old-fashioned one, from the days when the station needed live music. We can have people in to see the show—there's plenty of room in there for an audience."

Jerry brought up telephone calls. How about a delay system like Long John Nebel's? Callers on the air would be something really new, really different. WMEX would be the first with it in Boston.

Mac knew about the delay system—he'd heard Nebel's show, too. He was sure his engineers could figure out how to make something like that work. But it would have to be a system using wire recorders. Couldn't afford those new tape machines yet.

Mac couldn't see Jerry's face as he grimaced—the guy was cheaping out already.

Finally they started talking money. Mac cried poor. "Look, dad, this station is going to be big, but we're starting small. You'll get a fair buck, and a piece of the ad money so you can grow with us. What was IBG paying you?"

Back and forth, each one of them lying a bit, until they had a deal. Mac was going to pay Jerry $250 a week, plus some change for each spot sold on his show. Not too bad. It was a job, thank God.

So Jerry packed and moved to Boston, taking along his boxer, Clicquot, the last remaining member of the old menagerie. Rosica and he parted professional company, but they remained friends as John segued into the world of record promotion. Teri stayed with her folks, trying to make them feel okay about losing her to another town.

What did he know about Boston? What everyone knew about Boston in the mid-fifties. The Sons of Liberty. One if by land, two if by sea. Faneuil Hall, the Cradle of Liberty. Ben Franklin. It had a lot in common with Philly, and not just history. Old-machine politics. Lots of ethnic neighborhoods. Brick and stone.

When Jerry got there and started driving around, he was underwhelmed. It didn't lay out like a city. As you drove along the Delaware in Philly, you knew you were Someplace. There was a big muscular river, almost as big as the Hudson, on one side, and a broad swath of unmistakably urban territory on the other, with a couple of monster bridges.

Here in Boston, you kept looking for the city and not finding it. When you drove alongside the Charles, it was like driving along the Schuylkill, Philly's second river, bucolic, quiet, curvy. It looked like Cambridge was just a stone's throw across the Charles, and frankly, Cambridge looked a little classier than Boston did. The bridges looked like they dated from the turn of the century— at least from the forties.

The park (Hey, Jer, call it the Common, willya?) was a postage stamp. The only rational street grid was in the Back Bay, with all those nice old brick and brownstone houses. When you looked down along the river to where the center of the city was supposed to be, there was the gold dome of the State House, and a tall spire that someone called the Custom House, and a lot of low buildings. Not a single skyscraper. If you turned around, there was a chunky tower in the Back Bay, the offices of the John Hancock Insurance Company, twenty-six stories high, with a column of lights on the top that were supposed to give Bostonians a color-coded weather forecast. That was it for office towers. A low-rise town in red and pale gray. It looked a little the worse for wear, to tell you the truth.

Another thing: you couldn't drive in this burg. Not rationally. Not sensibly. The streets ran every which way, as narrow as the worst Philly streets, but not so straight. A couple of the major thoroughfares had trolley tracks running down the center, with MTA trolley cars that looked like they were designed in the 1930s, wobbling back and forth every few minutes alongside your car. Brooklyn had gotten rid of trolleys decades ago, for Chrissake. The signage? Forget it. You had to learn the weirdness of every intersection for yourself.

Not to mention the driving habits of Bostonians. If someone was waiting at a light to make a left-hand turn, he'd jump out in front of oncoming traffic as soon as he saw the green, instead of waiting for cars on the other side to pass. First time someone did that to him, it nearly gave Jerry a heart attack.

And those Bahst'n accents. This was like London, he supposed: upper-class and lower-class people spoke two different dialects.

Jerry found an apartment—one floor of a little gray stone place on Bay State Road, cheek by jowl with other three- and four-story apartment buildings shaded by trees, just behind the glowering Gothic monstrosities Boston University had constructed along Commonwealth Avenue, buildings that looked a little like Erasmus Hall. Jerry could walk to the WMEX studios from there, though he usually drove. It'd do for a while. Who knew how long this job was going to last?

Teri came up to visit, and they walked the city, just to get the feel of it. On foot, it made more sense—the statues, the greenery, the elegance. That fall the weather was perfect, dry and fresh, not too cool. A horde of college kids came into the area as classes began, surrounding the building where they lived, walking from class to class with transistor radio earpieces stuck in their heads. The whole area felt young. Jerry started to like it. Teri did too.

From the first time Jerry walked into WMEX, he knew he was going to have trouble. It was some schleppy place, up a long flight of stairs, near a bowling alley, just a few walls away from where the Red Sox played. Rock 'n' roll was blaring. Mac's office was a pigsty, right down to the floor, since he smoked cigars constantly and let the ashes fall anywhere. Jerry was dressed in his sharpest, most fashionable suit, ready to turn on the charm, and the boss looked like he hadn't slept all night, hadn't shaved in three days, and had chosen his clothes with the lights off.

Still, there was something about Mac when he talked about radio—not charisma, by a long shot—but a kind of no-bullshit authority, a kind of drive. Mac was young enough to be in touch with the new spirit of radio, smart enough to know what it should sound like, and fixed just well enough so that he could make it happen the way he thought it should be. He believed in listener service, too—on his own terms, and as long as he could make money at it.

Mac showed Jerry around the WMEX operation. Outmoded, outdated equipment. There was a small studio where the DJs worked, with sleeves of platters and sheets of instructions for the jocks stuck on the walls all around the audio board. A few steps away was the old performance studio, a silent, cavernous room with a big organ that had been used for "musical interludes" and live shows. On one side there was a table with a couple of mics, a telephone, a little board, and a couple of metal boxes. Wooden chairs and benches were scattered around. The walls were bare and institutional. A window looked out on Brookline Avenue.

Mac said, "This is it, dad. Your studio. And you'll have an audience, just like Steve Allison at WPEN." Jerry did a quick think. A studio audience—they could probably get a couple of hundred people in here. Within a few blocks of the studio there were at least three hotels, thousands of apartments, the whole Back Bay, really. Plenty of warm bodies who might decide to take a walk down to WMEX and see what he was doing. Not like Tendler's, not in the middle of the action, but maybe . . .

"Up there, dad"—Mac pointed to a glassed-in room, probably a clients' booth at one time—"there's your engineer and your seven-second delay."

They went inside. There was the system Jerry and Mac had discussed, a wire recording rig that would capture the studio sound and the voices of people on the telephone and spit them out on the air seven seconds later. There would be just enough time for Jerry or the engineer to kill the call if somebody got smart and decided to use dirty words. There was a box on the desk in the studio and one in the engineer's booth with the panic buttons, the devices that would cut off the call.

Jerry looked around, nodded. "When do I start?"

"Labor Day."

He'd started in so many markets now—Bristol, McKeesport, Allentown, Camden, and Philly—that his process of acclimation to Boston was almost automatic. Get the papers, read the columns, find out who's who and what's what. He had to get familiar with the styles of the different rags, their editorial positions, all the important local writers, what they said, and how they said it. The *Globe* was stuffy, Harvardy. The *Herald,* a solid second-level paper. The *Record*—a tabloid, but not *Daily News*-style—working-class, it felt like. The *Traveler.* The *Transcript,* an evening paper. The *Christian Science Monitor* was published in Boston, but that didn't really count as a local paper. There were ethnic papers, neighborhood papers, special interest papers— Jerry was particularly interested in the *State House Reporter–City Hall News,* a kind of political gossip sheet.

He quickly settled into a routine. At 11:00 A.M. or noon, he'd drive from his apartment over to Boylston Street, a big thoroughfare a couple of blocks away from the station. He'd park, feed the meter, figure out when he'd have to come out and pump more money into it, and then walk into Kenmore Square and buy the papers and any of the weekly newsmagazines that he didn't have yet. His first stop was the Triangle Cafeteria, across the street from the station. That was where he'd read the papers, have a sandwich, smoke a few cigarettes, watch people, talk to the regulars, think about the show, and read some more. Sometimes people could see him moving his lips, testing how this column or that article might sound if he read a paragraph or two on the air.

In the mid-afternoon, he'd come into MEX, check his messages, make a few phone calls trying to line people up for the show, and disappear by four or so to have dinner with Teri. Finally, at quarter of ten at night, he'd drive back to Boylston Street.

The politics of Boston was legendary, and Jerry had to go on the air with at least the major players and the basic outlines clear in his mind. He knew the old days of ethnic rancor in town were passing. It was no longer Irish Democrats versus Yankee Republicans, James Michael Curley cronies versus downtown bankers. Now there was a different kind of struggle going on, between the "New Boston" types and those who liked things just the way they'd been. Not so different from what had been going on in Philly.

He got to know the players and their styles.

Governor Foster Furcolo was a liberal Democrat, elected just the year before. He was the first Italian American governor of the state. The more Jerry found out about him, the more he liked him—although they didn't always see eye to eye on policy. Furcolo was a jolly good fellow, as they used to say.

Senator Jack Kennedy was a force to be reckoned with because of his powerful family. He had the good looks, the warm smile, some kind of magic.

Then there were the other members of the congressional delegation: a Yankee senator, Leverett Saltonstall, and a host of well-entrenched U.S. reps—Torbert Macdonald, John McCormack, Tip O'Neill.

Below that level, it got complicated. Johnny Powers, president of the Massachusetts Senate. Mike Skerry, Speaker of the House. The fractious City Council—with one member from every one of Boston's twenty-two wards, who could keep them all straight? And the small-townish School Committee, where neighborhood rivalries were played out as bitterly as if the parts of Boston were villages at war in the Middle Ages.

The heart of WMEX's coverage was the city of Boston, and Jerry needed to understand the one man making the big decisions affecting the lives of most of his listeners, the guy locals called the Mayah, John Hynes, who'd been in office for seven and a half years.

He was in the job almost by accident. The boys on Beacon Hill picked Hynes to keep the seat warm for a few months while James Michael Curley took a short vacation in prison, and he was perfectly fine with that deal until Curley got back to town and began telling the press what a do-nothing Hynes was. Two years later, in 1949, Hynes was elected mayor and Curley was history.

Hynes was surrounded by a new political generation, the "New Boston" crowd—including people like Gabe Piemonte, a young lawyer and aspiring pol whom Jerry got to know very well. The way they saw it, the city was down-at-the-heels, seedy, shabby. The population was declining. They wanted to see lower taxes, better housing, some real urban redevelopment. They envisioned a new image—gleaming buildings, some skyscrapers, some modern architecture to relieve all that brick, new businesses to build the tax base.

By the time Jerry arrived, Hynes and the New Boston boys had accomplished a lot—not that everyone was happy about what they had done. Planners were gobbling up land in the heart of the waterfront and building a new elevated roadway that was supposed to relieve the congestion on downtown streets. They were eyeing an extension of the new Massachusetts Turnpike into the city to provide a fast way for suburbanites to get into town. The city's planning board wanted to clear out the dilapidated Quincy Market buildings and replace them with something fresh and exciting. Hynes and his friends had enticed Prudential Insurance (with some generous tax breaks) into buying an abandoned rail yard in the Back Bay to build the first major new office building in Boston in decades. The city had built housing projects in the city's neighborhoods to help out the poor. They weren't very pretty, but they seemed to be serviceable. And they had ambitious plans for a swath of the city that looked particularly bad to them—the burlesque theaters, tattoo parlors, and sailors' flophouses around Scollay Square, and the adjoining ethnic enclave of run-down apartment buildings known as the West End.

Jerry pored through the newspapers every day at the Triangle, getting the feel of the city as quickly as he could. He knew he wouldn't grasp all the nuances at first. But that was fine—in fact, it might be something of an advantage. He would just talk to his listeners, as honestly as possible. He would be an ordinary guy from out of town trying to understand the mysterious world of Boston politics. He'd ask the callers to help him cut through the official party lines and get to the truth.

That was one of the ways he got the conversation started in his first weeks on the air in Boston. Obviously, this show would build on what he'd done at WIBG, with commentary, interviews, the issues of the day at the center of the action every night, but there was an essential difference. Now the calls from his listeners were at least as important as the other elements in the show. No one else in Boston was putting callers' voices on the air. Damn few people in broadcasting had ever done it, and only a handful around the country were ballsy enough to try it as a regular part of a radio show.

The competition? Well, there was none, really, except for ol' Sherm. Sherm Feller was still doing his showbizzy conversation show, which was now a ten-year-old institution in town. In 1953 he'd moved from WEEI to WVDA (which was soon to change its name to WEZE). By the time Jerry got to town, Sherm had bowed to fashion and started taking phone calls—he was still doing them the old-fashioned way, paraphrasing the unheard people on the other end, the way Jerry had on WKDN and WIBG.

Another guy made a name for himself following in Sherm's wake—Kenny Mayer, or "the Night Mayer," as he sometimes called himself on the air. Mayer was a Walter Winchell–style gossip columnist, supplementing his rep with a restaurant show from Ken's in Copley Square: one-way calls, showbiz schmooze, comics, some laughs.

TV wasn't really a competitive factor. At that point, watching television was still special, and not everybody had one. The family didn't plunk themselves down in front of the tube and glue themselves to whatever was there. They'd gather at specific times to watch the big shows—but their idle moments still were spent with the radio. And lots of people went out. They were going to clubs and cabarets, dancing and drinking.

Jerry could sum up the other local media outlets in a few words. There was a smart young anchor on Channel 7 who looked pretty good, Dave Rodman. Downtown there was the radio station owned by the *Herald*, WHDH. Westinghouse had a monster station, WBZ, with a morning music host who was an institution, Carl DeSuze, and a fine John Cameron Swayze–style newsman named Streeter Stuart. Across the street from WMEX was the headquarters of the Yankee Network, a big operation owned by a guy named John Shepard, with one of the area's most important radio and TV outfits, WNAC. And there were a few great DJs scattered around on other stations. Jerry especially liked Bill Marlowe and Stan Richards.

Though the managers of other radio stations didn't know it, there were two huge holes in the Boston market: a format that young people could call their own, and controversial, issue-oriented, telephone talk. Whatever you might think of Mac Richmond, he read those tea leaves perfectly.

If Jerry's first impressions of Mac as a boss were negative, his second and third impressions went south from there. When he got his first payroll check, the gross amount was $125, not the $250 Mac had promised. He was furious, but Mac was matter-of-fact. "Don't get excited, Jer. It's just that I'm not gonna pay you what I said I would. You'll get this $125 as salary, and a dollar more for every spot we sell on your show. Take it or leave it." Jerry knew that even if they sold out his show, that would add only $60 more to his pay each week. He yelled. He stormed. Mac just sat there. "You don't like it, dad, you can always go somewhere else." What was he gonna do? Tell Teri to start packing again? Mac had screwed him.

He did the math. If he was lucky, even counting the dollar he'd get for every spot, he'd make $9,000 a year. If Mac was lucky, he'd sell more than $90,000 in ads during Jerry's time. He vowed to make the most of it and never to trust the guy again.

Mac and Jerry agreed on one thing, at least: the telephone calls should be the heart of the promotion for the new show. Mac sprang for some ads, showing Jerry's grinning disembodied head, touting the novelty of the concept: "Your voice will be heard right over the air!"

The studio audience saw this: down in front of rows of uncomfortable chairs, Jerry at one end of a splinter-ridden table, dressed in a very sharp suit with a very nice tie, the image ruined by a pair of ugly black headphones wrapped around his carefully-groomed hair. On the table, an old Graham McNamee–era RCA microphone for him, a little worse for wear, a couple of other mics for his guests, a little audio board, and, to start with, just one black telephone in front of him.

Jerry prepped them: don't applaud, don't ask questions. Only he could hear what people on the phone were saying, but if you'd like to listen in, you can take turns with a set of black plastic headphones available at the far end of the table, hard as little round rocks.

He was always amazed at the crowd that showed up, especially on Friday and Saturday nights. Who would come in from the night to watch a guy talk to people and answer the phone? People would wander in and out during the broadcast. They'd stare at him like he was an exhibit in the Museum of Radio. Sometimes he felt a little apprehensive. What would prevent some nut from coming in and taking a swing at him?

Each show began with a stentorian warning—in the tone of "Abandon hope, all ye who enter here": "The views and opinions expressed on the following program do not necessarily constitute the views and opinions of the management or its sponsors. It's time for the new Jerry Williams show, for comment and controversy."

In those first few shows, he did little set-up monologues, using stuff from the paper, to introduce himself and the concept. He also tried to chase the rock 'n' rollers away—or at least to weed out the ones who couldn't think. He'd have guests a couple of times a week—nobody special quite yet. And every night, after things were warmed up, he'd say, "Let's open our phone lines now and take some of your calls and comments on the new WMEX."

Taking a call was more than just picking up the phone and saying "Hello!" He had to throw a couple of switches and coordinate with the engineer-producer up in the booth. And there was a Moment of Truth before he'd increase the volume of the telephone pot. He'd have to listen to the caller's voice and make a split-second decision about whether there was any point in putting the person on the air.

He got to know the voices of kids or pranksters in half a heartbeat. After a while, he could sense what sort of caller was on the phone by the sound of his or her breathing. The kids and the losers never made it on the air. "Don't waste your time, sonny! Next call!" He'd bang the receiver down, wait a beat for it to ring again, pick it up, and say "Jerry Williams, hello!" Sometimes this would happen two or three times before he'd twist the pot and bring up the volume of the call on the air. Then the game would begin.

"Jerry!"

"Yes, you're on the air." He almost immediately put an edge on his voice. The caller had to know that this was showtime, and there was no room for hesitation.

"Jerry!"

"Go right ahead."

"Jerry! I can't hear myself."

"We're using a delaying system, sir." When he said "sir," everyone could hear his annoyance. "You'll have to turn down the radio. You're not going to hear your own voice. Just go right ahead."

"Oh. Well, just a minute."

This stuff drove him crazy. He wanted to get to the substance, what the person called about. He'd fill time waiting for the person to get back to the phone—"You're on the new WMEX in Boston, 1510, COmmonwealth 6-2525 is the number."

"Jerry! I wanta say somethin' about this plan to tayah down all them West End apahtm't buildings . . ."

In the first few months, he gave little lectures to the callers—don't waste everyone's time, be ready to make your comment, be brief and to the point, please. We're trying something new, an open forum, the first time in Boston; that means you have to speak right up. This eventually solidified into his rules—the ABCs, he called them—"Be accurate, brief, and concise." (Yeah, the last two words meant the same thing, but what was he gonna use for the "C"? Cockamamie?)

When he finally got someone with something to say, a different kind of game would start. He'd ask questions to get a feel for the person on the other end—Where do you work, sir? Do you have kids at home, ma'am? Do you live in the West End yourself?

He could prompt, probe, prod—if nothing was happening, he could wipe the slate clean with "Next call!" Then the bang of plastic on plastic. Then, "Jerry Williams—hello!"

People could hear him hang up. The technology for smooth transitions hadn't yet been invented, so the receiver would clatter into its cradle fifteen or twenty times a night. The phone noise, just off-mic, sometimes with a little clang from the otherwise-silenced bells inside the phone, became a signature sound. He learned to make it loud or soft as a punctuation mark at the end of a call, a sound effect that added to the drama.

Almost from the start, he wasn't polite or impartial. Instead of *The Jerry Williams Show*, the words *Comment and Controversy* appeared on the station's official log. Jerry also occasionally called it "New England's Town Meeting of the Air"—he wanted people to understand that this was a place where regular people could have their say and their fellow citizens could listen to them. It would be noisy at times, like a real town meeting. But something worthwhile would come out of it.

When he agreed with a caller, he often rephrased his or her words more eloquently as a way of moving the conversation ahead. When he disagreed with someone, he gave the person a hard time—often much more than the caller had bargained for. A lot of people who never considered actually picking up the phone couldn't believe how tough he was on those people calling him. He wasn't a nice man at all. They called Mac in the mornings and complained. Another group saw him as a progressive crusader, and they began to compliment Mac on his importance, to thank Mac for bringing him to Boston, to say how much they needed him. His audience began to divide into partisans—people who loved him and people who hated him.

Three hours after the station disclaimer, Jerry would wrap it up. "Good night, good luck, good morning." Then there'd be that same ominous voice, closing the door of the Inner Sanctum: "The views and opinions expressed on the preceding program did not necessarily constitute the views and opinions of the management or its sponsors." And WMEX would sign off for the night.

He soon discovered that it actually was harder to control the show with the new system than it'd been when no one could hear the callers. The people calling in weren't as important as the thousands who were just listening. Most folks tuned to 1510 between 10:00 P.M. and 1:00 A.M. were *never* going to call him, and they wanted to hear something worthwhile. That meant he had a responsibility to make the show move, to milk each call for its excitement and interest. But in this format he couldn't camouflage the dullards or smarten up the inarticulates. Not to mention the fact that Mac's cheap wire recorder system made the callers (and Jerry, for that matter) sound like they were talking through woolen masks. So he constantly pushed his callers to speak clearly, make their points, and move on. And if he couldn't sharpen up the caller, he made his impatience part of the show.

Others took notice. Within the first few months of the show, a columnist for the *State House Reporter–City Hall News* named Anthony Broderick wrote, "Jerry is a personable, youthful lad, who goes through what seems to me an ordeal, in an intelligent and very calm manner. . . . [He] and his program are intellectually stimulating and I believe he is becoming very popular and deserves success."

Finally, in November, a week and a half before Thanksgiving, Jerry got his wish. Therese Iezzi became his wife. He went back to Philly for the weekend (Mac gave him Friday and Saturday off!), lived through the whirlwind of family kisses, welcomed Herbert and his folks to town, made sure their rooms were all right, went through the simple ceremony, stood around grinning while the few pictures were taken, tried to be the Groom with the Most at the reception at the nice new Sheraton Hotel, spent the wedding night there, and then packed Teri's remaining things into the car and hustled back up to Boston by Sunday night. No honeymoon. Mac just laughed. Are you kiddin', Jer? I didn't tell ya t' get married, did I? It was back to work the next day, and Jerry added "Good night, T" to the signoff as he had in Philly because he knew she was listening.

They didn't get a break for quite a while. Because he was working six nights a week, there was precious little time for fun. Boston had an active pre-Broadway scene and a little theater district, but Jerry's job meant that his theatergoing had to be limited to matinees or Sunday nights. And, in fact, despite his love of acting, he didn't get a great thrill out of seeing others onstage. It was a lot like watching Steve Allison in Philly. He kept thinking, "Why isn't that me up there?"

Leisure for the Williamses was an occasional dinner out. Teri wasn't the world's best cook and they were on a very tight budget, so they looked for inexpensive places to go. At the same time, Jerry was always looking for potential sponsors, knowing that every new spot would put a dollar in his pocket.

Jerry found Jack & Marion's pretty quickly. This was a deli that had all the trimmings—the free stuff on the table, like good bread and pickles, that took him back to dinners his dad had sprung for in Brooklyn, the huge "fresser" sandwiches, the giant menu, the Jewish home cooking specialties like latkes and kishke and knishes, and big, rich desserts.

Occasionally, they could take a ride up to the North Shore for fried clams at Woodman's in Essex. They could go to the North End for cheap Italian, and if they had a little extra money they could go into fabulous Joe Tecce's. For a splurge, there was always Bob Lee's Islander in Chinatown (a tiki restaurant to beat them all, with the dark decor, the sweet and sour, the exotic drinks, the complete package), or Durgin Park, with its wiseass waitresses.

The Ritz and Locke-Ober were out of Jerry's price range, but they didn't want to advertise on WMEX anyway. Jack & Marion's, Bob Lee's, the No-Name Restaurant on the Fish Pier—they all showed up on Jerry's show, and he pitched them so well that people's mouths started to water almost as soon as he began one of their spots.

His first two years on the air in Boston, through the end of 1959, were Shakedown Time. Controversy brought people into the studio, and the novelty of calls on the air attracted listeners, but Jerry knew he would have a precious few chances to make an impression, and he wanted the show to knock people over. He worked on every element of the show with a passionate drive.

In February 1958 Mac got the first ratings. Everyone at WMEX was ecstatic. The Top-40 format and Jerry's controversial nighttime show had pushed the station from nowhere into the top ten.

On the strength of the numbers, Jerry and Mac had lunch at the Triangle to talk over improvements in the show. They needed two lines and two phones, Jerry said, so that there'd always be a call waiting. Mac agreed that it would smooth out the sound of the show if Jerry could segue from one call to another without waiting for the light on his solo phone to flicker on again. He said he figured he could afford to have the phone company put in another line. And *tape* delay, Jerry said. The calls sounded like shit using this wire system. Mac said he'd look into it.

Those were the days when Jerry's tuna fish sandwich cost seventy-five cents, but he was making only $125 a week, before taxes. Maybe the total bill was a buck and a half, or two dollars if they had dessert. Who paid? Please. No matter how many times they had lunch, Jerry would be the one who would always make the move for the tab, and Mac would never fight him for it. The guy was pulling at least five grand out of Jerry's show every month and he couldn't spring for a lousy lunch.

Mac said, "I'll get the tip." He left a dime on the table. Jerry thought: not even 10 percent! When Mac got up to leave, Jerry put another coin, sometimes a quarter, next to Mac's dime.

The numbers confirmed Mac's decision on another improvement—a small investment in a jingle package for WMEX, including one that would highlight Jerry's show. Jerry didn't have any say in the copy for his jingle, but at least it reflected the response he was getting. The company had put together a song, sort of, sung by a chorus of voices. The first thing listeners heard were these singers, warbling in harmony over a big-band backup, with a cheery "Do you disagree?"

Then there was a female speaker, probably one of the singers, whining over the music: "I think he's terrible!"

The singers came back in harmony: "Or do you agree?"

Another female speaker gushed, "Yes, he's wonderful!"

The chorus wrapped it up, singing, "Well, whatever you think, feel free to let us know. Just call us, WMEX, Color Radio—[big finish, the whole group excitedly speaking:] *The Jerry Williams Show!*" (Mac had stolen the phrase "Color Radio" from KFWB in Los Angeles to show how up-to-date his station was.)

It was the fifties, after all.

Jerry found his issues, stumbled into them, really, and it turned out that they were the real key to his success.

Take the time he saw his car being towed away. He had just miscalculated a little, left it a few minutes too long on Boylston Street. He looked at his watch, realized he had to pump more money into the meter, hustled down the couple of blocks, and saw a truck hauling his car away! What a pain in the ass *that* was. Getting someone to drive him to the tow lot, out in the middle of nowhere, shelling out hard cash to some grimy city employee, just to get his car back. So that night, when the on-air light went on, he just started talking about it. "Listen, folks, I wanna tell ya about something that happened today. I came to work as I always do, found a good spot for my car over on Boylston Street. And I goofed. I admit it."

He suddenly found a groove. He slowed the words down, started spiking some of them with the upper tones of his voice.

"I [a little pause] *let* [another pause] the *meter* [a longer pause] *run out.* And the cops *towed* my *car!* Why? *Why?* Listen, I didn't park in a no-parking zone. There was no sign saying, 'Park here, buddy, and you're gonna get towed.' It was a *legal* parking space. Why, Mr. Mayor, *why?* Do you really need my money *that* badly? You're gonna hold my car for *ransom?* Hey, I'd *fix* the ticket if I could. You can fix *anything* here—except a tow. Because it means money for the city, right? You have to picture this: there I am, standing on the street, watching my car fade away into the sunset. I'm waving my arms— 'Stop! Stop!'" He put a little sad music into his voice, picturing poor little Freddie Bartholomew, abandoned, cold, lonely. "But they wouldn't stop. And there went my car.

"Y' know what? I think I'll *sue* the city. That's it. I'll sue them."

People *loved* this stuff. Suffering Jerry, just like them.

Callers: "Hey, that happened to me, too, Jerry." "If y' think that's bad, wait'll y' hear *this.*"

Cars. Cars. Of course! Cars were central to Americans' lives. He knew where to take this. The traffic in this town. Where are the signs that tell you where to go? And the lack of courtesy from other drivers. And the cabs—what about those *bombers* that the city lets out on the road?

And the insurance? When Jerry saw his first auto insurance bill, he went ballistic. Off the air. Then he went ballistic *on* the air. It's not *right,* this cozy relationship between the insurance companies and the agencies that're supposed to regulate them. And who gets it right in the teeth? You know who.

And the dirty streets. Folks, just look at what they let sit there in the gutters. For *days!*

"Jerry!"

"Yes!"

"Y' talkin' about the streets theyah. Y' oughta come down heeyah to the South End. They ain't cleanin' the streets heeyah."

"Well, how long has it been since they've come through?"

"'Bout thirty yeeahs."

Later on, another caller, from out in the suburbs, Wellesley. "Hey, Jerry! Y' know what I do?"

"No. What?"

"I take alla my gahbage, put it in the wagon, drive inta town, and throw it in the South End."

"I believe it, sir. I believe it."

Of all the elements—his personality, the callers, the guests, the monologues, the tone, the forward momentum—it was the issues that made the show distinctive. He came to know instinctively when something was hitting people where they lived. He listened to what people said, and he let his callers show him what they considered important. He also knew which were the right issues for his own personality. If there was something to which he could bring his own experience, his own sense of outrage against the injustices of the world, it clicked.

Everyone in the area had an opinion about this redevelopment of the West End. The New Boston boys were convinced that the little rat-infested ethnic neighborhood ought to be wiped off the map and replaced by nice new apartment buildings. Maybe the old residents of the neighborhood wouldn't be able to afford to live there afterward, they said, but there were plenty of other places to live. Wait just a minute, Jerry said. These Italians, Jews, Greeks, Poles, Russians, Albanians, Ukrainians who lived in the West End—some of these folks were DPs from the war. Was this the way America treated refugees? He thought (and said) that these little people were being sold a bill of goods. Where was the city going to relocate them? To those ugly, crowded, housing projects, the ones that were already falling apart just a few years after they were built? He listened to residents of the neighborhood complain about being pushed out, about city services being cut off to their apartments, about their homes being bulldozed. "Doesn't anybody care about this?" he fumed.

National issues worked, too. Almost as soon as he was on the air, civil rights started to heat up. What was going on down there in the South? Jerry asked his listeners. Didn't they know the Civil War was over? When he started taking calls about this, he was surprised at how many white Bostonians sounded uneasy about blacks voting or sitting right next to their kids in school—or going on dates with their daughters. He'd push them, trying to get them to have a little humanity. Some of them didn't like that. Some of them were downright ugly about it.

He started showing off his anger with hostile callers or stupid callers with exclamations ("Sheesh! They're out there tonight!") or by smashing the telephone down onto its cradle they way they did in the movies. It wasn't too long before he actually was breaking phones. Mac loved that. He told the engineers to stockpile a few extra phones in the station's shop just in case.

Mac wasn't so even-tempered about controversy. Jerry was saying things that made him nervous, so he sent the station's lawyer, a man of ample girth and unimpressive demeanor, to watch the show and "advise" Jerry periodically.

"Jerry, Jesus, don't talk about, don't talk about the mayor," he said. "For cryin' out loud, don't talk about the Church. Ooo! Don't talk about the archbishop. Whooo! Don't talk about the governor. We don't need that. I mean, Furcolo's a nice guy. And oh! Jerry, don't talk about the City Council. I wanna see that you get along here in Boston. You're new in town. You keep saying 'Boston *Commons*,' when it's 'the Boston *Common*.' You keep saying 'Beacon Hill' when you mean 'City Hall.' Whooo! Don't talk about the police commissioner. Whooo! And don't talk about the district attorney. Oooo, don't talk about Garrett Byrne."

The lawyer was right about Garrett Byrne, but in that particular case Mac didn't agree with him. Suffolk County District Attorney Garrett Byrne and WMEX Talk Show Host Jerry Williams became mortal enemies because of . . . Corruption? Civil rights? Fixed parking tickets? No. Because of rock 'n' roll.

You see, Garrett Byrne tried to stop a rock 'n' roll concert from taking place at Boston Arena in May 1958. It was part of the Big Beat Tour, a series of concerts organized and hosted by Alan Freed, one of the first disc jockeys to make a fortune on the new music. Boston was supposed to be a major stop on the tour, but Byrne didn't like that idea at all. There'd been trouble at these concerts in other cities. Black kids and white kids were dancing together and what all. Sometimes there were fights. This Freed wanted to put Buddy Holly and Danny and the Juniors, who were white kids, onstage with Chuck Berry, a black. It was a recipe for trouble.

Jerry got right up on the freedom of expression horse. This was the music that WMEX was playing all day long. It was like Byrne was calling them degenerates or something. He scoffed at Byrne on the air. This was more of that old Boston stuffiness, the "banned in Boston" business, bluenosed shock at the rock. Let the kids have their fun!

Byrne didn't have a radio station to fire back. He did not like being attacked on the air, night after night. Who *was* this Jerry Williams, anyway? A strange voice in town, an out-of-stater. He sent a couple of investigators and an assistant district attorney to Philadelphia to look into Jerry's past. Where'd this guy come from? Where'd he work? The folks at WIBG got a visit. Ben Gimbel and Major Compton got calls. Whaddya know about this Williams? Not his real name, is it? Jacoby, right? What's that, Jewish? Got married here?

Oh, *second* marriage. Must fool around, huh? Of course, it got back to Jerry. He knew lots of people in Philly. It was pretty scary, what Garrett Byrne was up to.

But he kept on about Byrne on the air. He said that Byrne was trying to build a career on an illusion. Rock 'n' roll was just *music*, for heaven's sake. Or maybe it was something uglier that was bothering you, Mr. Byrne. Let's get our cards on the table. It's about race mixing, isn't it, Mr. District Attorney? That's what's makin' you crazy, isn't it?

Then the funny noises started on the phone at 189A Bay State Road. Phone tapping in 1958 was pretty crude, and every time Jerry picked up his home phone, he could tell there were a lot of people listening. There were so many others on the line that he considered selling commercials. He asked someone he knew on the police side to investigate. The fella listened. He said, "Somebody's there." So Jerry made a point of saying hello to his new audience every time he made a call, and pointedly told his friends and acquaintances they'd better not discuss the commie plot they'd been working on because the line was tapped.

Byrne gave in. The concert was held. Six thousand people came out to rock 'n' roll. But guess what, Jerry? After the show, there *was* some violence. And not a little. A guy got stabbed, some people got hurt. Quite a few got robbed. Three subsequent Big Beat concerts were canceled. Mayor Hynes banned rock 'n' roll in public venues in Boston. Alan Freed had to quit his great job at WINS in New York as a result of the fracas. Byrne indicted him for inciting a riot, and Freed's career spiraled downward into payola and disgrace.

Jerry didn't talk about Garrett Byrne for a while after that. Sometimes silence is smarter.

Jerry heard a lot about Father Leonard Feeney, the Boston priest who stuck to the idea that there was no salvation outside the Roman Catholic Church long after the Church fathers, including Boston's archbishop, Richard Cushing, had backed away from it. Feeney was expelled from the Jesuits and his St. Benedict Center was placed under official interdict back in 1949, and yet the guy kept on preaching on Boston Common right up to the time Jerry got to town. One night there was some discussion about Father Feeney on the air. Jerry said that the guy was a rabid anti-Semite, of course. He'd seen this sort of thing before—Father Charles Coughlin's radio broadcasts out of Chicago during the war, Reverend Carl McIntire down in New Jersey. Religion as an excuse for hatred. Not very pretty. (Listeners who didn't know it already had pretty good reason to understand from what was said on the air that Jerry was Jewish.)

Not too long after that, when Jerry was leaving the station at 1:00 A.M. as usual, making his way down Lansdowne Street, there was a group waiting for him. They looked starry-eyed and odd. One began talking to him about Father Feeney, and then the others chimed in. He was making a mistake. He ought to watch what he said on the air. They followed him down the street. Jerry talked fast and moved toward his car. One man got ahead of him, perceived where he was going, and stood menacingly between him and his car. It was a tense moment. For a second, he wondered if this bunch was going to rough him up. He moved in a businesslike way to the driver's side, got in, closed the door, talking all the time—gotta get home now, thanks for your opinions, really appreciate it, gotta go. And he slowly pulled away from the curb, watching them in his rearview mirror to see if they might follow him. Whew.

It wasn't long after that that someone smashed the windshield and damaged the hood—and he'd just bought that car, too. Somebody else threw a brick through the window of his studio. The blame could never be pinned on anyone in particular, but Jerry was sure the incidents had to do with the things he was saying on the air.

This controversy stuff could have an effect on his health.

He started taking Clicquot to work with him. The dog's fierce look—that tough-mug quality that boxers have—made it look like he had protection at his feet, even though Clicquot was a sweetheart.

It wasn't all fireworks. He also connected with the showbiz PR people in town. When well-known entertainers came through Boston, Jerry wanted them on his show first. In his initial six months, Pat O'Brien, Tony Martin, Louis Armstrong, and James Mason all came to the studio and talked with him. He was comfortable with them, and their celebrity added to his.

Then one night a guy named William McMasters dropped in to see the show. Like so many others, he simply showed up at the station, walked in through the studio's side door, and took a chair in the audience. Afterward, he introduced himself.

He said he was an old Boston broadcasting veteran—Jerry believed that he was old, all right; the guy looked like he was in his eighties, and he sounded like a nineteenth-century orator who'd arrived in 1957 in a time machine. Apparently he'd been a news commentator for WNAC, the station across the street, and he'd hosted his own discussion show there. He said he'd done three thousand broadcasts in Boston, which Jerry took with a shakerful of salt. He said he was intrigued with what Jerry was doing and wanted to do a profile of him for one of the local papers.

As they talked, Jerry's opinion changed. This old man *got it*. He really was a broadcast professional, and he really understood what Jerry was trying to do. So he gave McMasters an earful—high-toned stuff about his broadcast philosophy.

A few days later, McMasters sent Jerry a proof of his article. Jerry was impressed. This guy knew his stuff. "Only a broadcaster" (Go ahead, Jerry thought, pat yourself on the back) "can really appreciate the enormous effort and adaptability needed to keep up a program like the one that Williams is pouring over the 1510 beam, six nights a week."

Jerry laughed a little at "pouring over the 1510 beam"—where did this guy get this stuff? But McMasters was right when he talked about how much work it was. "I have caught the Jerry Williams program several evenings and it strikes me that he has developed a new pattern that is so different and so elastic that it will never lose its appeal." Well, thank you, Mr. M!

Jerry read his own quotes, nicely set off in boldface type. He got a kick out of the way McMasters had cleaned up the stuff he'd said in the interview and made him sound tweedy:

Naturally, with Boston University, Harvard, Boston College, Tufts, Northeastern, Brandeis, Radcliffe, and scores of other smaller institutions of learning, we have more intellectuals to the square mile than can be found anywhere on earth. But we also have a practical crowd of young and older men and women who want to know what it is all about. They take life seriously. They are deeply concerned in the future of their state and country. They hate confusion and want to fight their way through the enveloping fog of doubt and distrust.

You see, this is a participating program. The listening audience is invited to call the station and ask questions or make pertinent observations on the topic that has been introduced by some speaker or an entire panel. Whenever we accept a call on the program, the conversation becomes two-way for the benefit of other listeners. Listeners can hear the entire conversation.

I have not hesitated to take up controversial subjects. Everybody who listens in can learn something.

You couldn't buy publicity like that. After the piece appeared in the paper, Jerry was talking with another old hand in the Boston newspaper business. He mentioned McMasters, laughing at his mannerisms and what he'd written. The other guy said, "Don't you know who William McMasters is? He helped bring down Charles Ponzi in 1920!"

After nine months or so on the air, WMEX was a sensation. Despite the station's odd and spotty signal, kids were doing everything they could to hear the music. And their parents were talking about Jerry Williams.

Mac stoked the fire. He knew that one of the best ways to get someone to write up a station event was to make it a benefit—so there was a WMEX campaign for "Tons of Toys" for needy kids at Christmastime, or a gala for the Jimmy Fund (the pet charity of the Red Sox), or a telethon for the Cystic Fibrosis people or the Heart Fund or one of Cardinal Cushing's projects. And Jerry always was expected to be there.

One facet of Mac's generosity cut him where it really hurt. Mac felt that it would be good business if the WMEX Good Guys would make personal appearances on their own time, for free. Jerry got calls all the time asking him to speak—from the library association, the political clubs, the temples, the churches—and he was only too happy to meet his listeners. But Mac had put it out that Jerry would make personal appearances "with no remuneration, but as a public service for the community good." It took more than a year of complaining and carping to Mac to undo the PR effort so that Jerry could start another income stream.

He learned a lot from that emceeing and moderating and lecturing. One of his earliest engagements was an address in front of a group of psychologists. He gave them a serious, tough talk in his usual on-air style, with familiar themes—government doesn't have enough concern for ordinary people, we have real injustices in our country but the politicians want to spend their time raising taxes and looking under rocks for commies—and these guys picked up on how angry he was. And then all these headshrinkers came up afterward saying, "Are you all right, Mr. Williams? You know, if you want to talk about it . . ." He realized that people who came out to see him didn't want an angry speaker. They wanted someone who would be entertaining. So he dusted off some of the old lines from the Gag Busters, added some borscht-belt jokes to his repertoire, slipped in some character voices and stories, and pretty soon he had an act. He could still get political, but he had to keep smiling and make sure the crowd was smiling with him.

More advertisers joined the Williams fold. Bernie Garber's travel agency began sponsoring tours to Miami with Jerry and Teri as hosts. Moe Ellis, Ellis the Rim Man, the proprietor of an automotive supply shop, became a regular, even though he couldn't pick up MEX in his house and had to go out to his car late at night to hear his own commercials. These, like most of Jerry's advertisers, were not highbrow businesses. Most of the sponsors with whom Jerry developed personal relationships had started out as small shopkeepers or restaurant owners, a lot like Samuel Jacoby. Jerry knew what they needed, and he knew how to talk to their potential customers. And a lot of people came in to those businesses saying, "Jerry sent me."

The months went by fast. He made quite a few influential friends—his sponsors, some lawyers, Democratic Party activists, even a few names among the state's Republicans. One night James Michael Curley himself, the legendary Mayah, called the show to comment on something, and then, every three or four weeks, Jerry would get another jingle from Curley. It was a little sad, he thought, this guy who once had the world (or Boston, at least) by the tail, calling to offer his comments to a thirty-four-year-old Brooklynite who'd never had the chance to vote for him.

As a matter of fact, the local pols loved the show—both as listeners and as guests. Frankie "Sweepstakes" Kelly was one of the first to take advantage of Jerry's invitations to come up and talk. He'd been the youngest city councilor in Boston's history, then attorney general, and then Don Quixote, tirelessly promoting the idea that taxes could be reduced by instituting a state lottery. Every year, Frank would manage to get a lottery bill filed in the legislature. The *Globe* would make fun of the idea. The Massachusetts Council of Churches would call it immoral. Every year it failed. Even so, Kelly taught Jerry an important lesson in 1958. The perennial bill was up for a hearing, and Frank encouraged Jerry's listeners to go to Gardner Auditorium, at the Massachusetts State House. Hundreds of people showed up. "We want a state lottery. We want a sweepstakes." The bill failed anyway. But Jerry saw just how much influence the show had, and what Bostonians would do when they got behind something.

As the first anniversary of his show appeared on the horizon, a lawyer Jerry knew named Mitch Mabardi suggested that there ought to be some kind of commemorative event. Pretty soon there was a committee of people organizing a First Anniversary Banquet and Testimonial Dinner—including Julius Ansel, a Democratic state rep from Dorchester; the political columnist Joe Malone; Kenny Mayer, the columnist and restaurant show host; Eddie McCormack, the state's attorney general; Gabe Piemonte, Jerry's personal attorney; and good old Frank Kelly. They'd have a pleasant dinner on October 26, 1958, at the Sherry Biltmore. There would be a few tributes, Jerry would make a speech, and everyone would go home happy. The $7.50 ticket price (more than fifty bucks in today's money) would cover the expenses, besides providing a reasonable speaking fee for the Man of the Evening. When Jerry presented the idea to Mac, the boss said that WMEX would spring for the promotion and office help.

The event turned out to be far more than the intimate dinner they first envisioned. The committee sold more than fifteen hundred tickets and packed the hotel's function room a few days before Halloween 1958. There were guest appearances by Governor Foster Furcolo, Mayor John Hynes, Senate President John E. Powers, future governor Chub Peabody, Republican heavy-weight Leverett Saltonstall, Father Norman O'Connor (the "Jazz Priest," known for his radio shows), and Jerry's old Philly friend and business partner Sam Hatoff. When your friends give you a dinner, it's a very nice thing.

The station roared into 1959, as Mac signed one of Boston's great Top-40 origi-nals—Arnie "Woo Woo" Ginsberg—away from WBOS. He was given a prime spot for the teen audience, 7:00 until 10:00 P.M., where Jerry had ample opportunity to hear and watch him work. Jerry was amazed by Arnie's energy, his personality, his style. Here was a guy with a thin, nasal voice and a kind of sing-songy delivery who had invented an on-air sound that was pure genius. He had a box of noisemakers in the studio, and one or more of them were always right there, under his hands, for him to use as attention getters. "Woo Woo" jumped on the ends of records, ran a nonstop stream of patter between tunes, punctuated his words and commercials with bells, whistles, ratchets, and other sound effects, and pulled listeners along with him whether they wanted to go or not.

Jerry also admired Arnie's guts. He didn't change his name, didn't mind if his listeners knew he was Jewish. And he was so confident that he could bring advertisers with him from WBOS, and attract even more on WMEX, that he got Mac to agree to give him a straight 25 percent of all the spot revenue he brought in, in lieu of salary.

Arnie and Jerry were on-air personalities with their own passionately loyal fol-lowing, but Mac didn't want other jocks to get the wrong idea. Like many other owners, he told new staff they'd be using WMEX names, not their own. The morning man was Fenway, whether he was really Ed Heider or Jack Gale. Melvin X. Melvin would always be Melvin X. Melvin. Dan Donovan would always be Dan Donovan—and pronounce that Bahst'n style, dad. It's Dunnuhv'n.

There was a little bit more in Jerry's check every week, funded by his dol-lar-a-spot deal with Mac, but he always looked at the amount with suspicion. Mac forced him to keep a log of his own spots, writing down the name of each one and the day it aired, as justification for his extra pay—so it would be Jerry's fault if the check was short. After Arnie was hired, Jerry began agitat-ing for an improved deal. This dollar-a-spot thing was nuts. He wanted a straight percentage in addition to his salary. Eventually he got it—Mac start-ed small, with 5 percent, but Jerry kept chipping away. He still was nowhere near the $250 a week Mac had promised, but it was a step forward. And Mac finally caved on installing the tape delay system, so the show began to sound much better. It was progress.

In early 1959 Jerry heard about Governor Foster Furcolo's plan for a sales tax. Furcolo wasn't a bad guy, but a 3 percent tax on everything you buy? Even if food and clothing were exempted from the tax, did the governor think most people could just magically up their income to pay higher prices on their appliances, their furniture, their cars, their gas, toys for their kids? Jerry had just furnished an apartment, and he had only a wife and a dog, and a baby on the way. He knew how much you could spend on this stuff. And what about gas? Gas was already thirty cents a gallon! The governor wanted to tack on another cent or two a gallon? If taxes had to be broadened, why not use the income tax?

"Let's hear what you have to say about this. Just send me a postcard—no letters, please! Just a postcard, to Sales Tax, Jerry Williams, WMEX, 70 Brookline Avenue, Boston 15. Just write 'Yes' or 'No' on the back."

The flow began—a trickle, then a stream, then a torrent. Hell, *no* one wants new taxes. Jerry took a page from the Frank Kelly playbook. He talked about the legislative hearing coming up, and he told his listeners they were welcome to attend. He was going to be there, and he was going to take their postcards.

WBZ's newsman Streeter Stuart was in the hall when Jerry Williams arrived at the State House on March 30 with bags and bags and bags of cards. Jerry got up to give his short speech against the tax, and he climaxed it by having people from the station lift up the big canvas mailbags that contained the negative cards and put them on a table. Here are the No votes, gentlemen. Seven thousand, three hundred and seventy-three Nos. Then he took the twelve Yes cards out of his jacket pocket and put them down next to the negatives. His people applauded. Streeter Stuart wondered: who *is* this guy?

The tax went down to defeat.

Then there was the night that Boston first heard the F-word on the air, just a week before Jerry's daughter Eve was born.

Jerry had heard from Boston's NAACP leaders that Daisy Bates was going to be in town in May, and he wanted to speak with her. Mrs. Bates and her husband, Lucious, were the publishers of the *Arkansas State Press,* out of Little Rock, one of the most important papers for the state's black community. She'd been very close to those kids who'd integrated Little Rock's Central High School, just a few weeks after Jerry started on WMEX. She was also president of the Arkansas Conference of Branches, the umbrella organization for Arkansas's chapters of the NAACP. She answered Jerry's questions about Central High, Governor Faubus, desegregation of the schools, and the serious racial tension in her hometown. She also pointed out that being outspoken about civil rights in Arkansas had some unpleasant consequences—a boycott by white advertisers had almost put her paper out of business. They had a lot to talk about, and Jerry had to work hard to get it all in, because she could spare only one hour.

Jerry opened up the lines in the next hour to get some reaction. Everything went fine for a while. Then a guy, smooth, no edge to his voice, led Jerry right into a trap. "Jerry, I certainly enjoyed hearin' Mrs. Bates theyah. It was very int'restin'. Y' know, I really enjoy it when you have these folks on tellin' us about what's happenin' down South." Then the guy shifted gears, just like that. "And you're a goddamn bastahd and she's a fuckin' niggah bitch." Then, gone into the night.

There was a shock moment, when everything slowed down. He jabbed at the panic button on the table. He dropped the phone into its cradle like it was burning a hole in his hand. He looked up at his engineer. Hey, what's he doing? The button was a signal for him to act, to shift from the delay to live so that Jerry could take control and they could omit what the caller had said. This guy doesn't seem concerned. He's *not paying attention*. He's got his eyes somewhere else, doesn't see Jerry vigorously slicing his finger across his throat. Jerry realizes he's not listening to the live feed—he's listening to the delay, what's coming out over the air. The seconds are going by, Jerry can't get his attention, and here it comes . . . "she's a fuckin' niggah bitch." Jerry sees the guy jump out of his seat. Ah, too late now.

That was the first time the F-word had been on his air, probably the first time it'd been on WMEX, maybe the first time it'd ever been on the air in Boston. Jerry apologized and kept going with the show. And that was it. Not one caller mentioned the F-word or the N-word. Not one criticized the man who'd said them. Not one said he or she was going to call the manager the next day. Mac never mentioned it.

During the fall Jerry got a call from a reporter at the *Boston Globe* named Paul Benzaquin. Jerry had seen the name in the paper, but he didn't know him. Benzaquin said he was working on what he hoped would be the definitive history of the Cocoanut Grove fire, the November 1942 Boston disaster that people were still using to define their lives seventeen years later. Paul said he'd been listening to Jerry for years—in fact, it seemed to him like Jerry had always been on the air in Boston—and would he like to do a prepublication interview before the book came out in November? Jerry would.

Paul's appearance prompted dozens of moving calls—people who remembered the fire, people who worked in hospitals that night, people who knew people who had died. A powerful show. Jerry liked this guy Benzaquin. Good voice, too.

Also in 1959, Jerry got a call from a dotty old woman who identified her-self as Grace. She didn't seem to understand the names of the area pols or the important issues. Jerry tried to straighten her out, but she persisted in her wacky points of view. Some time later she called back, and then again. Jerry started to look forward to hearing from her. Then, when he was in the office one afternoon, a young guy named Bob Ness gave him a ring. Bob told Jerry that *he* was "Grace," and he proved it by doing her voice and mannerisms on the phone perfectly.

Jerry was stunned at first, then delighted. How old are you, kid? Just in his teens. Jesus, you have talent. Bob said he was just trying to break into radio, and could Jerry help him? Help him? Did he want to keep doing Grace? Ness hadn't considered the idea before—he just wanted to get on the air. Come on, Bob, we'll have some fun with it. I'll be your straight man.

Jerry recognized that Bob could be a regular character, filling a role like that of Bud Smith, but without the hassles of equal billing or salary. So they made a deal—Bob would call when the show didn't have any controversial guests or serious topics, and Jerry would feed him lines and ideas. The next time Bob called, Jerry dubbed the character "Grace, Queen of the Cockamamies," and they were off to the races. Ness refined Grace's person-ality, making her Boston's own Mrs. Malaprop, seventeen years before Gilda Radner's Emily Litella character did the same thing with Chevy Chase on *Saturday Night Live*. Some people guessed that Grace was a put-on, but thou-sands of Bostonians accepted her as a real Beantown nut case, a neighbor with more than a few loose screws.

Jerry was coming up to the two-year mark. His 1958 testimonial dinner had been big, but this year—why not go all out? And to make sure it's a success, work the charity angle with Mac. The proceeds would go to the one hundred neediest families of greater Boston, selected by a multidenominational com-mittee of clergy, under the auspices of the Cardinal Cushing Charity Fund— it couldn't hurt to get the cardinal's imprimatur. Mac's promotional machine went into overdrive.

Jerry roughed out a few words for the invitation summarizing his feelings about where the show stood in the fall of 1959: "Two years ago, I inaugurat-ed the 'Jerry Williams Show' over WMEX with one idea in mind—to use the medium of radio to add new dimensions to the concept of the public forum. . . . People from every walk of life have used the 'Jerry Williams Show'. . . to push, prod and sometimes pummel their fellow citizens into wakefulness about events affecting the well-being and progress of the Greater Boston com-munity. I am very grateful to these average citizens . . . for making the 'Jerry Williams Show' a success."

This time the guest list was huge. The invitations landed in mailboxes just after Election Day concluded a brutal campaign for Mayah in which John Collins defeated the president of the Senate, John E. Powers. Jerry's event made for a nice no-hard-feelings kind of occasion. A raft of political enemies and friends, community leaders, cronies, and hundreds of ordinary folks joined Jerry at the First Corps of Cadets Armory, a big stone building in downtown Boston that imitated a medieval castle inside and out. They had an informal dinner, some comedy, some nice speeches—and wrestling! It was a Very Big Deal, and it made a tidy sum for the needy families. The guest of honor enjoyed himself quite a bit.

The second dinner confirmed it: it was officially Star Time for Jerry in Boston. The next three years were magical for him. His show was the number one media venue, the place you aimed for when you wanted exposure for your idea, your client, or your cause. His monologue at 10:00 P.M. was a yardstick against which you measured your own opinions about your city and the country. His program showed you what people in New England were thinking. He provided great and consistent entertainment, six nights a week. Going to see him perform was the best cheap date in town.

And no one in Boston even tried to compete with him. He was untouchable. He was the King.

Or maybe not. Even though the Red Sox and WMEX put out fund-raising postcards for the Jimmy Fund sporting a picture of the two Williamses, Ted and Jerry, he still couldn't get any ink from the *Globe*. And there were precious few mentions in the other major rags, although Bill Buchanan, the TV and radio columnist for the *Record*, paid some attention from time to time. Jerry clipped his mentions in the *Back Bay Ledger–Beacon Hill Times*, the *State House Reporter–City Hall News*, a paper from Cambridge called *Around the Square*, and the *Christian Science Monitor*, underlining his name in red whenever it appeared. Why weren't the others paying more attention? He had good guests and big names on his show. His crusade against the sales tax had stymied the Beacon Hill boys. He'd made some noise supporting the drivers in Boston's longest-ever bus strike. His shows on abortion, homosexuality, and alcoholism dealt with don't-touch issues seriously, compassionately. He was Boston's most outspoken public voice: against police bullying, against property taxes, against political inside deals, against capital punishment, against the Bay State's insurance establishment, for civil rights, for personal freedom, for individual liberty.

Every payday the injustice gnawed at him. He was the biggie in town, but his salary felt puny. It wasn't, really; he was getting around $175 a week, and

Promotional photograph created for the Jimmy Fund: Ted Williams and Jerry Williams in the WMEX studio, 70 Brookline Avenue, Boston, summer 1959.

his cut of the ads brought his take up to $15,000 or so. That was decent money in 1960—in real terms, he was clearing about as much as he did when he was flush in Allentown. But now he had a wife and child, he had to have a new car every couple of years, and he liked to dress well, and Teri liked to dress well . . .

He kept finding new angles to press Mac for more money. If you won't raise my base salary, hike my percentage of the ad revenue. If you won't do that, raise the ad rates. If you won't do that, give me some nonsalary money for my expenses. If you won't do that, at least let me make something on the side as a speaker and emcee. Mac gave in on the speaking fees, and Jerry hired Lordly & Dame, one of the area's top personal representation companies, to get him gigs. By the end of 1960, he was doing all right with these things, adding another fifty or seventy-five dollars about once a month.

But he was a *star*. This was nickel-and-dime stuff. Where was the fine residence he felt he deserved? He and Teri would drive through Brookline, look at those magnificent houses, and sigh. What the hell did these people do for a living?

Their own living situation did improve a bit. By the start of 1960, he and Teri had just enough to rent a little two-story row house, a step up from their Bay State Road apartment. It was on Aberdeen Street, a tiny cul-de-sac very close to Kenmore Square, nice and quiet, except on days when there were Red Sox games and the area was flooded with fans. Jerry could walk to MEX in about five minutes from there. There was room for a nursery for seven-month-old Eve. He set up an extra bedroom as an office, so he could spend some quiet time there reading his newspapers and prepping for the show. There was enough room there for a second child, too, and Teri loved being a mother, so . . .

There were some occasional nonmoney perks to the job as well. Jerry helped Chuck Sozio launch his appliance store in Revere ("Jerry, you are doing a *fantastic* job. You're *fantastic!*"), and he figured Chuck would give him a break when it came time to furnish a house. The family were regulars at the No-Name Restaurant, where Nick Contos had taken over for his dad and refused all Jerry's attempts to pay for dinner. A guy named Moe Eagerman, who had a bagel shop in one of the western suburbs, started bringing Jerry and the crew shopping bags full of green bagels on St. Patrick's Day.

By the spring of 1960, Jerry had more than 200,000 people tuning in to his show nightly. One of every 20 people living in the area was a regular listener. He was dominating nighttime radio and doing quite well against the rising tide of evening TV.

The noise about Jerry—his big dinners, his charity work, his political friends, the shows on civil rights, his examinations of abortion and homosexuality—had reached the ears of one of Boston's most powerful men, Richard Cardinal Cushing. Cushing's people let WMEX know that the cardinal would like to meet this young man so many people were discussing.

The cardinal had a unique status in his community in the 1960s. His charm was legendary. He was consulted by the mayor and the governor, especially around election time. The observers of Church politics opined that if there ever was to be an American pope, Cushing was the most likely prospect. Not to mention his actual role as spiritual leader of a diocese of several million that was still very observant. He spoke to and on behalf of that considerable flock, and he held lifetime tenure in his job. In some ways, he was the most powerful individual in the city and the state.

Jerry made the appointment to visit the cardinal at his magnificent residence in Brighton. *That* was a house, set back from the road, way up on a hill, surrounded by vast grounds. And Cushing disarmed him completely, as he had so many others. He asked Jerry questions about himself, his background, his family, his goals. Cushing knew already that he was Jewish, of course. Jerry was impressed by the way he showed respect for his heritage without condescending, how he mentioned his friendship with rabbis and the need for there to be regular cooperation among the faiths. He thanked Jerry for the exposure given to the Cardinal Cushing Charity Fund in his second anniversary dinner, and the generous contribution to the one hundred neediest families. For a while, Jerry was in awe, but when he got his courage up, he began to do a little interviewing in return, asking about Cushing's youth in South Boston, his rise in the Church, the nature of the city as he saw it. Jerry felt that they actually got to know one another. They talked about the struggle of blacks for equal rights. Jerry felt a kinship, a bond. Finally he said, "I hope someday you'll do the program."

Cushing replied, "Well, just ask me."

Jerry said, "Consider yourself asked."

It took weeks for Jerry to deal with the cardinal's secretary and find an open spot in his schedule, but by the end of 1960, Cardinal Cushing had made his first appearance on the show. As far as Jerry could determine, it was the first time an American cardinal had ever agreed to appear in a live interview program and take phone calls from the public. Jerry felt that Cushing's willingness to come to WMEX and sit in his big dumpy studio was a sort of blessing, a stamp of approval that he needed. In effect, he thought, the cardinal was saying, "This guy's legit. He's okay. I don't like everything he says, and I don't like everything he does, but I sort of approve of him."

Cushing apparently had a good time on that show, and he surely appreciated the significance of the platform. In subsequent years, he was a guest on three more occasions, and Jerry reciprocated by helping out with some of the cardinal's pet charity projects.

Cushing always was gracious, kind, and witty on the air. He was never daunted by Jerry's questions about the Church's wealth and why it wasn't doing more on social issues. He patiently explained the Church's position on birth control when Jerry challenged him. He was more than a match for his interviewer—and he shared a lot of his interviewer's progressive ideas.

One night the subject of beano came up. Everyone knew that the authorities were winking at illegal games of chance with cash prizes that were regularly being used to supplement parish income, but many people resented the double standard—if gambling was breaking the law, then the Church was breaking the law. So in comes a call from a lovely little lady (not Grace, Queen of the Cockamamies—this was a real call). "Fathah," she said, "I just came from the beano game at St. So-and-so's—"

Cushing cut her off deftly, with a smile: "Please, my dear, don't tell me the name of the pastor." They all laughed.

Senator Jack Kennedy's run for the White House was a seismic event in 1960. Everyone knew that if a Massachusetts politician, especially one so well connected, got to be president, there'd be a flood of Bostonians to Washington to fill positions in the new administration. So everyone in town was backing Jack.

Jerry was, too, but more because he hated Nixon, the Republican candidate. That guy couldn't look comfortable in a suit. He couldn't look comfortable at all. Jerry took every opportunity that year to point out the growling, raspy voice, the hard little eyes, the creepy way he smiled when he was trying to ingratiate himself, the way he couldn't hide his fear and his scorn when he spoke in public.

He would have loved to get Martin Luther King Jr. in person. The best he could do was a phone hookup, using the conferencing technology he'd badgered Mac to install. King's profile was rising almost by the minute, as he was seen more and more as *the* spokesman for civil rights for American blacks, a leader within the Baptist Convention, and a galvanizer of protests wherever a forceful presence was needed in the South. The demands on his time by the movement and his church were enormous. When Jerry asked for an interview, King's people were always very pleasant, but there were more important things than *The Jerry Williams Show.*

Malcolm X was more available. The man once known as Malcolm Little, who had lived a criminal life in Boston's Roxbury neighborhood for a while in the forties, was now a principal minister of the Nation of Islam and one of Elijah Muhammad's most effective representatives. He had become known nationally in July 1959 when a five-part documentary called *The Hate That Hate Produced* aired on local TV in New York and then on CBS. The words spoken in the show by Elijah Muhammad and Malcolm electrified white Americans. Here were men who referred to Negroes as blacks, who pulled no punches about accommodation with white America. They weren't careful with their words the way Martin Luther King was. In Boston the respectable media outlets considered Malcolm "irresponsible" and "fringe." The *Globe* and *Herald* did not interview him. But Jerry wanted him, and beginning in April 1960, Malcolm X had repeated opportunities to speak at length on WMEX about the Nation of Islam and the situation of American blacks as he saw it.

Jerry paid him the supreme compliment: he was great radio. After a while, they got to some real give-and-take on the issues, and Jerry felt that Malcolm was treating him with a modicum of respect—if Jerry was a devil, Malcolm was at least giving the devil his due. Especially when Malcolm was on, Jerry heard from his black listeners, and he was careful to show them the courtesy they deserved. Those Malcolm shows built Jerry's credibility within the black community and turned occasional listeners there into fans.

Mac liked those shows, too—though his reason, as always, was that WMEX was getting attention. One night when a show with Malcolm was going particularly well, Mac called the engineer's booth between midnight and one. "Tell Jerry t' keep that guy on for another hour. Let the overnight guy go get some coffee and wait a while."

Malcolm had little if any respect for the white people who interviewed him and the less outspoken black folk with whom he appeared on panels. They were "devils and Ph.D. puppets," as he says in the autobiography he put together with Alex Haley. When hosts are mentioned by name in the book, they're usually castigated for their agendas or their ignorance. Not Jerry Williams. The one reference to Jerry in the autobiography is matter-of-fact. "Not long before [Elijah Muhammad and I made our last public appearance together, in late 1963], I had been on the Jerry Williams radio program in Boston, when someone handed me an item hot off the Associated Press machine. I read that a chapter of the Louisiana Citizens Council had just offered a $10,000 reward for my death." Considering the choice words he had for Mike Wallace and others of the time, and the contrast with the white folks in the South who wanted him dead, it is almost as though he had written, "Jerry Williams? Not a bad guy."

Most folks who listened to the show for any length of time thought they knew Jerry's political orientation. He was a liberal, of course. But he himself was uncomfortable with labels. He took each issue on its merits, the way he thought most Americans did. On race relations, it was time for justice and fairness—in fact, that time was long overdue and it was necessary to act immediately to make things right. On the other hand, he thought that the structures of government—local, state, national—were shot through with corruption and cronyism. You couldn't trust people with power, so you always had to watch them. Every plan for an "improvement," whether it was a social welfare scheme or a new road, meant that someone, somewhere was getting a kickback or a sweetheart deal.

Jerry represented the center, as he saw it, and he invited far right and far left guests on the show for the excitement they brought to it, not necessarily because he agreed with them, although his listeners heard far more folks from the left than from the right. One of the most visible of the regulars was Gordon Hall, the so-called anti-anti-Communist, still fighting the McCarthy battle. Then there was Gus Hall (no relation), the head of the American Communist Party. And, even though he disliked her personally, Jerry made room frequently for Madalyn Murray, who filed her famous lawsuit challenging Bible reading in U.S. public schools in 1960 and finally won it in 1963.

Jerry Williams atop a WMEX car in a Boston motorcade, ca. 1960.

When you're a Star, they start trying to pull you off the pedestal.

In 1962 the WMEX team made its annual appearance in the South Boston St. Patrick's Day Parade. Someone in the crowd had planned well and pasted Jerry with a chocolate cream pie. Scratch one suit.

Shortly after one of Malcolm X's appearances on the show, someone sabotaged the WMEX transmitter site. Scratch the air for a day or so.

And just after midnight on May 23, 1962, Jack Molesworth invaded Jerry's studio. That was more than a scratch. It became one of the great Jerry Williams stories, a tale he loved to tell.

Those were the days when the Jewish Democrats of Ward 14 and their buddies from all over the city would gather at the G & G Deli on Blue Hill Avenue, often presided over by Representative Julius Ansel, a genial if somewhat mush-mouthed Figure of Influence (okay, ward boss, if you insist). Julie had been a friend of Jerry's almost from the first month of the show and a regular guest. Jerry liked to call him his "eyes and ears on Beacon Hill." Julie happened to be at the WMEX mic when all hell broke loose.

That month, the legislature was working on a change to the state's policies on auto insurance. Since anything having to do with his car got Jerry's attention, he'd been working the issue for more than a week, with guests pro and con. On the evening in question, May 22, Jerry and a Democratic rep named Bill Keenan were carping about the bill on the air. Julie Ansel was there in the audience watching Jerry go at it, waiting for his turn later in the show. He had a friend with him, a guy named Saul Walters, who was supposed to give him a ride home. At one point, Jerry said he'd provide equal time to responsible representatives who wanted to defend this bill.

Meanwhile, out there in the dark, at his home in a nice stretch of Beacon Street, a Republican state committeeman named Jack Molesworth and his wife are listening to the show. Jack is a philatelist, a dealer in rare stamps and other collectibles, with a little shop downtown. Thanks to his position in the Republican Party, he is also an old hand at jousting with Jerry on the air.

After a few minutes listening to Jerry and Keenan, Jack stands up and heads for the door.

"Where are you going?" his wife asks.

"To the post office," Jack says. The post office? At 11:45 at night? Well, Jack's the stamp guy. He must know of something going on down there.

Jack doesn't go to the post office. He drives down the street a few blocks to Kenmore Square and then down Brookline Avenue to the MEX studio. He walks right into the big room, the way anybody can. By this time, it's about ten past midnight and Keenan is gone—he probably passed Jack on his way in and had no idea what was about to happen. Julie Ansel is sitting at the table talking about reform of the state's blue laws, saying that if they let the stores stay open on Sundays, it'll be good for business and good for tourism, and blah blah blah . . .

Jack wants to talk to Jerry. He wants equal time on the insurance bill. He figures he'll ask Jerry right now, while Julie is talking. He walks right up to the table and starts whispering in Jerry's ear.

Jerry is amazed at what's going on. No one has ever tried this before. He's on the air. Julie is talking but Jack has a big voice, and Jerry knows that listeners can hear this muttering in the background.

He decides he has to go public with this and interrupts Julie. "Excuse me a minute, Julius, because somebody in very bad taste, who walks in now, at ten minutes after midnight, Jack Molesworth, wants to go on the air." He turns to Jack. "Now, do you think that's fair, Jack?"

Jack takes this as a challenge. A debate starts, with Jerry on mic, trying to keep his voice steady, and Jack bloviating off in the distance. Jack says Jerry offered equal time and he wants to defend the insurance bill against tonight's attacks. Jerry says Jack can have time if he'll just call during the day. Jack says Jerry doesn't return his phone calls. This is true, actually—Jerry hates to talk to Jack. So Jerry gets angry. "I'm not going to discuss it with you, Jack, in the middle of a broadcast."

"I'm not attempting to discuss it in the middle of the broadcast. I'm talking to you personally."

Jerry's thinking, is he *nuts?* Where does he think he *is?* He says, "Well, please get out. Will you please get out of the studio?"

But Jack doesn't go. He stands there and keeps on talking. The audience sitting in Jerry's studio doesn't know what to make of it.

Jack starts questioning Jerry's fairness. "Jerry, you will not allow the other side to be heard. That's your position. You misrepresent the bill."

Them's fightin' words. The conversation gets less rational, if that's possible. Jerry starts trying to argue Jack down and get him to leave at the same time. His show is in shambles. He has to do something.

"Please leave the studio."

There's a silence. Jack stares at him without moving. They're sizing one another up. Jerry thinks, This guy has about six inches on me, and he's a tough customer.

"Please leave the studio, or I'm gonna have to have you ejected from the studio." Jerry looks up at the engineer in the booth, a heavy-set guy who can handle himself, and waves at him to come down. The guy is nonplussed. Jerry wants *him* to throw Molesworth out? He didn't sign on for *this*. But he takes off his headphones anyway and heads for the door.

Jack just stands there. Jerry keeps saying, "Please leave the studio." The two of them are glaring at each other. It's one of those moments when you know something ugly is going to happen. Saul Walters decides to come to the rescue. He stands up while Jack and Jerry are going back and forth and comes up to Julie at the table. Julie mutters to Saul to escort Jack out.

Jerry is waving his arms now. "This is our private property and I'm asking you to leave the studio. I wouldn't pop into *your* office in that manner."

"If I invited you, and you came in, you'd be welcome."

"I didn't invite you, Jack!"

Saul Walters is now at Jack Molesworth's elbow, way off mic. He says, very nicely, trying to calm things down, "Will you leave, please?" The tide seems to be turning. It looks like Saul is getting somewhere.

But Jerry can't stop himself from talking. He's got to put Jack in his place. "Nobody in the history of this program or any other program ever walked in here in the middle of a broadcast to try to get equal time. There are—these things are done in responsible ways. You're a good letter writer. You woulda gotten the equal time, Jack, but not under these circumstances."

Now the engineer is down there, too, and both of them are trying to ease Jack out. They've got him almost to the door. But Jerry is pouring on the sarcasm now, grandstanding for the audience, pointing to Jack. "Jack Molesworth, Republican state committeeman, a man of manners and courtesy and dignity . . . you can do your rabble-rousing at the Republican State Committee, as you usually do."

Jack stops, incensed. "*You* are the rabble-rouser."

Jerry tosses a bomb back at him. "Just get out of the studio. You can go with Major General Walker and the rest of those cats."

Major General who? Time out. With those three words, Jerry was nastily tying Molesworth to one of the poster boys for the hard right. Among other things, Major General Edwin Walker had organized protests against the enrollment of James Meredith at the University of Mississippi, and he'd been relieved of his command by President Kennedy after being accused of distributing John Birch Society literature to his troops. A few weeks before Jerry fired this shot, Walker had finished last in the Democratic primary for governor of Texas, where he'd run with Barry Goldwater's blessing.

That does it. Jack doesn't want to be associated with segregationists or Birchers, and he gets completely fried now. "Major General Walker is no friend of mine."

Jerry is insolent. "No?"

"I have nothing to do with him." He steps forward with a hard look. "I insist—"

"Will you please leave the studio?"

"—that you stop maligning me over the air or I will stop you."

Jack strides toward Jerry. Jerry stands up. Someone throws a punch, and then the two of them are tussling, on the air, with grunts and thuds and chair scrapes and odd miscellaneous sounds, and *no one talking for nearly ten seconds.* Jerry and Molesworth are on the floor, rolling and tumbling. People listening are wondering, *What* is going *on?*

Saul and the engineer get involved and the three of them wrestle Jack out of the room, while Julie Ansel tries to take charge. Of course, the engineer hasn't turned his mic on. Julie doesn't know he's talking into a dead hunk of metal and just adding to the confusion, as he says, "Well, that'sh what happens when—uh—"

Jerry reappears and moves toward his mic, but Molesworth is right behind him, and they start fighting again. For another fifteen seconds, which seems like an hour, the strange noises continue as Jerry and Saul and the engineer try to pull Jack out of the studio, down the stairs, and into the street. People can hear Jack, way off in the distance, saying, "You laid your hands on me!"

And Jerry, equally distant: "I told you ten times to get out of the studio!"

Finally, Julie is there alone, and the noise is far away. He tries again, still into the dead mic. "My friendsh, it was an unfortunate inshident in the studio and—uh—that'sh what happens, I suppose, when these sortsh of conflictsh develop, and—uh—I'll resume in a moment."

The faraway bedlam goes on for another thirty seconds, Julie making another stab at a sentence or two and Jerry's audience murmuring quietly, not knowing whether to leave or stay put until the authorities come.

While almost nothing is on the air, Saul, the engineer, and Jerry are working Jack down the stairs, well out of range of the mics. When they get to the street, Jack stalks away, shouting, "This is assault and battery! I'll sue you!" Saul stays down below, guarding the door. Jerry and the engineer start running back up the stairs. The engineer says, "What should I do?"

Jerry shouts, "Get back to the booth and call the *Globe*!"

The engineer sprints for the control room, and Jerry strides to the table, completely winded. He looks at Julie. He can't say anything until he gets his breath. So he gives the floor to Julie with one gasping word: "Julius?"

The engineer is back in the booth, and Julie's mic is on. Now he talks.

"Well, I'm in the midst of the heat of battle here, at the studio of Jerry Williamsh." He recaps everything, how he came up to talk about the blue laws bill, how Molesworth came in and interrupted, how Jerry offered to talk to him off the air during normal office hours. Julie's watching Jerry, just filling the time until he can start talking again.

Jerry finally finds his voice, still panting. "Well, this whole situation came about when, last night—you were here, Julius—Representative Keenan and myself . . ." And the show is back to normal. Sort of.

The papers loved this story. A *Boston Traveler* reporter (who didn't get a byline on his piece, unfortunately) wrote a lead Jerry cherished: "A professional stamp collector took a licking early today when he walked into a Boston radio station and demanded air time."

Jack Molesworth was not amused. He'd had to drive himself to Massachusetts General Hospital, sit in the emergency room, get X-rayed and prodded, and read about himself as the villain in the piece every day in the newspaper. He wasn't kidding about legal action. It took six years for Jack's $300,000 lawsuit against Jerry to work its way through the courts. By the time it was over, the John Birch Society was old news, no one remembered that auto insurance bill, Julius Ansel was dead, and Jack's time in politics had passed. Jerry won.

Christmas is trouble. You can't do controversy at Christmas. It's family time. What can you do? In the time-honored tradition of radio, you do a Christmas special.

Jerry came up with something he'd heard Dylan Thomas do in the late fifties—"A Child's Christmas in Wales." Thomas had written it to perform on his own radio show, so it was natural for the voice, once you'd worked out all the descriptive tongue twisters. It had a wonderful unity and a great sense of unfolding surprise. Because it was so improvisational, you could hear it over and over again, and pick out new details every time.

It started out like one of Henry Morgan's monologues, a little off-kilter, sort of in the middle of things. Thomas remembered how all the Christmases of his childhood were so much alike, segued easily into an anecdote about planning to throw snowballs at cats on the afternoon of Christmas Eve, suddenly introduced a very specific memory of a smoky kitchen fire at a neighbor's house, brought in the voice of a little boy he could speak to about the way things are now and the way they used to be. Then the postman's arrival, the useful and useless presents, the litany of details of Christmas Day at home—uncles and aunts, mistletoe, fire, walnuts, watching neighbors walk by, after-dinner naps and cleanup, trying out the toys. Finally came the best parts: the after-dinner boys' expeditions out into the cold to make mischief, their evening caroling before a "haunted" house, family music making, and bedtime. As close to music as prose ever gets. Great radio.

It blended elegant poetic description and down-to-earth detail. It was full of great things to put in your mouth: "a dumb numb thunderstorm," "crunches, cracknels, humbugs, glaciers," "iron-flanked and bellowing," "a small, dry, eggshell voice." Best of all, no baby Jesus or evergreen trees or Santa or Tiny Tim or nutcrackers. As Jerry ran through it, first idly, then seriously, he heard the great radio actors in his head—William Conrad, Orson Welles, the guys who really knew how to deliver a text. They had better low notes than Jerry, but if he worked close to the mic, he could bring out some deep tones—not molasses-rich exactly, but maple-syrup mellow. He knew it would surprise a lot of listeners.

When he finally did it on the air, he made the spaces between the sentences sing. He set the pace with the first words, slow and nostalgic: "One Christmas was so much like another . . ." Taking his time, giving the words a chance to breathe, speeding up in the exciting parts, pulling back for hushed moments. "The bells that the children could hear were inside them . . ." Anyone listening between the words could hear the melancholy. "Years and years and years ago, when I was a boy . . . " He sang the first lines of "Good King Wenceslas" in a touching falsetto. He put you right into bed with little

Dylan, and pulled up the covers. "I said some close words to the holy darkness, and then I slept."

Dylan and Jerry put a lot of lumps in a lot of throats with those words, and an engineer bringing up a chorus singing "Wenceslas" usually brought out the tears.

How a Jewish kid raised in Brooklyn could bring that near-Dickensian Christmas to life! But maybe it wasn't that different. Or maybe he *thought* it wasn't that different. Maybe that's why it worked so well. Maybe that's why he kept doing it every year.

Let's face it. When you're a Star, you don't have a lot of time for family.

Like his father, Jerry was consumed by his work. He expected Teri to be like his mother—to accommodate the man of the house, to keep the home running smoothly while he was out earning the bread. He didn't know how to relate to his two little girls, and they couldn't yet understand what Daddy was doing all day long and very late at night. Maybe his dad never taught him how to care. Maybe that fire of ambition inside him could be satisfied only by public love.

In any case, the magical woman he'd fallen for in Philly was now Wife and Mother. He had kept the promise he made that she would never have to work, and she gave him the support and caring he wanted. She always listened to the show, and she liked to talk it over with him when he got to the house, but he felt curiously empty when he returned home, uncommunicative, sometimes surly. She had to get used to the fact that all the performing juice of the day had been wrung out of him.

He had managed to cajole and bully Mac, step by excruciating step, out of around $25,000 a year. With the money from his speaking engagements, he was bringing in something equivalent to $150,000 in today's long green, not much when he and Teri began thinking about moving to Brookline, with its leafy streets and top-level schools.

The beautiful houses there cost seven or ten times what he was making and the property taxes were ferocious. He figured he could afford the four-bedroom brick house they saw at 90 Clinton Road. It wasn't the fanciest one on the block, but it was up on a slope, so he could look down on the world a bit. It offered an easy drive to WMEX along Route 9, and it was just a five-minute walk from the Runkel School, a terrific public school where the kids were sure to get a good education.

But the loan officer at the bank looked at all that commission money and fretted about whether he really could make the payments. They could give him a small mortgage. And they had to ask him for 25 percent down, please. Maybe he could find a smaller house? Nah. The house on Clinton Road was what he and Teri both wanted. A really quiet, tree-lined street.

What to do? He had to ask his folks for a loan. He'd do a half-and-half, with part of the money from a bank mortgage and part from Samuel and Frieda. I just need twenty thousand. Don't worry, dad. I'll pay it back. I'm doing fine. Good, good, Gerald, but let's make it official, put it down on paper, a good businesslike arrangement. He might be the biggie in Boston, but he couldn't shake the feeling that he was still a little unstable and untrustworthy as far as his dad was concerned.

When they finally moved in, Teri was genuinely happy for the first time in years. At last she had a place of her own to furnish instead of a temporary residence that she knew she'd just have to pack up at some time in the future. Jerry had a bigger room for his study. Eve and Susan had a room. The house had room for a piano.

As soon as they could find babysitters they could trust, Teri started going with Jerry to the speaking engagements and charitable functions—the Jimmy Fund, the Massachusetts Heart Association, Cystic Fibrosis Research, United Cerebral Palsy . . . She turned heads. *Mrs.* Jerry Williams? Oh, how do you *do?* Her figure was still great, her smile still gorgeous, her clothes sense unerring. Jerry was always glad to be seen with her.

Some time in 1961 or 1962, Mac started the Friday Game. That Jerry Williams check he had to sign every week kept getting bigger and bigger. He was giving Jerry money for "expenses" and his salary, and an ever-growing piece of the ad revenue. One day the thought struck him: every week that I kick out these bucks to Williams, I'm losing a few dollars on the float. If I could just hold onto it until Monday or Tuesday . . .

So Jerry would come by for his check Friday afternoon, and Mac would put him off. "Ah, Jer, I'm so busy. Gotta go out. Lemme get it to ya Monday." The first couple of times, it was such a surprise, Jerry let it go. But then it became a regular thing, and a real pain in the ass.

Here he was bringing in three or four times the money Mac was paying him, and the guy was delaying shelling out the dough. Here he was, every week, laboriously writing down all the names of the sponsors, all the times they aired, the cost of the spots, figuring out the percentage, drawing the line with how much Mac owed him, doing the work of the bookkeeper, just so Mac could blame Jerry if the numbers were off. Jerry had bills. What did Mac think he was gonna do, tell Boston Edison to wait until he got his check on Monday?

And even when he could pin Mac down, when he could back him into his office and stand there while the guy wrote the numbers down and signed his name, Jerry could see the pained look on Mac's face when he'd finish writing the D on "Richmond." Mac even started giving a little regretful sigh after a while. He just *hated* to give Jerry all that money.

Not that it was all that much.

"Mac, it's Friday. Can I have my check?"

"Uhh, Jerry, I'll give it t' ya on Monday."

Jerry couldn't hold it in. The anger was just behind the door, ready to jump out, and Mac unlocked the cage. Jerry's voice would tighten in rage. He sounded like Howlin' Wolf on one of those old blues records: "Give it t' me *now*, Mac! I want my check *now!* I got bills! Gimme my check *now!*"

And Mac would kind of sidle away, slip down the steps, trying to escape. Jerry would pursue him down the stairs, out onto Brookline Avenue, into the crowd of Red Sox fans if there was a game that afternoon, yelling like an idiot: "My *check*, Mac! I want my *check!*"

Mac would just keep walking. "I'll give 't' ya Monday."

There was a day Jerry had to pin Mac up against a car to stop him. "Let's go upstairs *NOW* and *get—my—check!* I'll take you to the Labor Board, I swear I will!"

Which he eventually had to do to get Mac to stop the Friday Game.

The topical topics came and went. They rose up through the headlines, onto the air, into Jerry's monologues. They were urgent, then dealt with, then history. Did Israel have the right to try Adolf Eichmann for his Nazi war crimes? When was the Prudential Tower going to be built, and how much was it going to cost Boston in tax blackmail to the people at the Pru before they'd agree to break ground? What were we going to do about the Russian missiles in Cuba? Who would be the best man to fill out Jack Kennedy's term as senator? When would they do something about the city's archaic property tax system?

There were more memorable moments during the Star Time years, so many that lots of them have been forgotten. Jerry stored away a couple of them, though. Like the time that former President Eisenhower passed through town and came to the studio. *That* was a thrill, though Jerry couldn't help feeling like a private again.

And then there was that senatorial candidates' debate that Jerry helped to set up in South Boston in August 1962. Who should sit in JFK's seat? He was convinced that the younger brother, Edward Moore Kennedy, just wasn't ready for prime time yet. Jerry's friend Eddie McCormack was a better man, and putting the two of them onstage together should prove it. No doubt, Eddie was in good form. Pointing over at Kennedy, he scoffed, "If his name was Edward Moore, with his qualifications—with your qualifications, Teddy, your candidacy would be a joke." Later on, he gave Ted another hard shot: "You never worked a day in your life." But the strategy backfired. It didn't matter that Teddy was out of his depth; people just liked his style on TV. Conversely, even though Eddie knew what he was talking about, he still looked like a pol on the tube. When Jerry did a post-debate phone poll of his listeners, Teddy was the winner. It wasn't the first time Jerry misunderstood TV, and it wouldn't be the last.

By the end of 1962, with five years under his belt in Boston, Jerry had done something that few in radio have ever achieved. The guys in the business would say that he had "created an audience."

Sometimes the public is ready for a change or a new point of view. That readiness is inchoate, hanging out there like a fog, ready to congeal around something that will make it a trend or a format. In Boston, looking back, you can see the signs—the postwar generation's itchiness to take the controls, the general dissatisfaction with the city's highly stratified society. Most cities around the country were experiencing their own local versions of the Great Awakening, but not very many of them had someone like Jerry Williams on the air, someone who was throwing out provocative statements every night, charging the atmosphere with the electricity needed to catalyze the change.

In Jerry's five years, Boston's average people had gotten used to the idea that there was a place on the radio for them to speak their minds, to hear issues kicked around, to take the temperature of their town and their country. Most people couldn't remember when it *wasn't* there. That's what creating an audience is all about: making something so pervasive and significant within the realm of media that people think they have a right to it, that in some way they *own* it.

In those five years, thirty-eight-year-old Jerry Williams and a handful of others around the country had birthed issue-oriented talk radio. But no one else was so dominant in his market. No one else so convincingly showed that this was the Right Way.

By the end of 1962, Boston's Sherm Feller and Kenny Mayer were hanging in with one-way talk, but they were sounding very old-fashioned in comparison to Jerry.

Another talker present at the Creation, Mary Margaret McBride, had left New York City for the sticks, but she kept her hand in with three interview shows a week on a little station in Kingston, not far from her Hudson Valley home. WOR, where Mary Margaret had started as "Martha Deane," was edging closer to an all-talk format; Jean Shepherd was doing his monologues around midnight, and Long John Nebel was floating in outer space all night long. In just a few months, WOR would hire a new gun named Bob Grant for the early evening, and Jerry's mother would become one of his fans.

They had to compete with the prophet of talk radio in New York, Barry Gray, who was tackling controversial topics, interviewing newsmakers, and jousting with phone callers in the later part of the evening on WMCA, the town's big Top-40 outlet (sound familiar?). Across the continent, one of the other prophets, Joe Pyne, was doing Rude Radio in Los Angeles at KLAC, where Ben Hoberman, the station's visionary manager, had abandoned music programming and cobbled together a proto-news-talk format that included straight news, commentary, "homespun philosophy," financial and health advice, and general-topic phone-in shows.

There were some interesting characters coming up in other markets. Larry Zeiger was now Larry King, the host of a houseboat-based Miami interview show and a color commentator for Dolphins football broadcasts. A twenty-two-year-old fellow with a British accent named Michael Jackson had gotten some notice in *Time* for his all-night radio show in San Francisco that included a couple of hours of conversation with listeners.

As for the young'ns, not one of them had yet cracked a mic. An erudite twenty-two-year-old David Brudnoy had recently graduated from Yale with a degree in Japanese studies, an affinity for Libertarianism, and an inconvenient sexual orientation. Don Imus was looking around for real work after a Wild Oats stretch of passing bad checks, drifting through odd jobs, and making a record with his brother Fred called "I'm a Hot Rodder and All That Jazz." Bill O'Reilly was in eighth grade on Long Island. Rush Limbaugh III was in sixth grade in Cape Girardeau, Missouri. A ten-year-old kid named Howie Carr had become a fan of Top 40 on WMEX and also liked hearing Jerry tear it up at night. A toddler named Sean Hannity was about to begin his Terrible Twos in New York.

For King, Jackson, Brudnoy, Imus, O'Reilly, Limbaugh, Carr, and Hannity, Jerry Williams was the Now to their When.

Was the craft perfect? No. He was still working on the details. But when you listen to the tapes of those early sixties Boston shows, you hear it in full flower, done as well as anyone else would do it for the next forty years: Real Talk Radio. It's all there—the spellbinding rhetoric, the dramatic exchanges with callers, the tough and perceptive interviews, the savvy about the world, the sense that Something Important is on the air. The Achilles' heels are there, too. When a caller or a guest starts scoring points, he sometimes loses his head, dissolves into bluster, even damages his credibility by trying to cite precedents in law or history where he's on shaky ground.

But he's incontrovertibly Great Radio. And he's shown everyone else in the country how to create an audience.

Most Boston radio execs didn't know what to do about Jerry. They kept looking at those nighttime numbers—and WMEX's Top-40 ratings during the day—and saying, "This is gonna pass."

Finally, in 1963, the ice began to break elsewhere on the Boston radio dial. WEEI put that reporter-columnist Paul Benzaquin on the air in the afternoons with a radio vet named Howard Nelson. *Listen!* was a different concept that Jerry liked, principally because Benzaquin and Nelson weren't trying to imitate him: they had the news, Benzaquin wrote clever commentary, they did in-depth interviews, and they didn't take phone calls. Benzaquin came up with a name for what they were doing, a term so logical that almost no one gives him credit for being one of the first to use it: "broadcast journalism."

Westinghouse hired Bob Kennedy to do a show on WBZ in the earlier part of the evening—phone calls and interviews, pretty obviously in Jerry's wake. Then WNAC moved Haywood Vincent, who'd been doing a weekend show, into a slot to compete with Benzaquin.

Stan Kaplan was WMEX's sales director at the time, and he had big plans. He was gonna make Ol' Mac's station into a modern operation and eventually run the place. Jerry took him aside after he'd sized him up. He said, "Stan, listen to me. In one year you'll be a *raving maniac.*"

Stan was a big guy with a big, barrelly voice: "Jer, ya gotta gimme a chance. Things'll be great. You wait and see."

Jerry held his tongue for a while. Then Stan came up with an idea to build station camaraderie: a group holiday present for Mac. He cruised the office, going from one open-partitioned cubicle to another, taking up a collection. For Mac's Christmas present. Jerry listened to the patter as he got closer.

Jerry thought: Mac's idea of a Christmas present for the staff was some piece of garbage like a tie rack, nothing he had to pay for—something he could get in exchange for a couple of free commercials. One year he actually gave away LPs and 45s—this is a Top-40 station, where record promo men would give you any tune you wanted and as many copies as you wanted, just for the asking—and Mac gives out records as the holiday gifts.

Stan turned the corner into Jerry's cubicle. "Jerry, we're taking up a collection for Mac's present."

Jerry unloaded. The whole office could hear Jerry screaming. "Get outta here! I'm giving you *nothing!*"

Mac was up at the end of the hallway, with his door open. Jerry knew he could hear. "You'll get nothing from me. *Nothing! Zero!* And I don't want anything in return. Keep the fucking presents!"

While Stan was in the saddle, Mac came up with one more masterstroke for Boston radio: Larry Glick. Glick was a candy dish for WMEX to pass around after Jerry's three-course meal of issues. Jerry was yang and Glick was yin.

Glick's forte, the concept that he virtually invented in Miami, was the all-night companion show, an all's-right-with-the-world assurance warming the radio next to your bed. The man had an inexhaustible well of good fellowship. He didn't comment on the news, but he was curious about everything. If someone gave him the number of a phone booth in London, he'd call it to see who would pick up, and then he'd somehow get that person in London to tell his audience all about himself. If Jackie Mason came on the show, Glick brought up Mason's early years as a rabbi in the South, not his feud with Ed Sullivan. He had the psychics and the UFO experts and the people with advice whom Long John Nebel had, but he also parodied the psychics and the UFO experts and the people with advice. He told jokes, laughed at himself, and said, "Lemme check," while clutching his groin every time someone said, "Is this Larry?" He made you think that all of life was a great game, and when you were listening to his show, you could play too.

So Mac hired him, and the one-two punch of Jerry Williams followed by Larry Glick became one of Boston's most enduring radio combinations.

It was good that Glick arrived when he did, because people needed some relief from the headlines. In June 1963 the Boston chapter of the NAACP began its challenge of the Boston school system. To the area's black leaders, Martin Luther King's efforts to dismantle the systems in the South that kept the races apart and disenfranchised blacks went only so far. The time had come to bring these issues home, and if that made some people uncomfortable, so be it.

Everyone in Boston knew that the schools were segregated, just as the neighborhoods were segregated. Guests on Jerry's show had been saying it for years. But doing something about it was another matter. Irish and Italian pols fussed. This wasn't the South. Here the issue was neighborhood rights, not racism.

The summer heat didn't make things better. Dr. King delivered a speech everyone would come to remember in front of two hundred thousand people in Washington, a gorgeous poem of ideals, freedom, brotherhood. But Boston School Committee Chairwoman Louise Day Hicks, an unlikely combination of Irish matron and battleship, saw the matter in stark street terms—crime and property values and black boys dating white girls and cracks in the walls that kept decent folks protected from the ghetto. There was trouble ahead.

Jerry was sitting in Jack & Marion's at Coolidge Corner, a nice halfway point between his new Brookline home and work, reading the papers that November afternoon, when people started buzzing, "Kennedy's been shot." You don't need to hear something like that twice. He paid his bill and got over to the station as fast as he could. As he drove, he listened to Benzaquin and Nelson on WEEI, to the news team on WBZ—this was a time when having a network affiliation really helped.

Still, Mac had built a good local news staff, and he made the good decision to suspend music that day and give them the reins. Dick Levitan, Paul Smith, and Len Lawrence usually just produced and reported the hourly newscasts, but now they were filling the air with the latest developments, impromptu live interviews, and anything else that would keep people informed. The jocks— Larry Justice, Melvin X. Melvin (who at the time was inhabited by Jim Makrell), and the others who'd never handled news or talk—were put into the studio to fill the gaps between news reports with somber platitudes and listen to Bostonians express their shock on the air.

Jerry heard that Theodore Bikel—the folksinger, actor, and political activist, a guy who'd been on the show a few times—had decided to cancel his concert in town that night. Jerry got Bikel at his hotel. I'd like to have you on tonight. We'll talk about JFK and what it all means.

By ten o'clock that evening, the news was over. People had been transfixed by the reporting and then exhausted by the horror of it. No one knew the why or the how, or what was going to happen next. So that's what Jerry and Bikel talked about. Was the right wing somehow involved? Could this have been related to the Bay of Pigs? With the Texan Lyndon Johnson as president, would the commitment to civil rights be slowed or reversed? They were both gloomy.

Night after night, people mourned on the show. Jerry read editorials and in memoriam pieces from all over the country on the air. Lee Harvey Oswald was captured and then killed by Jack Ruby, and it didn't make anyone feel any better. Jack Kennedy's wake simply would not end.

The audience started sending him poems and in memoriam pieces of their own. Jerry thought a lot of them were just as good as what had been published in the paper, and some of them were better. An idea came to him—a memorial book of some sort, using the best of these pieces. Herb Connolly, president of United Cerebral Palsy of Massachusetts, offered to coordinate the project. They decided to sell the book for a nominal amount to benefit CP research. Jerry announced the idea on the air. They got hundreds of submissions.

Teri got involved as an aesthetic advisor, working with the ad agency to get the right layout and order. Obviously, this needed photos. The United Cerebral Palsy folks and the ad agency used their influence to get as many as they could donated from the *Globe*, the *Herald*, the wire services. They chose three kinds of texts—formal eulogies and remembrances from public figures such as Cardinal Cushing and House Speaker John McCormack, JFK's own words, and the amateur poems from students, a bus driver, a nurse, a secretary.

A lot of people bought the book.

Those few months following the JFK assassination confirmed the place of the show. When the numbers came out in early 1964, they were hard to believe. During the winter book, three-quarters of the people who had their radios on between 10:00 P.M. and 1:00 A.M. were listening to *The Jerry Williams Show*.

The last two years of Jerry's WMEX run were Competition Time. Not that he ever had to worry, but the Big Dog finally had some poodles yapping at his backside. Ad rates went up on the strength of his numbers, Jerry made a much better deal for himself, and life was good—except for the insatiable ambition inside him and the downward spiral of the news.

The prospect of the 1964 national election gave Jerry nothing to be enthusiastic about. He viewed Lyndon Johnson with great suspicion. Here was a consummate wheeler-dealer, a southerner in a time when racial justice needed a champion. The Republicans could have nominated Henry Cabot Lodge, a centrist whom Jerry respected. But the right flank of the party pushed for Barry Goldwater and they got what they wanted—a choice, not an echo.

And the battle over civil rights was polarizing the country, Boston included.

In March 1964, at the annual St. Patrick's Day parade, some tough guys in the South Boston crowd started throwing stuff at the NAACP float, which just happened to be next to WMEX's. Jerry was there. He was almost in the path of some of the debris. A lot of people didn't like what he had to say about it when he got on the air.

In April 1964 Martin Luther King and other civil rights leaders were arrested for protesting in Birmingham, Alabama. Sheriff Bull Connor became an icon of intolerance, and some people in Boston compared him to Louise Day Hicks.

In June 1964 Chaney, Goodman, and Schwerner, those three well-meaning kids who just went to the South to help blacks register to vote, disappeared. Probably killed. For helping people register? What is *happening* to our country, folks?

Late in 1964 Malcolm X broke with the Nation of Islam. He had been to Mecca, had seen the brotherhood of Muslims, and now believed that hatred wouldn't solve anything. Jerry invited El-Hajj Malik Al-Shabazz, as Malcolm would prefer to be known, on the air to talk about it with Louis Farrakhan, one of the rising ministers in the Nation of Islam. Another great show.

Early in 1965 Malcolm came back to the show for another stimulating conversation. A few weeks later he was shot to death. Jerry remembered him on the air, and he regretted that he hadn't recorded and preserved all those programs they'd done together.

On March 7, 1965, in Selma, where so many of the streams of the civil rights movement converged, a mostly black march organized by Martin Luther King Jr.'s associate Hosea Williams ran into a mass of Alabama state troopers, who'd been ordered by Governor George Wallace to turn them back. They used tear gas and clubs, leaving more than a hundred people injured and bloody. That night ABC-TV interrupted a broadcast of *Judgment at Nuremberg* for almost fifteen minutes of stunning, violent coverage. On Monday, March 8, King put out a nationwide call for clergy of all faiths to come to Selma and witness.

Boston was particularly moved—because it was a liberal town, because it had a strong component of students, because many young clergy were getting their degrees at the area's seminaries and universities, and not least because of what Jerry Williams had been saying about racial injustice. Groups of clerics assembled—some spontaneously, some more organized—to take plane flights to Alabama. Rabbis and ministers, most of whom could make their own decisions about their actions, were the first to respond to King's call. Catholic priests, who were subject to bishops and cardinals and the heads of religious orders, were represented in smaller numbers. They boarded planes in Boston and got to know each other on the way down. On one of those planes, a priest who'd appeared on Jerry's show, Father Tom Carroll, got to know some Unitarian ministers, including a young guy named Reverend James Reeb.

Carroll, Reeb, and many more Bostonians found solidarity and a remarkable moment in Selma. On March 9 Martin Luther King led them on another march to the bridge where the state troopers had charged two days earlier. This time there was no violence because both the troopers and the marchers pulled back. But afterward, as a few of the Boston Unitarians lost their way in Selma, they ran into some unsavory white characters. Jim Reeb was knocked down by a roundhouse blow to his head from a club. Within hours, it was clear that he had a major concussion or something worse. He was taken to Birmingham to be hospitalized.

Tom Carroll flew back to Boston on March 10.

On March 11, just before 7:00 P.M., Reeb was pronounced dead.

The news was all over the air by the time Jerry signed on that night at 11:00. Callers blamed Alabama's Governor Wallace and his state troopers. They blamed LBJ for not reacting quickly enough. They blamed Klansmen, southerners, bigots. Then Jerry got a call from Tom Carroll.

Carroll sounded tired and sad. In that near brogue that for generations marked the speech of Boston's Irish Americans, he started preaching. He urged Jerry's listeners not to blame others but to look to themselves. "I want to say to your listeners: How many of them have turned down the Negro who wants the home? How many of them have moved out of a neighborhood because a Negro is moving in? How many of them have heard the stereotype of the Jew and the Negro . . . how many of them have laughed at the joke?" Jerry knew better than to interrupt. He let Carroll write his own music. "I didn't know Reverend Jim Reeb that well. We were on a plane together going down . . . He went to bear witness . . . He wanted to give the Negro the opportunity he deserves as a fellow human being . . . Boston (and the suburbs and the exurbs) needs to examine its conscience if the death of Jim Reeb is to mean anything. Your listeners have to say: Where do they stand?" The show was no longer just a forum. It had become a place where people came to testify.

Over the next couple of weeks, the progressives in town worked with King's people to set up a march of protest against the violence in Alabama on April 23, at which Dr. King would speak. Jerry talked it up, brought in the organizers, said it's important to stand up for justice, said he would be marching.

On April 22 King came to Boston to prepare for his first major civil rights demonstration in the North. That afternoon he addressed a joint session of the Massachusetts legislature. Then he rode in a motorcade through the Back Bay, through Kenmore Square, right past the WMEX studios, to speak at an evening service at Brookline's Temple Israel for the last night of Passover.

The next day Jerry marched in the intermittent rain with more than twenty thousand others from Carter Playground at the corner of Camden Street and Columbus Avenue in Roxbury to Boston Common, where King spoke. That night he came back to the mic to give his own testimony.

The combination of talk at night and Top 40 during the day had put WMEX in a dominant position in Boston and put a lot of green into the pockets of the Richmond brothers. So Mac did some real estate shopping. He found an interesting building in Bay Village, the part of town where the big movie studios used to have screening rooms and local offices in the heyday of Hollywood. The building even had a big auditorium that would be ideal for the Williams show. But Mac couldn't anticipate the Machiavellian idea percolating among the execs at WEEI, the CBS radio affiliate downtown.

General Manager Donald Tregiser, Program Director Dan Griffin, and the other guys at WEEI were bright—very bright. They saw that talk had a future, and they began to look for talent. But if they were going to commit to talk, they had to deal with Jerry Williams, the gorilla of the market. Jerry's contract specified that he was locked in Mac Richmond's grip until October 14, 1967; even if by some miracle they could persuade the Richmond brothers to let Jerry come work for WEEI, Mac would make them pay in blood. The best way to break the talk market open in Boston would be to get rid of Jerry Williams.

How could they do that?

Say, wasn't CBS's Chicago station WBBM having trouble holding its own against the other outlets in the Windy City? Wouldn't it be collegial of Boston's CBS affiliate to suggest a move that could be mutually beneficial?

Shortly after the big civil rights march, they got the word to Jerry about the plan. Chicago? Not bad, Jerry said. Go ahead, see what happens.

Jerry was checking in one day with Tregiser on the phone, and Don said, "Jerry, say hello to some new competition." Don had one of those new speakerphones in his office, and he had a visitor, so it was obvious they weren't going to talk about Chicago. He introduced a young guy with a big, powerful voice who was going to join WEEI in the afternoons, Gene Burns.

Jerry started telling Gene about the realities of talk radio. He'd just recently gotten another threat, one of many he'd received over the years. He warned the new man: everyone who has talk on the air in town has to be concerned about this stuff. There's a lot of racism just beneath the surface. He'd had one of the South Boston community leaders on his show—Mrs. Louise Day Hicks. She was tough as nails, and some of the guys on the street in Southie were a lot tougher. Burns got his two cents in: hey, death threats and such are just part of the job, aren't they? After all, don't you just have to let 'em roll off and go on?

There was a silence. Tregiser smiled, a smile that said, "Here it comes, Gene. This is what Boston knows and loves." Jerry unloaded. "Gene, you don't know what it's like to work in this town. I've been confronted on the street, had my car vandalized, had my transmitter sabotaged, had stuff thrown through the studio window, been pelted when I was part of the St. Patrick's Day parade, for Chrissake. This is Boston. It's *no joke*."

Gene got the message. He remembered it.

Primed by their colleagues in Boston, the folks at WBBM in Chicago took a long, hard look at Jerry Williams. They'd heard of him, but they hadn't actually looked at his numbers. Impressive. Maybe they'd like to talk to someone who'd commandeered 75 percent of the ears listening to the radio at night.

Ernie Shomo, the head of WBBM radio, called and made Jerry an offer. When Jerry and Ernie had finished talking, WBBM was prepared to guarantee him more money than he was earning from all the different streams he'd managed to pry out of Mac, and they would start him off with a big professional ad campaign.

Jerry contemplated Mac's stinginess, the Friday Game, the double-dealing, the disdain. He thought about his new daughter, Andrea, born just a few months earlier. He needed to take another step up, and this looked like the offer he'd been waiting for. He didn't have to think about it very long. After telling Teri, he dropped the bomb on Mac in May.

Mac was angry. Not just angry, boiling. Jerry's last contract was ironclad, and it was the most generous deal he'd ever given anyone. Jerry said he was going to Chicago and that was that. Mac could break the contract for nonperformance, but why would he want to go through the expense of suing Jerry? Jerry was leaving whether Mac liked it or not. Or would he match what CBS had put on the table?

Mac absolutely would not meet the CBS offer. He couldn't. It'd be giving up far too much. If Jerry wanted out, he'd have to make some guarantees. They'd have to do a termination agreement.

For two months Mac and Jerry wrangled. Mac kept finding new ways to tweak it, new things to ask for. The worst was the out clause. Mac wanted an outrageous five-year term of noncompetition—Jerry had to agree not to work in Boston again until October 1970. Jerry was furious. The bastard was turning the screws every chance he got. To fight back, he leaked the news of his departure to Paul Benzaquin. Paul wrote a farewell column in the *Herald* while the negotiations were still going on, including the projection that Jerry would be leaving on June 1. (What Paul said about him was so nice that Jerry had to pinch himself to make sure that it wasn't an obit.) But Mac didn't budge—oh, it'll take so long to get a good replacement, look at all we've invested, you have to help in the transition. Jerry began to parry concerned calls from BBM execs asking when they could seal the deal, get the promotion going. They sounded nervous.

Jerry never had the patience for drawn-out discussions. Finally, the lawyer repping him in the negotiations, Irving Sheff, told him to give up. Sheff said the out clause was unenforceable. No court would ever uphold it. So swallow your pride, sign it, work until the end of August the way Mac wants, and go. Jerry hated to give Mac the victory, but he accepted the deal, bad as it was.

The great transition began. Jerry and Teri put the Brookline house on the market.

Mac had heard a couple of younger guys he wanted to try out in Jerry's slot. Guy LeBeau and Fred Dreyfus did some shows in tandem with Jerry, and some solo shots. Dreyfus got the nod.

They passed papers on sale of the house on August 23. Teri, Eve, Susan, and baby Andi left Boston and got settled in temporary hotel accommodations in Chicago.

On the evening of Friday, August 28, 1965, Jerry turned the reins over to Fred.

On Saturday, August 29, MEX sponsored a farewell affair—another glory moment for him—at one of the big hotels. Listeners, guests, friends, station people, all turned out to say good-bye. No hard feelings, Jer? Sure, Mac, sure. And good riddance.

On Sunday Jerry left Boston.

Dreyfus didn't last long. Mac fired him a few months later because he did a program with an author who thought sex before marriage was a good idea. Mac liked the show when it was on the air, but when the complaints started rolling in, he decided Fred was expendable. The new host, the latest cast member in the Richmond soap opera, was a guy named Steve Fredericks.

When Jerry heard about it, he had a long laugh. He was free of Mac's clutches at last, already shaking things up in the heartland of America.

6 CHICAGO

Men hate each other because they fear each other. They fear each other because they don't know each other. They don't know each other because they can't communicate with each other. They can't communicate with each other because they are separated from one another.
—*Reverend Martin Luther King Jr., address at Highlander Center, New Market, Tennessee, September 2, 1957*

CBS decided that Jerry Williams would be introduced to Chicago with a professional media campaign, state-of-the-art for 1965. Young & Rubicam got a budget of $50,000 for newspaper ads alone, about $300,000 in today's money—more than Jerry's annual income at MEX, including all the commissions he made from the spots on his show, his weekly "expenses," and his speaking fees. It was a nice taste for a local ad campaign designed to introduce a nighttime show. Obviously, the folks at CBS thought Jerry had potential.

They were right.

Y&R told CBS that Jerry should be portrayed as a maverick, a provocateur. He was the guy who had shaken up Boston. He could be expected to do the same in Chicago. Give him a whiff of danger.

Jerry's first Chicago glossy made him look more like a private eye than a talk show host: dramatic lighting, a cityscape backdrop, cigarette smoke curling in front of the WBBM mic, a suspicious glance out of the corner of his eye, a thin wisp of hair falling over his forehead. Except for the microphone, it would have been a perfect promo still for *Richard Diamond, Private Detective*, the late-fifties TV show starring David Janssen.

From Jerry's viewpoint, the press release said all the right things. "The hottest, 'no-holds-barred' contribution to night time Radio programming ever

*"The Professional Provocateur":
a publicity shot created under the
direction of Young & Rubicam
for the debut of* The Jerry
Williams Show *on WBBM,
Chicago, ca. August 1965.*

created. . . . Past master at shooting down 'sacred cows' . . . finder of skele-
tons in political closets and dauntless needler of the collective consciences of
major metropolitan area leaders! . . . A *consistent #1 position* . . . (not to mention a punch in the nose from an irate politician who crashed into the studio
while he was on the air)." And there was a civics lesson that sounded like
Jerry'd dictated it: "The JERRY WILLIAMS SHOW is designed basically to
give the 'little guy' an opportunity to question, praise, complain about or
exchange ideas freely on a wide range of subjects—via the telephone."

Best of all was the money: $45,000 a year, a great salary for a nighttime
radio host in 1965. And he never had to chase anyone down a flight of stairs
for his check.

Chicago stuns the newcomer. Its bursting-with-commerce downtown, its wide
thoroughfares offering dozens of bullet-straight routes out into the ethnic

neighborhoods and even the suburbs, its sense of centrality within the Great Plains, its limitless horizon along Lake Michigan—this is Big Town, the way it's supposed to be.

Just a few blocks north of Chicago's commercial heart, nearly at the lakefront, there's a strange low-rise building that occupies half a block of prime real estate. It's got funny peaks in the roof, an odd array of windows and facade features, and a brick-and-stucco exterior. Before the Depression it was the Chicago Riding Club, outfitted with stables and a horse arena. In the forties it was a dairy barn; in the fifties, a roller rink. When Jerry got to town in 1965, it had been CBS's Midwest HQ, home of WBBM Radio and Channel 2 TV, for nine years.

If you'd been Jerry, driving to work, you might have cruised along Lake Shore Drive, not too far from the region's most prestigious shopping, the Magnificent Mile. As you surveyed the skyline, you'd see a few landmarks pushing upwards—the Wrigley Building, the Chicago Tribune Building, the Drake Hotel, the Civic Center, maybe eight or nine more. As you turned corners to navigate onto McClurg Court, you might have seen a city bus with "Jerry Williams has a big mouth!" plastered in huge letters across its side. Then you'd see the block-long covered entryway to 630 McClurg. With all those glass doors, it looked like the entrance to an old-fashioned movie palace. You could even imagine a marquee above it. You'd pull into your precious place in the parking area for CBS employees across the street. When you walked toward the building, you wouldn't have to fight through crowds of people trying to get into a baseball park. You'd pass through the reception area, smiling at one of the stunners who were always installed at the front desk. You wouldn't have to climb a flight of stairs to get to your office—there was an elevator! When you got to WBBM Radio, shlubby Mac Richmond would not be there. Instead, Ernie Shomo, a beautifully dressed, top-level CBS executive, would be your boss. You might see young, dedicated John Callaway through a studio window, toiling away on one of his radio documentaries. Maybe you'd say hello to Mal Bellairs, who did the afternoon *Tie Line* show, or Rick Weaver, who did *Sports Line* in the early evenings. All professional, straight-arrow radio guys who knew that you were there because you'd been a Star in Boston. Working here wouldn't hurt your self-esteem.

In 1965 WBBM was an also-ran. The leading stations in Chicago were WGN and WIND, with their rival morning men, Wally Phillips and Howard Miller. Phillips and Miller were both personalities in the style of the midsixties, playing adult-oriented hits, managing chunks of news, sports, and weather, talking in the gaps about whatever came to mind. Miller got political on occasion, with right-wing comments that made him no friends among

Jerry Williams in the lobby of the headquarters of CBS Chicago, 630 North McClurg Court (home of WBBM radio and television), ca. 1966.

the city's minority communities. Phillips was more fun and funnier. These were the guys that most Chicagoans listened to as they showered and shaved and made breakfast for the kids and drove to work. The rest of the top five usually included WVON ("the Voice of the Negro"), a white-owned station with a huge audience among African Americans, and WLS, where the kids went for Top 40.

WBBM, as a CBS O&O—the shorthand everyone in the business used to designate a station that was owned and operated by one of the networks—was supposed to be a leader in its market, or so William Paley, the head of CBS in New York, believed. Anything less than top-three status was an affront to the brand, and local management knew it. They had tried to make it into a talk station, sort of, but the strategy wasn't working. Bud Kelly, who had a run-of-the-mill music-and-talk program in the morning, was not a factor in the morning race, and the rest of WBBM's broadcast day consisted mostly of noncontroversial hosts like Mal Bellairs and the child-care expert Dr. Freda Kehm, along with a couple of CBS network shows. Paul Gibson, a monologuist who'd once been the station's morning host, had been whittled down to a half hour at 7:30 P.M. Before Jerry got there, the dark hours were muddling along with *Tempos for Tonight,* a generic announcer-with-records program, and Jay Andres's long-standing all-night music show.

The only bright spot in the weekly schedule was John Callaway's *Nightline* on Sunday, an innovative combination of documentary, interview, and thoughtful call-in that grappled with tough issues from a serious journalistic perspective. It was a must for the thinking folks in town, and it had a solid audience across the country as well, thanks to the station's 50,000-watt clear channel signal and the peculiarities of AM reach at night. The station recognized the show's importance, airing it without commercials (which wasn't that big a deal, since the sales guys couldn't move spots on Sunday nights, anyway) and giving Callaway a full (if small) salary to produce and host it.

Except for Callaway, WBBM was at least five years removed from the most dynamic ideas in radio. It was in serious need of Jerry Williams.

Jerry dug into the papers—four big dailies duking it out every day—and he used his well-honed political savvy to get oriented. Who was influential? Irv Kupcinet, "Kup" to everyone, a *Sun-Times* columnist and television host, an icon. The *Daily News*'s Mike Royko, a legend in American journalism. Hugh Hefner, publisher of *Playboy.* John H. Johnson, founder of *Ebony* and *Jet,* national magazines targeting blacks. John Sengstacke, owner of the *Defender,* the city's African American newspaper. Paul Harvey, a throwback to the old days of radio news and comment, on WLS. A dozen terrific city and national reporters on the *American,* the *Tribune,* the *Sun-Times,* and the *Daily News.*

Who was important? Everett Dirksen, the centrist Republican senator with a voice like the low notes of a pipe organ, the guy LBJ now had to negotiate with to get anything through the Senate. Governor Otto Kerner. Representatives Dan Rostenkowski and Bob Michel. A rising state senator named Paul Simon. Some other lesser lights—a fella named Don Rumsfeld, who had held the U.S. Rep seat for the Thirteenth District for a couple of terms.

Who held the power? There was one man above all others, the man who dominated, outfoxed, or co-opted anyone who mattered. The Honorable Richard J. Daley, mayor of the City of Chicago and chairman of the Central Committee of the Democratic Party of Cook County. A guy who made James

Michael Curley look like Casper Milquetoast. The head of a mighty political machine more suited to the Kremlin than America. The Boss.

What was under the surface? Race, race, and race. The Chicago metropolitan area was one of the most rigidly segregated in the country. The fast-expanding ghetto neighborhoods of Chicago's West and South Sides were coming into conflict with traditionally Irish, Italian, Polish, and Lithuanian communities inside the city limits and in adjoining lower-middle-class suburbs. Real estate people were terrifying whites with the prospect of a black plague sucking the value out of their homes. To whites, Martin Luther King's civil rights movement looked like a nightmare about to come true on their own streets. To blacks, the movement looked like a long-awaited megaphone for their complaints about housing, schools, and wages.

Starting on BBM wasn't the same as it was on MEX. Jerry already knew how to select the hottest topics for discussion, how to set things up in an hour, how to strike sparks in interviews, how to smoke out and shape good calls, how to keep the momentum going. Despite the fact that Chicago was vastly bigger than Boston, there was a familiarity to the machine, the corrupt politicos, the ethnic mix. National issues hadn't changed—civil rights was just as important in Chicago as it'd been in Boston, if not more so. The same wrongs still needed to be righted. The same Vietnam problem was waiting in the wings.

The big differences: he was now just one of many talk show hosts. Telephone calls on the air were commonplace here. John Callaway was already taking on controversial issues.

There were a couple of other factors: nighttime TV was becoming a habit for Americans, so he had more competition from the little screen. And, even though management would always be primarily concerned with Chicago numbers and Chicago ad revenue, Jerry knew he was going to be speaking to thirty-eight states.

Jerry saw his goals clearly: get listeners into the arena right away, become a lightning-rod personality whom people couldn't ignore, give the show a national flavor without neglecting the base audience, and, above all, get out ahead of the issues. The show had to be immediately topical, even make news if it could. He talked it over with the producer BBM gave him, a tough, politically savvy guy named Paul Fanning. Paul got what he was trying to do right away, and he promised to give him the benefit of his living-in-Chicago experience.

The first show was on Labor Day, September 6, 1965, competing directly with the top TV network shows, at 8:00 P.M. As WMEX had, BBM led the show with a disclaimer: "The views and opinions expressed on the following program do not necessarily constitute the views and opinions of WBBM Radio and the participating sponsors." It worked the same way the MEX announcement had—distancing the station and the advertisers from Jerry's opinions, but creating a sense of anticipation, giving listeners the impression that they were about to experience a new kind of radio show, something fascinating, modern, even dangerous.

Then the recorded announcer wrapped it up with a flourish: ". . . America's largest town meeting of the air, with your host, the Speaker of the House, Jerry Williams." The studio light went on.

"After that fantastic buildup in the newspapers, I can hardly wait to hear what I'm going to say." Then he did the usual hellos. A pause. A deep breath. A manifesto:

> Since this is a new program, I would like to preface this, our opening show, with an explanation for its being, because it is a new concept in Chicago radio.
>
> This program will strive to give *full* vent to freedom of speech, where all points of view, including highly unpopular ones, may be heard. [Jerry stepped up on the soapbox and adopted the Royal We.] We will attempt never to delve into controversy for its own sake. However, if we do find ourselves swimming in a sea of controversy somewhere, on some issue, it is only with a broad eye to the future, that is, how we may remedy a particularly foul situation, how we may lighten the burden of an oppressed group, how we may enlighten the general populace and start them thinking.
>
> You, of course, will be free to call in to discuss anything at all on our open forum nights. These are the nights when we will have no guests at all. All we ask is that you be accurate, brief, concise—the ABC's, accurate, brief, concise—and in good taste.
>
> This program will strive to be the pulse of Chicago, and the Midwest, a reflection in the mirror of public opinion. Now, at times the image may be ugly, for there are those who would seek to preclude this concept of freedom of speech, because they are adamant in their *own* views and opinions. We will resist their efforts and, in so doing, attempt to give them broader scope to their own narrowness. For those who will not see the light, we say, "Alas."

Pretentious? You bet. John Callaway, driving around at night, listened to the guy who was going to host the six other nights of the week on BBM, the man who would be his colleague and his competition at the same time. He heard the brash approach, the aggressive interviewing so different from his own style. He thought: I've earned my stripes in Chicago, print and broadcast. Who does this guy think he is?

Jerry's day-to-day agenda was set by the news, and there was plenty to talk about—mostly civil rights at first.

Jerry waded into it right away—frankly, before he was fully informed on the local nuances. But his point of view got immediate attention, and listeners weren't afraid to mix it up with him. Less than a month into the show, black Chicagoans were already talking about this new guy, a white man who was unequivocally on their side. On September 25 the *Defender* prominently published a letter to the editor suggesting that the show was "a program that each Negro in the city should hear. . . . On the last show many of the white race called and really gave him a rough time. But he stood his ground and did a wonderful job defending the rights of Negroes."

Opinions about the involvement in Vietnam hadn't hardened yet. Johnson had started bombing North Vietnam in February 1965 and sent the first combat units into the country in March. The pacifist left began making noise about the escalation right away, but the big trouble was yet to come. It was hard for most Americans to figure out exactly why we were getting involved in this little Asian country, and their pundits gave them conflicting analyses. Jerry was willing to hear critics and defenders of the war, but he himself was skeptical about it.

Civil rights and the war. They were always on the program—foreground or background.

But the first notoriety came to the show from another quarter entirely. Jerry invited one of the most unreconstructed right-wingers out there, Richard Cotten of the Committee of Christian Laymen, to appear on November 1, 1965. Cotten didn't cavil. He assailed the pernicious forces at work in America, including the "Zionist lobby controlling virtually every facet of our lives," black agitators like King, and the Marxist plan for world domination destroying our country from within. And he rolled over the others Jerry had invited to provide alternative viewpoints. After three hours, Cotten retired from the field, encouraging people to write Jerry with their reactions.

Thousands of cards and letters came in to WBBM, and Jerry kept the pot simmering by reading some of the riper ones on the air. Jerry had seen stuff like this in Boston, but never so much of it: "There were no Jews, Catholics, troublemakers in the Pilgrams and *no Negroes.*" "The honorable Germans have finished paying their reparations but not so with Israel, because as the saying goes, 'There is no honor among thieves.'" "You really fell flat on your hooked nose." "Perhaps you now have a bit of feeling that we in the South have when your northern press, television, etc. crucify the white man here." "It was a fair sample of how the Jews try to gang up on anyone who has the brains and the courage to show them up for what they are." "Generally, your kind of Hebrew are overaggressive . . . violent in your emotions, hate, and are hostile, greed for money, money, money consumes you, everything must be ostentatious, vulgarly showy to draw attention to yourselves. . . . Hate and inner conflict are your master and greatest enemy. Until you *conquer yourselves,* your *own turbulent inner sickness,* you will *never* be *like other human beings.*" "It doesn't matter what the pope of Rome says about absolving the Jews in the death of Jesus Christ. They were the ones that crucified him. . . . The Jews are just as anti-Christ today as they were then." "God help America if it ever falls into the hands of people such as you seem to prefer."

The stuff came in from Rome, Georgia. Madison, Wisconsin. Grand Rapids, Michigan. Forest, Louisiana. Hattiesburg, Mississippi. Columbia, Missouri. Gardendale, Alabama. Duluth, Minnesota. Corpus Christi, Texas. Nashville, Tennessee. Springdale, Arkansas. Man, he thought, that signal really travels.

And they're *out there* tonight.

In late 1965 a book called *Unsafe at Any Speed* appeared on Jerry's desk. It'd been written by an unknown consumer activist named Ralph Nader who was criticizing the quality of American automobiles in general and nailing the Chevrolet Corvair specifically. Jerry considered himself a connoisseur of cars, and he actually liked the little Corvair quite a bit, but Nader said that the thing was a deathtrap by design. He resolved to get Nader on the air. John Callaway was on top of the book too, and he beat Jerry to the punch, giving Nader his first Chicago exposure, three full hours on the Sunday night show.

That Monday, there was a lot of talk in the halls about management's reaction. Old hands pointed out how risky it was to criticize the auto industry in the Midwest—a lot of ad money came out of the Big Three, and you didn't want to kill that golden goose. Some folks had heard that GM was being pretty direct about it, trying to freeze this Nader off the air by putting pressure on ownership at other stations. But everyone could say one thing for sure: when Ernie Shomo heard Nader on Callaway's show, he blew his stack. People could hear him yelling at John, "What the fuck are you doing with Ralph Nader?"

So Jerry knew where he stood when he invited Nader to appear. Naturally, he didn't tell Ernie. But it was a matter of principle. Management couldn't strong-arm programming. It would ruin his credibility if his audience ever found out that he'd caved to advertiser influence on an issue like this. So he did the show. And say what you will about Nader's fashion sense (Bad haircut, Jerry thought when they shook hands), the guy knew his stuff cold. He was a walking research lab, and he had a curious intensity that got people fired up. Best of all, he was on the side of the little guy against the big companies. It was exciting radio.

Jerry and Ernie had a talk afterwards, and Shomo let Jerry know how unhappy New York was about that show. He suggested that Jerry take a couple of days off to think things over. Jerry said he would, but he also said that Ernie shouldn't have any illusions. Nader would be back. People wanted to hear the guy.

Thanks to Jerry, Nader moved quite a few books and managed to break through the media wall. And Jerry didn't hear anything more about it from Ernie.

A few months later, a minister untied Jesus' loincloth on the air, and for a few days *The Jerry Williams Show* was Chicago's number one topic of conversation.

The June 15 program wasn't supposed to be a big deal. Jerry wanted to discuss new trends in religion and the new generation of activist clerics. He invited three clergymen to the studios—Robert Claytor, Joseph Scheuer, and Malcolm Boyd, an Episcopalian minister who had written a book of modern prayers called *Are You Running with Me, Jesus?* They got into a conversation about Jesus as a real person. Reverend Boyd matter-of-factly said that people had to deal with the fact that Jesus was a man, and that he had all the standard physical parts of a man—head, arms, armpits, legs, a penis . . . Nobody said *penis* on the air in 1966. Jerry had seven seconds to decide whether to cut the word, and he let it go.

They didn't print *penis* or *testicles* in the papers in 1966. Even writing *armpits* wasn't exactly decent. So when Dean Gysel, the *Daily News* media columnist, told his readers how "the shock waves still were being felt" five days after the broadcast, he was forced to write, "Father Boyd emphasized that, physically, Christ was a man like anyone else, with . . . sweat glands and reproductive organs, for which he used a very specific word."

Because that show featured three clerics, it polarized the opinions of religiously oriented people about Jerry. For example, lefty Catholics, the people who supported change in the Church, civil rights, social justice, all the usual causes—they were behind Jerry 100 percent and not offended by the word at all. On the other hand, to Father John Banahan of the Chicago Archdiocesan Office of Radio and Television, that show was an outrage. He wrote about it in *Catholic New World,* filed protests with the FCC and the National Association of Broadcasters, and was still exercised about it more than a year later when he wrote a letter to the editors of the *Sunday Tribune.*

To lighten things up, there was a visit from Dr. Gilbert Holloway.

Long John Nebel, Larry Glick, and a host of other late-night entertainment talkers had made minor celebrities out of mentalists, psychics, astrologers, advice mavens, religious seers, and the like. These folks were always good for a talk show, since they offered listeners the chance to get a "spiritual" take on a personal problem without crossing a fortune-teller's palm with silver. Jerry used them sparingly and thought of them as a kind of relief from the serious topics that were the show's meat and potatoes. He liked financial advisors and stock pickers for the same reason—and he put them all in the same category when it came to his personal life. Others might actually take the advice being offered, but Jerry reserved his own judgment when it came to matters of the heart and the pocketbook.

Dr. Gilbert Holloway was different. His gift of extrasensory perception or whatever you wanted to call it wasn't yet widely known when Jerry heard about him and put him on WMEX years before. Back then, Jerry was skeptical about this stuff—there were a lot of snake-oil characters out there who were certifiably nutty. But Holloway had surprised him. He had an avuncular gravitas, a sort of inner calm. He wasn't out to prove anything to anyone. He gently resisted being put in any category. He simply believed that he had been born with a gift that allowed him to help people, and he wanted to use it. (Jerry understood that he did public appearances and personal counseling, and that sometimes offerings were made. Hey, the guy had to make a living.)

He only asked Jerry to set things up for him by telling his listeners to say the phrase "Tell me something about myself" when they called in. Holloway would then begin to share what he felt or sensed about the person's nature, character, background, and aptitudes. Unlike the medicine-show types, he wasn't afraid to ask questions to get more information about people's pasts— when they were born, whether their parents were alive or dead, that sort of thing. It was a kind of intuitive psychology. Holloway frequently came up with surprising insights into a person's weaknesses or strengths, traumas or triumphs. And callers loved the guy. So whenever he was in town, he'd call Jerry and they usually worked out a mutually agreeable guest shot.

What was special about his visit to WBBM in the summer of 1966 was that Jerry was able for the first time to measure his significance, thanks to a system BBM had to count the number of times callers got a busy signal. The system couldn't distinguish between twenty individuals who found the BBM lines busy and one person who made twenty calls in a row, but it was at least a rough tool showing how popular a topic or a guest was. Holloway racked up 29,000 busy signals, which was pretty damn good.

For the rest of Jerry's career, Holloway found his way onto the show regularly, usually once a year or so.

Month after month, the ratings and sales improved. In February 1966 Bob Smith of the *Chicago Daily News* wrote the first big piece on Jerry for a Chicago rag. For the title, the headline writer picked up a phrase Jerry particularly liked—"Radio's Professional Provocateur." Smith documented how well the show was doing: "Since Williams arrived, WBBM has jumped from seventh to fourth place in the evening ratings. . . . And Williams has drawn five commercials for every one that WBBM had without him in that time period." He quoted Jerry about his on-air philosophy: "'I like to get emotions flying . . . but I don't want to force it. It's right only when it's there naturally. I want a show that makes people think . . . that makes people turn up the volume on the radio and say, "Shhhh! I want to hear this."'"

There were more and more requests for Jerry to speak, and BBM transferred a young woman named Pam Clayton from TV sales to Jerry's office to work as an assistant. Within a few weeks, she was bringing in more outside appearances than Jerry had ever had before. Church groups (especially those from Jewish temples), professional associations, PTAs, colleges, country clubs, fraternal organizations—they all wanted Jerry. Once things got rolling, he often had three or four appearances in a single week, each one putting two or three hundred dollars in his pocket.

Shows like Cotten's or Boyd's or Holloway's got people talking about Jerry and helped them remember him, but the factor that truly drove his listenership was exactly what it had been on WMEX—the daily news.

Many in Chicago thought the city would be an ideal venue for Martin Luther King's first northern campaign, a springboard for another piece of national legislation like the Voting Rights Act. Ultimately, King chose to use the city as an example of discriminatory housing practices. There were plenty of easy targets—realtors who prevented blacks from seeing apartments and homes in white neighborhoods, building owners who let ghetto apartment buildings decay, developers and managers who built substandard project housing and ignored basic maintenance, and city officials who winked at the rules and regs that were supposed to apply equally to everyone. In January, King, his wife, Coretta, and their kids moved into a tenement apartment at 1550 South Hamlin Avenue on Chicago's West Side, one of the worst buildings King's people could find, to dramatize the conditions of ghetto housing in the city. In February King led a march to another building that had been the subject of numerous complaints and took it over symbolically, saying the rent the tenants usually paid to their landlord was going to be put into property improvements.

On the air and off, Jerry spoke out boldly about King's housing campaign, perhaps a little heedless of the fact that open housing was a real hit-'em-where-they-live issue for northern liberals. When people from the ethnic white neighborhoods living near the ghetto called in or came out to hear him speak, they often pointed their fingers at the wealthy hypocrites living in the lily-white suburbs who were so eager to give King what he wanted: how come they didn't sell their homes and come live next to the Negroes they loved so much?

How come *you* don't live in the city, Jerry?

That question didn't get on the air very often. It was one of the ugly things people said to hurt you. They didn't really care where you lived. It was a way to get personal: You wouldn't be so high and mighty if you had to live next to 'em every day, lemme tell ya, Jerry.

And the answer to the question was . . . because I don't have to. Because I at last have the money to live in that house I've always dreamed of. Because my wife wants a beautiful showplace home and my kids deserve it. Because I'm a Star.

Until the middle of 1966, Jerry, Teri, and the three kids had lived in an apartment. And what an apartment! Their rental agent had found them a place at one of *the* prestige addresses, 3240 Lake Shore Drive, a massive, elegant, redbrick McNally & Quinn masterpiece dating from 1929. The apartment was on the Lake Michigan side of the building, surveying unobstructed miles of shoreline and cityscape as far as the eye could see, and there was room for live-in help.

They became familiar with the city from that vantage point, as much as Jerry ever did. Frankly, he didn't really enjoy a night out unless he was the featured speaker or a restaurant owner gave him the big glad hand when he walked into a place. But he found a small slice of Brooklyn out in a western neighborhood once populated by small businesses owned by Jewish merchants—one of the last ones was Sam Braverman's deli. Braverman's had giant (I mean, *giant*) corned beef sandwiches. They were so vast that Sam had to put a sign up saying he wouldn't sell extra bread—if you ordered a sandwich, no sharing! Not coincidentally, Sam was a sponsor, and he was always pleased when someone came in and said, "Jerry Williams sent me."

Another place, much closer to the apartment building, was the Ivanhoe. The kids loved going there—it was so kitsch, it was fun. They'd done this building up like a little Tudor castle—turrets, moat, drawbridge, pennants. Inside, they had a restaurant and bar on the main floor and a couple more bars in the basement, which they called the Catacombs.

Still, living inside the Chicago city limits was just temporary—just to see if the job lasted. They had owned their own home in Brookline, and once you've owned your own home in a nice residential neighborhood, an apartment in the city just won't do.

The home they finally found, a few months after Martin Luther King started his housing campaign on the West Side, was in Glencoe, a North Shore suburb. This is a town with one of those "charming" little business districts, where the buildings are all carefully maintained and coordinated in style, and the nice houses radiate out from there. But Jerry and Teri didn't settle for "nice." They got an estate, a David Adler country house once known as "The Gables." As Irv Kupcinet described it in his June 13 *Sun-Times* column, it was "a Glencoe showplace."

It's one of four vast houses built by a man named Moses Born in the 1910s, originally designed by Howard Van Doren Shaw and renovated in the early twenties. One of the area's premiere domestic architects, David Adler, turned it into a French Norman manor, faced in clean beige stone, with a conical turret and steeply pitched roofs. It had an entry gate with ten-foot columns and an ornamental iron arch that led to a courtyard that could easily accommodate ten cars around a handsome fountain. Out back there was a swimming pool big enough for one of those Hollywood movie star parties. The formal entry had a spiral staircase. There were columns in the living room. The kids' bedrooms had silk wallpaper. Jerry's study, where he reviewed the newspapers and mouthed the columns he planned to read on the air, had a mammoth carved black oak desk and soft red velvet on the walls. The place had *wings*, for Chrissake. Norma Desmond would have loved it.

Once the Williamses got it furnished and hired the help and started to have parties there, people's jaws dropped when they visited him. Jerry Williams lives *here?* A radio host, here in a home once owned by bankers and philanthropists? This guy must be doing all right. They didn't have to know how much debt Jerry had shouldered to afford it.

And Teri made the image complete—a stunning hostess, sexy, charming, gracious, beautifully dressed, yet down-to-earth too.

So when did you start cheating on your wife, Jerry? And why?

Well, when was it? Probably in Chicago. You see, when you've perfected all those lady-killing lines that worked so well in Philly, and you see a woman who's a little younger, and she gives you one of those why-don't-we-get-to-know-one-another looks, you say, "What the hell? I'll just do it to see if I've still got it." And then, maybe you do it again, because you've gotten away with it. And then you get in the habit of doing it. And after all, you're a Star.

July 1966 was hot in Chicago, the kind of midwestern hot that grabs the back of your neck like a big sweaty hand. Martin Luther King's housing campaign was making ethnic whites uneasy, and a stupid little scuffle between West Side residents and the police over whether kids could cool themselves off in fire hydrant water started a wave of violence that rose and fell for weeks. There was a riot in mid-July that left two people dead and caused more than two million dollars in property damage. Near the end of the month, a march for equal treatment in housing ran into hundreds of white protestors with eggs, bottles, and rocks. The next day, a Sunday, another housing march led by King's people was met by thousands of furious whites throwing bricks and firecrackers and shouting, "White power" and "Burn them like Jews." Forty of the marchers and two policemen were sent to the hospital. John Callaway of WBBM was there with his mic and tape recorder. He captured the sounds of the march and the sounds of the crowd, and he shared them with his audience that night.

Jerry saw the papers on Monday, August 1. This was like one of those scenes down South, and here it was in his own hometown. He heard about what Callaway had done on the air the night before, and he considered the situation. His own show was at a disadvantage because he was always in the studio, invariably using others as his eyes and ears. Callaway had street time and street experience. Because this melee happened on a Sunday, he'd gotten the whole story on the air that night and been able to get listeners' reaction right away. What if it had happened on a Tuesday? Would he have to sit on that tape for five days?

When Jerry next saw Callaway, he made an offer—if something like this happened on a weekday or a Saturday, would John be willing to bring raw or minimally edited tape to Jerry's show that night and talk about it?

It didn't take long for Callaway to say yes. The ideas of having a timely outlet for his work, exposure on the hottest show in town, and a public display of respect from Mr. Hotshot were very appealing. You bet, Jerry. Let's keep each other informed.

King announced the movement's next step—he would lead another housing march on Friday, August 5. Jerry and Callaway touched base. If something happens . . .

Something did. That evening five thousand whites showed up to vent their anger, throw things at the marchers, and fight with the police. The violence continued for two hours. Martin Luther King himself was hit by a rock. John Callaway was just a few steps away, taping and reporting. As the marchers retreated and the trouble dissolved into sporadic attacks on police cars, Callaway rushed downtown to BBM and joined Jerry on the air. He told everyone what he'd seen and he played them the sounds he'd heard. Some listeners were horrified—Martin Luther King attacked *here?* Some said he had it coming.

That was some show. When it was over, the two of them promised that it wouldn't be the last time they worked together.

WBBM gave Jerry three votes of confidence in September: a party at the prestigious Tavern Club to celebrate his first anniversary on the air in Chicago; a new, hour-long interview show called *Contact* from 4:00 to 5:00 P.M., Monday through Friday; and the recasting of the Saturday night show into a "best of Jerry" so that he could finally work a five-day week.

And there was recognition from another source, too, one he particularly prized. He was invited to give an address at a meeting of the Radio and Television News Directors' Association, which convened in Chicago that fall. Jerry didn't consider himself a journalist, and yet, here he was speaking in front of one of the country's most prestigious journalistic fraternities. He worked hard on that speech. He wanted to draw a line between reporting of the news and involvement in the news. He wanted to cast himself as a progressive, someone who felt that observing from the sidelines in these times was just not enough. He wanted to shake these guys up a little.

When he was introduced on September 30, he started out with a quote from an unlikely source: Mayor Daley. "I'm told that the mayor chastised you gentlemen for being 'preoccupied with conflict' and held you responsible for a large part of the racial disturbances in Chicago this past summer.

"I'm surprised to see you blamed. When the disturbances were taking place, the mayor, and others, laid the blame squarely at the feet of 'outsiders.' . . . To politicians, newsmen are 'outsiders'—'outsiders' who dispute the fact that the president, or the mayor, or the precinct worker knows best what 'the people' ought to be told." Then, up popped something he remembered from those days at Erasmus Hall. "I'm sure civics classes still read about [John] Peter Zenger and the continuing battle for a free press in a free society."

He shifted his tone. More sarcastic:

It is the nature of government to manage news . . . to release only that information that gives "the right image." . . . When the mayor of Cicero says it's a peace-loving town, good newsmen should take his word for it—instead of photographing peace-loving citizens peacefully throwing bricks and firecrackers. Good newsmen shouldn't cover marches, because, if they didn't, people wouldn't throw bricks, marchers would stay in their ghetto, and, as far as the politicians are concerned, the problem would be solved. . . .

The mayor says newsmen are "preoccupied with conflict," but *avoiding real* conflicts makes for dishonest reporting and dangerous ignorance. . . . Too much coverage of a riot may distort its importance—but politicians' indifference *started* it! Obsession with "where's the action" may be today's mistake—but a century of belief that "ignored problems" would disappear has produced the inhuman conditions and unbearable frustrations which erupt into action.

"Where's the action?" It's right here, Baby, and it won't go away, even if the newsmen do!!!!

The reaction of the journalists is not recorded.

The grim events of the summer of 1966 had an effect on Jerry's listenership similar to that the JFK assassination had had on his numbers in Boston. When that era's gold standard in audience measurement, the Pulse ratings, were released in the fall, the CBS sales force began touting the fact that Jerry's *nighttime* numbers were beating the numbers of some of the other top-ten Chicago stations *in morning and afternoon drive time.* And the salespeople helpfully pointed out that WBBM's nighttime ad rates were a bargain in comparison with the other stations' daytime rates.

Jerry and his producer, Paul Fanning, kept the formula working. The closing months of 1966 and the first part of 1967 featured Hazel Smith, the editor-publisher of an African American newspaper in Mississippi; the LSD guru Timothy Leary, touting his new psychedelic religion; the columnists Roland Evans and Robert Novak, comparing the presidential qualities of Lyndon Johnson and John Kennedy; members of Chicago's Mattachine Society, discussing discrimination against homosexuals; a debate on gun control with Carl Bakal, author of *The Right to Bear Arms,* one of the earliest books on the subject, and Robert Kukla of the NRA; Chicago's godfather of the left, Studs Terkel; a roundtable on whether abortion ought to be legalized; and two old reliables, the Communist Gus Hall and the atheist Madalyn Murray O'Hair.

He interviewed Dr. Sam Sheppard, who'd just been acquitted of murdering his wife; Kay Jarrett, an ex-madam who'd written a book; the playwright Garson Kanin; Hunter S. Thompson, a young writer who'd done a book on the Hell's Angels; and the TV producer David Susskind. And he rolled out the red carpet for the political comedian Dick Gregory, who managed to be entertaining and provocative at the same time.

By January 1967 management had seen a full year of Jerry's numbers. This guy was no flash in the pan. Like him or not, he was WBBM's hot property. One day someone came up with the notion that he could be moved to a more prominent place in the broadcast day. Since Bud Kelly's low-key music and banter in the morning were not cutting it against Wally Phillips on WGN and

Howard Miller on WIND, maybe Jerry could succeed there. Even though Miller was occasionally controversial and Phillips took an occasional phone call, Jerry had the market cornered on the combination of the two, wrapped in that very distinctive personality. He had a strong profile that might play well against the big guys in the market.

And then there were the inevitable economic arguments. Maybe setting him up in prime ad rate time would make his big salary more cost-effective. Maybe they could find some younger talk host to continue the hot stuff at night more inexpensively.

The ideas took shape over the course of the next few weeks. Finally, Jerry was brought into the conversation. What could he say? Being offered morning drive time was the ultimate compliment in radio. Of course, he wouldn't have to do the afternoon interview show any more, and they would give him more money (always a plus). Would Paul Fanning continue to produce? Well, they wanted Paul to keep the continuity going at night with a new host. But they had a real can-do guy named Herb Howard to handle the mornings. And the morning show would be an hour longer than his nighttime gig, and they wanted him working live on Saturdays again.

Four hours a day, six days a week. Well, when you're a Star . . . If he had any misgivings, he didn't let on. Who would do the night show?

Had Jerry heard of Don Cannon?

Cannon? Oh, yeah. He'd worked with Don at MEX. In fact, the kid was a sort of protégé—he'd started a Jerry Williams–type show in some small New England market, and done very well with it, Jerry heard. Where was he now? Hartford? He'd be good, sure. He knew how to do a talk show.

The announcement went to the press on February 21. Ernie Shomo did the interviews—this was a change of focus for WBBM, so he was out front as the official spokesperson. The ads followed right away, and again it was a big splashy campaign. But the "professional provocateur" was gone. The Little Guy was gone. The civics lesson was gone. WBBM was now emphasizing the dynamic Jerry, not the dangerous one: "Up and at 'em, tiger! Here's Jerry, with two-way morning radio like you've never heard before! You'll never know what to expect! Listen . . . talk it up . . . MO 4-8660. The latest news, frequent time and temperature, helicopter traffic reports. Jerry Williams, 6–10 A.M. Mon–Sat. The Talk of Chicago. WBBM Radio—780."

Morning work began on March 6. It was an adjustment—turning his normal day upside down, being in front of the news rather than reacting to it after a day of reflection. And the content parts of the show—"the Elements," as radio people call them—were always bumping up against him, cramping his style, interfering with his rhythm. First of all, there were big, weighty

CBS network newscasts taking a bite out of the top of the hour, where he would have preferred doing provocative stuff to grab people's attention. You couldn't forget the weather. And the guy in the helicopter with the traffic. And a lot of commercials.

Not that they had constructed the format to make Jerry crazy. This was reality. The standard radio wisdom was (and is) that you had to deliver news, weather, sports, and traffic frequently to make sure you were serving the folks tuning in, getting coffee, showering, dressing the kids, driving to work, and so on. Listeners just don't have a lot of time or patience in the morning, and their attention span is limited. So Jerry's first three hours would have short interviews, a few calls, and the usual mix of information and spots breaking things up into small segments. At 9:00 he'd be able to stretch out, but only for an hour. At 10:00 he'd be done, the news would come on, and then it was Old Radio again—Arthur Godfrey and Art Linkletter.

The rest of the day didn't make much sense as talk radio, either—Freda Kehm was still hanging in with her child-care show. Mal Bellairs and Tom Clark did their noncontroversial daytime talk. John Callaway, now the station's news director, was trying to make *Newsday,* a news and feature show, an attractive option for afternoon drive. Early evening was a mess—a half hour of sports, an hour of *Ask a Banker,* commentary with Art Mercier, and finally Don Cannon to put the day to bed. For some reason, they stuck Ken Nordine's clever *Word Jazz* monologue show at 11:00 P.M. and then gave the night back to Jay Andres, the guy who'd been doing *Music 'til Dawn* since Eisenhower was in office.

They were calling it "total talk," but you needed a road map to figure out what was going to happen from minute to minute. The signs weren't good.

Still, he got some good press out of it. And a surprise—a personal note from Howard Miller himself. No matter what Jerry thought of Miller's politics, this was a classy gesture. Miller wrote: "Welcome to the land of the living dead! . . . I was tuned to your show last night when you made the announcement. . . . Any performer who wants identification must seek out the maximum tune-in hours, and in our media [*sic*] that is ONLY 6–10 A.M. . . . I'll look forward to seeing you at breakfast after March 6th . . . at Pixley's on Ohio. I'll introduce you to all the cops, purple boys, ladies of the night and lousy coffee!"

Just twelve shows into the new morning gig, the American Federation of Television and Radio Artists, the nation's biggest union of broadcast talent, called for an announcers' strike against the big networks and the stations they owned. Since Jerry was a dues-paid-up AFTRA member and CBS owned WBBM, he had to walk. For two weeks the strike went on, at exactly the wrong time for him to establish himself in his new role. The ad campaign was wasted. The build-up momentum in the press might as well have been forgotten.

Len Schlosser, the program director, was pressed into service as Jerry's sub. He had no idea how to do a morning show or controversial talk. And he sure as hell wasn't going to discuss the strike. To make matters worse, neither WGN nor WIND was affected by the strike, so Jerry's competition continued to broadcast as usual. Jerry had to listen sourly in Glencoe as Wally Phillips merrily offered to set up a soup line for the strikers.

Exactly in the middle of the time Jerry was off the air, on April 4, Martin Luther King gave one of the crucial addresses of his life, his definitive statement of opposition to the war in Vietnam. Before a crowd of almost four thousand people at Riverside Church in New York, he declared: "I could never again raise my voice against the violence of the oppressed in the ghettos without having first spoken clearly to the greatest purveyor of violence in the world today—my own government. . . . Somehow this madness must cease." Jerry was stuck in his mansion, without a mic to talk about it or money coming in.

The strike finally was settled, and Jerry was back on April 11, a little more than a month after the morning show had started.

There's only one word for the following six months: weird. It was the only time that Jerry Williams hosted a morning radio talk show, and it was wrong for him almost from the first minute. If he hadn't already been a Star, if this were a small market where he could try out ideas with relative impunity, if management wasn't constantly looking over Jerry's shoulder, if New York management wasn't constantly looking over Chicago management's shoulder . . . maybe he could have eventually made it work. But the scorekeeping and second-guessing started immediately, and Jerry became a cork bobbing on the CBS ocean.

Despite fair-to-middling ratings for the new morning show, there was a sea change in New York that made Jerry's performance almost irrelevant. Some time that summer, Bill Paley, the chairman of CBS, heard a rumor that Westinghouse's Chicago station, WIND, was going to go all-news. At first, this seemed hard to understand. WIND was the station with the commanding morning lead, the station with Howard Miller. But Paley decided he couldn't ignore the whispers. Three years earlier, he'd watched skeptically as Westinghouse's New York station, WINS, converted to all-news, only the third station in the country to try this new idea. At first, that seemed a foolish risk—who would listen to the same news stories recycled hour after hour? But Westinghouse made it work. They had research showing that radio use was changing, that people wanted to have a station they could depend on for news and information twenty-four hours a day. Paley's WCBS, boasting some of the world's greatest radio journalists and a huge news budget, had to eat WINS's dust. So Paley did not ignore the hints from Chicago. He decided that WBBM would beat WIND to the punch. WBBM would be Chicago's news station, no matter how high the Chicago staff had to jump and how fast they had to run.

Jerry who?

Jerry Who was kept out of the loop, and there's some evidence that the plan was so hush-hush that not even top Chicago management knew what Paley wanted. In early August Jerry saw a disquieting squib in Herb Lyon's column: there were "racy trade rumors" that CBS corporate planned "major local brass changes," a WBBM shift to all-news, and Jerry's return to nights. Ernie Shomo was quoted as "flatly" denying the rumors, but he must have seen what was coming. A month later he had found himself another job and Bill O'Donnell was the new vice president and general manager of WBBM. There was handwriting on the wall, but Jerry chose not to read it.

After all, he'd been delivering some pretty good shows. That was the Summer of Love, the summer of the riots, and the summer of the Six-Day War. He'd had State Senator Paul Simon speaking out on Vietnam, Lerone Bennett of *Ebony* reviewing black history, and Robert Lucas of Chicago's CORE talking about civil rights. The show had plenty of star power, with some of the biggest names in comedy dropping by—young talent from Chicago's Second City, his fellow Brooklynite Pat Cooper, the team of Jerry Stiller and Anne Meara, even Steve Allen and Jerry Lewis. He got so comfortable as a morning personality that he called Wally Phillips on the air, and for a few minutes WGN and WBBM were semi-simulcasting.

The nonradio career was flying high, too. He'd had almost thirty speaking engagements in those six months. He'd won awards from a local branch of the NAACP and the City of Hope. He'd been to a benefit event at Hugh Hefner's house. He was a guest on Irv Kupcinet's TV show. He'd been signed to do a character part in a play—a dinner theater production of George S. Kaufman's *The Butter and Egg Man,* starring Tom Poston, at the Ivanhoe. Best of all, he'd had the chance to fill in as a TV host, and the folks at Channel 2 had made noises about having him on the tube regularly.

But the pendulum had already swung. By the middle of September 1967, just six months after Jerry had moved to mornings, just about the time he turned forty-four, the word came down from the new vice president, Bill O'Donnell: the station was going all-news in the mornings. Jerry would return to the old stand at night—which would now be a four-hour show, running until midnight—and they were moving Don Cannon to afternoons.

*Jerry Williams interviews Jerry Lewis in the WBBM studios, Chicago, ca. May
1967. Lewis is demonstrating his ability to catch a cigarette in midair.*
"PHOTOGRAPHY BY ERNEST"

He had a month of transition time. As always, he put a good face on it for
the listeners. No one cares about your troubles—they've got problems of their
own. Yes, it was a shame he didn't have more time to prove himself in the
mornings. And those TV shows, which he considered such a good opportunity to show off his talent in another medium, hadn't worked out so well—the
phones died during the first one, and he never had the time to get comfortable
under the lights. Another blow: working nights again meant that he couldn't
do that play, and who knows when he'd get another chance to do something
like that?

But life goes on, and you have to roll with the punches.

On October 23, when Jerry went back to nights, he hit the air at 8:00 P.M.
as if there were no place else he'd rather be. That first week, Paul Fanning
(now producing both his show and Cannon's in the afternoons) scored an
interview for him with Bobby Kennedy, who was accompanied by Dick
Schaap, the author of his biography, *RFK*. Of course, Kennedy wouldn't say
whether he was running for president, but he had plenty to talk about—misgivings about the war, the need to do more to alleviate poverty and hunger and
racism in America, the legacy of his brother.

In March the noise of CBS's internal politics got louder and louder. The
rumors wouldn't stop. John Callaway was elevated from news director to program director. Even the engineers were saying that CBS must be planning to
go all-news. Nearly every day, Don Cannon or Jerry would walk into Callaway's

office. What do you hear? When is it happening? Callaway had been sworn to secrecy, and he had to keep lying. No one knew that his own show, the Sunday night program that he'd been so proud of, was going to get the axe as well.

In mid-March Gene McCarthy turned in a surprisingly strong showing against Johnson in the New Hampshire primary, not beating him but showing how powerful the antiwar movement was becoming. Bobby Kennedy was in it as soon as he saw that LBJ was vulnerable. At the end of March Johnson pulled out. The Democratic Convention, coming to Chicago in just a few months, looked like it was going to be a free-for-all.

Two days before Johnson made his announcement, Bill O'Donnell called Jerry into his office. Then he called Don Cannon into his office. Then the two about-to-be-out-of-work talk show hosts went out to lunch. What're you gonna do, Jerry? I dunno. What're you gonna do, Don?

Six weeks' notice.

After Johnson's announcement, there was euphoria on the left for four days. On April 4 Martin Luther King Jr. was murdered in Memphis.

Jerry was winding down his Chicago show as the city's black neighborhoods (like those in more than ninety other communities around the country) exploded. Nine were killed. Twenty blocks were devastated by fire. A few days later, Mayor Daley let it be known that he would brook no more disturbances in his city, and ordered the police "to shoot to kill any arsonist and to shoot to maim or cripple anyone looting."

Many people in the black community, who valued Jerry's show because it featured a white man who was outspoken about civil rights, felt that WBBM ought to reconsider its decision, especially considering the tension in the city. They launched a petition drive. A young woman named Wilma Phipps pushed the petitions, and she even became a kind of spokesperson in the effort to save Jerry's show. CBS stood firm.

But Jerry had already made his peace with the changes. He appreciated the support of his listeners and thanked them repeatedly on the air, but he knew there was no chance to turn things around. Yeah, he said to himself, he was up to his neck in debt and he'd soon be out of a job. But there were important things to talk about on the radio. He knew that the best legacy he could leave Chicago would be serious discussion of the state of the country, the next steps for black Americans, the war, the next president. So he dug into the issues and put the personal stuff aside.

One week before the end, antiwar protestors mounted a demonstration in the city that was bigger than anything seen during the civil rights marches, and the crowds were of a different stripe—younger, wilder, scarier to the forces supposed to keep order. Mayor Daley knew that there were a lot of unpredictable radicals among the eight thousand protestors. It was necessary for the police to keep order. Some people described what happened as a police riot. From Saturday night through Monday night, people who'd been in the crowd called Jerry, John Callaway, and Don Cannon with stories of merciless brutality. The controversial style for which WBBM had become known might be sputtering out, but people still wanted that forum. They still wanted to share while there was a vehicle available to do so.

Finally, on Saturday, May 4, it was time for the last show.

He pulled out a 1942 piece written by the *Daily News* columnist Howard Vincent O'Brien. The *Daily News* had reprinted it because of Vietnam, and Jerry had read it on the air a couple of times. It was published originally as "So Long, Son," but it also became known as "On Seeing a Son Go Off to War." He read:

There was no band, no flags, no ceremonial. It wasn't even dramatic. A car honked outside and he said, "Well, I guess that's for me." He picked up his little bag, and his mother said, "You haven't forgotten your gloves?"

He kissed his mother, and held out his hand to me. "Well, so long," he said. I took his hand but all I could say was "Good luck!"

The door slammed and that was that—another boy gone to war. . . .

I sat down and thought how time had flown. Why, it was only yesterday when I had held him in my arms! . . . I thought, too, of that last inarticulate "good luck," that last perfunctory handclasp; and I wished that I had somehow been able to tell him how much I really loved him.

Had he perhaps penetrated my brusque reserve?

. . . Well, curlyhead, you're a man now, bearing your bright new shield and spear. I hated to see you go out of my house and close the door behind you, but I think I would not have halted you if I could. I salute you, sir. I cannot pretend that I am not sad; but I am proud, too. So long.

As he read, he thought about his own father's brusque reserve, his own years at war. He took a pause. He reminded his listeners that O'Brien's son Donel had died in combat a few months after the column was written. He said that the heartache of parents seeing their sons go off to war is always the same, no matter how noble the cause. He asked them to consider whether the suffering of Vietnam parents was going to be worth it. And, finally, he said good-bye.

On Sunday, May 5, 1968, for the first time in ten years, Jerry Williams was out of a job.

He had been making more than a thousand dollars a week. It wasn't top money in radio, but it was a very good living. To make that kind of money now, you'd have to get more than five grand every Friday. When you add the extra cash he got from speaking engagements and adjust the total for inflation, Jerry was making more than $330,000 a year in today's dollars.

It really hurt. Although he never thought that his knock-'em-dead success of 1965 and 1966 would continue forever, the wind had shifted brutally. As long as the money was coming in, Jerry could easily afford his big house in Glencoe. But that mortgage was going to be a serious problem very soon. Teri loved the house, with its ample square footage for their growing collection of antiques. Jerry told her they had no choice. WGN was putting a talk format on the air, but they had decided it would be "noncontroversial," and they told Jerry he wasn't going to fit in. A few other calls proved that there was no place for him to go in the Midwest that wouldn't be a big step down in prestige and money. He had to change cities.

The next day, Monday, he opened the *Sun-Times* and saw a farewell column from Roger Ebert, the film critic. Ebert had been on the show a couple of times, out to the house for a party, even been a guest on Cannon's show. The headline showed how significant Ebert and the headline writer thought the format change was: "Demise of Talk Radio Is Graceful, but Sad"—as if "talk radio" could only be the controversial style that Jerry had made so popular.

Ebert was a fine writer, Jerry thought. This would sound good on the air . . . oh, wait.

It had been a noble experiment, and a successful one. . . . When *Daily News* columnist Mike Royko suggested, jokingly, that the listeners buy Williams a radio station, some even sent in dollars. Williams forwarded the money to Martin Luther King's SCLC, a typical gesture. . . .

WBBM's talkers sought and encouraged controversy. The phone-in format permitted the citizens of the city to talk to each other publicly, and in a time of racial tension and a breakdown in communication between the leaders and the led, that was good. . . .

When the police attacked the peace marchers on April 27, Chicago news media didn't adequately report the story. But dozens of WBBM callers gave eyewitness testimony on Saturday, Sunday and Monday, and by Tuesday [April 30] the police behavior was a public scandal. . . .

On his last program . . . Williams was optimistic . . . but his callers were not. Some wept over the telephone. Some joked. A few were old regulars, calling in to say goodbye. Sidney Lens, the radical peace worker, called in. So did

Paul Powell, the Secretary of State. So did Sam Braverman, whose corned beef sandwiches Williams often extolled. . . .

The all-news format . . . will not, I believe, be able to express the great democratic voice of the city as the talk format did. We will not hear that voice again.

Thanks, Roger. Thanks a lot.

He worked the phones from Glencoe during the day—every contact he had in every major market. He knew it was good to have as many offers as possible for his services, the better to play station managements against each other. And one thing in his favor was that no one in radio ever considered losing a job to be a black mark. Jerry had a great story to tell. His numbers were strong; it was just that the station was going all-news.

He had some nibbles in San Francisco and Miami. He considered going back to Philadelphia. And there was serious interest in Boston.

Jerry talked with Jim Lightfoot, who had just taken over as general manager of WBZ Radio. Jerry liked WBZ's huge radio signal—one of the earliest in American broadcasting, a clear channel on 1030 that allowed the station to reach thirty-eight states at night, as big a reach as WBBM's. Even more, Jerry liked the idea that WBZ also had a TV station with major-network affiliation—and that Westinghouse's radio-television combo was one of the leaders on both sides of the Boston market. He wanted to maintain his presence on a signal at least as good as WBBM's, and he wanted the chance to do television on his own terms. A deal with BZ could put him in the right place to do them both.

But KABC in Los Angeles made a hard offer first. KABC was a pioneering talk station—in the early sixties, when it was known at KLAC, the station manager, Ben Hoberman, had taken it "all talk," even though Joe Pyne was really the only classic talker they had at first. The station had an opening after Joe's show—the execs thought that Jerry might be the guy to fire up their late nights. Jack Meyers, KABC's program manager, pitched him, and Jerry weighed the prospect of a sunny February out west against that of a gray New England winter. On the one hand, coming home to a heated pool; on the other, unpredictable nor'easters casually dumping a foot of snow in his driveway. Southern California was very appealing.

They came to terms in just a few weeks. Myers said they couldn't match what he was getting in Chicago. It would be $800 a week, a 20 percent cut in his base salary. But there were some good incentives—a piece of the ad revenue the show brought in, and 50 percent of the syndication profits if KABC decided to take the show national. KABC's lawyers drew up the signature copies of the contract. Jack Meyers wrote Jerry an enthusiastic cover note, looking forward to helping him and Teri find a house in the area. His secretary put everything in an envelope and mailed it on the morning of June 5, 1968.

That night Robert F. Kennedy won the California Democratic primary. He went to the Hotel Ambassador in Los Angeles for a victory party, and Sirhan Sirhan killed him.

Meyers got on the phone to Jerry the next day. Maybe they'd have to put things on hold for a bit—not too long, but who could say what was going to happen? Jerry couldn't wait. He had to sell his house. He had to get settled somewhere else so the kids could start school properly in the fall. If the country was going to explode, he needed to be on the air. And he knew that his people in Boston, mourning another Kennedy, needed him more than those strangers in LA ever would.

At least he had a draft contract he could use for leverage. He called Jim Lightfoot again.

7   BOSTON AGAIN

A jaunty-looking person, . . . evidently a stranger, said . . . , "This was what I heard: 'Boston['s] State-House is the hub of the solar system.' " . . .

"Sir," said I, "I am gratified with your remark. . . . The satire . . . is essentially true of Boston, and of all other . . . places with which I have had the privilege of being acquainted."

—*Oliver Wendell Holmes*, The Autocrat of the Breakfast-Table

Jerry and Lightfoot danced. Jerry wanted more than just radio—a TV show had to be part of the deal. Lightfoot would do what he could, but he had no authority on the other side of the building. Yes, they were planning to bounce Tom Kennedy to make room for Jerry, and yes, Tom was doing morning TV on WBZ-TV as well, so they could cut him loose from both gigs at the same time. Jerry said, "Gotta have TV." Jim said, "I'll talk to Win Baker, the TV GM." The final deal: a two-hour radio show on WBZ from 10:00 P.M. to midnight, Monday through Friday, plus a TV tryout (a color broadcast, Jer, to show off those new suits and ties) from 9:00 to 10:00 A.M., to be produced by Jerry's WBBM colleague Paul Fanning. He wouldn't be getting much sleep.

When Jerry finally saw the cold language of the new contract, he was disappointed. It said nothing about the actual number of hours on the air. It had no specifics, radio or TV. He was simply designated a "staff announcer," required to work up to thirty-five hours a week, as Westinghouse determined. There was no share of advertising revenue. There was no guarantee of a piece of syndication—in fact, no mention of syndication at all. And BZ could get out, no strings attached, at the end of each year of the contract. What could he do? He signed for the same money KABC had offered him—$800 a week—but with fewer perks and fewer guarantees.

Comparing his last payday at WBBM with his first payday at WBZ and adjusting for inflation, he was swallowing nearly a 25 percent cut in income. Westinghouse agreed to guarantee an escalation of his salary each year over the five years of his new contract, but it wouldn't make up for lost ground or inflation. By 1973 he would still be making fewer dollars than he had been making when he left WBBM in 1968.

Teri packed up the kids and the antiques and got temporarily settled in the Sonesta Hotel in Cambridge (on BZ's nickel), and began looking at houses in the Boston area. Jerry transported his cherished 1957 Chrysler 300-C convertible personally. As he drove through Ohio, New York, and Massachusetts, he had hours to think. He was confident about the radio program—because he would be on the air deep into the night, the show would have national reach throughout the year. That meant he could concentrate on the national issues there: the war, civil rights, and the 1968 presidential race. Both of the party conventions were coming up fast—the Republicans' show would be in the first week of August (his second week on the air) and the Democrats' at the end of that month.

The big challenge was the new television show. He needed to define what it was going to do, how it should be positioned. Mid-morning was still housewife time, soft TV time, but he didn't want to do a schmoozy, chummy show. He would make it as hard as TV management would permit. Because the show wasn't yet going to air outside the market, it would necessarily have a local focus—he could pick up where he'd left off with Bay State politics and regular-folks-versus-big-government issues. Race was hot in Boston, too. There were riots in Roxbury that summer, and Louise Day Hicks was more visible than ever as a symbol of white resistance to school integration.

As soon as the promotion started in early July, WBZ heard from Mac and his brothers, who still owned WMEX. That damn termination agreement had come back to bite him in the ass. The Richmonds said that Jerry had agreed not to work in Boston radio again until October 1970, and they filed an injunction to stop him from going on the air. The briefs flew.

The Westinghouse legal staff told the judge that the noncompete clause was onerous and that WMEX would suffer no harm as a result of Jerry's new show on WBZ radio. Jerry's lawyer, Irving Sheff, concentrated on the $4,000 in commissions and expenses that Mac still owed Jerry—he told the judge that was a breach of the contract, and as a result, the noncompete clause was invalid.

Of course, all the lawyers knew that enough compen$ation from Westinghouse to the Richmonds would make the matter go away, but WBZ had no intention of paying any more for Jerry than was absolutely necessary. So the three sets of attorneys went to court on Thursday, July 25, 1968; Jerry was scheduled to debut on BZ the following Monday. The judge said that the Richmonds couldn't stop Jerry from going on the air, but he'd let the matter go to trial.

Ironically, the lawsuit cemented Jerry's relationship with WBZ. The Westinghouse lawyers had put a clause in a side letter that would allow them to can him immediately "in the event that any action is brought against us and/or you by the Richmond Brothers, Inc." But the ads touting Jerry's show were in the newspapers. To cut bait would mean a huge public relations mess for Westinghouse. In a weird way he felt secure, at least for the moment. But if the judge upheld the noncompete clause, he had no doubt that he would be out on the street in a heartbeat.

Jim Lightfoot couldn't worry about a lawsuit that probably wouldn't be in court for months. He had a radio station to run, and he wanted Jerry Williams to start off right. Lightfoot had a talk with Jerry Wishnow, Jerry's producer-to-be. Lightfoot told Wishnow that Jerry was a tough customer, and it was up to him to stand in for management and rein in Jerry's self-indulgences. Lightfoot told Wishnow that he needed Jerry's debut to be big, with special guests. Wishnow could even spend some money for travel and hotel stays if that was necessary.

On July 29, 1968, the Beatles recorded the first tracks of what would become "Hey Jude" at Abbey Road Studios in London. The Vatican released Pope Paul VI's encyclical *Humanae Vitae*, which condemned the use of condoms, diaphragms, the Pill, and other artificial devices for birth control. The leaders of the USSR, Leonid Brezhnev and Alexsei Kosygin, met with Alexander Dubček of Czechoslovakia; they criticized him for allowing "democratization" in his country and thus paved the way for a Soviet invasion. Minnesota students founded the American Indian Movement. Jefferson Airplane played a concert in San Francisco. There were riots in Seattle following a police raid on an office of the Black Panther Party.

In Vietnam, Lieutenant Douglas Orvis, Sergeant Alfred Davies, Sergeant Terry Robinson, and Sergeant Willard Pack were killed by gunshots from guerilas hiding in concealed positions on a hilltop in the Hai Lang district of Quang Tri province. Private Michael Glasford died as a result of shrapnel wounds in Thua Thien Province, west of Hue. Staff Sergeant Jerry Auxier was lost in action, probably as a result of a booby-trap bomb, northwest of the city of Tam Ky.

Jerry Williams's first WBZ television show ran at 9:00 A.M. that day. That night, the guests for his first radio show were the raconteur Henry Morgan at 10:00 and Muhammad Ali at 11:00.

When forty-four-year-old Jerry Williams said "Hello, America" for the first time into a WBZ microphone, there was no one in the country better at talk radio. Larry King had a nice little career going in Miami, dividing his time among radio, TV, and a newspaper column. Don Imus was just two months into his first radio job, at KUTY in Palmdale, California. No one in broadcasting had yet heard of Bill O'Reilly, who was between his first and second years at Marist College in Poughkeepsie, New York, considering a teaching career. Rush Limbaugh III was about to be a senior at Cape Central High School in Cape Girardeau, Missouri. And a kid named Howard Stern was counting the days before he entered high school in Jackson Heights, New York.

If you were making lists of star talkers in 1968, you'd be hard pressed to find more than a handful with a national reputation. Barry Gray would be there, simply because he was on a New York station with a huge reach. Long John Nebel was well established in syndication, his bailiwick still confined to the weird and wacky. Jack Eigen was doing a sort of offshoot of the restaurant-celebrity style he'd pioneered in New York when Jerry was working in Philly, but he styled himself more "controversial" now and cultivated the image of a swinger. Joe Pyne had become a syndicated TV star, a nasty carnival barker skewering the freaks brave enough to appear with him. And the hip crowd lionized Jean Shepherd, not yet the author and narrator of "A Christmas Story," a guy who simply went on the air and talked about his youth, his life, the people he met, the things he saw, digressing and digressing and yet always tying things up in the last seconds of each show.

If you were making lists, you had to include Jerry Williams, no matter how he had left Chicago. This guy had been a huge star in two major markets, and he had built his rep on issues, the hardest talk medium of all. Long ago Jerry had figured out the answers to all the questions the new talkers were wrestling with, and he'd proven that he could bring in ratings and revenue as well.

By this time in radio history, the talk show was well established as an idea, but it had a lot of growing to do. Younger hosts and radio managers were grappling with the relatively new issues it had generated. What was the host's proper role—an active advocate, a contrarian, a moderator? How should a host deal with the Fairness Doctrine and the Personal Attack Rule and Equal Time, provisions in the FCC regs that were still so broadly defined that no one really knew how to apply them? And, if you were a program director trying to keep your talent in line, how did you get the hosts to follow your lawyers' interpretations of the rules?

Jerry had already thought this stuff through. His goal wasn't to muzzle contrary opinion, but to provoke it. Lively public discourse and the clash of ideas made for good theater. Throughout his years at WBZ he made what he did perfect, but the rest of the business gradually caught up to him.

Studio Z, where Jerry would spend the next eight years of his working life, was drab, like the one at WBBM, but smaller. It was about seventeen feet square, with blue industrial carpeting like that in the BZ hallway, a no-nonsense table, functional chairs for the guests, and a better-than-average office chair (adjustable) for the host. No logo, no fashion, no style. It was consistent with a principle of Westinghouse broadcast (or "Group W," if you preferred the new corporate identity) management: if there wasn't some demonstrable benefit to the bottom line, you could live without it.

In the control room Wishnow put the first hour's commercials in order, matching them against those scheduled on the program log. Because of strict union rules, the only technical devices he could touch were the black producer's phone (sporting a set of four call buttons and a red "hold" key) and the intercom that allowed Jerry to talk to the control room when his mic was off. As they closed in on 10:00 P.M., he took his place in the producer's chair and began talking to people calling the station's talk line. Jerry had already begun laying down the law to Wishnow: "This is a national show, so put anyone who's calling from outside the area at the head of the line—the farther away they're calling from, the faster they should get on the air."

Precisely at 10:05:00, the newscaster finished his copy, and the show began. The first thing listeners heard was a low buzz, like an old-fashioned telephone dial tone. Then a voice emerged, fading up to full volume: "2-5-4-5-6-7-8. 2-5-4-5-6-7-8. 2-5-4-5-6-7-8." Finally, there was a snippet of music that repeated and repeated until Jerry's voice finally came in over it. "Hello, America! This is Jerry Williams."

Bob Oakes, the production director, had prepared the opening especially for Jerry, following Lightfoot's instructions for something dramatically different from the canned music themes that were used for almost all show intros at the time. Lightfoot drummed his fingers on his desk, repeating the on-air phone number rhythmically. Oakes liked what he heard, so he recorded Lightfoot saying the phone number and added the telephone sound effects. He capped it with the voice of WBZ's newsman Gary LaPierre saying the number at full volume. It was a great attention getter.

Jerry had a private guideline for a good interview: if possible, feel superior to your guest. He imagined that it was going to be hard to live up to that standard in his first encounter with Henry Morgan, his childhood idol, the monologuist who demonstrated by example how much fun it was to break the rules of radio. Fortunately, Morgan cut himself down to size that evening by showing up tipsy and getting even drunker when Wishnow took him out to dinner. That gave Jerry all the edge he needed. After his opening hellos to all those old Bostonian listeners, he got into a friendly rhythm with his guest, prompting Morgan into acerbic remarks about contemporary mores and sharp reminiscences about his iconoclastic broadcasts before the war—even if his guest did get a little testy when reminded of his age.

Muhammad Ali was on the phone during the second hour. That conversation turned out to be more serious than the interviews they'd done in Chicago, since Ali was now fighting for respect as a conscientious objector to the war in Vietnam. He'd gone on the record with "No Viet Cong ever called me nigger," and he'd then been stripped of his title and livelihood for acting on his beliefs as a member of the Nation of Islam. That gave Jerry the chance to hit race and the war in the same hour.

Then it was midnight. Jerry thanked Ali, thanked Henry Morgan in absentia, thanked his listeners for their attention. In the last seconds, he signed off with the words he'd used in Chicago and on WMEX: "Good night, good luck, good morning, good night, T."

At the end of the following week, after a few days of orderly suspense covered live by WBZ Radio, the Republicans nominated Richard Nixon in Miami Beach, along with his handpicked candidate for vice president, the governor of Maryland, a political unknown named Spiro Agnew.

A few weeks later, the Democrats gathered in Chicago for their convention and BZ provided a week of live coverage once again. Inside the convention hall there was a political struggle of a new stripe, at least by twentieth-century American standards. The Gene McCarthy–George McGovern forces looked scruffy and unruly. Humphrey's crowd looked tired and old. Mayor Richard Daley's police, acting as security for the convention, sought to impose order in their inimitable way, and they roughed up a young reporter named Dan Rather as they were giving him the bum's rush out of the hall. Outside the building, there was revolution or something like it in the streets. Abbie Hoffman, Jerry Rubin, Daley, and the Chicago cops became fixtures on television.

Jerry followed it minute-by-minute, watching the TV coverage with horror and fascination. Chicago was a world away from him professionally now, and yet it felt intimately close. Something about the ranks of police and the unruly kids was profoundly disturbing. He began asking a question on the air that he would repeat over and over again for years: "What is happening to this country?"

Within Jerry's first couple of months at WBZ, he found out that his old friend Larry Glick, the guy who'd done the all-night show on WMEX, had parted company with Mac Richmond. Glick had a six-month noncompete deal with WMEX. While he waited it out, performing around town in nightclubs with a hypnosis act, Jerry pitched him hard to Lightfoot. Listen, we should get this guy over here. People love him. He's got a five-year track record, so he'll start with built-in numbers. You think Long John's got a following? Wait 'til Glick gets on a clear channel station like BZ.

Lightfoot pondered. People love him? We can use that. Let's give the guy a shot for a few months. We'll put it out that we might hire him full-time if our listeners like him. So, as soon as Glick was free of Mac's clutches, BZ put him on the air. We're giving Larry Glick a tryout, folks. Whaddya think?

All the old Glickshtick moved right over to 1030, and the regulars came with it. The word went out among the Glickniks. People started piling into the BZ parking lot with signs, chanting and cheering, "Hire Larry Glick!"

Which didn't really matter to Lightfoot. Almost as soon as he heard Glick work, he knew: this guy was one great air talent. They came to terms well before the end of the trial period, but Lightfoot let the picketing go on right up to the last day. Then—the people have spoken! WBZ picks up Glick!

It was like old times for Jerry, finishing up his shift and walking into the DJ booth where Glick did his show, standing up like the daytime jocks, Carl DeSuze, Dave Maynard, and Larry Justice. If Jerry was feeling good, there'd be some back-and-forth banter. If Jerry was in a foul mood, he'd just wave good night.

He went home to another grand house, a forty-room place he and Teri had found in Milton, Massachusetts. Milton was not as tony a suburb as Glencoe, and the new house was not as splendidly isolated as his old one was. It was on Blue Hill Avenue, a street that led toward the city and got rougher and rougher the closer you got. Still, that was another Wow House.

The Chicago antiques took their places. Teri set up each room carefully. They hired some live-in help. The kids got into school. As the foliage season arrived, he took the family on excursions to New Hampshire and Vermont, looking for bargains in the antiques stores, introducing the kids to the Old Man of the Mountain, rediscovering the unmidwestern scenery, the classic churches, the village greens, the country stores, the pleasures of driving in New England. It was boring for the kids, but he needed to do it, to reestablish himself in that old environment.

September 24, his forty-fifth birthday, came and went. He was middle-aged, no denying it, even if he hated the idea.

During those first few months, it quickly became clear that his TV show was running on empty. Paul Fanning hadn't made friends with BZ management, and he wasn't coming up with the kind of exciting guests Jerry wanted. In fact, BZ had asked Wishnow to bail Fanning out and take a hand in producing the TV program as well as the radio show, and the two producers did not get along. To make matters worse, Jerry's vision and on-air style didn't fit with management's ideas. By Election Day, Jerry was done as a TV host. Baker was businesslike, but firm—no hard feelings, it's just not working out.

Jim Lightfoot was conciliatory. The radio show would be expanded, adding two hours so that Jerry would be on from 8:00 P.M. to midnight. It would be the centerpiece of WBZ's nighttime programming. Jerry would still have a lot of flexibility in his personal life, because hockey and basketball games would cut the show in half on many nights in the winter and spring. Lightfoot said he could prerecord commercials to be used in the sports broadcasts, so that he wouldn't have to be physically inside the building to be announcer on duty.

Jerry stormed. They hadn't given the TV show enough time. And all those sports broadcasts were ridiculous: day-to-day pacing would be destroyed; listeners wouldn't be able to depend on him. If Lightfoot really wanted Jerry Williams for four hours, can the sports and let him make something happen. Jerry didn't give a shit what they did with the games—they could put them on their FM station, for all he cared.

Lightfoot said he wanted Jerry to work with it. He said they should see how it goes, keep talking, check in after a few months for another heart-to-heart talk.

Jerry was furious, and he let Wishnow know it. He felt trapped. He didn't want to be filling the evening hours as an afterthought to sports. He never would have taken the WBZ job if the TV show hadn't been part of it. And Nixon was going to be president. He fumed and stewed for a month.

Eventually, the old routine reestablished itself—reading the papers in his home office in the morning, practicing material for the air, barely acknowledging the kids, grimacing at interruptions from their friends, going into BZ in the afternoon for a while to catch up on mail, coming in as close to 8:00 P.M. as possible, working until midnight. He worked to differentiate himself from the growing number of Boston talkers, zeroing in on issues and sparking controversy whenever he could. And he got some unexpected help from the community service projects created by Jerry Wishnow.

It wasn't that Wishnow or Jim Lightfoot woke up one morning and decided to make WBZ a paragon of issue-oriented promotion. The two shared an ideal of station service, and Lightfoot thought stationwide campaigns were a great way to give unity to the station's music-and-news format. Wishnow, now sporting the title of Creative Services Director, came up with ideas and cultivated the area's most influential community leaders. The momentum built from the end of 1968 to fall 1973, as WBZ took a stationwide approach to one local issue after another—race relations, illegal drugs, physical fitness, auto pollution. Each campaign featured special programming, and Jerry's show was always central to the effort. Over time, what had been just another radio station became a kind of Good Corporate Citizen, sending out ripples in Boston broadcasting that are still felt today. Along the way, and partly because of those special efforts, it got huge ratings and made a ton of money.

The first campaign was a marathon discussion about race in Boston—an all-day affair modeled on the T-groups of the time, followed up by conversation on the Williams show. The second was an all-station mobilization during one of Boston's biggest blizzards—the first WBZ Storm Center. After that, Wishnow was expected to come up with something major every year. Whether he liked it or not, Jerry was on the team, and those campaigns got his name in the paper as more than just a rabble-rouser.

On January 13, 1969, Jerry's brother, Herbert, died of cancer at the age of fifty. The brothers weren't exactly estranged, but they had drifted apart. Herbert had put his business degree to work with the International Telephone and Telegraph Company, and he had prospered as Harold Geneen turned ITT into an international conglomerate. By the time Herbert became ill, he was living in Tenafly, New Jersey, with his family and had risen to become director of governmental negotiations for ITT's Space and Defense Group, the part of the company that was running the hotline from Washington to Moscow, the Defense Early Warning system, and other big-time projects. He was, in short, a straight arrow, a Responsible Character, a Contributor to Society. He had Samuel's respect. If you were writing his story, you would expect him to keep on rising in the company, get the gold watch, say the respectful words at his parents' gravesides, be surrounded by grandkids in retirement, pass away quietly in his bed. You wouldn't expect the smoking, stay-out-late, fool-around brother to be the one with the longer life.

Even though Jerry didn't talk to Herbert frequently, even though his kids were much closer to their maternal aunts and uncles and cousins, even though he resented Herbert's standing in his parents' eyes, he looked at the stone in the cemetery and felt more alone than he thought he'd ever been.

A year later, Jim Lightfoot was dead. He'd handed off running WBZ to Sy Yanoff, a more typical general manager out of the successful sales director mold. Bob Oakes was elevated to the position of program director. Lightfoot went West, ready to conquer new territory, maybe build a chain of radio stations, and then was cut down by disease. Lightfoot and he had had their run-ins, but Jerry really liked the guy—he was one of the few radio GMs who understood that programming was more than just a vehicle for advertising. A troupe of BZ people went out to California for the funeral. The shock of it hung over the station like a cloud.

The first three years of Nixon. The war's going to be over soon. Peace with Honor. Paris Peace Talks. Student strikes. The death of Ho Chi Minh. The My Lai massacre. The Pentagon Papers. The March on Washington. Four college students killed by National Guardsmen at Kent State University. George McGovern announces his candidacy for president. Lieutenant William Calley is tried for war crimes and convicted. A Vietnam veteran named John Kerry testifies before Congress, asking, "How do you ask a man to be the last man to die for a mistake?"

There was more than enough to talk about. Jerry read the articles, provoked discussion, became more and more an opponent of the war. He asked for someone to provide sensible reasons for the United States to fight this war now, questioned the wisdom of ever having gotten involved in what was really a civil war, detailed the amount of money being spent, reminded listeners that they were paying for it. Usually, he tempered his tone with sympathy for the kids being drafted against their will, the soldiers who were dying or coming home torn up, the families who were suffering the losses, and the people of Vietnam, whose country was gradually being destroyed.

There was a lot to cover in Boston over the same three years. Kevin White, the Mayah elected while Jerry was in Chicago, said he was going to turn Boston into a world-class city. Frank Sargent, a rangy Yankee, became governor. The city dedicated a grotesque new Boston City Hall, an incomprehensible building floating on a desolate stretch of barren brick—the last of the New Boston projects. Ted Kennedy drove his car off a bridge on Martha's Vineyard and a young woman drowned. Louise Day Hicks moved from the School Committee to the City Council, and then from City Council to U.S. Representative from Massachusetts. Mayor White ran for governor with a state rep named Michael Dukakis as candidate for lieutenant governor; they lost, and White went back to being mayor. Work began on the renovation of the Faneuil Hall Marketplace.

On slow news days, Jerry kept trying to roll those old boulders up the hill and watched them roll back down despite his best efforts. Boston driving—how can we stand it? These taxicabs—the city ought to be ashamed. The cost of gas. Property taxes and valuations—a system that didn't work before the Depression, and we're still using it today. The horrific parking situation downtown, and the gouging going on at parking garages!

As always, Jerry didn't know whether to laugh or rail.

Another drama continued off the air as the Richmonds' noncompete case crept through the Massachusetts court system. Finally, in 1969, they went to court. Jerry testified, Mac testified, and finally Superior Court Justice James C. Roy ruled that the Richmonds had been unreasonable in their noncompete restrictions on Jerry. He dismissed the case with prejudice. But the Richmonds appealed.

In January 1970 the Supreme Judicial Court of Massachusetts, the highest court in the commonwealth, agreed to hear the case. Two months later the decision came down. Judge Jacob J. Spiegel wrote, "We are of the opinion that the restrictive covenant in the 1965 contract is no longer reasonably necessary for the protection of the plaintiff's business."

When Jerry had a chance to read the decision, he especially liked Judge Spiegel's quote from a 1916 case, *Herbert Morris, Ltd. v. Saxelby:* "A man's aptitudes, his skill, his dexterity, his manual or mental ability . . . are not his master's property; they are his own property; they are himself."

Have a nice life, Mac. Good-bye forever.

Jerry kept refining, polishing. He stimulated "comment and controversy," as WMEX used to say. If he felt strongly about an issue, he cited others who took that position, such as Jack Anderson and other outspoken columnists. When he questioned a policy, he asked provocative rhetorical questions on the air addressed to the mayor or the governor or the president, implying that the big shots were always welcome to come on the show and defend themselves. He mixed it up with callers, giving them plenty of air time and using their contrary opinions to sharpen the focus of discussion. Because of the chances he had taken and the skills he had mastered over more than fifteen years, he always felt that he was staying within the guidelines set down for broadcasters by the FCC, even in the heat of an argument. But his point of view was far from settled policy.

When Jerry began at BZ, the FCC was looking over broadcasters' shoulders more carefully than it does today. Under the Personal Attack Rule, if a public figure was attacked by name on the air, the station had to give the public figure time to respond to the attack. Under the Fairness Doctrine, stations had to "afford reasonable opportunity for the discussion of conflicting views of public importance."

The rules affecting content were set aside by the FCC in 1987, but they were very much alive during Jerry's BZ years. Broadcasters hated and feared them, especially since the FCC wasn't afraid to levy reprimands, fines, suspensions, and losses of license against transgressors. Prodded by the attorneys trying to protect the value of their clients' holdings, owners and hosts in radio and television were looking over their shoulders constantly, worried that the FCC might pounce on them for a thoughtless word. The bigger the station, the bigger the revenue. The more there was to lose, the bigger management's apprehension.

No one got very intellectual about it back then, but the fact is that the FCC's approach to content was based on an understanding of the media that was essentially flawed. What's said on a single broadcast outlet just doesn't have much power in shaping public opinion. Sure, some people will believe anything that's on the air, but most folks are cherry pickers when it comes to the media. Even back in the earliest years of the twentieth century, when the first content rules were devised by the Federal Radio Commission, most Americans had many sources of information available to them. Broadcasting just took its place among them.

In Boston in 1968 there were three major daily papers and three television stations with nightly network newscasts. The leading radio stations, such as WBZ, tapped into robust international networks of reporters and editors—NBC, CBS, and ABC still had the staff to give radio a few substantive reports each day, and some veterans like Lowell Thomas were still doing nightly radio newscasts with a thoughtful approach, even though stations were starting to emphasize a faster, up-to-the-minute approach to the news. No radio station in Boston had yet opted for an all-news approach. "Educational radio" was still a haven for amateur announcers, classical music, and earnest but dull discussion; *All Things Considered* wasn't even under consideration.

Opinion leaders got their breaking news from the radio, their first comprehensive report from the network TV newscasts, and their details from the local paper the next morning. Many read *Time* and *Newsweek* and *U.S. News and World Report* to fill in the shape of the stories and to get perspective. Some Bostonians read the *New York Times* daily because they wanted more international news. Those who wanted additional depth in news reporting consulted the journals of opinion—*National Review,* the *New Republic,* the *Nation,* and others with particular slants. They knew that these publications provided information with an editorial point of view, but they also knew that the points of view were explicit and undisguised.

Americans wanted help sorting and sifting the news. That was where Jerry's show came in. His listeners wanted to learn details they'd missed. They wanted to hear from newsmakers and from people with valuable perspectives. They wanted to hear what Jerry had to say. They liked the action—Jerry's rhetoric, the fire, the combat with callers. And they wanted to weigh in, too.

Jerry knew from experience and instinct that listeners wanted a personality at the center. His success proved that an opinion-oriented approach (with a veneer of "public discourse") would easily trump neutrality. His way of working was consistently ahead of what people heard on other stations. As the seventies moved forward, the style that Jerry pioneered gradually became the norm in talk radio.

In 1971 Wishnow spearheaded something really ambitious—a comprehensive discussion of drug abuse and an attempt to reform the drug laws in Massachusetts. The Williams show was the sparkplug and centerpiece of the campaign.

Even though the local press and some skeptics inside WBZ scoffed at the idea of a lowly radio station having an influence on public policy, the campaign actually produced a draft drug law that incorporated some groundbreaking provisions suggested and shaped by Jerry's listeners. One woman said that drug offenders should work off their time in some sort of service to the community, something useful that would show them the effect of drugs on other people's lives. Others liked the idea that an offender's record of conviction might be expunged after he or she had served whatever penalty was appropriate. The drug law began a long slog through the mire of Massachusetts politics, emerging two and a half years later with both of those ideas still in place.

The drug campaign proved that radio *could* have an influence on public policy, and Jerry filed that lesson away for the future. Even so, he knew that the minor thrill of drafting a bill on the air evaporated in the tedium of governmental deliberation. To really mobilize the people, he knew you had to have a clear yes-or-no issue and a simple means of response, like those postcard polls he'd done during his WMEX days. And you needed an issue that had some resonance with the Little People.

Jerry's folks came to Boston to celebrate Thanksgiving (and Susan Williams's eleventh birthday) in November 1971. On Friday Samuel suddenly became ill and had to be taken to the hospital. On Monday he was dead.

Jerry's emotions about the old man were conflicted, to say the least. From him he had taken a love of radio, a fondness for puns and vaudeville jokes, a

Depression-era survivor's suspicion of the stock market, a small business-man's concern about bad deals and big competitors, a discreet pride in his Jewish heritage, an equally discreet pride in being an American, and a tire-less work ethic. They'd had their battles—over the family store, over his choice of career, over the girls he chose, over his spending. Worst of all was the man's reserve. Even after Jerry fought his way to success in Boston and stardom in Chicago, his father held back his praise. It always seemed to be criticism, except when the old man talked to others and Jerry heard it sec-ondhand. He's proud of you, you know. He thinks you're something.

So Jerry went to New Jersey for the services and stood by the grave with his mother. He cried. But he felt a little relieved, too.

Just a couple of weeks later, Jerry got the news about Mac Richmond. The same month as his father—death number four while he was at BZ. This time, though, it wasn't tragedy; it was farce. He and Glick laughed about outliving Mac. You would have thought the old bastard was immortal, the way he fought the WMEX staff for money. Jerry called MEX veterans all over the country with the news about Mac. They all cheered.

In January 1972 the Williams show finally got a new producer. Jerry had been bugging Bob Oakes, the program director, about it. Wishnow had been booking during the day and supervising directors at night, but that didn't give Jerry the kind of control he wanted. Network Ned Foster and the others who were screening the calls didn't care enough. He needed someone to work with him, to be part of the show.

Oakes kicked the problem around with the station's operations director, Clark Smidt. If they could find someone young and hungry, someone who would work cheap and work hard, they could keep Jerry quiet on this score, anyway. Smidt suggested Steve Elman, a grad student working at BZ part-time who'd helped get sound for the drug documentaries. Elman had shown he wasn't afraid of drudgery. He was helping to prepare some of the documenta-tion for the station's upcoming license renewal by listening to hours and hours of low-fidelity tapes of WBZ's FM station and doing scut work in the traffic department. He was already a known quantity. He'd seen Jerry in the hall and they knew each other well enough to nod hello.

If Jerry had any reaction to his new producer—twenty-four, long-haired, pudgy, owlish—he didn't show it. He said they'd get along fine and he'd show him the ropes. "You'll get it," he said. That was it. No orientation, no philosophy.

Oakes and Elman had a brief conversation, much like Lightfoot's talk with Wishnow when Jerry had been hired four years earlier. Jerry was something of a lone ranger. Elman should understand that he was management's guy. He would also have to monitor the content of the programs to make sure that WBZ was living up to the promises it had made the FCC, and prod Jerry into doing shows on some topics he might not be enthusiastic about, such as education, housing, and health care.

Elman didn't know Jerry's work or his rep or his importance. He was a big talent, sure, but just another talk show host—and hadn't that telephone call-in stuff been around forever? But by the end of the first month, George McGovern's staff had said "yes" immediately when he'd asked for an interview. He'd spoken with Jack Anderson, the muckraking columnist; Senators Ernest Gruening and Vance Hartke; the playwright Garson Kanin; and U.S. Representative John Ashbrook. And Jerry had been mentioned and quoted in a *Newsweek* profile of the nation's leading talk show hosts. Whoever Jerry Williams was, he was a lot bigger deal than Elman had thought. Even more, Elman was astonished by what he saw Jerry do night after night, interview after interview, call after call. He could create interesting radio as if by magic.

His monologues were especially thrilling. He could take a topic that sounded like nothing—the meaning of success in America, for example—spin ten or fifteen minutes on it (drawing on his experiences, current comment in the press, and the things he'd learned from listeners), and make it so compelling that listeners were practically forced to call. They had to tell their own stories, add their perspective.

In 1972 no one was asking anymore if we were going to get out of Vietnam. The issue had become *when* we would leave and how ugly it would be. For Jerry, Nixon's own deviousness was a bigger issue than the war, and he delighted in exposing anything that tarnished the president further. In early 1972 he seized on the juicy near-scandal of the ITT affair as he would have attacked a fresser sandwich at Jack & Marion's. He first heard about it when Jack Anderson revealed the contents of a memo written by Dita Beard, a Washington lobbyist for ITT, in which she crowed that ITT's partial funding for the Republican National Convention in 1968 had influenced a 1969 Justice Department antitrust ruling that favored her company. Anderson was on Jerry's show the day after his column came out, and the story took on soap opera aspects in its details. Could the Republicans' Justice Department really be bought and sold? Was Nixon in on it? Jerry was alternately outraged by the influence peddling and thrilled to catch the administration with its hand in the cookie jar.

As the wave of anti-Nixon feeling in the country grew, Jerry rode it like a surfer. Nixon was the perfect villain. Jerry began closing his show with "Wake up, America!"

The 1972 campaign heated up and the war dragged on. And on Saturday night, June 17, 1972, a group of White House operatives were caught by a security guard in a simple little burglary of the Democratic Party headquarters at the Watergate office building in Washington, D.C.

When the implications of this operation began to emerge, Jerry could hardly contain his pleasure. This wasn't like the ITT business, in which there was only an *appearance* of influence, and you had to connect A to B to C to D to get to Nixon. This was a group of White House stooges trying to bug the telephone of the chairman of the opposition party. It was an abuse of power that started right down the hall from the Oval Office. Jerry first mentioned Watergate on Tuesday, June 20, 1972. For the next two years, the unfolding drama of presidential cronies engaging in cheap and stupid shenanigans, then clumsily trying to cover them up, then cravenly pointing fingers at one another—and the president himself first hiding inside a prison of self-pity and recrimination and then falling from power in the most ignominious way—gave Jerry more great raw material than he could ever have hoped for.

Not that the war ever went away.

Labor Day, September 4, 1972, was a night when callers to *The Jerry Williams Show* were wrangling as they had many times before about staying the course in Vietnam or getting out. Elman screened the calls as he always did and picked up one from a man who said he was a Vietnam veteran from East Boston. The veteran went into the queue, and twenty minutes or so later, it was his turn.

Jerry said, "Hello."

The caller began, in a broad Boston accent, "Yeah, I'm a, a Vietnam veteran. I got out in March, and I'm also a little nervous. Um—y' know, I've heard the program tonight, and I, quite a people—quite a few people call up an' talk about Vietnam and—uh—" He stopped briefly, "I, I, I don't think the American people really, really understand—uh—war, and what's goin' on.

"Uh—I, I think about—uh—in order to, t' blow up something like the Tobin Bridge—ah—they, they, they drop enough bombs to wipe out everything from the Tobin Bridge to Kenmore Square." His voice took on a sudden urgency. "And there's nothing left."

Jerry furrowed his brow. Things in the control room became very quiet. The caller had described a grotesque excess of violence with a metaphor that most Bostonians could quickly appreciate. Thousands of cars pass over the Tobin Bridge every weekday commuting to and from the city. During the summer, thousands more use it on the weekend getting to and from New Hampshire and Maine. Because it passes over land and two strips of water, the Tobin is actually two and a quarter miles long, but most New Englanders would understand the bridge proper to be the eight hundred feet of roadway above the water of the Mystic River. The bombing the caller imagined, wiping out an area from the bridge to Kenmore Square, would devastate about three and a half miles of the city's most fashionable and densely populated land. It would kill tens of thousands of people.

Jerry began to reply: "I've tried to dramatize this as best I can—"

But there was something pushing the man's words forward, and it seemed that he had not even heard what Jerry said. "We, we would go into villages after they drop napalm and—uh—human beings were fused together, fused together like pieces of metal that had been soldered. Sometimes you couldn't tell if they were people or" (his voice took on a higher, more urgent note) "animals."

He breathed in heavily. "W—w—we have—ah—ah—jets—uh—that drop rockets, and in, in the shells they have penny nails. And those nails are one nail per square inch f—for about the size of a football field. Uh—I—uh—you, you can't believe what they do to a human being."

His voice had cracked on "being," and it seemed as if he were about to sob. "And I was there a year, and I, I never had the courage to say that was wrong. I, I *condoned* that. I, I, watched it go on. Now I'm home, and sometimes I, my, my heart, it—it bothers me inside, because—" he paused and sighed, "—I remember all that. And I never had the courage then to say it was *wrong*. And I hear people call up, and talk about killing, and they, they wouldn't mind their son going over there and doing that. T' other human beings."

His voice quivered and cracked. "It doesn't matter what the Viet Cong—the Viet Cong are *bad*. But that doesn't make it right for *me* to be bad. Or f' someone t' say that they should send their son, or their husband, or their brother to go over there—it'd be just as vicious.

"It's unbelievable. Y' know, people—people don't understand what that does t' your *mind*. You, you, you, you go into a, a village that's had a thousand-pound—" he inhaled sharply "—a thousand-pound bomb, that's called a daisy-cutter, a thousand-pound bomb dropped on it. Y'—you don't worry about taking pris'ners, because there *are* no pris'ners. You don't know if you killed Viet Cong, because you can't put the people together."

He stopped for a moment. Then the words came out in a rush: "That's what the people in this country've got t' understand. That's—that's what Americans are doin', and, and when you're over there, when you're over there in the middle of it, you think it's right because it's goin' on ev'ry day, twenty-four hours a day." He slowed again. "You rationalize it, you think it's right, and when you come back, and you see your own wife," he said, his voice cracking, "or your own family, then you understand what you did."

He inhaled sharply. "You, you understand what would happen i—if someone dropped napalm—uh—where you lived. And he bailed out, if you'd be *kind* to 'im. Or if you'd wanna send him back an', an', an', an', that, that's what they want American boys to do. And that's what we've *been* doin', an' it, it's not right." His voice faded to a whisper. "It's not right under *any* circumstances. Because that's—it's *wrong*."

He seemed overcome with emotion. "I, I'm sorry I got so upset."

Jerry spoke calmly and quietly, in the low register of his voice. He did not want to interrupt, but the man needed to know someone was listening. "Uh—where were you stationed?"

The question seemed to catch the man off guard. He struggled for a moment and then gained more control: "Well, I, I, I was I—I was in An Loc and in and around that area."

Then it seemed as though he was seized again, back in the experience of the war. "And—uh—you, you, you take an aerial photograph, y' know, you think of CBS, an' NBC an', an' ABC, an' they do such fantastic programs—they should let th' American people understand—y' take an aerial photograph of a place like Quang Tri and then, you, you take an aerial photograph after—after the B-52s have been over it, you—" he began to speak in a higher pitch, with greater urgency, "—you can't believe what, you can't *believe* what happens. You can't *believe* it. You go into a village—I—not even the *bugs*. You, you can't find *bugs!* That's how fantastic and devastating it is.

"And what bothers me is when you're there, you can't believe it—" his voice shattering, "—when you're there, you, you, you rationalize it, you *condone* it. You say it's *right*, because they're the enemy." His voice faded to a whimper. "And then when you come home, you can't believe that you didn't have the courage to open your mouth against—" he gasped harshly, "that kind of *MURder*. That kinda devastation. Over people, over animals.

"You don't know if they're Viet Cong. You can't *tell*. There's no bomb that's smart enough to blow up an entire village so that there is *nothing left*, not even the bugs that knows what it's killed, Viet Cong—" his voice suddenly hushed, "—old people, children."

He paused again, and then began speaking as if he had forgotten something important. "Napalm—there's no way people in this country can understand what napalm *is*. You, you, you go into a place, and, and, and there's noth—the people, they're just *burnt*. It's incredible, it, it's, y' know, I, I, I, talk to people who, who remember the Cocoanut Grove fire, a long time ago, and they said it was incredible—the bodies, the way they were brought out." He paused, and then in a hoarse whisper said, "That's *nothing*. That's *nothing!* When you go to a piece of something, and you have no idea whether it's a human being or an *animal*. That's what's been done to it.

"And you have to come home and *live* with that, because y' didn't have the *guts* t' say it was wrong. A lotta guys had the guts. They got sectioned out." He spoke more steadily for a moment. "They got sectioned out, on a 208. An' on the discharge was put that they were unfit for military duty, unfit, because they had the courage." He became more urgent, and his voice broke again: "Guys like me were *fit,* because we *condoned* it. We *rationalized* it."

He stopped. "That's all I have t' say, Mr. Williams. Thank you."

Jerry replied, "Thank you." He sat in silence. The studio, the control room, seemed dark and empty. After three seconds he said, "There really is nothing you can say after that. We'll return in a moment."

The commercials were a relief. As soon as they were rolling, Jerry hit the intercom. "Save that tape. Cut it and put it on cart. We're gonna need it."

For the next five weeks, Jerry replayed the Vietnam Veteran's call. Some listeners said they heard it that first night and needed to hear it again. Those who missed it the first time, the second time, the third time, asked for a rebroadcast so they could hear it for themselves. It polarized listeners. Some felt that it was a cry from the heart, the voice of a decent man in a cruel and brutal place. Some felt the man was a coward, a traitor, a disgrace to all his comrades who had died. The Veteran brought the war home in a way no informed guest, no rhetorical flourish ever had.

Jerry hoped that he would call again, and he said so on the air. If the Veteran didn't want to deal with getting an open line at night, he could call the office during the day and they would arrange a time to put him on, when it would be convenient for him. Weeks went by. He asked Elman, "Did you hear from that guy?"

"No, not today."

Late in September, the McGovern campaign called with the news that they had a major appearance set for Boston on October 11 and 12. The 11th was going to be billed as McGovern-Shriver Day in Boston; both candidates were scheduled to attend a rally in the evening. They hoped something could be worked out for an interview with Jerry. Jerry was going to be on vacation that week. Still, he could come in that morning, tape a half hour or so with McGovern, and Elman could roll it as part of the show that night. "I want to give him a copy of the Veteran's tape," Jerry said. "Dub it onto cassette so that he can take it with him." This was unusual. Definitely not standard operating procedure. Elman did it anyway.

The interview on October 12 went well. McGovern and Jerry had talked on the phone a number of times over the past few years, and they both were relaxed and casual. When it was over, Jerry said, "Senator, I want you to hear something." McGovern made his excuses. He needed to stay on schedule. Jerry said he understood. He explained about the Veteran's call, gave McGovern the cassette and said he should listen to it when he had the time.

That afternoon, aboard his campaign plane, McGovern pulled out the cassette. The press guys aboard the plane watched as he borrowed a machine and played the tape. After a few minutes, his eyes filled with tears. He turned away and looked out the window. He pulled out a handkerchief. Several savvy reporters, including Mike Feinsilber of United Press International, the *Boston Globe*'s Tom Oliphant, and a *New York Times* stringer named Christopher Lydon, knew that they had a great story. They took notes on what they'd heard and they asked McGovern's people for a copy of the tape.

McGovern took a short nap, and he then told his staff he had decided to play the tape at his next stop, a rally at the University of Minnesota in Minneapolis.

When they arrived, the advance team scrambled to get a tape recorder connected to the PA system. After McGovern delivered his prepared speech, he told the crowd he had something he wanted them to hear. He said, "I think it comes a great deal closer to what's going on than what we keep hearing from Nixon."

The Veteran's words reduced the crowd—variously reported at from 12,000 to 25,000 people—to stunned silence. Oliphant heard a young black man say, "Man, that was deep." McGovern closed the rally with an exhortation: "Well, I guess there's nothing much more to say after that except that this young man spoke the truth. Now I think it's up to us to take the next step that can change the leadership that put this young man in the position he just came back from." The crowd sang Woody Guthrie's "This Land Is Your Land."

Oliphant wrote, "The entire episode had all the makings of the kind of genuinely electric scene that happens so rarely in presidential campaigns, as television crews scrambled to ship their film to their networks and newspapermen dove for telephones to call their offices."

The real noise began after that. Questions about the Veteran began almost as soon as the tape had been played. Lydon asked McGovern whether anyone could establish the man's truthfulness. He wrote, "Mr. McGovern said he was relying on Mr. Williams' word that the voice was authentic." Oliphant went to WBZ for comment. His story said, "As of last night, the young man had not been identified, so there was no way of knowing for certain that he was a veteran of the war. . . . The policy of the show, as on many of this genre, is not to ask callers to identify themselves."

Excerpts from the rally appeared on the network TV newscasts. By 7:00 P.M., the Associated Press and UPI had run long stories about the dramatic tape provided to McGovern by Jerry Williams. Editors all over the country took it up, and the story appeared on the front pages of many papers the next day. Tom Oliphant's piece was on page 1 of the *Globe,* next to a Sal Micciche story about Nixon's campaign swing through Atlanta. The *Globe* transcribed the tape and printed the transcript on page 24. Lydon's *Times* story appeared on page 20. A week later, the Veteran's words and Jerry Williams's name were on page 34 of *Time.*

This was the kind of press Jerry had gotten in Chicago—only better. Normally he couldn't get the *Globe* to put a mention of his show in the wasteland of the TV/Radio column, and here it was on page 1. And in the *New York Times.* And on the networks! It was a glorious few hours.

The general manager, Sy Yanoff, called Jerry on October 13, the day after the McGovern rally. He said he wanted Jerry to come to his office for a sit-down, and it had to be that day, even though Jerry was on vacation. Jerry arrived around three o'clock in the afternoon. Sy told Jerry he had to stop playing the tape. In fact, Sy told Jerry he'd heard the Vietnam Veteran for the first time on the previous day, on the network news.

Jerry couldn't believe it. He recalled the conversation later:

"Sy, I've only played it fifty times. This is the first time you've heard something that's been on your own station for more than a month? I've been playing it all along."

"Well, I'm gettin' calls from New York."

He said he was getting calls from the chairman of the board, saying, "Who was that guy who played that tape? Y' know, we don't need that, the campaign is almost over. For cryin' out loud, get sumpin' better on. Sumpin' more entertaining." So, Sy told me never to play that tape again.

I said, "Sy, it's been *played.* People have *recorded* it. What's the difference?"

And he says, "Well, I'm gettin' calls from the network, and the network doesn't want to hear it any more, and thank you very much."

Jerry left the building without talking to Elman.

A few minutes later, Elman was called into Yanoff's office. Bob Oakes was there too. They were stern. Elman had violated company policy by giving a WBZ tape to McGovern, even if Jerry had told him to. How did anyone know this guy on the phone was legit? Elman was to make sure that all copies of the Vietnam Veteran tape were erased. Anything they had in the studio, anything he had personally in his apartment. He was to get any copies back from Jerry and get them erased. The Vietnam Veteran would not be heard on WBZ again. The matter was closed.

Elman was terrified. WBZ couldn't fire the number one talk show host in town, but they could very well dump the boy producer. He did as he was told—except in regard to Jerry. He knew there would be no point in trying to get a tape that Jerry had taken home. Elman figured that something in Jerry's personal possession was Jerry's business. Westinghouse wasn't paying him enough money to fight *that* battle.

The Thursday and Friday shows were tense. Elman was actually glad Jerry was on vacation that week. Maurice Lewis, an affable WBZ newsman, was filling in for him, and they both understood there would be no discussion of the Veteran's tape. Elman eliminated callers who wanted to raise the issue and Maurice sidestepped it whenever it threatened to come up on the air.

By the end of the week, Jerry had received a telegram from Westinghouse that left no doubt about where things stood. He was officially informed that he had violated company policy and that disciplinary action was being considered. It was signed by Don McGannon, president of Westinghouse Broadcasting. He fumed. This was bush-league management, being called into the office and getting dressed down, and then receiving a telegram, as if he were some rookie they could push around. He knew he couldn't go against a direct order from his superiors, but he was determined to find another way to make the experiences of veterans real to the listeners. Guys were fighting this war and agonizing about it every day. Why not get some other vets on the air? Give them the time to talk, let them tell their stories. The more he thought about it, the better he liked the idea.

Elman tried to forget the show over the weekend. On the following Monday, when Jerry came in, he confided that Yanoff and Oakes had read him the riot act about the tape. He told Jerry how worried he was. Did Jerry think that they might fire him?

Jerry was confident. This was going to blow over. "They can't touch us," he said. "If they decide to fire us, we'll stage the loudest, noisiest press conference you've ever seen." He seemed to enjoy the fantasy of taking a freedom of the press issue to the people. Elman swallowed hard. It wasn't exactly reassuring.

One week later, twelve days before the election, Secretary of State Henry Kissinger announced a tentative agreement on a cease-fire in Vietnam. Many analysts had predicted that the administration would try to broker some kind of peace deal at the last minute; reporters had asked Nixon about it the week before the Veteran called the show, and the president had been noncommittal.

But now it looked like he was about to achieve his goal of "peace with honor," and suddenly the Vietnam Veteran looked like yesterday's news.

On November 7 Nixon buried McGovern. Only one state ended up in the Democratic column—Jerry Williams's Massachusetts.

Jerry did a burn about the results. How could the American people be so badly fooled? But the contest was over, and the show moved on.

In the days and weeks that followed, Jerry moved back to local issues—property taxes, prison unrest, legalized gambling, food prices, drunken driving, a plan to address racial imbalance in the Boston schools. Jerry was restless. They needed something to fire up the show again. He suggested some sort of special with an audience, maybe from Boston's "Cradle of Liberty," Faneuil Hall, where he had done previous live broadcasts. Elman thought that the show might focus on freedom of the press. He got approval from BZ management, found an available date, and began lining up guests.

1973. Watergate.

On January 8 judicial proceedings began before Judge John J. Sirica against the seven fall guys accused of doing the break-in at the headquarters of the Democratic National Committee. Sirica started by offering deals to the defendants. Howard Hunt went down first, with a guilty plea on January 11. Four days later, the henchmen—Bernard Barker, Virgilio Gonzalez, Eugenio Martinez, and Frank Sturgis—also pled guilty. That night, Jerry and Jack Anderson talked on the show about the implications of the scandal. Jerry began asking the questions that would occupy the air for much of the year: how high did this thing go? Did Nixon know about it?

The chief burglar, James McCord, and Gordon Liddy, the guy running the Plumbers (the men who were supposed to plug the leaks) at the White House, hung tough, stood trial, and were convicted on all counts by the end of January.

Lower-level White House aides began to cave shortly thereafter. The smell of decay wafted upward—Jeb Magruder, John Dean, John Ehrlichman, H. R. Haldeman. They all came under suspicion of condoning or knowing about or covering up. Nixon spoke to the nation on April 30, announcing that Attorney General Richard Kleindienst, Dean, Ehrlichman, and Haldeman were all out. But the bloodletting did not stop the questions about Nixon himself, especially on the Williams show. By May the Watergate conspiracy occupied more than half of Jerry's time on the air, and he was regularly closing the show with "Wake up, America!"

A special Senate committee, led by Senator Sam Ervin, began hearing testimony. John Dean, now former White House counsel, testified in June. He said that Nixon, his aides, his campaign staff, and people in the Justice Department had all conspired to cover up the Watergate affair. He also revealed the existence of a Nixon "enemies list." It became a badge of honor for media people to be on it—Ben Bradlee of the *Washington Post,* Robert Healy of the *Boston Globe,* the columnist Mary McGrory, CBS's newsman Daniel Schorr, George Frazier, Jack Anderson, and many others were proud that Nixon thought enough of them to call them his enemies. Frazier wrote a column for the *Globe* about it, saying that Jerry belonged on it, if he wasn't there already.

In July the Reverend Robert Drinan, who was one of the Massachusetts reps in the House, filed the first motion for Nixon's impeachment. He appeared on Jerry's show that night.

In a garden-variety corruption sideshow to Watergate, Vice President Spiro Agnew was indicted on kickback charges that went back to his time as governor of Maryland, and he went down on October 10. Ten days later Nixon fired the guys appointed to conduct the administration's internal investigation—Archibald Cox and William Ruckelshaus—and Kleindienst's replacement, Attorney General Elliott Richardson, resigned in protest.

As the year closed, the long knives came out.

Despite the fixation on Watergate, and even though the United States and North Vietnam had signed a peace pact in January, the war was still there. Jerry's guests addressed the issues of possible war crimes committed by U.S. forces, "orderly withdrawal" of American troops, what was going to happen in South Vietnam, the fate of the returning veterans, and amnesty for draft avoiders. They did a four-hour show on the vets, with a psychologist, representatives of the Veterans Administration and veterans' organizations (including John Kerry, head of Vietnam Veterans against the War). One of the guests who identified himself as a vet was a local labor leader, Domenic Bozzotto.

At midyear 1973, the show on WBZ was as hot as it had ever been, still the leader at night in Boston radio by a comfortable margin and boasting a younger demographic than Jerry's competitors. Jerry had a new three-year contract, which finally brought his salary back up to the dollars he had been making when he left Chicago (though they were worth considerably less, thanks to five years of inflation). But BZ had been hearing from listeners, advertisers, and senior Westinghouse execs that Jerry was too much of an advocate, too liberal, too outspoken. The decision came down to find some conservative voices to fill in when Jerry was on vacation. There was a libertarian commentator named David Brudnoy—a tweedy, pipe-smoking intellectual with a persona like William F. Buckley's—on the public television station, Channel 2. A new-style conservative named Avi Nelson—intense, charismatic, combative—was rising in the ranks of Massachusetts politics. They both got their first shots at talk radio in 1973 as fill-ins for Jerry, and both went on to successful careers as Boston talk hosts. Jerry said that fill-ins from other perspectives ought to be given some time as well. He and Elman agreed that John Kerry had come across well on the air, so Kerry hosted a series of shows.

The recession worsened. Advertising revenues went down more than they usually did during the summer, and many of the Westinghouse stations were having serious cash-flow problems. There were some hard decisions to be made, and New York decided that all the Group W stations would have to find ways to economize. Elman found out about the new austerity in late July, when the operations director, Dave Graves, called him in for a conference. "We've just had a budget meeting, and you're not in it." The producer's job would be gone by September 1.

When Jerry got the news, he was angry, but he could offer little comfort to Elman. His own contract was in the final stages of negotiation, and he didn't want anything to upset its progress. After all, everybody gets fired in broadcasting, sooner or later.

Still, he felt bad for the kid. On August 31, Elman's last night as producer, Jerry told Elman to come into the talk studio while it was on the air. He told the audience that Elman had been through some tough situations as producer, that he was going to be leaving the show, and that Jerry wanted to show his appreciation. He said, "When you retire, they usually give you a gold watch. I know you're not retiring, but I think you should have a watch anyway." Then he gave Elman a small black box and told him to open it. Inside there was an antique Waltham pocket watch from his own collection. Engraved on the back was "To Steve Elman from Jerry Williams with gratitude." Elman was dumbstruck. When Jerry asked him if he had any parting comments, he stammered out a few sentences of thanks.

A woman named Lynn Rashkis took over as director at night, paid by the hour. She and Jerry did not get along. Some other young women followed in her wake over the next couple of years—Cathy Bayless, Laura Debowski, Cathy Shapley—and Jerry eventually got the position back to full-time. Rick LaPierre produced for a while, and then a young guy named Ken Cail.

Why did the Williamses need a new house? Maybe Teri thought the kids should have more room—Eve was fourteen, Susan twelve, and Andrea nine— all getting to be grown up, in their ways. The antiques were taking over. Maybe Jerry and Teri missed the prestige of their Chicago home and they wanted a New England version of the same. Jerry could see the decline of the neighborhood a few blocks away. He may have felt that it was time for another step up, another way to spend the increase in his income.

And there were the death threats that would come into BZ late at night. "We've got a bomb at your house." The help at Jerry's mansion would have to bundle up the kids and get them out while the police searched the premises.

In October 1973 they spent $96,000 on a brick mansion on Churchill's Lane in Milton—presiding majestically over a terraced, quadruple lot with loads of trees that was probably five acres big, a two-and-a-half-story carriage house that could have been a pretty nice dwelling all on its own, and a three-car garage (which still wasn't big enough to accommodate all the cars Jerry wanted to buy). It had a view of the Blue Hills. It had a couple of old-fashioned monster fireplaces. It had all kinds of fancy interior detailing. It had been designed by the architects who'd done the reproduction houses at Colonial Williamsburg. Quite a place. It'd cost you three and a half million, maybe more, to get a house like that today in the Boston area.

The location gave Jerry a sense of security. The house itself took him back to his Chicago status. Once they got everything in place, Teri hosted parties and get-togethers and Jerry invited prestigious guests from the show to visit. They both enjoyed watching people gape at the opulence.

But Teri tried to keep the kids from getting the impression that they were rich. They had to take people's coats when there were parties. They had to address the live-in help with respect. They didn't get everything they asked for. On the other hand, they knew they lived in a pretty special house, and they didn't mind that the kids from school who came over to visit were impressed. Hey, those Williams girls have a couple of rooms that are just *empty*, no furniture or nothin' in them—and their parents let them keep those rooms as messy as they want, even write on the walls if they want to! Jeez, Mom, why don't *we* have a place like that?

Some visitors and neighbors were put off by the pomp and circumstance. Some were envious. Some thought that this dwelling wasn't quite harmonious with Jerry's man-of-the-people image on the air. Ah, well, when you've got it, tongues will wag.

A year or so after they'd settled into the Churchill's Lane mansion, as their annual antiques-hunting vacations began bringing in too many things even for that residence and Teri began holding mammoth yard sales that showed she had more than a little entrepreneurial ability, Jerry presented her with an idea: what about opening a store? Would she like doing that?

Was it just the antiques, or was it that old shopkeeper's gene? Like his grandfather Julius Post and his father, Samuel Jacoby, Jerry Williams soon had his name on a place of business—"Jerry and Teri Williams Antiques," in

*Teri Iezzi Williams and Jerry
Williams at a Boston-area
social event, ca. 1972.*

Milton, Massachusetts. Teri didn't think this idea broke Jerry's promise about
her not having to work for a living. Since the store didn't make a lot of money,
it was as much a hobby as a job for her, and once she got it stocked, she liked
going in every day to show people around and occasionally make a sale.

But if someone was looking for a target, a way to get to Jerry Williams for
all those things he was saying on the air, this was a pretty inviting one. Who
needed to bomb his house?

In January 1974 there was another one of those incredible calls. Once again,
the person screening the calls didn't have any inkling of what was about to
happen.

Jerry had been urging his audience to write to the TV networks to put the
congressional hearings on the Watergate mess on the air live—hell, the only
place Jerry could hear what was going on was on the little public radio station
at Boston University. This was a big story, more important than the soap
operas. People should make their voices heard! And they did.

But he'd also been hearing for months from management that he was hitting Watergate too hard. Bill Cusack, who had followed Sy Yanoff as general manager, was by no means as sympathetic to Jerry's approach as his predecessors had been. Watergate was the same thing every night. It would work itself out, and Jerry could talk about it when it was all over. It was dull radio—like a soap opera. With all these characters, who could keep them all straight? Lighten the show up a bit.

Jerry asked himself whether Cusack was hearing from Westinghouse brass, where it was rumored that Nixon had friends in high places. This call came in at just the right time.

He took it with his usual sharp "Hello!"

A man with a broad New England accent:

I listen to y' program onna way home from work ev'ry day . . . I think I'm a good American. I've raised a family, four children, a wife. I live in a small home inna suburbs, fifteen thousand dollar home. I put [in] four years inna Marine Corps. I did my duty inna Far East. I work at Newport Naval Base. I'm bein' told that I'm being fired because the base is being closed . . . I work two jobs . . . I can't put up a fence in my yard unless I have a *permit*. And den I see people like Mr. Agnew, Mr. Nixon, the Plumbers get away wid all these things. And you know, I'm tired. And I'm ready for a revolution. I think it's time that the people in this country stood up and fight like they were taught when they went into the 'Merican service, to take back their Constitution and the American flag. They're ours. They belong to us. Not to a buncha hypocrites who stand on a platform and tell us lies. . . .

I tell people, "Look, if something happens that you don' like, send a telegram. Explain," y' know, "Tell th', your, your representatives how you feel."

You know what they tell me? They tell me, "It's not going t' do any good."

This whole thing's come about because it is our fault. We sit in our little home, in our yard, wid a fence around our property, and we don' care what happens acrossa street. . . . You might as well take the crosses down inna churches and put up dollar bills because this is all the American people seem to be int'rested in. . . .

This is a great—the greatest country inna world. And if we sit by idly and let Mr. Nixon and his administration do what they're doing and stay in office, I feel sorry f' dis country, because is it [*sic*] in terrible trouble . . . It's our own greed f' money and power dat is causin' 'is.

That's all I have t' say.

That's all I have t' say. Why did this sound so familiar? Did Jerry hear it? Did he realize that the Vietnam Veteran had concluded his call with exactly the same words? Did he hear the same kinds of rhythm in that voice, the familiar cadences? Did he suspect that this was the same man who'd called fifteen months earlier?

He certainly reacted in a similar way. "Dub that call to a reel!"

A few days later, Mike Barnicle, a *Boston Globe* columnist, published a partial transcript of the call, suggesting that the guy was a kind of Everyman, summing up the average guy's feelings about the Watergate sleaze. If he got a copy of the tape from Jerry, he didn't say.

This time Jerry's show didn't get into *Time.*

May 1974 saw the beginning of impeachment hearings against Nixon. In July, the hearings were live on radio and TV. By the end of July, three articles of impeachment had been recommended, and it looked like a trial would take place in Congress. On August 9, Nixon threw in the towel.

Jerry did not gloat. It was too serious for that. He analyzed it politically: the country had been through an ordeal, and it was time to move on. Nonetheless, Nixon supporters blamed Jerry personally, and death threats against him came in to the WBZ switchboard.

In June Judge W. Arthur Garrity ruled that Boston schools were segregated de jure, making them no better in the eyes of the law than the southern schools Jerry had been criticizing for a decade. The Boston School Committee appealed the ruling, but the state's highest court agreed with Garrity. There was so little time left before the school year was to start that Garrity had to use an off-the-shelf scheme to begin desegregation in 1974 while a comprehensive plan was developed for implementation in 1975. It looked like the fall was going to be tense.

Jerry defended the ruling. He cited the racial polarization in the city, which he could see personally as he drove along the border of white and black neighborhoods on his way home. Roxbury, Dorchester, and Mattapan looked bombed out. The housing stock there was decaying and the absentee landlords didn't seem to care. There were loads of unemployed people on the streets. The city had shortchanged schools in minority neighborhoods, and parents there didn't have the clout or the money to get the School Committee's attention. Besides, the School Committee was controlled by the political sons of Louise Day Hicks, people who favored the schools in white parts of the city and used neighborhood rights as a smokescreen for their own personal bigotry. There were two educational systems in the city, one for minority kids and one for white ones. The black kids deserved a fair chance to learn. Boston had to take its medicine the same way the southern schools had.

When black kids from Roxbury were bused into South Boston for the first time that September, there was a near riot. Southie parents began by protesting the arrival of the buses. The protest escalated to egg throwing, tomato throwing, stone throwing. The windows in some buses were broken. Some people shouted, "Go home, niggers!" The next day Roxbury parents began escorting their kids to school in the white neighborhoods.

Tension in the schools remained high for months. In December a black student stabbed a white student at South Boston High, and in a matter of a few hours the school became a battleground. Students divided into groups along racial lines. A crowd massed outside, shouting, "Niggers eat shit!" Black students were isolated in the principal's office as a security measure, and Roxbury parents had to escort them home.

A little later that fall, Jerry got acquainted with a genial political junkie named Mark Shields, who was leading study groups at Harvard's Institute of Politics. Shields had worked on the campaigns of Bobby Kennedy and Ed Muskie, and he had a lot of interesting and provocative opinions on national affairs. Jerry had him on the show a couple of times, and he gradually turned into a regular, sometimes appearing with Mike Barnicle from the *Globe*. Both had broadcasting in their future—Shields on CNN and Barnicle with his own Boston talk show. *The Jerry Williams Show* wasn't a bad place to learn how it was done.

In November the young Greek American who had listened to Jerry's very first talk show on WKDN when he was at Swarthmore got himself elected governor of Massachusetts. You could tell he had big ideas. Jerry would have preferred that Frank Sargent stay in office, since he liked the idea of a Republican counteracting the excesses of the Democrats who controlled the legislature, but Dukakis seemed like a pretty straight arrow.

That fall and winter saw the first of several incidents at Teri's store in Milton. The broken windows and graffiti were not necessarily connected to the racial tensions, but the coincidences made both Jerry and Teri nervous. It wasn't just the security of the business they were worried about, but their personal safety and that of their daughters.

This wasn't the first time Jerry's radio work had affected his personal life, but it was one of the few occasions when the show prompted unwarranted attention to his family. As had been the case in Chicago, the most venomous callers and letter writers questioned Jerry's personal commitment to racial equality. They said he was one of those armchair liberals who wouldn't practice in private life what he was preaching on the air. They pointed to his big house in a safe suburb, where he didn't have to deal with city dirt and city crime. They accused him of sending his kids to private schools. Some even knew about the place on Cape Cod where Teri and the kids spent much of the summer.

He couldn't deny that he liked the pleasures his income allowed him and that he wanted his family to be secure. He could tell the carpers that his kids had always gone to public schools, but they'd come back with "Milton ain't Boston."

These personal comments, along with the attacks on Teri's store, penetrated his professional armor, although he never let the callers or letter writers know it. He knew it wasn't right for the problems of desegregation to fall inequitably on working-class and poor families. Like many other upper-middle-class people in eastern Massachusetts, he felt a bit guilty that he could afford a life away from the city's school system and the city itself. If it read like hypocrisy to his critics, he couldn't do anything to resolve the discord. Whenever the sniping started on the air, he waved it away angrily. "What difference does it make where I live, sir? We're talking about centuries of injustice here."

The troubles continued through 1975. The second phase of busing started in September, when black kids and Latino kids were bused into previously all-white Charlestown High School, and Charlestown kids were bused into Roxbury. Again there were protests, anger, boycotts. That November Louise Day Hicks was once again elected to the Boston City Council, with more votes than any other council candidate.

The city's racial tensions seemed to inflame other events as well. When a black man named James Bowden was shot and killed by plainclothes members of the Boston Police's Tactical Patrol Force on January 29, 1975, it set off a bitter court fight. The TPF's actions had been witnessed firsthand by a *Boston Phoenix* reporter, Dave O'Brian. He documented the actions and attitudes of a group of tough, snap-judgment cops who never doubted that what they did was necessary to enforce the law. They staked out a car that looked like one involved in a robbery; when the driver showed up and backed down the street, they cut him off. They thought he was trying to escape. They thought he had a gun. They shot him. But it turned out that Bowden was a husband and father, a guy with a regular job who was working when the robbery was committed, and that he was unarmed when he was shot. In March the Bowden family hired the attorney Lawrence O'Donnell to sue the cops and the city. Antibusing conservatives tended to side with the police, though they admitted the TPF might have been hasty. Liberal voices supported the Bowden family's call for a damage award. Jerry was with the Bowdens.

It took nine years for the case to be tried and appealed, for the amount of the judgment against the cops to be established, and for the City of Boston to agree to pay it. The Bowdens eventually got $750,000. During those nine years, Jerry worked on three different Boston radio stations, but he never forgot about the case. He repeatedly spoke about it with Larry O'Donnell and his son, Lawrence O'Donnell Jr., who wrote a book about it called *Deadly Force*. He castigated Kevin White for stonewalling the family after the judgment was set and praised the new mayor, Raymond Flynn, for finally getting the city to do the right thing.

WBZ gave Jerry one more great moment before things began coming apart. Since the days when Bob Oakes was program director, station management had had a touching fondness for the traditions of radio—unlike so many other stations, where history goes back only to last year's ratings.

Westinghouse had celebrated the fiftieth anniversary of the 1920 debut of their first station, Pittsburgh's KDKA, with an elaborately produced six-record boxed set of radio memorabilia—with a free copy for every employee of a Group W station. WBZ celebrated its own fiftieth anniversary in 1971, and Jerry was in the thick of it. Ken Meyer, a new producer with a passion for old-time radio, was deputized to round up every star of the thirties and forties who was still drawing breath for Jerry to interview—Bob Hope; Art Linkletter; Ben Grauer; the comic actors Jerry Colonna and Gale Gordon; Jack Benny's announcer, Don Wilson; Burns and Allen's announcer, Harry von Zell; Herb Morrison, the man who witnessed the fiery demise of the *Hindenburg* zeppelin; the sportscasters Bill Stern and Mel Allen; Bob Elliott and Ray Goulding; and even cast members from the original *Howdy Doody* radio show.

Then, in the early 1970s, BZ re-created the classic days of Top 40 on the air with *Grease Weekends,* bringing Arnie Ginsberg, Dick Summer, and other well-known Boston jocks back to the mics for adventures in nostalgia and demonstrations of radio techniques that were already thought of as "classic."

In 1975 they came up with a different concept—a series of live broadcasts over the Fourth of July weekend re-creating the feeling of the big band radio performances that were ubiquitous in the years Jerry was growing up. In all his fantasies—from seeing Benny Goodman at the Paramount to wearing the white jacket with Jerry Russell and the Band to grabbing the mic in the Army whenever he could, he always hoped he'd someday be able to be the announcer for one of those big band broadcasts. Ken Meyer was producing again as a reconstituted Jimmy Dorsey Band led by Lee Castle held forth at Dunfey's in Hyannis, on Cape Cod. There, wearing his best retro outfit, was "Yours truly, Jerry Williams, welcoming you to an evening of swing, featuring the song stylings of Bob Eberle . . ." A dream come true.

In 1976, as a new presidential campaign heated up, Jerry's deal with WBZ foundered.

He was primed to talk about the campaign as he always had, ready to interview the candidates and handicap the race. Frankly, it looked dull as dishwater, with Nixon's goofy successor, Jerry Ford, apparently about to be pitted against one of the nation's up-and-coming-but-not-too-well-known Democrats, maybe Milton Shapp of Pennsylvania, or that nuclear engineer–peanut farmer from Georgia, James ("Call me Jimmy") Carter.

It was also contract renewal time. Jerry's first deal with WBZ had been for five years. The second one covered 1973 through mid-1976. It had been a tough negotiation, but he felt he'd gotten a pretty good deal. This time, as the end date of the 1973 contract came closer and closer, Jerry was amazed at Group W's resistance to even a slight increase in his salary.

WBZ agreed to give him a thirty-day extension while they haggled, then a second thirty days. Then a third. It dawned on him gradually. They didn't want to renew. They weren't going to put it in so many words, but he was being canned. Westinghouse was taking away the best platform he'd ever had, his longest run ever at one station. He had come to think of that ugly studio as home, and Group W was evicting him.

Until the end of his life, Jerry believed that his strong positions on civil rights, the war, Watergate, busing—positions that had him branded for better or worse as a "liberal"—put him at odds with Westinghouse brass and made it uncomfortable for BZ to keep him. He had good reasons to be suspicious— early on he'd been pressured to avoid criticism of the nuclear power industry, where Westinghouse had big investments. But it could have been much simpler. Contract renewal is always the time for cost-benefit considerations, and WBZ clearly thought that Jerry Williams wasn't worth what they were paying him. Although he had great ratings and his show was almost always loaded to capacity with commercials, the ad revenue at night simply didn't justify big expenses, and there were younger talk hosts coming up who would work Jerry's shift for a lot less.

Also, the audience was in a period of transition. The "long national nightmare," as Gerald Ford had put it, had exhausted Americans. The United States had seen its forces leave a war zone in defeat for the first time ever. Busing went on in Boston and racial tension kept simmering. Mayor Kevin

White's power was firmly established, and he seemed impervious to Jerry's barbs.

In October 1975 *Saturday Night Live* premiered, turning politics and news into a weekly joke. Even though he and Teri sat on the couch each week with little Andi, laughing at the arch ironies and admiring the new generation's cool satire, the show's rise was one more indication that what Jerry did, and what he wanted to keep doing, had lost its edge.

Maybe the most important reason was one that no one wanted to talk about: Jerry Williams was past fifty. Executives may have begun to see him as an old man in a young person's game.

They worked out a more or less amicable parting, and Jerry made a few calls. He tried to be positive. Maybe this was his big chance to take another step up—to break into New York at last. And WMCA, one of the best stations in The City, was interested. They agreed to give him a weekend slot on Sundays. If he played well, there might be a chance to do something full-time.

Good enough. But what about regular income? The noncompete clause in Jerry's contract specified that he couldn't take another job in the Boston market for at least sixty days. Jerry worked his contacts, and it didn't take long for WTIC in Hartford, Connecticut, to show some interest. But with only thirty-day contract extensions to work with, he had no leverage. He had to agree to one of the toughest shifts of his life—thirty-five hours a week on the air, Monday through Saturday, 7:00 P.M. to midnight. WTIC at least agreed to limo him back and forth from Milton, and there would be a lot of sports in the schedule, but still, he'd be working seven days a week. Good thing he had to do it for only two months. He'd have to find something easier, but he was set for the short term.

WBZ's management made an extraordinary concession: as he prepared for his last show, they let him promote his new station and mention its call letters on the air—normally a cardinal sin in commercial radio.

On September 20, 1976, he began making the announcements on the air. His last ten shows on WBZ: every night, sad and loving farewell calls. Then, thousands of letters from all across the country start coming in. Did Westinghouse management care? Well, Jer, it's probably best for all of us if you just stick to the plan.

The last week he did something he hadn't done since he composed his Chicago manifesto in 1965. He began working on a written text to read on the air, a farewell address. He wanted to thank everyone who'd helped make BZ such an important experience, and to say the right things about this medium he'd helped to create. As he looked back, he found that he was choking up. All these people. All that work. On Friday, October 1, he practiced, polished, tried to drain off all the tears. At 10:05 P.M., two hours into the last show, he read what he'd written:

It is with great sadness and reluctance that I leave WBZ in Boston, and Massachusetts. I've spent most of my adult life here, half of my radio and TV career. I married my wife, Teri, in 1957, my first year in Boston. And all my children, my three girls—Eve, now seventeen, Susan, almost sixteen, and Andrea, who just turned twelve—were born here at Massachusetts Memorial Hospital and they truly do not know any other home. And so I'm leaving Boston *again*. This time, most unwillingly, although my family will continue to live here.

It is difficult to recall all that I would like to at this moment. What an exciting time it's been for me. Truly an education, for me, and I hope it's been the same for you. Because after all, this is the function of this program, to inform, and to entertain you who listen.

I will miss all of you because this is really my home, and though I may not have been born here, it is the place of my choice, and it will be most difficult to adjust at this point in life to anything else.

The thanks began. Jim Lightfoot, Tony Graham, and Bob Oakes got a tip of the cap, but no other successors in management, and no one higher up. He'd deal with the nameless and faceless Group W execs later. Then, the producers—Paul Fanning, Jerry Wishnow, Steve Elman, Cathy Bayless, Laura Debowski, Cathy Shapley, Ned Foster, Rick LaPierre, Tessel Collins, Kenny Meyer, and Ken Cail. Office staff and folks in the background. All his studio engineers: Lee Holbrook, Warren Aulenback, Don Tortorella, Charlie Dinsmore, Fred Stroud, Dwight Macomber, Carol Jeffrey, Alison Frisbee, Frank Edmunds. The air staff: his colleagues Carl DeSuze, Bob Raleigh, Dave Maynard, Guy Mainella, Bob Wilson, Johnny Most, Lovell Dyett, Dick Pace, Bill Smith, Larry Glick, Jim Sands, and Larry Justice. The news guys: Gary LaPierre, Don Batting, Stephen Smith, Ted Larson, Listo Fisher, Ann McGrath, Darrell Gould, Harry Savas, Art Gardner, Nancy Koplofsky, and Ed Bell.

"It's the best news staff I've ever worked with." His voice began to crack.

He cataloged the many issues that had taken center stage on his show. Then: "The concept of people being able to express themselves and to talk to one another by simply using the telephone as a microphone—that has always excited me. . . . People who participate are an amazing cross section of America. Just people. All kinds of people. And isn't it about time that just people had a forum of their own? I truly believe in this form of radio, and I do hope it stays with us."

He told his listeners he wanted to share with them some of the pressures of the job, and he started with a veiled slash at the suits he felt had pushed him aside: "Now, being a social critic is not an easy role. You make enemies. Many of them in high places. Pressures upon you are constant, sometimes insidious, both covert and overt. And when you are the employee of a large communications organization, one never knows the source of the pressure or criticism."

He spoke of the other pressures:

From people who listen to the program and do not like what is being said, and would in effect like to silence the voices of dissent. They are dangerous to America. . . . Sometimes, pressures from advertisers, but rarely these days. . . . And of course, there's the pressure of the nightly performance. Many nights . . . I do not feel like doing the four hours. It takes an enormous amount of discipline to psych oneself up for the night ahead. Then, of course, the obligation to the audience to be as accurate on the issues as one possibly can be. And one of the most obvious pressures is to keep it entertaining and humorous when the occasion arises. Some observers feel, looking from the outside in, that nothing could be easier than sitting down for four hours and battin' the breeze. And you still have to perform the commercials and hawk the goods that are necessary to your survival. And then, there's of course the ratings. If you don't get them, you don't exist.

I'm not crying the blues, because I love the work and I would not do it if it was not satisfying and stimulating. But I did want to let you know what goes on behind the scenes as well.

My ambitions have somewhat dimmed with age. I've always wanted to do more television. But as luck will have it, that has not occurred. Perhaps I will get a further opportunity, and if not, it no longer disturbs me as it did when I was younger. I think now less in terms of career ambition but more in terms of life fulfillment, family, friends, children, and only with age and maturity do you find out that that is truly what life is all about.

His voice began tightening. "And if only I could find my island—" Choking with emotion, he pushed the last words of the sentence out: "That would be nice."

The audience heard Jerry Williams sob. Then there was a long silence. He recovered.

"I love the Cape, and someday, that might be my island, or maybe one of Florida's great beaches. Who knows? I'm still searching—" his throat clenched again, but he mastered it. "And I don't know for what."

But the most important factor in what I do is you, the listener. Without your participation and acceptance, this type of program could not exist. The essence of freedom and the first amendment are embodied in this form of radio. Not many places are left on earth where one can speak out to hundreds of thousands of people about their own government and the high public officials who run their lives. This should not be taken for granted. Don't let it be. There are very few courageous radio and television stations or broadcasters around where true free speech is heard, so we must be ever-vigilant about protecting this right.

I thank you for everything. It's been a good eight years. I have no regrets, just sadness at this moment. This is a time, by the way, of the year for new beginnings, and new challenges, and atonement for one's past mistakes. So on October the eleventh, I begin again, and perhaps I should leave you with a bit of personal philosophy:

There is a glorious sun. Not the sun you see in the sky. But a sun which is within ourselves, which is much brighter than the sun you see in the sky. When the sun comes out, it only dispels the darkness. But when *this* sun comes out, it dispels the darkness and ignorance both. It is much brighter than the sun that shines out. It is all within us. Just within us.

A parade of guests said good-bye. Ken Meyer, Larry Glick's producer, who had given Jerry those memorable shows with the old-time radio stars and his chance to be a big-band announcer at last. Glick himself. The TV anchor Tony Pepper. The sports producer and host Jimmy Myers. Streeter Stuart, WBZ's venerable veteran newsman, who had seen Jerry take his first bag of mail to a legislative hearing in 1958.

There were lots of sad farewells from his listeners. Then, just before midnight: "This is Jerry Williams, and for the final time, wake up, America! And good night, good luck, good morning, good night, T."

H. V. Kaltenborn had been dead for twelve years. Edward R. Murrow had been dead for eleven years. Lowell Thomas had retired from radio five months before. Radio wasn't old time anymore, and radio talk shows were everywhere. Some three hundred people were earning their livings talking on the radio in America, and Boston had become one of the country's best markets for talk. Paul Benzaquin was a recognized local icon, almost as respected as Jerry himself. Avi Nelson and David Brudnoy, who had cut their radio teeth filling in for Jerry, now had their own Boston shows. Some stations were flirting with the idea of talk twenty-four hours a day. The concept was so widespread around the country that some people in management thought that it had peaked. Little did they know that the people who would remake talk radio were just revving up their careers.

Larry King was forty-three, rebuilding his status in Miami after a few years of combating some embarrassing charges of influence peddling, passing bad checks, and white-collar larceny. Don Imus, thirty-six, was on the air in the morning on WNBC-AM in New York, riding the success of three comedy albums, but not quite in control of his own inner demons. Rush Limbaugh was twenty-five, with three years behind him as a rock 'n' roll DJ, working under the name Jeff Christie. Bill O'Reilly had graduated from Boston University's School of Public Communication in 1975 with a master's degree in broadcast journalism; by the end of 1976, he was a TV reporter in the Scranton–Wilkes-Barre area. A twenty-two-year-old Howard Stern had BU on his résumé, too; he did his first radio on the university's low-power AM station, got his under-grad degree in 1976, and then landed a job on a weak AM outlet in Boston's western suburbs. And Tom and Ray Magliozzi were failing as the owners of a do-it-yourself garage in Cambridge, Massachusetts, without a clue that they would be radio personalities a year later.

Jerry Williams was fifty-three. In October 1976 he had become just another voice in the crowd. He was still a master of the craft, but Bostonians—even Bostonians who remembered the WMEX shows—had come to take him for granted. Those who'd discovered him in the WBZ years might be forgiven for not recognizing all that he'd done to make talk radio what it was.

He would have to live through five years of hard times and self-doubt before he reclaimed his throne.

8 EXILE

What went wrong?

October 1976 should have been the beginning of a new wave of success for Jerry Williams. Vietnam was over, Nixon was gone, and Jimmy Carter looked ready to oust Gerald Ford. Carter was the first presidential candidate since JFK to cultivate a style of casual geniality. He had blown in from outside the Beltway, seizing the electorate's willingness to take a chance on new blood. He was just one year younger than Jerry. He knew how to dress, how to use the media—why didn't both of their stars ascend at the same time?

Because what's young in politics is old in radio.

What happened to Jerry was nothing new in broadcasting, where fifty tends to be the Career Grenade for men. (Women, as always, have it tougher—if they hold their jobs past forty-five, they're lucky.) It's not just the priorities of the business that makes the Grenade so dangerous; your body's working against you, too. You're not as sharp, your reflexes slow down, you can't deal with the unexpected as effectively.

If you're in radio, you have to deal with the Grenade in one way or another. Some people get off the battlefield. Some suffer the explosion and put themselves back together again. Some soldier on.

Jerry didn't know how to duck the Grenade. It blew him up.

His exile started in Hartford, where he spent two months in 1976—two months that seemed like a year. Hartford is a schizophrenic little city—it has a tiny but handsome center, a classic colonial statehouse for Connecticut government, lots of civic pride, and suburbs that grow tonier as you move southwest toward the Apple. But it also has a gritty underclass, a struggling working class, and quite a bit of desolate urban real estate sliced apart by miles of expressways.

The city's name used to be synonymous with insurance. In fact, WTIC, the station that put Jerry on the air beginning Monday, October 11, got its call letters from its onetime owner, the Travelers Insurance Company. The studios and offices were in the Travelers' landmark tower. TIC management was thrilled to have a talent of Jerry Williams's stature on their air. They'd given him a very nice deal for a small market. For those with the right temperament, there are worse things than being a big fish in a small pond.

But Jerry's own advice to John Rosica, twenty years before in Philadelphia, came back to haunt him. He didn't want to be a star in a little theater group. No matter how lavishly he'd praised WTIC in that last WBZ show, calling it "another great radio station" and touting its fifty thousand watts, he knew that it would never have the prestige of a major-market station. Just saying "WTIC, Hartford" made him feel small. For Jerry, it could never be anything more than a place between New York and Boston, a place you passed through.

The question was: which direction would he be going?

He still thought he might be able to parlay that bit part on Broadway into a conquest of the Big Town. That's one of the reasons he undertook the Sunday show on WMCA, even if it meant working seven days a week for a couple of months. Forty-seven-year-old Bob Grant and sixty-five-year-old Long John Nebel were both on MCA, so he was in the company of acknowledged talk pioneers—eating their dust, it's true, but at least on the same station. MCA had some good up-and-coming talent, too, including a thirty-three-year-old woman named Sally Jessy Raphaël. Jerry told Dennis Israel, his boss at WMCA, that he would be ready for a full-time job whenever something opened up.

The New York gig had another advantage—at last his mother could actually hear him work. For decades now, Frieda had told him how she never missed Barry Gray on WOR, how much she loved listening to Barry. Inside his head, Jerry always heard a version of her voice saying, "And you'll never be as good as he is."

But nothing materialized at MCA right away. After a couple of weeks in Hartford, he knew he had to get out. The day came when he had to pick up the phone and call WMEX. Dick Richmond, Mac's brother, was the owner now, but he left day-to-day operations in the hands of a guy named Joe Scallan. Jerry felt he had some rapport with Dick, even if it was humiliating to think about going back to the place he'd started in Boston. He made a deal, telling himself it wouldn't last long, just until WMCA came through. And he got one good thing out of it: MEX agreed to give him the afternoon drive slot—no more working nights, thank God. Unfortunately, he had to leave Kenny Cail, who'd come with him to Connecticut to produce the show, high and dry.

WMEX had long ago moved away from Fenway Park. Now it was in a dismal little gray building on the border of Bay Village, a small area of brick row houses that had been adopted by the gay community, which was still a somewhat closeted society in 1977. The local homeless folks liked to sit on the WMEX steps. It was another kind of nowhere, even though it was in the middle of Boston.

In December 1976, when Jerry debuted there for the second time, no one heard his dissatisfaction on the air. That wouldn't have been professional. Besides, he knew how to work the Boston audience, and he had been out of the market for only a couple of months, so there was no need for a new manifesto or a honeymoon period. But his new producer, Jack Kirby, got an earful from the first day of his return to WMEX. The signal was terrible. He was going to have to concentrate on local issues when there was nothing happening. He was going to have to work hard to create excitement on the air. He had to listen to Guy Mainella, who was great at sports but way out of his depth on issue-oriented talk, struggling to do Jerry's old shift at WBZ. And Dick Richmond was so cheap. Sidney Lumet's film *Network* had just been released, with Peter Finch playing the crazed anchorman Howard Beale, fulminating that he was "mad as hell." Jerry saw the movie. He felt just like Beale, except that he wasn't crazy.

In the midst of the ice and snow of 1977, working at WMEX, dealing with the drunks and weirdos who congregated on the station steps, Jerry slipped on a patch of ice and came down hard, cracking his elbow and a bone in his foot.

And he was not getting along with Joe Scallan. Joe was making noises about reneging on the deal, moving him to nights, again wedging his show between and around sports broadcasts. Jerry had put up with that at BZ because of the huge national reach. He had put up with it at WTIC because he had no other choice. But he sure as hell wasn't going to put up with it at WMEX.

He pleaded with Dennis Israel at WMCA to help him out, and Israel agreed to make some moves. It was a little inconvenient, and he had to ruffle some feathers among his own staff, but Jerry sounded good on Sundays. Israel figured it was a gamble worth taking.

Three months after his second return to Boston, Jerry left WMEX again for that long-coveted full-time job in New York City. Yeah, he was back in a late-night slot, but at least he wasn't an afterthought to basketball or hockey. And he was leading into Long John Nebel, one of the most durable talents on the air.

It wasn't easy. Despite his Sunday night shows, despite his Brooklyn credentials, no one really knew him in the big town. The talk audience there already had their gods—Gray, Grant, Nebel, Shepherd, Barry Farber, Joe Franklin, Bernard Meltzer, and all the rest.

He looked around the city—again, trying to be the Little Guy, trying to see what the average person saw. In addition to the *New York Times,* he was reading the *Daily News* and the *Post,* trying to get a handle on local issues. The housing was crushingly expensive, and most of it was in rotten shape. The educational system was disgraceful. The taxes were punishing. The subways were decaying. The air pollution from the traffic, the poor quality of municipal water, the press of people everywhere you went . . . Where was the old pride in the Greatest City in the World?

Whaddya think now, Ma?

You know how proud I am of you, Gerald. But did you hear Barry Gray today?

Two and a half months after his weekday show on WMCA debuted, Frieda Jacoby was in Englewood Hospital, the place Herbert had died. Pancreatic cancer, the doctors said. For fifty-one days, throughout the early summer, she gradually got worse. Jerry went to see her a couple of times a week, driving through the city, marveling at how dirty it had become. When she felt well enough to talk, she would tell him she'd been listening and say, "Are you sure you should get so *mad?*"

When all hope for her recovery was gone, Jerry took Teri and the kids to New York to say good-bye. On July 14 Frieda died. The Williamses, along with Herbert's widow, Diana, and his son, James, accompanied her body out to New Montefiore Cemetery on Long Island. Jerry stood at the grave, grim-faced. Here I am in New York, Ma. Finally. Where are you?

Then the tedious, horrible business of clearing out her apartment, dealing with her bills (every goddamn doctor wanted another couple of thousand dollars! Shouldn't the insurance or Social Security take care of this?), the lawyers, the taxes. He argued with Diana about the effects. No wonder he wasn't at his best on the air.

He took a ride through Brooklyn one day. Nostrand and Church. A big hardware store where Jacoby's Kiddie Shop had been. The neighborhood decaying. The imposing apartment buildings on Linden Boulevard, the little brick house on Martense Street, all the old places grim and decrepit. Even Erasmus Hall looked down at the heels. And there were a lot of dangerous-looking characters on the street. What was he *doing* here in New York? You can't go home again. Give it up, Jer.

So the pendulum swung back to Boston, and he made phone calls to Joe Scallan and Dick Richmond. I'll come back to WMEX. But I need a guarantee that you won't put me on nights.

OK, Jer. You got it.

He wrote to Dennis Israel on July 26. It was a remarkable letter:

> After much soul searching, I've decided to return home to Boston. It is with
> deep regret that I take this action. . . .
>
> 　I had always wanted to work in New York. . . . However, it has not been an
> easy year. . . .
>
> 　I have decided not to dislocate my family. They like Boston and this is
> where they have been most of their lives. Eve is entering college and Susan is
> finishing high school this year. Teri would be happy in New York if there were
> no one but us and is most reluctant to give up house and business for what
> could be another temporary situation. . . .
>
> 　No more job chasing for me. . . . I've made a life decision which puts
> career and job in a secondary position. . . . I've discovered that New York is
> not for me or my family. Assessing all the facts, housing, education, job,
> taxes, environment, etc., . . . it is not worth it.

Jerry Williams, family man? Maybe he meant it. But sometimes you can't
live up to your ambitions. Sometimes you say what you hope is true, knowing
in your heart it's not really so. Sometimes you just lie.

It surely wasn't all sweetness and light at home. Teri knew about the casual affairs, but she tried to ignore them. She knew he still loved her in his way,
and she still loved him, but his absences made everything worse. Nine
months of job turbulence had made her the sole manager of the big house at
the same time she was trying to make a success of the store, now known as
Eclectic Antiques, to disguise Jerry's association with it. Even more than
before, Jerry wasn't there when she needed him.

As for his daughters, despite his best intentions, he was making the same
mistakes with them that his father had made with him. He was somehow
unable to be as affectionate as he wanted to be, as he felt he should be. He
had tried to protect them, not to ask too much of them, to give them a real
childhood even though he was so publicly exposed in Boston. He hoped they
knew how much he loved them, he hoped they could penetrate his brusque
reserve, as Howard Vincent O'Brien had put it—but when it came to hugs and
kisses, something stood in the way.

At this moment he and Eve were fighting bitterly about her future. They'd
had some huge blowouts over her wild parties in Milton and at the Cape
house. She wanted to go to Emerson College and pursue a career as an
actress. He refused to pay for it and told her she'd have to attend a state
school with low tuition. Eve fought back. If she couldn't go to Emerson, she

was at least going to go to a school with a decent drama program. So she got herself a scholarship to Bridgewater State College.

The next year Jerry had the same discussion with Susan. A college with a dorm? Too expensive. In 1982 it was the same song with Andi. You don't know what you want to be; go to a community college, close to home. The girls knew he was a tightwad. But none of them knew he hadn't graduated from high school, that his older brother had gone on to advanced degrees and left him as the also-ran son. College. Bah. It was just too much money, that's all.

For years his home hadn't been a real sanctuary, but it hadn't mattered so much, because he always had his show to fall back on. As he came to WMEX for the third time, he needed a sanctuary and he knew how much he himself was to blame for not having one. He was angry with the business for screwing him, angry with his family for not being more understanding, and angry with himself for making all the problems worse.

On August 1, 1977, Jerry picked up where he left off at MEX. Local issues came first now, with national ones holding a strong place in the background.

Two things in particular occupied the next year.

First, there was a scandal involving Joseph DiCarlo, Democratic floor leader of the Massachusetts Senate, and Ronald MacKenzie, the Republican whip. Both of them were accused of taking bribes from a construction company, McKee, Berger and Mansueto (abbreviated to MBM), to fix contracts for the University of Massachusetts campus at Columbia Point in Boston. Both senators were convicted of extortion and conspiracy. This was prime Jerry material—bipartisan corruption at the highest level. Everyone knew this went on every day in Massachusetts, but this time identifiable snouts were in the trough. Jerry railed at these political hacks. He said that there ought to be an independent investigation, one of those blue-ribbon commissions, to find out everyone who was involved, to clean things out, top to bottom. He got people writing, and eventually the pols did what he'd suggested. Not that the commission really did clean house—the Bay State's legislators are too foxy for that.

The second issue was the civil trial of Boston Tactical Patrol Force officers accused of liability in the death of James Bowden. This case was already two years old, and it was starting to seem like justice on ice. This elite unit of police had guessed wrong about Bowden—they thought his car had been used in a robbery, and they shot him dead without asking the questions they should have. So the family was suing the City of Boston for damages. Their lawyer, Larry O'Donnell Sr., appeared regularly on the show to keep Jerry posted on the progress of the trial. This was perfect Williams fodder: give the police a lot of discretionary power, close your eyes to the dangers, and you're almost surely going to have abuses, whether they happen in Selma or Chicago or Boston. As usual, he blamed the man at the top, a guy too removed from the day-to-day to do right by ordinary people—Boston's Mayor Kevin White, dubbed "Mayor Deluxe" by the *Herald* columnist Peter Lucas.

He had good guests during those fourteen months, too. Edward Brooke, the first black man elected to the U.S. Senate. Daniel Ellsberg, the guy who leaked the Pentagon Papers. Marvin Kalb, one of the great TV journalists. The mayor of Jerusalem, Teddy Kollek. And then there was the afternoon Abba Eban paid a visit for an exclusive interview.

Eban was foreign minister of the State of Israel, on a promotional tour for his new autobiography, and Jack Kirby had worked hard to make sure that no one else in Boston was going to be scooping Jerry's show. As the time for Eban's arrival neared, Jerry looked around at the facilities and realized, too late, that they weren't really very impressive. He pleaded with Dick Richmond: "Dick, you've got to get the alkies away from the entrance. Think of what it's going to look like." So Dick deputized Norman Solomon, who had been WMEX's in-house troubleshooter since the Mac Richmond days, to guard the door.

And then there were the lights. To save money, Dick maintained only the barest illumination in the WMEX hallways. Jerry went around snapping switches on, which made the station's $1.98-a-square-yard indoor-outdoor carpeting look even worse. Richmond was baffled. "Why are you turning on the lights in the halls?"

"Dick, to *see!* To *see!* Abba Eban will be here in just a few minutes!"

"Oh, that reminds me. Jerry, get me his autograph, willya?"

"You have the book?"

"Well, don't *you* have a copy?"

"Why dontcha go out and *buy* the book? It's down in the store here, y' can get a book. It's, y'know, $12.95, and I'm sure he'll be happy to autograph it for you. But first, we have to turn on the lights."

"Well, if you have to . . ."

That was the last of the Richmonds. A few months later, Joe Scallan bought WMEX from Dick and retired the old call letters. The new station would be weather, information, talk, and sports—WITS. An agreeable fellow from the south named Pat Whitley was the new program director, but Jerry still had to deal with Scallan, and they still didn't get along.

Controversy and entrepreneurship were an uneasy combination, and people were still making the antiques store a target for their hostility toward Jerry. Late in 1977 they started shooting at it. This was no joke—the front window was shattered twice. Even though Jerry hated to give the creeps any satisfaction, he and Teri decided that the danger just wasn't worth it. Some of the antiques went back to the house in Milton, and some of them got sold off in the going-out-of-business sale.

Teri had nothing to fill the loss of the store. She had good friends in the area and a pleasant social life, but with the two older kids growing up, she was feeling more alone and disconnected.

Funny thing, memory. Jerry had a conversation around the beginning of 1978 with Larry King, but Larry doesn't remember it the way Jerry did.

It was a big moment for King. Mutual, the radio network without a TV arm, had been doing pretty well with *Nitecaps,* an overnight show out of Salt Lake City hosted by Herb Jepko. Mutual could see that talk radio was gaining momentum, and they figured that a more substantive program might get wider acceptance around the country. Only fifty stations were doing a substantial amount of news and talk, but the format was growing. And if you were a station owner and you wanted to go with news or interviews, and there was a show that could fill those overnight hours inexpensively . . .

So Mutual pitched Miami's star interviewer, Larry King, to take over for Jepko. He was smart, he had good contacts, he did a solid news interview, and he had good rapport with the showbiz types. He hadn't done much work with phone calls, but caller input wouldn't be at the heart of this show anyway.

Jerry remembered that Larry King called him for advice while he was considering Mutual's offer. It was as though Larry were coming to one of the Old Hands to assess this new opportunity. What did he think of this idea—a syndicated nationwide radio talk show? Would Larry be wasting his time? Wasn't TV where the money was?

Jerry remembered telling Larry that it was a great concept. He said, "If you don't do it, I'll call Mutual and tell them they should hire me." That was enough for Larry. *The Larry King Show* debuted on January 30, 1978, and you should know the rest of the story—how that made King's reputation nationally and led to his towering success today.

Except that Larry doesn't remember talking to Jerry about it. Maybe he called a lot of people for advice or reactions, and the discussion with Jerry was one of many—it could have just slipped his mind. Maybe he wasn't really asking for advice, just sharing a moment with an old colleague in the business. Maybe he thought Jerry's comment was a joke. Maybe the conversation was a lot more important to Jerry than it was to Larry King. Funny thing, memory.

The rest of 1978 was a mess.

Things at WMEX had never been good, and they were no better now that it was WITS; Jerry began arguing with Joe Scallan, threatening to go elsewhere.

Then he talked to a guy he knew from his WIBG days, Jack Dash, who was now sales manager for the first FM station to go all-talk, WWDB in Philadelphia. They had an opening for on-air talent and a program director. It would be a step down, but Dash and the station's owner, Dolly Banks, at least treated him with a little respect. They were willing to build the format around him and give him the afternoon shift he craved—a three-hour block ending at 6:00 P.M., just before the city's TV news programs hit the air and stole a lot of the available radio listeners away.

But WWDB was housed in a dismal little facility, and they couldn't pay him what he wanted unless he agreed to be program director, too. He see-sawed. Some time during the summer they actually had a deal in principle and were proceeding to contracts. Jerry pulled out at the last minute. He wrote another remarkable letter, beginning it with almost exactly the same words he had used writing to Dennis Israel at WMCA:

> After much soul searching, I've decided to stay in Boston. It is with deep regret that I take this action.
>
> This is not a career decision; it is a family decision. . . . I'm sure you realize that with daughters aged 19, 18, and 14, the decision making process is no longer solely mine. . . .
>
> I have tried desperately over the last few weeks, to convince everyone concerned of the benefits of this move . . . but I have not been successful. The two older girls . . . have refused to accept the change as I thought they would. We did discuss the possibility of my commuting for a year or two, like a Congressman, but concluded that simply would not be fair to anyone. . . .
>
> Hence, the hard decision had to be made. . . . Should I stay in Boston and keep my family happy or return to Philadelphia for a new career challenge?
>
> I decided to make the sacrifice. . . .There are times in one's life when "family" means more than career. . . . I am involved in a personal trap from which there does not seem to be any escape at this moment.

If Eve and Sue Williams had read this letter in 1978, they would have laughed out loud. There had never been any family conferences. The kids were never consulted about Jerry's job prospects. They had no idea he was even looking for work out of town. In fact, there had never been any situations in which Jerry had made job choices based on what his family wanted. He bailed, pure and simple.

Why? Maybe it was because he got the chance to do a tryout on WOR in New York, doing Barry Gray's shift while he was on vacation. But *that* bite of the Apple ended in angry exchanges with the management and another burned bridge.

He publicly reaffirmed his commitment to Boston and to WITS, and Scallan made nice noises in return, but privately it was no good—Scallan was willing to make a long-term deal, but Jerry would have to take less money and go back to nights.

Then he happened to talk to Mort Sahl, a guy who'd been on the show a dozen times, a biting political comic, someone Jerry liked and respected. Mort told him that WRC, the NBC station in Washington, D.C., was going talk. Mort was going to have a show there. They were staffing up—why didn't Jerry give them a call?

Jerry paid a visit to WRC. This was a real station—a facility with all those network extras he hadn't seen since he'd left WBBM in Chicago. They needed a night man, and Jerry took the bait. He turned his back on WITS so fast that he started at WRC before Mort did.

In October 1978, two years after he'd left WBZ, Jerry debuted in the nation's capital, bringing seventeen-year-old Jack Kirby with him from Boston to produce the show. But he soon found out that he'd neglected to get some crucial information. Since WRC was owned and operated by NBC, he assumed it had a great signal, but the reality was a shock. The station operated at reduced power at night. His show was going nowhere. He was reaching only a small part of Maryland. He couldn't be heard at all in Virginia. WRC wasn't even covering the entire District of Columbia. And to make matters worse, it was clear that WRC had fallen in love with Mort—Jerry was second banana to a guy who'd never done a talk show before. The final insult was that WRC management decided to split Jack Kirby's time between the two talk show hosts. The only good thing about the job was that Larry King had relocated to the area to do his all-night show and the two of them could have lunch and talk politics regularly.

As soon as he could, Jerry started calling Jack Dash at WWDB in Philadelphia again. They still needed a program director. They were still willing to do the deal. This time Jerry's family considerations mysteriously disappeared. With the new year, he and Kirby were gone from Washington and back at Jerry's Square One—the market where he'd had his first nighttime talk show twenty-two years earlier.

If you want to set an arbitrary date for the Great Segregation of the Radio Bands, 1978 is as good a year as any. By that year, FM had finally penetrated enough homes and cars so that it was an almost universal alternative to AM. And as soon as a new medium gets enough penetration, its advantages begin to define it in the minds of consumers, and by default those advantages redefine the old media as well. FM's superior sound quality was obvious to everyone by 1978, and it had become the preferred medium for music. In addition, the segregation of music on the FM dial accelerated the process of narrowcasting—the restriction of music stations to tight little format niches that delivered a dependable style of a particular kind of music twenty-four hours a day. These developments drove AM to become the exclusive province of news and information, and they drove individual AM stations to greater niche identity in talk.

But there are always exceptions. WWDB in Philadelphia had bucked the trend by becoming one of the first FM stations—if not the first—to go all-talk. They made the move three years before Jerry joined the staff, when the owners, siblings William and Dolly Banks (the WDB of the call letters), switched format from all-jazz to all-talk. They staffed it up with announcers who reflected Dolly's personality—brash, outspoken, a little rough around the edges. The only remnants of the jazz days were the very profitable Sinatra shows hosted by Sid Mark, the station's operations manager and a Philadelphia institution. WWDB was making some headway against news-talk WCAU, but it still needed someone who could help it achieve its potential. Enter Jerry Williams in March 1979.

WWDB was broadcasting from a Quonset hut on Conshohocken Avenue, a few blocks from the Main Line and in the shadow of two big radio-TV complexes. That made it convenient for the producers to get big-name guests to come by for interviews after they'd finished up their spots on the morning TV shows.

There were a couple of veterans on the air—Frank Ford in the mid-morning hours and tough-talking Irv Homer, a true Philly character, on the night shift. Wynn Moore did the mornings, Dominic Quinn preceded Jerry, Don Henderson had a sports show in the early evening, and there were a few wild cards on the weekends. Sid Mark was still doing eight hours of Sinatra in two shifts on Friday nights and Sunday middays.

As program director, Jerry was called on to give the station some continuity. He had a limited budget, but one of the first things he did was to remake the studio. The long tables, the microphones on shock mounts right in your line of sight, guests at ninety-degree angles, where you couldn't make eye contact—he told the WWDB engineers that he'd had it with the way engineers designed studios, and he showed them how to set things up for optimum performance. The host and the guests should always have a clear view of each other, so that the host could keep control over the guests and the guests could read visual cues from their studio mates. The in-studio board should be compact

Jerry Williams on the air in the studios of WWDB-FM, 3930–40 Conshohocken Avenue, Philadelphia, ca. 1980.

and simple, angled like a cockpit so that the host could get to everything quickly and easily. One button to get calls on the air. One button to get them off. The cutoff control should be the biggest thing on the board, a big rectangular panel on the right side that you couldn't miss even if you had to hit it with your elbow.

They did the renovation exactly as Jerry wanted it—except for one thing. Because orange was Frank Sinatra's favorite color, Sid Mark had the whole thing surfaced in orange Formica. At least people stayed awake in there.

Jerry had to deal with some significant disadvantages—no 800 number, for example. To keep costs down, WWDB wanted callers to pay their own way. They thought it would be sort of user-friendly to set up three different numbers—one for Philly itself, one for the western suburbs, and one for New Jersey. But that meant a long list of numbers on the air. Jerry put that problem in the hands of Ken Nordine, as part of the design of a new audio identity package for the station. Jerry had known Nordine in Chicago, where his quirky, spacey *Word Jazz* show was a late-night treat for the hipsters. Since that time, Nordine had used his incredible voice and prodigious production skills in ads, presentations, commercial work of all kinds. The package for WWDB used the Nordine trademark effects—whispers, overlaid multiple tracks of that amazing voice, synthesizer effects—it was modern, attention getting.

One of the basic problems Jerry faced was the longevity of the staff. After four years on the air, Moore, Ford, and Homer all had significant followings and set ways of doing things. So he rode with the staff he had for most of 1979, trying to coach them and coax them into doing the job the way he thought it should be done.

What remained of Jerry's marriage dissolved when he relocated to Philadelphia. He found a large, handsome apartment in a modern building close to the center of the city—a real residence, not a commuter stop. Within a couple of months, he gave up the pretense of "commuting" to Boston. He began a relationship with a newswoman at WWDB. He found a deli down the street from the station he could depend on for good samwitches. As he began to be heard in the city and known as a radio personality, he patronized local institutions and station sponsors such as Cent'anni, an Italian restaurant in South Philadelphia, where he came to be recognized and welcomed. It was as if he were trying to put in place the things that were most important to him and start his life all over again.

But he and Teri never talked about divorce, or if they ever did consider it, they didn't tell the kids. Instead, the relationship became a kind of formality of mutual convenience. Jerry would provide all the money Teri needed to live life as she liked. Teri wouldn't comment on Jerry's affairs. She wouldn't go to any lawyers. He would retain control of the finances. She would take most of the responsibility for raising the kids. He would have the freedom to remake his life and change cities when he felt he had to. And he could always say he was married when it was convenient to do so.

After six months or so, Jack Kirby moved on, and a kid named Alan Tolz got the job producing Jerry's show. Like so many of Jerry's producers, Tolz gradually came to realize that the old guy in there was somebody special. And by this time Jerry had thirty years of broadcasting stories with which to entertain a green guy in the business.

One day Jerry noted that *Cosmopolitan* was publishing the results of a survey on the sexual habits of its readers. He was fascinated by the results, amazed at the things these anonymous women said they were doing. Was there some way to take this to the air? Bill Ballance had done sexy talk for years out on the West Coast, but Jerry had never seen that vaguely smarmy approach as something that he wanted to incorporate in his repertoire. Instead, when Jerry had dealt with sex, he'd emphasized some controversial aspect—homosexuality and prejudice, abortion and women's rights, contraception and the Catholic Church, the *Playboy* philosophy, prostitution as a victimless crime, even the merit of extramarital affairs. He and Tolz talked it over. If the setup was right, they might be able to adapt *Cosmo*'s survey for radio, getting female listeners to call in and answer the frank questions the magazine had posed about their sex lives. They invited *Cosmopolitan*'s editor in chief, Helen Gurley Brown, to be on the air for a full-hour interview; they'd launch the radio version of the survey in the following hour.

Brown was perfect in setting it up, not prurient, just matter-of-fact. This is real life. This is what people do. When he finally began asking the pointed questions, Jerry maintained a neutral tone, encouraging frankness but avoiding any leering. The results were better than they'd hoped. Once the ice was broken on the air, it seemed that every woman in Philadelphia wanted to tell the city how early she had done it, how often she had done it, whether she had engaged in oral sex or anal sex, what positions she had used, and what rooms of the house she had done it in. It was a great show—and in a way, a turning point. This was a new way to push the envelope. Maybe the audience was ready for something different from Jerry Williams.

He and Tolz cooked up some political satire with local comics, getting them to parody Mayor Frank Rizzo and President Carter, among others. Jerry played the straight man, asking the questions that allowed the comics to deliver their zingers. He wanted to hold on to the substance of issues as always, but he also made his approach a little tougher, a little younger, to stay current with the audience's expectations. Along the same line, he took one of the station's liabilities—the multiple phone numbers—and turned it into a piece of shtick, identifying people calling from South Jersey as yahoos and baiting them to call in on the Yahoo Line, the one with the New Jersey area code.

In the fall of 1979 Jerry came to the conclusion that there was no point in maintaining the big house in Milton any more. There were no more big parties, the kids were there less and less, and it was time to take some of the money he had earned out of that big property. He also thought that relocating the family might solve the problem with little Andi. She'd taken to hanging around with some characters at Milton High who made her parents more than a little uneasy.

So he found Teri a beautiful (if less palatial) home in Palm Beach, a short ride from the shopping on Worth Avenue and a few steps from the ocean. She agreed with the wisdom of the move, but she hated the weeks of drudgery that it meant. As she packed, she told herself she'd miss those autumn days when she could walk among the fallen leaves.

By now Eve was on her own at Bridgewater State, but Susan and Andi went with their mother. Susan was philosophical—it was just a shift from one small college to another, and she'd be living at home as usual. But Andi was beside herself—she was being uprooted from friends in the Boston area and the only home she'd ever really known. She was being transferred to a small private school because she was a problem kid. She raged and sulked. It came to a head a few days after they got to Florida.

Jerry responded in kind. "You're in one of the most beautiful places in the country. You're two doors from the ocean. What's wrong with you?"

Teri tried charm and reason, only to hear her youngest daughter call her a bitch. That tore it.

Jerry shouted, "Don't you dare ever call your mother that!" He hit her.

It was the only time Andi could remember her father raising his hand to her. Apparently, it was as much of a shock to Jerry as it was to her. That night he stopped by her room on his way to bed for a makeup talk. He became tender, speaking in a tone he rarely used with his kids. "If you love somebody, never go to bed mad at them."

That brought them closer, but it still didn't stop her from running away from Teri's house to be with her friends in Milton a couple of times, as Jerry had done when he was unhappy in Flatbush. He always said Andi was more like him than either of the other two.

When the smoke cleared from the big family move, Jerry took stock. Buying in Florida had used up most of the money from selling in Massachusetts, but he was able to put $55,000 in the bank, and he still owned three of the original four lots in Milton. Not bad.

A few days after the closing on the Palm Beach house, a mob of Iranians seized the U.S. embassy in Tehran. Sixty-three Americans were among the ninety people who were taken hostage and imprisoned in the embassy. As it was to so many other Americans, the news was unwelcome and baffling to Jerry. On its face, this looked like another one of those holdovers of the bad old Cold War days. We'd propped up this tyrant for decades because he was a dependable Bulwark against Communism, and now there had been a revolution overthrowing him, and we were getting some of the fallout from it. But what was the point of taking over the embassy? What were these people so *mad* about?

Conservative talk show hosts of all stripes, from people who were reasoned and careful like David Brudnoy and Barry Farber, to people who were blue-collar or ideological like Irv Homer or Lester Kinsolving, got a big boost from the Iranian hostage crisis. The momentum of talk, the weight of the audience, the confidence of investment—all began to shift to the right.

Bob Grant, one of New York's monster talk radio hosts who, like Jerry, was one of the Prophets, was among those who now looked like they had been right all along. His tough approach, part of the legacy of Joe Pyne, had occasionally been a problem for management—he'd had nothing nice to say about Martin Luther King, for example. In 1980, as happened at some other times in his career, he went too far. This time he suggested that some of his colleagues at WOR got their jobs primarily because of their color or sex. That didn't sit too well with RKO General, the station's owners, who were battling the FCC on a completely different issue at the time and didn't need Bob rocking the boat. They told him to take a hike while they decided whether they should can him altogether.

Jerry heard about it and gave Grant a platform at WWDB. Despite the fact that he and Jerry didn't agree politically, they respected each other professionally. Jerry knew Grant could be outrageous and entertaining at the same time; the bottom line was that he was good on the air, period. Jerry shook up the air schedule, moving Wynn Moore to the weekend and Dominic Quinn to mornings. He slotted Bob Grant in just before his own show. The two of them excoriated Carter from different angles. Grant thought that some tough military action was needed to knock some sense into those ragheads (as he called the Iranians). Jerry wasn't so sure that you could solve this with troops, but the administration seemed to be just dithering around, and that would just give troublemakers in other countries some bad ideas.

After several months, Grant tired of commuting from North Jersey and playing second fiddle to Jerry. When he left, Jerry moved Irv Homer up from nights to middays and brought Stan Major in from Miami to do nights.

The modest gradual improvements Jerry had made bolstered WWDB's position. A solid overall audience of more than three hundred thousand, bragging rights as Philadelphia's number one talk station, a strong showing for his own show . . . maybe he'd proven everything he could prove in Philly. He began looking around again.

WNWS in Miami made an offer, and Jerry took it. After twenty-two months on the air in Philly, he said good-bye without a tear. Was he more cynical about the business now, or was it just that he had learned—as the syndicated talk host Bruce Williams liked to say—not to love something that couldn't love him back?

He'd done some good shows. That old Watergate conspirator G. Gordon Liddy was on with him in November 1979, and they really mixed it up. Phil

Donahue visited in March 1980. Barbara and George Bush came on in April 1980, before George was nominated to run for veep with Ronald Reagan. He had Al Franken and Tom Davis in October 1980—funny guys, with lots of barbs about Mr. General Electric and Fancy Nancy Shmancy.

There were some good entertainment guests, too. Maynard Ferguson, the high-note jazz trumpeter and leader of a latter-day big band. The opera singer Anna Moffo. Carol Channing, now an old friend from all her appearances on the show through the years.

"G'bye, cheese steak samwitches and soft pretzels. G'bye, Betty Berneman. G'bye, Alan Tolz. G'bye, Philadelphia."

What was the point of working in Miami? Sure, the weather was appealing—when you're fifty-seven, the prospect of another long, cold northeastern winter can be genuinely depressing. But was that the only reason for leaving an FM talk station where momentum seemed to be building? Maybe he thought that he should play his ratings success in Philadelphia into more money while he could. Maybe he thought his on-air options were dwindling and he would have to build his résumé as a program director. And winter was coming.

Those eight months in south Florida at WNWS, from November 1980 through June 1981, are a puzzle. This station was only two and a half years old, and almost two years of its life had been spent in trying to make it a news outlet (hence the call letters). The facility was grim, like a machine shop. Cement block walls. Industrial carpeting. There was a gas station outside.

It *did* have some good talent. A year or so before Jerry arrived, they'd nabbed south Florida's free-form, openly gay, scatological Neil Rogers, a commanding presence in the market. They moved a former NWS newsman, Al Rantel, to a talk seat, and he had established himself as a smart, energetic personality. But there was room for improvement.

Jerry put himself in afternoon drive time. And he commissioned Ken Nordine to do a new package for the station, along the lines of the one he'd done for WWDB a year and a half before. The identity line turned out to be a good one—"*The* Talk Station," Nordine intoned, giving the station a Voice-of-God credibility.

It was in Miami that Jerry watched the Reagan revolution begin, where he interviewed the Chicago Seven activist Jerry Rubin, the futurist Alvin Toffler, and the feminist Erica Jong, and where he re-interviewed G. Gordon Liddy. It was where he did another sex survey on the air, where Dr. Gilbert Holloway visited again. Where Nothing Was Happening.

There were afternoons when it seemed no one was listening except people over eighty. They wouldn't respond to his monologues. They obsessed about crime. Schleppers and shmendricks and alta kochers! They wouldn't talk into the mouthpiece of the *telephone!* Jerry Williams couldn't strike sparks on the air. What was *wrong* with these people?

He got himself another one-person apartment. His feet started to hurt and he was diagnosed with gout. He took up with a Latina cop from North Miami. Jerry Williams? Sleeping with a *policewoman?* This really must have been a midlife crisis.

By May 1981 his frustration was all over the air. No good calls? No interaction? A sudden inspiration: Okay, folks, I'll do everything myself. It was late in the month, the day after a particularly fruitless afternoon of pushing and prodding the audience for something, anything. He started with a monologue—what a sad state of affairs we were in. Didn't anybody care? He'd seen apathy before, but never like this. Things ain't what they used to be. Wasn't that an old Ellington song? Well, they ain't. You wanna hear how things used to be?

Miami Beach. It used to be a special place. Now—pah! God's waiting room.

The stories started coming out on the air. Stories Jerry had told to John Rosica, Paul Fanning, Steve Elman, Alan Tolz, his other producers and professional colleagues, all those stories started coming out over the air. An hour went by—that was nothing, really. Jerry had done hour-long monologues many times before.

As the second hour opened up, he asked the audience rhetorically if they thought he could keep talking for the full four hours. Hey, wasn't that the plot of a book? It was like that book Stanley Elkin had written back in the late sixties—*The Dick Gibson Show.* Did they know Elkin had dedicated that book to Jerry and Long John and Barry Gray and Jean Shepherd, among others? There was this all-night talk show, see, where all the guests gradually stop talking and the host has to fill the air by himself—so he just does it, tells the audience anything and everything. But nobody had actually done it in reality. But why not? Jerry Williams presents the world's largest monologue. A long march of words from 2:00 until 6:00 P.M. Call the people at the *Guinness Book of World Records.*

He posed questions for people to answer off the air, just to be sure there were a few individuals still with him. What were PT-19s? What was the distance along the right-field fence at Ebbets Field? What is Xyloprim? (A couple of hours later, the answers: a PT-19 was a trainer airplane, the kind he'd flown in Texas; the right-field line ran 297 feet; Xyloprim was a drug to control gout.)

Then he trolled for opinions on his performance. Y' never know in radio if you're not getting instant gratification with phone calls, y' know. D' y' wanna hear a tape of his interview with Van Lingle Mungo? Should he keep talking or take a call?

By the five-to-six hour, he was digging deep. He remembered Joanne McCoy, who was the reeeal McCoy. He recalled the original name of the show he did with Bud Smith, the show that became *The Gag Busters.* It was *Quaker City Capers!* Wouldja believe that? He rhapsodized on Brooklyn and the great Nathan's hot dogs of old.

"When I say the Nathan's hot dogs of old, it's because they ain't what they used t' be. . . . Those Nathan's hot dogs in my youth were the greatest. They were only a dime. And in the dead of winter, you'd hang out in Coney Island, and get those Nathan's hot dogs, with just some mustard, and sort of a weak-looking orange drink, but it was good. And it was fun. And they were great. But all the things you remember from your youth, even if you're only thirty, and you can reckon back to . . . the time when you were twelve or fifteen, things have changed so much that it's not fun to go back to those days and think about how things were, because they never are going to be the same. Nathan's hot dogs are not the same. Sorry. They're not what they used to be."

Free-associating, through Philly steak samwitches, chili con carne at places his dad used to take him in Brooklyn for a treat, the Famous Restaurant—that Florida throwback to the old days in New York, when they used t' put all that stuff on the table for free, a nine-course, a ten-course meal, and it only cost you a buck eighty-five. But things ain't what they used t' be.

His father's Essex, and the cigars he used to smoke. Kaiser rolls in Chicago. The way that Brigham's Ice Cream in New England had reduced the size of their cones to save money. His Hudson Hornet and the Allentown accident.

And then a parade of the cars he'd owned. The green DeSoto. An Austin-Healey. A Volkswagen Beetle. His Jaguar. That Chrysler 300-C. What a car: "The guy demonstrated it to me by taking me down the Edens Expressway in Chicago and putting it into third gear. Y' know, this is the one with the push buttons. Had push-button transmission. And I tell ya, in second, I think, he took me up to eighty. I was frightened to death, but this car—the front end used t' take off. This was Kelly green, white-leather interior—beige-leather interior. With a twin-hemi engine. Unbelievable. It got about six miles on the gallon, something like that."

His 1972 Mercedes 280 SE. His 1967 Cadillac limousine, which he drove around himself in Boston, like a chauffeur who'd stolen the boss's car. Speaking of that, what about that 1972 Lincoln Continental Mark IV? "I once drove it up to a hotel and gave it to the guy at the hotel, and y' know, thinking he was gonna park it. Guess what? It wasn't the doorman! He stole it! *Stole* the *car!* . . . Never saw—yes, I *did* see the car again. It wound up in Roxbury in Boston, and they'd taken everything off it. Tires, everyth—stripped it, stripped the car down. Wouldja believe—that's a funny way to steal a car, isn't it? To wait at the door of a major hotel, say, 'Take y' car, sir? Yes, sir, take y' car!' Put the key in and drive it away."

The stories kept coming. Six o'clock arrived and he hadn't even scratched the surface.

Jerry's dissatisfaction with Miami, which had always been at a barely-under-control simmer, bubbled over in mid-1981. He was tired of his cheesy office, the absolute lack of decor. So he used his position as operations and program director to authorize a modest makeover. The most expensive renovation he had in mind was new carpeting, not a big deal, fifteen or twenty dollars a square yard. He came in late on the day the guys were supposed to move his furniture around and put in the new rug, expecting that at least *something* about his situation had improved. When he walked in, he was stunned. The general manager had countermanded his design decision and told the flooring guys to hold off on the expensive stuff. So there on the floor of the program director's office was more of the cheap, tacky outdoor junk that everyone else at WNWS had, about as stylish as an off-the-rack suit from Bob's Discount Menswear.

Jerry stormed into the GM's office, shouting and waving his arms. What was the *idea?*

The carpet he'd ordered was an unauthorized expense. Jerry should know that these things had to cross the GM's desk first.

He leaned over. He grabbed the lip of the boss's cheap desk, a rattle-and-bang piece no better than the stuff Mac Richmond used to buy. He pushed the desk over into the GM's lap. Papers, pictures, mementos, everything spilled onto the floor.

"That's it. I'm leaving."

Fifty-eight years old—that's still young. If he found another job in Miami, he'd turn into an old man. *Got* to get out of here! What's going on in Boston? he wondered.

Funny thing. Remember Top 40? Believe it or not, Top 40 or something like it was still on the air in Boston—WRKO had stuck with it, and stuck with it, and stuck with it, but they were finally ready to acknowledge the new world and throw in the towel.

Jerry talked with Bob Fish, the general manager of RKO—which everyone in Boston called "Arko," as if it were a dog food or something.

Look, Jer. We're gonna take this station all-talk. Remember Charlie Van

Dyke? He's our program director. This isn't gonna be like WEEI. We'll have real talk personalities, let 'em go for it, push the envelope, do it the right way.

Bob, you know what I've been *doing* for five years? Listening to talk, all over the East. Most of the people who're doing it sound dead. The *right* people, you can make it work. We've got a concept down here that sounds great. *The* Talk Station. I'll send you some of our spots.

(A pause.)

Hey, Jer? You wanna come back? You want afternoon drive?

How much, Bob?

(Then the usual haggling, the number finally landing at $70,000.)

You know what, Bob?

What, Jerry?

I can't fuckin' wait.

9 BOSTON FOREVER

Outrage is not enough.
—*Lou Dobbs, in an interview with Jon Stewart on* The Daily Show, *October 10, 2006*

"I'm back, Kevin. I'm back."

Not "Wake Up, America." No statements of principle or pronunciamentos. This time it would be personal.

The Jerry Williams who arrived in Boston in mid-August 1981 was no longer idealistic and headstrong, as he was in 1957, when he began his first WMEX show. No longer the crusading leftie on his way to national syndication and his own TV show, as in 1968. No longer the local activist gripped by a midlife crisis. He had been seasoned and tempered and soured.

Jerry had been Out There for five years. He could hear that the younger talkers weren't doing things the way he had done them. The slaughter of sixties icons and the fecklessness of seventies idealism had left a great hole in the heart of America, which the Little Guys were now filling with religion, patriotism, anger, and beer. The talkers of the era were responding to that, building on Bob Grant and Joe Pyne—they were angry at the incompetence and folly of the people who were elected, skeptical about idealism and sentiment, soothing their disillusionment with bitterness and irony. They were slapping callers around because it felt good to hurt people, because the callers themselves had come to expect a little pain, and because the people who would never call had come to enjoy hearing others humiliated.

Jerry knew that the WRKO signal restricted his audience to eastern New England. He knew Boston's landscape of corruption and self-absorption. Debate on national issues and political philosophy? Let the Sunday morning

TV shows handle that stuff. He would view national and international issues through a local lens, or as a subject for satire. He had already encouraged the WRKO promotion department to bill him as "The Man You Love to Hate."

But Jerry was still old-fashioned in one significant way. He still believed in representing the Little Guy. He still thought that ordinary people needed an advocate, someone who didn't have money on a horse in the race.

He made Mayor Kevin White stand in for everything about life in Boston that was unfair, arrogant, unresponsive, vainglorious. And he wanted Bostonians to know that there was at least one guy who was going to make trouble.

So the first words he spoke on WRKO were: "I'm back, Kevin. I'm back."

He had the good platform, that 2:00-to-6:00 P.M. shift he'd fought for at WMEX and then at WITS and worked as program director in Philadelphia and Miami to have. The one concession he'd made to get more money was working the shift six days a week.

Jerry, PD Charlie van Dyke, and General Manager Bob Fish, agreed: WRKO could prove itself as an all-talk station only by showing well in one of the money dayparts—morning or afternoon drive. They didn't have a strong morning show yet, so Jerry was the key to launching the station's new identity. He'd set the stage and warm things up from 2:00 to 4:00, so by the time more news, traffic, weather, and sports were added for the drive-home crowd, the show's momentum would already be established.

Jerry's style, by its very nature, would tend to draw people of all ages with an interest in politics and issues. He could always count on older listeners— by now, it was almost gospel in the business that listeners over sixty-five would gravitate to talk stations for the company, if nothing else. Intellectually active stay-at-home moms (and sometimes dads) were another natural constituency. Some people could get away with listening to the radio where they worked, and a proportion of that crowd preferred voices in the background rather than music. Additionally, technology was beginning to change the way talk would be perceived by listeners in their cars. Phones in cars were proliferating—not cell phones yet, but phones with antennas.

If Jerry's identity was clear, the rest of WRKO ("TalkRadio 68," to use the station's positioning identification) was not.

The morning man was the most gentlemanly and sweet of Boston's air personalities, Norm Nathan, managing a magazine format of chat, news, sports, weather, and traffic. He was revered—no, loved—by his colleagues, but most people on the WRKO staff knew that Norm was too nice for talk and the wrong guy for A.M. drive.

Mid-mornings were occupied by Dick Syatt, whom Jerry remembered as a kid intern at WBZ. In less than ten years, the guy had turned himself into

Boston's Mr. Lonelyhearts. His radio show was a sort of personals-column-of-the-air, facilitating matchups between people looking for love, and it had a symbiotic relationship with Syatt's entrepreneurial activities as an organizer of mixer events at local watering holes.

From noon until 2:00 P.M., a psychologist named Dr. Harry Sobel did *The Thought Process,* a show devoted to personal issues. Sobel occasionally brought personalities into the studio to go "on the couch" and answer his let's-go-back-and-look-at-your-childhood questions. He led into Jerry's late-afternoon slot.

Jerry's old stablemate from BZ, Guy Mainella, was back in the early-evening sports chair, this time coming out of Jerry's show. Guy's subtle, ironic on-air style made his show one of the few things on the air in Boston that sports fans could listen to without feeling their brain cells dying.

The libertarian David Brudnoy, now less stuffy and more of a personality than he had been in Jerry's WBZ days, had been hired away from WHDH a few months earlier to do the late nights—that had been a good move, since thousands of people were loyal to him.

All these disparate parts did not add up to a station that spoke to the market with a coordinated voice, but that wasn't unusual in the early eighties. Talk radio in general hadn't found a defining identity. Everyone in the business knew that it was in transition from a world of mavericks and oddities to something that could be codified and measured, but no one could predict exactly where it was going.

Some big names had already begun moving the genre toward what it would eventually become. Larry King's all-night interview show had become a huge success nationally, primarily because of King's incredible guest list. Out in San Diego, Bill Ballance had pulled back a little after getting burned for his frank sex-talk shows, but he was still being naughty when he could. Don Imus was doing very well in New York with his sardonic attitude, a crew of regular characters, a little political humor. Sally Jessy Raphaël, taking a softer approach, was beginning to make a name for herself among the roster of syndicated talk hosts distributed by NBC's Talknet. And there was a growing crop of conservative or libertarian hosts, beginning with old-timers (that is, guys only a little younger than Jerry) such as Barry Farber and Lester Kinsolving, who had been keeping the faith for decades. A younger but mature Gene Burns was well established as a libertarian personality in Orlando. Neil Rogers was shifting to the right at Jerry's previous shop, WNWS in Miami. Neal Boortz had a rep in Atlanta.

But hot issues didn't define the genre. There were all kinds of talk shows on the air—chatty conversation, psychological counseling, financial and legal advice, cooking and gardening tips, paranormal phenomena. And a lot of today's famous names weren't doing talk shows yet. Bill O'Reilly was in the midst of a multistation, multicity TV odyssey, trying to establish himself as a TV reporter. Howard Stern was still officially a DJ because he was playing music every once in a while, but he was beginning to make a name for himself in the District of Columbia as the Guy Who'd Say Anything. Rush Limbaugh wasn't even on the air; he was working for the Kansas City Royals.

Within this forest of talent and styles, Jerry Williams was still a Mighty Oak. Twenty-five years doing something gives a man an edge.

The WRKO operation was downtown, sharing a facility with Channel 7, right on the doorstep of the urbanly renewed Government Center, which had replaced colorful and seedy old Scollay Square. Jerry's physical residence, at least temporarily, was an apartment in Charles River Park, the luxury buildings built on the ashes of the West End, just a few blocks from work. If there was an irony here—if anyone pointed out that Crusader Jerry of the fifties, who had railed against the heartless city planners displacing whole neighborhoods of urban poor, was now earning his living and making his home in the very buildings he once deplored—Modern Jerry got over it. He was in the best broadcast studios he'd seen since WRC, better than the ones at WBZ by a long shot. His apartment had a commanding view of the Charles River and pretty old Cambridge. He'd been on the outside looking in for five years. This was *much* better.

Through the end of 1981, Jerry tested and shaped the new show. Local identity was key, no doubt. Jerry knew that Bay Staters had moved right like everyone else in the country—on the same day in 1980 that Reagan won Massachusetts by a few thousand votes, the voters approved Proposition 2½, a hard-edged limit on the amount that cities and towns could raise through property taxes. The *Network* refrain that Paddy Chayevsky had written for Howard Beale—mad as hell, not gonna take it anymore—was a good place to start.

In the first weeks, Jerry got a welcoming call from good old Grace, Queen of the Cockamamies. Bob Ness, who had created the Grace character for Jerry at WMEX, was as funny as he'd ever been, and he fit well with the approach Jerry wanted to take. In a way, Grace's appearance was a marker—she'd been part of the furniture on the old WMEX when Jerry wanted the show to have a strong local feel, had faded into the background during the WBZ years, and now reemerged to take a position among the comics who gave the WRKO show its satire.

He told his new producer, Paul Yovino, about the fun he'd had with the sex surveys in Philadelphia and Miami; they would definitely do one in Boston, and soon. Almost all the tools were in place. All Jerry needed was a cause, a classic Williams campaign to show the community what his new show would be about.

Jerry was getting what he considered appropriate deference from the other RKO hosts—except for David Brudnoy. During the first few months, as Jerry listened to Brudnoy's show, he heard Brudnoy's complement of conservative callers bashing him as an old-fashioned liberal with tired ideas. Wasn't Brudnoy listening to the stuff Jerry was doing in the afternoons, the shots he was taking at the arrogant characters running Boston and Massachusetts *today*, right *now?* Jerry kept waiting for Brudnoy to say something in his defense. Instead, there was quiet, quiet as another caller put another needle in him. As he listened one night, he was thinking: Did this guy know what it meant to be professional, to support your colleagues in a format? As soon as he saw Brudnoy, he was talking.

"David, I'm really sick of it."

"What're you talking about?"

"I've got the radio on at night. I'm hearing the things you let people say about me on the air. We're supposed to stick together. It's not supposed to be a contest between the old fart in the afternoon and the new conservative at night."

"Oh, come on. You've got it wrong, Jerry. People have a right to their opinions. I'm not putting words in their mouths. Take it easy."

Brudnoy, the professor, elegantly pontificating—and patronizing someone who disagreed with him, as he so often did on the air. Jerry reacted the way he did to other people who'd gone to college and lorded it over the uneducated—he went nuts, ripping David's office phone off the wall, tossing it across the room. "You just make damn sure that shit stops!"

By the end of the year, Charlie Van Dyke was gone and Bob Fish gave himself the ultimate authority for programming as well as general operations. Jerry thought that decision was unwise, but he kept quiet about it while he worked on getting the show moving in the right direction. He told Fish that he wanted to shake things up with some new approaches, and they tussled about what would be acceptable and what wouldn't.

King Kevin conveniently launched Jerry's first big WRKO crusade for him. Beginning in late 1981, Boston police officers—surely pushed into it by Mayor Deluxe—were enforcing traffic regulations with a new verve. They ended their customary winking when cars were double-parked, or blocking bus stops, or tarrying too long in limited-time zones. They were nailing unsuspecting drivers on every infraction they could find, generating more fines than ever. And if the beleaguered drivers ignored their tickets, the city had a new weapon to torture them into submission, the Denver Boot. Why was all of this happening? Jerry knew why: it was Kevin White's version of extortion. He was undoubtedly ordering the papering of the city with tickets because Boston needed more income to support the Mayah's lavish vision of a "World-Class City." The Boot allowed White to hold citizens' cars for ransom.

Who better to sound the alarm than Jerry?

Jerry bemoaned the blizzard of tickets and the truckloads of Boots, sympathizing with the poor commuters and tourists who were being victimized. Give Kevin the Boot! Then he ramped it up with the Great Boston Ticket Party. "Send me copies of your tickets!" he said, and listeners were only too happy to respond. Bags of photocopies—and some original orange parking citations, too—piled up at WRKO.

While the tickets were accumulating, on January 13, 1982, Howard Stern made headlines, at least among broadcasters, when a jet fell out of the sky after takeoff from Washington, D.C., and slammed into the Fourteenth Street bridge. The news stations there swung into action with copters and live coverage, but Howard made the crash a subject for satire: he called the local Air Florida office on the air and asked a customer service rep for the fare from National Airport to the bridge. Talk radio was changing, all right.

The day after Howard's bad-boy prank, Jerry did the first sex survey in Boston radio history. He and Paul Yovino had been working out the details of the show for more than a week. But it seemed to some that Jerry Williams was jumping on a new bandwagon—a race to the bottom on the highway of bad taste.

The reality of the Sex Surveys was very different from their reputation. A lot of people listened to them, but even more talked about them or heard about them secondhand. In some ways, what actually was on the air was representative of Jerry's own attitudes toward sex. He loved the thrill of the chase when he was single, didn't mind using his radio rep as a springboard to the bedroom, and had never been particularly faithful to his wife. So he got a charge out of those shows, no question. But there was something more. Jerry had a deep and never-satisfied curiosity about women. What did they want? What made them tick? Were they essentially different from men or essentially the same? The Sex Surveys were not just about sexual practices. He didn't even want to hear from men, really. The surveys were excuses to have conversations with women about their private lives. They were part of his quest to answer the questions he could never answer any other way.

When Jerry kicked off a survey, he always warned that it was maturity time—if you were likely to be offended by frank discussion of sexual matters, go listen to another station. This was going to be serious, and it was going to be sexual. The rules were simple. As he had done in Philadelphia, Jerry asked questions taken directly from the *Cosmopolitan* survey. He invited any woman who wanted to share to call in and answer the questions. Not just the supposedly liberated *Cosmo* readership, but real women, average women, and only women, thank you very much . . . at least for the first couple of days of the survey. Why only women? Simple, Jerry said. "Men lie."

Women simply came out of the woodwork during the first Sex Survey. The voices weren't the low and sultry ones men might have been expecting. These women sounded in every way like the women callers Jerry always got. Except that they were talking about sex.

At least one psychologist in the city admired Jerry's interview technique. He didn't leer. He didn't smirk. But he wasn't clinical either. He was sort of cheery about it, pleasant, lighthearted. He seemed to put his women callers at ease, talking to them as if sex was no big deal. At what age did you first have intercourse? Uh-huh. Did you enjoy it? And are you married now? Is it more enjoyable for you now? How long have you been married? How often do you do it? Three times a week—well, that seems to be about average. How often do you have an orgasm? What are your favorite positions?

The questions weren't always the same. If Jerry got an interesting response—not something dirty, just something interesting—he'd follow up. If a forty-two-year-old woman said she'd *never* had sex, or if a woman said she had come twenty times in a row, or if she said she liked to do it on the washing machine sometimes, well, that was interesting. You *never* have an orgasm? Well, have you ever talked to your husband about that? Doesn't he want to *help* you have an orgasm?

In late January 1982, Jerry put out the call to his people to assemble for the Boot-and-ticket protest. He wanted listeners by the hundreds to gather at Faneuil Hall, Boston's Cradle of Liberty, where the Founding Fathers had given their speeches on freedom and where Bostonians had had public meetings for generations since. When everyone was present, Jerry would say a few words, and then they'd march down to the waterfront, just as the Sons of Liberty had done in their Tea Party, and dump all the offending (copies of) tickets into the harbor.

The Great Boston Ticket Party went pretty well, considering—although it got postponed for a couple of days by the weather and it turned out that they couldn't actually chuck the tickets into the water because of the antipollution laws. A nice crowd showed up, he got a chance to stand on the steps of Faneuil Hall and work the crowd with an orange T-shirt ("I Got Booted in Boston"), and the press gave the event some coverage (although only Jerry's arm made it into the *Globe*'s photo).

Jerry Williams at the head of the Great Boston Ticket Party, on the way from Faneuil Hall to Boston Harbor, February 23, 1982.
PHOTO PROBABLY TAKEN BY JOE DENNEHY

In April 1982 Vanessa Redgrave was scheduled to come to town because the Boston Symphony had hired her to narrate Stravinsky's *Oedipus Rex.* But the BSO hadn't given consideration to Redgrave's outspoken support for the Palestine Liberation Organization, including her endorsement of the concept of "right of return" for Palestinians that would have the practical effect of ending Israel's Jewish identity. Boston's Jewish community made a big noise about boycotting or picketing Redgrave's impending appearance, so the BSO canceled it. Redgrave went public with an elegantly managed embarrassment campaign, threatening to sue the orchestra for breach of contract.

This was a perfect issue for the new show. The BSO looked clueless, Redgrave looked radical—and all this over a musical performance that had no political resonance at all? Jerry told Yovino to find Redgrave—get her to come to Boston for a show on the controversy. Yovino got lucky; he called her agent, got to Redgrave in London, proposed the idea, and she said yes. As it happened, she'd be in New York in April, so it would be easy to make it to Boston. Would WRKO pick up the tab for the flight?

Bob Fish loved it. He okayed the expenses, rented a Rolls to pick her up at the airport, made it into a genuine media event. Redgrave would be in the studio for two hours—the first half would be a news conference hosted by Jerry, live on the air, and the second would be give-and-take with the callers. So on April 13, the newspapers and the major TV stations had to come to WRKO and build their stories around *The Jerry Williams Show.* Fish made sure that the station's biggest banners were strung around the studio so that the TV cameras couldn't avoid them.

In May, Fish relinquished half of his job, the program manager piece, to Mel Miller, an old hand in the business. Jerry approved of the choice. Mel was one of the survivors of the Mac Richmond MEX days, when he had been on the air as a Top-40 jock from 1959 to 1961. Before getting the RKO job, he'd been PD at Boston's first all-talk station, WEEI, one of those anemic "balanced" formats, but Mel welcomed the chance to build something more forceful. He put up signs in the studio saying, "Who cares?" to remind the air people that the audience came first and that they had to rein in their own indulgences.

One of Mel's first priorities was morning drive. Despite the fact that everyone loved Norm Nathan, he had to go. To replace him and change the tone of the mornings, Mel tapped Janet Jeghelian, a promising young host who had been exiled by WBZ to their all-night shift, and Tony Pepper, a guy with a strong background in TV news. Jeghelian was one of the first women to do talk in Boston since the days of the housewife-interview shows in the thirties, and the combination Mel put in place was one of the first man-woman morning teams in the country. Their mandate was to follow the news, get the reaction of the newsmakers, and express their opinions about what was happening.

By mid-1982 the basic elements of TalkRadio 68—*The* Talk Station—were in place. All they needed were ratings.

All during the first part of the year, Jerry had been talking with Teri off and on about their daughters: Susan's wedding and Andi's graduation.

In Florida, Sue had met Bill Hobson, who had asked for her hand on one of Jerry's visits. Jerry had unenthusiastically granted it ("Ah, live with her another year, why dontcha?"). They set a date and Teri began shelling out the Parents of the Bride expenses.

At the same time Andi was finishing high school, where she had done pretty well academically. Jerry groused to Teri about having to make two trips to Florida in the space of a month, but he was there for Andi's cap-and-gown party and then again to give Sue away in June. She looked beautiful in that dress, he thought. But he felt old. Good thing there was so much distance between Palm Beach, where he had to be husband and father (Lord, maybe grandfather soon), and Boston, where he could be single, sort of.

His womanizing had to be more discreet there than in Philly and Miami, since everyone thought of him as married—hell, he was still using the "Good night, T" signoff when he ended his WRKO show at 6:00 P.M., even though Teri couldn't possibly hear it.

An opportunity presented itself. Dick Syatt, RKO's mid-morning guy, asked Jerry to emcee one of his mixer parties on a Friday night, where an attractive young woman caught his eye, surrounded by interested men. Who's that? An acquaintance identified her: Sandy something, about thirty, newly divorced. Tell her I'd like to meet her. The intermediary returned a few minutes later. "Jer," she said, "if you want to talk to her, you'll have to go over there." Jerry played it cool. "Get me her number." He filed the name away. Sandy Nagro, not very impressed with the big radio star. Oh yeah?

The next day, he was prepping for the show at RKO, pulled out the number, dialed it.

"Sandy, this is Jerry Williams."

No clue.

"I saw you at Dick Syatt's party yesterday. I was the emcee. You don't know who I am, do you?"

"Should I?"

Well, *this* was new. "I'm on the radio. WRKO. Listen, my show's about to start. Why don't you tune me in and call me after?"

Sandy Nagro had moved to Boston in 1979 with her husband and two kids, when Jerry was working in Philly. She had been born Sandra Kohlmann, been brought up in New York City in the fifties, went to boarding school in New Jersey. Now she was divorced. She never had been in a town where she could have heard Jerry or heard of him. He was just another one of these guys talking on the radio, and she didn't even like that kind of stuff. But she listened anyway. His show that Saturday was fun, not political. She figured, what the hell. She had to start circulating somewhere.

The first date was on July 4. What can we do that's patriotic? Hey, you mean to tell me you've never been to Plymouth Rock? I'll take you out there, then we'll have dinner.

Sandy wouldn't give him her address—pick me up at that hotel where Dick Syatt had his party, okay? Jerry charmed her, played tour guide. There's a great place on the Cape, Anthony's Cummaquid Inn, let's go there. You know, my apartment overlooks the river in Boston, where they have the big fire-

Sandy Nagro, ca. 1982.

works. Why don't you come on back and watch them? This is the first time I'll have the chance to see them there myself.

You've seen the movie with the big romantic clinch and the fireworks all around—Hitchcock's *To Catch a Thief,* with Cary Grant and Grace Kelly? Jerry wasn't in that movie. Darkness falls, the Boston Pops are on the Esplanade playing at the Hatch Shell, and Sandy wants to go out on the balcony of Jerry's apartment. Go ahead, enjoy yourself.

What about you?

Nah. I'm a little afraid of heights, actually. Never go out there.

The fireworks start, Sandy watches them from the balcony, Jerry stays inside. After that, a clinch or two . . . it's a different movie.

In fact, it's a movie without a lot of romance in it. A month later, he confesses that he's married and they have a huge fight. But Sandy's hooked by then, charmed by Jerry's jokes, fascinated by the world he lives in and the chance to be a part of it. As things settled into a routine, she found out how little glamour there actually was. Jerry was fifty-eight and working six days a week. He'd come out of the studio spent, drained. Maybe they would go out to dinner at the No-Name or Rubin's Deli, places where he was known and could get a nice welcome. On Sundays they might drive to the Cape and go to an antiques auction or stop by the Brewster Country Store, a place Jerry loved to poke around in. Once in a while, she could get him to a Red Sox game. She found out that he really didn't like going somewhere unless it was a personal appearance or someplace where he'd be singled out in some way. Going to a show or a movie? Bah! A couple of times a year, if a big star was in town, or if it was a really big deal, but otherwise, he'd rather stay in. If Sandy was expecting show biz, she didn't get it.

It's hard to say why she loved him.

Only two weeks after Jerry met Sandy Nagro, Hizzoner made a personal appearance on *The Jerry Williams Show* and the shit hit the fan for the first time at TalkRadio 68.

Bob Fish was looking for ratings results. He had told everyone on the staff that he wanted the summer book to be big. Shows should be exciting, attention getting. Jerry immediately thought of Jim Morris, one of the comics who had done Frank Rizzo impressions for him in Philly. He'd already been on the Boston show once, and he'd been great.

What did Bob think of the idea of a gag interview with a comic imitating Kevin White? Jim Morris does a great impression. They'd have to do it on the phone because he's out on the West Coast now. Sure, great. Paul, set it up.

Yovino prepped Morris about the ground rules as they led up to the Friday, July 16, show. "We're not going to use Kevin White's name. Jerry's not going to say, 'The mayor is with us today,' or anything like that. Don't refer to City Hall or your wife, Katherine. You're just Hizzoner."

Morris had Kevin White nailed—the slightly hoarse tone, the tendency to bray—and he overlaid some sloppy pronunciation to suggest that Hizzoner might have had a three-martini lunch that day. Jerry set him up with some fairly straight questions. As the interview went on, Morris became more and more loopy. Calls started coming into the studio, and then to the RKO switchboard. The listeners weren't used to supposedly serious radio stations blurring the line like this. Was that really the Mayah? The guy sounds *drunk!* Get him off the air!

At the same time, calls were coming into City Hall. "The Mayah ought t' be ashamed of himself, behavin' like this. Someone over theyah should *do* somethin'!" The staff tuned in, and they were *not* happy.

Someone in Mayor White's office with a pipeline to an RKO vice president called the head office in New York. Did they know what WRKO was doing? This was outrageous. The mayor was furious. We demand a clarification *and* an apology. Yeah, yeah, we'll look into this right away.

So Bob Fish gets a call from corporate. And Mel Miller gets the word from Bob. And Mel delivers the word to Paul and Jerry while they're on the air. Of course, by that time, the segment is over. Jerry has already introduced Morris and explained that he does celebrity impersonations. Morris has already done Governor Ed King, President Reagan, and Julia Child. No matter. After the show—Fish's office. Both of you.

Uh-oh.

When Jerry and Paul walked in, Fish was still steaming about what had been on the air. This was a big guy, built like a linebacker, an imposing presence. Paul Yovino's severance check was already cut and signed. Fish thumped it down on the desk in front of Yovino. "Today's show was completely unacceptable, Paul. You're done."

The kid is white. Jerry can see him thinking, Jesus, they're *firing* me.

Jerry jumped up. "Bob, this was *your* idea. You told us to push the envelope, and that's what we did. No one in their right mind could have heard this as anything more than a satire of Kevin White."

"Jerry, you better not push me on this. You know damn well I didn't approve the shit you put on the air today. If you don't like it, there's the fucking door."

Back and forth, with the heat rising. Did Fish tell Jerry to take a hike? Ultimately, the two of them stormed out and Yovino went to clear out his desk. He got his stuff and was standing at the elevator. Fish saw him, came down the hall, fired a parting shot: "Tell Jerry t' show up tomorrow, or he'll never work again."

Yovino asked people he knew for advice. Get a lawyer, Paul. Go to the papers yourself. Get a lawyer *and* go to the papers. He talked to City Councilor Mike McCormack—a lawyer and not exactly a buddy of Kevin White—and discovered that there might be grounds to sue RKO. Then he did the interviews. He wasn't going to take this lying down, he said. Robert McLean of the *Globe* wrote about it. Howie Carr of the *Herald* wrote about it. The way it got played, Jerry Williams was one of the heavies, too, letting his poor producer take the fall for him. Jerry read Howie's piece on the air. He didn't make any comment of his own about it, but listeners could tell that the story choked him up.

Then it all went away. There was a new producer—a former WRKO reporter named Chris Ryan, temporarily assigned—and the lawsuit disappeared. Yovino ultimately came to see the humor in it. Life went on.

In fact, there was no time for anyone to brood. At the start of June, Israeli forces had begun an operation to push the PLO into northern Lebanon. By mid-June they were shelling Beirut. By the end of July, they were in control of Beirut's airport. A couple of weeks later the Israeli consul in Boston gave Bob Fish a call. Would any of the WRKO hosts like to join a government-sponsored trip to see the situation on the ground in Israel and Lebanon? Bob saw the conflict-of-interest issues immediately and turned the offer down—but then he realized that he had an opportunity in hand to rebuild the reputation of the Williams show. Would the consul assist WRKO in setting up some live broadcasts from Israel, which WRKO would pay for?

Bob Fish told Jerry and Chris Ryan that they were going to Israel. Two weeks later they arrived in Tel Aviv. For four days Ryan scrambled to bring guests to their improvised studio on the eighteenth floor of the Sheraton or to get them on the phone. He got former Israeli Prime Minister Yitzhak Rabin, the Lebanese journalist Rami Khoury, a Palestinian resident of Hebron, an Israeli settler, a member of the Lebanese Parliament, and others representing a broad swath of viewpoints, and most of their guests answered questions from listeners in Boston. Sixteen live hours originating from a country at war. The most dramatic show included taped conversations with members of the Israeli Defense Forces as Jerry and Ryan visited the ruins of Beirut's airport. As always, Jerry asked some difficult questions—so much so that a Jewish man from Texas came close to attacking him in the middle of a broadcast and had to be held off by Ryan.

Those four days in August 1982 were Jerry Williams's only broadcasts from a war zone, his only broadcasts originating outside North America. They were career milestones, and yet they brought more heat than light. Jerry had never been a journalist. His forte was How and Why interviewing, and the speed of this trip didn't give him the chance to familiarize himself with the territory so that he could do his best work. Perhaps the most important aspect of the shows from Israel was the opportunity he and WRKO gave to average Americans to speak to average Lebanese, average Palestinians, average Israelis: Little Guys talking to Little Guys. That didn't happen often enough.

Pages turned as 1982 came to a close. Leonid Brezhnev died and was replaced by Yuri Andropov. Lech Walesa, the former leader of Poland's Solidarity labor movement, was freed after eleven months of internment. There were more than two hundred stations, or "sites," in a new system of academic and governmental communication known as the Internet.

Michael Dukakis regained his position as governor of Massachusetts, older and wiser in the ways of Bay State politics; that Vietnam Veterans against the War guy who had filled in for Jerry back in the seventies, John Kerry, was his new lieutenant governor. Jerry delivered the first of his dire judgments on Mike Dukakis: the man was "boring."

With Sandy Nagro's help, Jerry moved into an apartment in the suburbs. WRKO relieved him of Saturday afternoon duty. He found a young local comic named Steve Sweeney who did a damned good Kevin White impression, and Sweeney was soon on the air as "Mayor Sweeney," naughtily mispronouncing the name of his community as the "Shitty o' Boston."

Bob Fish moved on, replaced by an experienced, smart, Boston-savvy general manager named Dan Griffin. Chris Ryan continued as Jerry's producer for a few more months, pushing the program toward newsy topics. In February he produced another road trip—an expedition to Washington, D.C., where Jerry interviewed Representative Barney Frank, the columnist Mary McGrory, Senator Morris Udall of Arizona, the columnist Jack Anderson, Senator John Glenn, Senator Ted Kennedy, the columnist Thomas Oliphant, Secretary of Defense Richard Perle, Senator Gordon Humphrey of New Hampshire, Senator Alan Cranston of California, and Senator Paul Tsongas of Massachusetts.

Good as those shows were, Jerry wanted his own man producing, and Ryan didn't really want the job anyway. He called Alan Tolz in Philadelphia, still at WWDB.

"I need you to produce the show."

"Jerry, I've got a good job here. This is my home."

"Come on, Alan. We'll do good things here. You wanna work at a little station all your life? This'll be good for your career."

"Look, Jerry, if WRKO will make it worth my while—if they'll double what I'm making now—I'll do it."

Somehow Jerry got Alan his money. By March 1983 he had the man he wanted behind the glass in Boston.

There was one more milestone in 1982.

The psychologist Dr. Harry Sobel talked Jerry into appearing on *The Thought Process* on November 11. As he had with other well-known guests, he joked about putting Jerry "on the couch," but his purpose was never hidden: he wanted to get Jerry to talk about his feelings—and Jerry agreed to it!

"What about the personal attacks, Jerry? You get a lot of them, and—"

"They hurt. They hurt . . . especially if somebody is getting at you ethnically or tries to demean you personally . . . Or they get at your kids, or your wife, or whatever. 'When you were thrown out of Philly,' y' know, those things. . . .

"Sometimes I do get angry. If you do four hours a day, five days a week or six days a week, if you don't display anger or quiet or *all* the emotions, why then . . . it's not real. . . . There are people on other radio stations who are—" Jerry slowed his pace and darkened his voice in a sinister fashion: "—

always fair. Reasonable. Well, life isn't fair and reasonable . . . I do get depressed. I *am* up, I *am* down . . . But when that microphone goes on, . . . I'm on the air and I have to start *performing* . . ."

"When you think back over your life, what do you miss most about your parents?"

"I just guess I just miss 'em being there, that's all . . . I feel sometimes, being the only member of my immediate family, that is, my maternal-paternal family, that I'm sort of left there. There's nobody but me to carry it forward . . ."

"How did they respond to you on the radio all those years? Did they listen? Did they get upset that you were so angry, and taking on so many issues?"

Jerry hesitated. "No, no, my mother would say, 'Are you sure you should get so *mad?*' My father was very quiet, and would be very proud to other people. He would say, ''Dja hear my son on the air? My son, Gerald, on the air?' But he would never say it directly to me."

"Jerry, you're a father of three daughters . . . What's that like?"

"They're all born here in Boston. One is twenty-three, Eve. One is twenty-one, going to be twenty-two, Susan, just married. And one is eighteen, Andrea . . . she's going to Palm Beach Junior College. They're all very nice. They've gone through the trials and tribulations, I suppose, of whatever I went through . . . Eve, the older one, wants really to be in showbiz, and she's taking a crack at it. Sue is married, of course, is the sensible one in the family. And Andrea's more like me, she's a real flip."

"So if I had them sitting here, and I said, 'Tell me the things you admire and love most about your father and the thing that you resent the most,' what do you think they would say?"

"They probably would say I was like my father . . . not unkind or unloving . . . just . . . like your . . . relative, who might not say kind things about you, but really loves you, and is proud of you, but never really displays it. And that's because you're always playing the role of 'Dad.' You're the leader, right? Macho? And you're playing that role all the time."

"What do you want us to remember most about you?"

"I dunno . . . I don't think people remember much after you're dead, anyway . . . I fought the good fight, and I was sincere about what I was doing, I guess . . . When I take on the, quote, 'the Establishment,' or the cronies, or the 'boys,' that they really know that I'm doing it because I mean it."

A new character occasionally appeared on the air as Jerry's sixtieth birthday loomed in 1983: the Ol' Curmudgeon. The Curmudgeon was a radio veteran, a guy who'd seen it all, a guy who knew the ropes, a guy who'd lived through the Good Old Days and could tell you why they were good, a guy who hadn't gotten his due. He joined Mr. Style, Crusader Jerry, the Defender of the Constitution, and all the other roles that Jerry Williams liked to play.

He popped up on particularly frustrating days, when callers willfully brought up their own self-interested topics instead of the ones Jerry had laid out in his monologue. After a couple of hours of trying to give the show direction, he'd bring the flat of his hand down on the table, let the sound ring for a second, shake his head wearily (people could picture that shake of the head), and say "I'm getting *out* of the business! Gonna find that island."

The Ol' Curmudgeon was a kvetcher, too. You take restaurants. Used to be, you'd go to a nice deli and there would be five or six dishes of free stuff already there for you to munch on—pickles and cole slaw and bread—before they even brought you water. Now? You go into a restaurant and they have these teeny . . . tiny . . . tables. You barely have room for your *plate.* And coffee! You cannot get a good cup of coffee. A really *good* cup of coffee. For a cup of coffee to be really good, it has to be *fresh!* But no one does that any more. And words! You take "gay." Now, there's a perfectly good word. "We had a gay old time," they used t' say. "When you and I were young and gay." Now, you can't say those things without somebody lookin' at you funny.

Then there was "I never had a dinner." The phrase was shorthand for "I've never gotten the recognition I deserve for my contributions to [fill in the blank with one of the following] the business, talk radio, civic discourse, personal freedom." Jerry stole the line from Red Buttons—and often credited Buttons on the air. Buttons had been using it as the foundation for a one-liner routine for decades, and it had come to the attention of most people in the early eighties because of Buttons's TV appearances on the Dean Martin celebrity roasts. The idea was to catalog all kinds of people through history who didn't get the recognition they deserved, usually with some sort of rim-shot twist, kicking each example with the payoff line. "You take Adam. One day, after Eve'd been around for a while, he looks up, says t' God, 'I got more ribs. You got more broads?' [Rim shot.] *He* never had a dinner."

So Jerry made himself one of the Great Ones Who Never Had a Dinner. He could be confident that no one in his audience remembered his WMEX anniversary banquets back in the late fifties or his awards testimonials in Chicago. His days of being on a pedestal were over, and, in fact, it made for better business to be an unsung hero.

It's one thing to be unsung. It's quite another to have low ratings. As a matter of fact, you can be unsung and still be *very* popular.

By 1983, for the fourth time in his career, Jerry Williams had become a dominant figure in a major market. This time was sweeter than the others, in so many ways: he had beaten the Career Grenade and resuscitated his career after five years of ignominy; a station had built a talk format around him—his style, his drive, his way of doing talk radio; he had found new approaches to his work that kept him sounding contemporary; he was triumphing over the competition in one of the most important parts of the broadcast day; he was setting his own course without much management interference, primarily because of his ratings success; and the station giving him the platform was improving its overall performance as well. Listening to talk rather than news during afternoon drive became a habit for so many area listeners that two later heavyweights—Howie Carr and Jay Severin—would propel their careers to major success reaping their own harvest from the field that Jerry Williams had first plowed.

During April and May 1983 Jerry's listeners heard three words over and over: "King Arthur Motel." He was following the day-to-day developments at a high-profile trial of police officers from Everett and Revere who'd been involved in a predawn brawl at a place officially called King Arthur's Motel, which was known for its after-hours activities. Almost a year before, a group of cops had decided to avenge one of their own who'd gotten involved in a fight, and the mess ended with one man dead and a world of hurt on several others.

You know where Jerry stood. What were these cops doing there, anyway? Who told the posse to take justice into their own hands? These are the guys who are supposed to *enforce* the law, not *break* it. During the six weeks of testimony, Jerry read the accounts in the press and provided pungent editorial comment. During the six days of jury deliberations, he told listeners that they'd have the news of the verdict as soon as he did. When two of the cops were finally sentenced to life in prison and a third to six to ten years, he applauded.

And then came the Washing Machine Lady.

It was during the annual sex survey shows that September. It started like the other sex interviews—how old are you, are you married, when did you have your first sexual experience, how many partners have you had, how often do you have sex. This lady sounded like so many others—in fact, she was so *ordinary* sounding, with her broad Bahst'n accent, that the answer to the next question caught Jerry completely off-guard.

"Have you ever engaged in sex outside the bedroom, or in any unusual locations?"

"On top of the wash machine, when it's in spin. And I don't mean that sarcastically."

Jerry chuckled. "You're puttin' me on."

No, no. She lived in the same house as her parents, sometimes she and hubby needed to get out of earshot, and one day, when the washing machine (or, as she said it, the "wash machine") was running, they decided to do it down in the basement, on top of the machine, and it turned out there was something special about that motion.

Jerry could barely contain his laughter. He tried to shift back to the prepared questions: "Are there any special accompaniments to your lovemaking—lighting, scent, music?"

"No, no. I just whistle."

The picture of the woman whistling during sex on her wash machine put him over the edge. From then on, the laughs just kept on coming.

"Whatta y' laughin' at?"

"Listen, I'm just tryin' t' get over the *last* laugh." By now, Alan was feeding lines to Jerry. "It all comes out in the wash, right? . . . You oughta get a show of your own." He got control for a second. "All right. Do you have multiple orgasms—" quick as a flash, he added this to the question: "—depending on the cycle?"

They were both out of control now.

"Just on the super spin."

"Oh, you're funny, really. I'm not gonna get through this."

The laughs subsided long enough for them to have a real conversation. She's had only one sexual partner—just her husband. She was amazed at the other women, the ones with dozens of partners and dozens of orgasms. Then Jerry heard a click on the line—oh, she had call waiting and someone else was trying to reach her.

"Hello?"

"Yeah, that's awright. Just, just let that call go. They're probably calling you because somebody—"

"I know, they probably hear my voice and reckanize me."

"Right. Well, it's time to turn the Tide. Listen, I enjoyed talkin' to you, really. Are you really serious?"

"Yes, I am."

Finally, he wrapped it up, barely able to get through the copy for "Something Extra," an off-price clothing store that happened to have the next commercial.

Later that year, WRKO's TV affiliate, Channel 7, hired Bill O'Reilly. O'Reilly had been knocked around in broadcasting a bit, partly because of his own take-no-prisoners attitude, at one point rising to the ranks of a CBS correspondent, but now trying to rebuild his career. Channel 7 gave him the helm of *New England Afternoon,* the station's newsmagazine show, and in mid-November the show spotlighted some local lights of talk, including Jerry.

O'Reilly hit a hot button during a roundtable discussion: "The people who anchor the news . . . they read off those TelePrompTers . . . and they make a lot more money than we make . . . Do you, Larry Glick, think that those people deserve that kinda money? Do you resent it?"

> GLICK: No! No! I'm for big salaries. I like big salaries and loose women. I'm *for* that, no!
>
> JERRY: You know, the only people who *don't* make that kinda money are guys on the radio who labor every day for three or four hours.
>
> O'REILLY: Somehow, I think that *you* resent the big salaries.
>
> JERRY: I resent them. I resent it—*deeply!* . . . When Glick and I do a program in radio, why, the guy sits down about thirty seconds before we go on the air, and we *wing* it. And we do it because we do our homework every day.

Speaking to Nancy Merrill, host of *People Are Talking* on Channel 4, he made an offer: "If you want to do the show, I'd be happy to have you come up and do it for four hours . . . if I can do *your* show."

A few months later, O'Reilly took that bait. "Jerry's going on vacation, you wanna try out talk radio for a change?" "Yeah, why not?" And that's how Bill O'Reilly did his first radio talk show, just as David Brudnoy had—as a fill-in for Jerry Williams. After his trial by fire in the WRKO studio, O'Reilly told Alan Tolz that doing four hours on the radio was a lot harder than it looked. "How long has Jerry been doing this? Twenty-seven *years?*"

1984 was the year that WRKO found the right voice and the right balance for Janet Jeghelian in the morning. Mel Miller knew the existing chemistry wasn't right, and the ratings showed it. Tony Pepper was forceful—maybe too forceful, since Janet did a lot of agreeing with him, and she was too genteel to muscle him aside for equal lip time. When Pepper went on vacation, Miller asked Ted O'Brien to fill in. O'Brien was a veteran TV anchor freelancing on weekends in New York; he'd done a little bit of talk in Boston at WHDH. Almost from the first show, Jeghelian and O'Brien were perfect together. Dan Griffin quickly made a deal with O'Brien, and when Pepper got back, he was gently told that his services would no longer be needed.

Ted 'n' Janet—the branding of the show became such common parlance in town that it almost turned into one word—took WRKO ahead by another huge step, making talk a real contender in morning drive for the first time. Since it was natural for the morning team to talk about the issues Jerry was discussing, their success gave his afternoon show a boost, too.

Alan Tolz settled comfortably into his role as producer. He had the advantage of being one of the few in that job not intimidated by Jerry's prestige or style. Jerry relied on Tolz's ability to think with him, to feed him words or ideas or names that he needed on the air. Every once in a while, Jerry would rope him into distinctly un-producing duties like picking up dry cleaning, but for the most part, it was a close if not quite equal friendship.

The year 1984 was when Tolz branched out, taking on production of Charles Laquidara's *Big Mattress* show on Boston's preeminent progressive rocker, WBCN. Like many other morning-drive shows on rock stations, this one had a significant entertainment component between the tunes. Charles enjoyed hosting local comics like the standup master Kevin Meaney, and he had fun with the guys who did celebrity impersonations. WBCN listeners heard Billy West doing Reagan or Johnny Most, the Celtics' sandpaper-voiced announcer, and Marcia Masters conjuring up Geraldine Ferraro or Dr. Ruth Westheimer. It wasn't too long before the comics were showing up on Jerry's show as well, especially on Fridays, when Jerry knew that the end-of-the-week commuters needed some fun in their lives.

The year 1984 was also when Fairness started to unravel and Alan Berg got shot to death.

The Fairness Doctrine started slipping with a complaint about TV programming from a pressure group. It was nothing unusual, just one of hundreds of broadcast complaints that had been delivered to the FCC over decades. This one came from members of the Syracuse Peace Council, who were steamed up about some editorials regarding a nuclear power plant that had aired on WTVH, an upstate New York TV station. The Peace Council thought that some contrasting views ought to be broadcast, but WTVH said no. So the Peace Council filed a complaint with the Federal Communications Commission, and the FCC said the council was right. Normally, that's where something like this would end. The station would meekly take its letter of reprimand or its fine, promise never to do it again, and everything would go on as it had before. But not this time.

WTVH decided to fight. Their lawyers asked the FCC to reconsider its decision, claiming that when the FCC required any broadcast outlet to air opposing opinions, it was violating the station's rights of free speech. WTVH said that the Fairness Doctrine, a thorn in the side of broadcasters since 1949, was unconstitutional. There were two years of court fights, FCC rulings back and forth, changes in FCC personnel, and even some attempts by

Congress to make the Fairness Doctrine into law, which were vetoed by President Reagan and then by the first President Bush. When the smoke cleared, Fairness was no more.

So what? So broadcasters no longer had to worry about "balance," that's what. As the intentions of the government regulators and the courts became clear to station owners and network executives and broadcast entrepreneurs during the long appeals process, the talk radio floodgates opened and Modern Talk rolled in. The manner itself became feistier, tougher, coarser. Don Imus was incensed when the USSR shot down a U.S. airliner for violating Russian air space, so he cut down Rockefeller Center's Soviet flag and auctioned it off to benefit the survivors. Howard Stern did a sketch about a dial-a-date service for the bestiality crowd, which got him bounced from the station where he did the skit—but a rival New York station was only too glad to pick up his show. It hadn't yet become the world of Michael Savage and Bubba the Love Sponge, but everyone could tell that things were starting to change.

If you were looking for a marker of the modern era of talk, you could hardly ask for something more dramatic than the shooting of the Denver talk show host Alan Berg on June 18, 1984. To most Americans, it was a minor news story at the time and it's even less important now. But if you look hard at it, it seems a nexus, a place where the tides of idea and the currents of trend flowed into each other and then out again.

Berg, so often described as a liberal talk show host, wasn't Jerry's kind of liberal. He was of the younger generation, harder and sourer, spiritually and technically closer kin to the young, confrontational conservatives than he was to the original WMEX Jerry. Berg baited his neo-Nazi adversaries. He dared them to act. He made himself a target. He laughed at them. And he did it on the air, in the West, where the idea of "government as the enemy," which had energized so many new conservatives, had become deadly serious for a few—in fact, had moved off the end of the political continuum as it was ordinarily understood in America. Berg's enemies were real enemies, people who stockpiled guns, Americans who wanted to overthrow American government, people who were forming themselves into isolated and angry militias or posses or whatever you wanted to call them—people who found the symbolism of that bearded, Jewish, aggravating talker irresistible as a target. That was one stream—the rugged individualism and citizen-soldierism of America transforming itself into right-wing fury.

Another stream took talk radio away from Town Meeting of the Air toward Verbal Rassling. Americans already took talk far less seriously than they once had. For them, the matter was still real, but the manner was more and more showbiz. Callers knew more than ever that they were part of the performance when they got on the air. Hosts were chosen for their ability to strike sparks rather than find consensus. For many of those who experienced talk radio as it truly was day-to-day in 1984, Berg's shooting was baffling. Could anyone take this stuff that seriously?

One more stream swept modern radio away from artisan's craft toward accountant's enterprise. The adventure and excitement and thrill of the medium as an idea, revitalized after the coming of television by on-air people and maverick managers willing to take new chances with the old form, crazy characters like Mac Richmond, inspired leaders like Jim Lightfoot, original talents like Jerry Williams, whose work refashioned radio from mass appeal to format smorgasbord—that great transformation had been completed by 1984. From that point on, it would be business: aggregation, consolidation, formula, and finance.

The most immediate consequence of the Berg shooting for Jerry was the sense at WRKO that a little more security might be a good thing. He did not see it as a watershed. He did not moderate his language or temper his approach in its wake. If anything, he would come to find that he had to work harder than he ever had before to get people in his audience to act rather than just sit back and enjoy the fun. But if he had been a man inclined to reflection, he might have seen that the demise of Alan Berg and the decline of the Fairness Doctrine marked the end of the innocence for talk and the end of the Good Old Days for radio.

By this time, two years into her relationship with Jerry Williams, Sandy Nagro had few illusions and plenty of disillusionment. On the one hand, their tastes were similar—they went to the blockbuster musicals that came through town and enjoyed them, and when they went to the revival of *Porgy and Bess* in 1983, they walked out because it was too operatic for either of them. She enjoyed Jerry's quests for great finds or great bargains in antiques stores, at least until she came to realize that his obsessive examination of objects and haggling with the owners were more about deal making than aesthetics. She loved his joke telling and his ability to entertain, when he felt like it.

On the other hand, she was frustrated by the subordinate position she had in his life. For a while, she had hoped that Jerry would divorce Teri and marry her. She even consulted with Dr. Gilbert Holloway on one of his visits to Boston, confessing her wishes for something more than being the Other Woman. Holloway didn't have to draw on any of his spiritual gifts to reply; he'd known Jerry Williams for twenty years. "Well, Sandy, the other party has problems, y' know, and obligations. I would follow the guidance of my feelings, for a time. But time goes by swiftly. Let's not make a mistake, this round."

When she actually spoke with Jerry about a divorce, he wouldn't hear of it. She learned that his principal motivation for staying married was the nature of divorce itself—the dividing of assets, the inevitable investigation into his private life, and the feeling that the process would impoverish him somehow. That whole scenario infuriated and terrified him, and it gave Teri a kind of irrational power in Jerry's mind. He felt he could never acknowledge Sandy in public, even as the Regular Girlfriend, for fear that his wife might find out. When one of his kids or Teri herself came north for a visit, Sandy would get marching orders from Jerry. Everything she'd brought to his apartment in Quincy would have to disappear; any trace of her existence that a prying eye might notice had to be carefully stashed. Often when they went out, Alan Tolz would accompany them as a kind of beard. "Listen, Alan, if we see anyone I know, she's *your* date."

As Sandy came to know him well, she saw that the fear of divorce was just one of the insecurities he let very few people see. Despite the dozens of interviews he'd done with economists and financial counselors, from Milton Friedman to the latest investment tout, he would never consider putting his money in anything riskier than a bank. He avoided health care except when it was absolutely necessary—his medical fears started with dentists, escalated through doctors, hospitals, and proximity to the dying, and peaked at death itself. In a hundred different ways, he was deeply frightened of not being in control.

And yet he was profoundly needy. Sandy heard his endless complaints— his fatigue, his gout, his back. She saw that he needed radio the way a junkie needs dope. She saw the way his eyes drifted to other attractive women.

She didn't know he was cheating on her, too.

In November Reagan and George H. W. Bush were reelected. Jerry gave up trying to satirize Ronnie and Nancy. What everyone said was true: this president was Mr. Teflon. Jokes just bounced off him. He and Ted O'Brien talked about it in one of the rare moments that their paths crossed off the air.

He was amazing, this guy. There was nothing there. He was the classic empty suit—all words, no substance. O'Brien watched Jerry's eyes as he seemed to slip into deep thought.

"And yet, you know, Ted, people *love* him."

Oh, well. Let it be local. Kevin White was gone. The next of Jerry's nemeses to fall was House Speaker Thomas McGee, who got into a leadership fight with another rep, the rotund George Keverian. And just incidentally, there was a personal angle to the scrap. Michael Goldman, a political consultant who helped Keverian unseat McGee, was a regular on the show, and Jerry gave him the résumé of a woman he knew named Rita Frankel. "Just see what you can do for her . . ."

Not too long afterward, Rita was working as a researcher for the Science Resource Office of the Massachusetts Legislature. It definitely could help your career to be a friend of Jerry Williams.

It was probably during his yearly holiday trip to south Florida that year that he walked by that empty antiques store next to a newsstand in Palm Beach and started griping. "What've I been saying for years? There's no good ice cream down here. In the midst of all this shopping, restaurants everywhere, but no place to get an ice cream cone. Someone could rent this spot and make a mint with it."

Eve was listening. "So why don't you do something about it?"

"Me? How? I'm up in Boston. *You* should do something about it."

So she and her sister Andi and Teri did.

It was the only one of Jerry Williams's hundreds of idle entrepreneurial schemes that ever made any money, and his daughters had to make it happen.

Not that he didn't have a say in it. The seed money—about twenty grand—came from the Mom and Pop account, to buy the freezers and the equipment and pay for a few months' rent. Along with the investment, there was what might be called advice. Jerry announced that the ice cream had to be Bassett's. Nothing else would do—Bassett's, a Philadelphia ice cream wholesaler, had the best, and that was final.

But how would they get it from Philadelphia to Palm Beach? Say, Alan, how would you like to drive a load of ice cream down the eastern seaboard? Just a few ten-gallon tubs. No big deal. Just keep the air conditioner running!

The business was set up in Eve's and Teri's names. They rented that storefront Jerry had pegged and bought the equipment they needed. Teri did the books at first, but after a while that was Eve's job. Andrea Williams was the first employee. The two sisters nearly drove each other crazy working side by side every day, but they made that business go. In six months of constant work, Sprinkles was driving the Palm Beach competition into the pavement. The shop became known for its white-gloved staff rolling fresh-baked cones in the front window where passersby could watch. That smell floated down Royal Poinciana Way and drew people out of the trendy restaurants like Testa's. No dessert for us—we'll go have a cone at Sprinkles.

Sure, they forgot to pay their taxes, they had trouble with undependable employees, they sweated the rent—all the usual stuff of a small business. But Eve managed to pull a little salary and a Datsun 280 ZX out of it after a year or so had gone by.

Susan didn't have time for ice cream. In March 1984 her first child, Jessica Hobson, had been born. Jerry and Teri were both there to greet the new baby.

In February 1985 Gene Burns arrived at WRKO, putting an end to the last service-oriented talk on the station and adding a formidable intellectual presence to the air. Burns had done talk in Boston in the late sixties while Jerry was on WBZ, worked a long time in Florida, and done a short stint in Philly. He was just coming off a Quixotic run for president on the Libertarian ticket. At first Jerry was skeptical about him. For one thing, he was outspoken on Palestinian rights and it seemed that he wasn't giving Israel a fair hearing. Eventually, Jerry came to respect his talent, to agree to disagree with him on some of the issues, to appreciate his controlled passion, to hear him out on matters about which he hadn't yet made up his own mind, and finally to admire the younger host. If anyone could be said to be carrying on the great traditions of talk that Jerry had started, it was Gene Burns.

In any case, 1985 marked the start of a new era at WRKO. The days of a schizophrenic talk format were over. RKO had gotten serious—all day, every day. That kind of thing was going on all over the country—special-interest talk shows migrating to weekends as issue-oriented programs were coming into the spotlight.

Larry King took another step up that year, as the host of an hourlong interview show every night of the week on CNN. Don Imus and Howard Stern were on the same station in New York City, and there was no love lost between them. A woman named Laura Schlessinger was dispensing psychological advice, sort of, on the air in California. And out in Sacramento, Rush Limbaugh was a year into a gig as the host of a daytime talk show on KFBK, where he had replaced Morton Downey Jr.

Downey wasn't yet on TV. He had built a modest name as a right-of-center talk host, and he continued working on his rep after leaving Sacramento. The following year he was working at WERE in Cleveland, and he had enough visibility to prompt the producers of *A.M. Chicago* to invite him and four other "outrageous talk show hosts" to talk about their work on May 22, 1985. They brought in Irv Homer from Philadelphia, Alan Burke from Miami, and that legendary pioneer, Jerry Williams, who was still remembered in Chicago for his two and a half years during the sixties. Almost as an afterthought, the producers recruited one of the brash new conservatives, a guy named Warren Freiberg, a ten-year veteran of WLNR, a small station in Lansing, Michigan. Freiberg had been on *A.M. Chicago* before, and he was known for bringing along surprise props to punctuate his performances. The host was a relatively new figure locally, a bright young woman named Oprah Winfrey.

It was an exciting hour.

Freiberg wasn't in the best shape, physically or professionally. Although only forty-five, he'd had a stroke and brain surgery three months before. And his station had a new owner, Johnson Publishing, the owners of *Ebony* and *Jet*, who probably were planning to boot him in a couple of months. It was said that John Johnson wasn't too impressed with this guy, since he could just be heard in Chicago's southern neighborhoods and he was fond of making very critical comments about black leaders in Michigan, Indiana, and Illinois. He'd been quoted as saying, "Perhaps black people can't help that their children are criminals and their streets are dirty," and "You can't take people out of the jungle for only a hundred years and expect them to be civilized." Well, maybe he was just a little ahead of his time with that stuff—shock shtick was still a novelty.

Once the conversation about "outrageous talk" got under way, Jerry and Freiberg went at it tooth and nail. Freiberg was characteristically provocative; he confirmed to one of the show's callers that he had joked on the air about dropping an atomic bomb on the Cabrini-Green housing project. He referred to the mayors of Chicago and Gary, Indiana, Harold Washington and Richard Hatcher, both African American, as "garbage."

Jerry made things spicy by talking about his Sex Survey shows and claiming he was the first talk show host to expose the G-spot. Freiberg claimed to be offended on behalf of decent women everywhere. Jerry got personal, calling Freiberg "the Hulk Hogan and Mr. T of radio." Freiberg fired back, characterizing Jerry as a "super-liberal" (which was pretty funny, considering Jerry used exactly the same term to describe himself in one of his speaking engagements fifteen years earlier in the Windy City). Oprah, standing in the audience, tried to keep the peace, but the show went from loud to worse.

In the second half, Freiberg pulled out his prop, a little tube of liquid soap, and announced that he was going to clean up Jerry's act. He stood up in front of Jerry and squirted the goo all over him, from scalp to face (getting some in Jerry's eye along the way) to shirt—on Jerry's clothes? This guy knew how to make a man mad. Jerry stood up, walked over to Freiberg's chair and (with Mort Downey's help) pushed him over.

Oprah called for a commercial.

When the show resumed, Freiberg was gone. Oprah apologized to her viewers and the show concluded without further fireworks. When Jerry got off the air, he called Alan Tolz in Boston. "Alan, get on the phone to the TV stations. Tell them to get the video. Channel 7! WLS!"

As they had in the past, the Chicago papers played him big. The video didn't run in Boston. Never had a dinner.

In early June the Boston papers and TV stations snubbed Jerry again, even though his show made some pretty big news.

At the start of 1985 Susan Wornick, a reporter for Boston's Channel 5, was working a story about six police officers from Revere, Massachusetts (a town long known for a relaxed attitude toward organized crime), who were accused of looting a CVS drugstore in the early morning hours. The cops didn't know that there was a guy at a nearby ATM who was watching them empty barrels-ful of stuff stolen from the store into the trunks of their cruisers. One night the witness, a man named Scott, called Wornick and said, "I have some information." The guy wouldn't go on the record—too scared of what could happen to him. So she convinced him to do an anonymous interview, with his back to the camera, so no one would see his face. For three months after that, the state cops worked through Wornick. She'd call Scott, Scott would call the state cops back, he'd give them some more info.

Ultimately, the case had to go to a grand jury, and at that point the state subpoenaed Wornick because Scott still wouldn't go public. Wornick wouldn't give him up, Channel 5 backed her, and it turned into a reporter's rights issue that the *Globe* and *Herald* put on their front pages. Jerry Williams owned the story on the radio. Day after day, he added new details. The police are sup-posed to *protect* us, not rob us. The guy who saw them had good reason to be scared—you know what happens to finks in Revere? This reporter was look-ing at *jail time.* Couldn't District Attorney Newman Flanagan find out who the source was without these strong-arm tactics? Yes, there's no law guaranteeing reporter's privilege. But the Constitution guarantees freedom of the press. This is what the press is *there* for. If they compel Susan Wornick to give up this guy now, what happens next time?

One afternoon in June, Jerry's guest was the attorney Larry O'Donnell Sr. They were talking about police power and the Wornick case because of O'Donnell's familiarity with another high-profile affair, the death of James Bowden. By 1985 it had been ten years since Bowden was killed by Boston Tactical Patrol Force officers. During all that time, Jerry had regularly interviewed Larry, the Bowden family's lawyer, excoriating the White administration for dragging its feet about cutting the check to Bowden's widow. Once Ray Flynn was elected, the city finally did the right thing and paid the judgment—which, thanks to interest and fees, had grown to $750,000.

Scott, Susan Wornick's source, was out there listening. He called the show, said he's the guy. What would O'Donnell advise him to do? Larry said, "Come on, they need you on the record on this. Call me off the air and we'll work something out."

It was Jerry's persistence on the issue that set the stage, Jerry's discussion that made Scott feel comfortable enough to call, and Jerry's guest who finally got the man to go public. Susan Wornick thanked Jerry for keeping her out of the clink.

But when the story broke, for the most part Jerry Williams wasn't in it. Other radio stations? No. Channel 4? No. Channel 7, the station in the very same building, credited only "a radio talk show." Never had a dinner.

There were some consolations. Late in the summer he began discussion of his contract renewal with RKO General. The prestigious entertainment and sports lawyer Robert Woolf was doing the heavy lifting for him, but his numbers were great, and the negotiations went pretty smoothly. He signed on for another hitch with a nice bump in salary.

By fall 1985 Jerry had established a commanding lead in his time slot, not just over news and talk stations, but ahead of most of the music stations as well. More than 7 percent of the people with their radios on from 2:00 to 6:00 P.M. were listening to him. Only the progressive rocker, WBCN, could boast greater pull in the afternoon.

But he wasn't complacent. Maybe he felt the breath of the bad boys of Modern Talk on his neck. Maybe he was just irritated at the way things were going in the Bay State.

The congressmen and senators were on a safety kick, trying to reduce highway deaths; they passed a law that required Massachusetts motorists to wear seat belts and gave the police the power to stop and inspect cars.

Jerry had always hated the self-important meddling of Massachusetts pols in the daily lives of ordinary people, and he'd long been resentful of the police's arbitrary authority. He loved the freedom, literal and symbolic, of driving his own car, resented any restriction on it, and projected his own feelings onto the mass of drivers who heard him every day.

In addition, there was Governor Mike Dukakis, who supported the seat belt law and annoyed Jerry for a hundred other reasons—because he had this professorial attitude, because he was fixated on policy and details, because he dressed so unstylishly, because he couldn't speak dramatically, because he'd surrounded himself with colorless technocrats and slippery PR types, because he never took Jerry seriously.

Jerry had already been on a tear about Mayor Flynn's enforcement of the city's parking regulations and Boston's squad of meter maids, so it wasn't much of a jump for him to start grousing about seat belts and the police. That seat belt law made a good subject for a monologue—he could include all his favorite themes: individual liberties, the cops, the Constitution, intrusion of government in everyday life. As he returned to it more and more frequently, it seemed to hit a nerve with listeners. People called in with their own experiences, not just about the cops and the belts, but all kinds of police intrusions—their imperious demands at drunk-driving roadblocks, their sneaky use of radar guns, their humiliating field sobriety tests, their insidious speed traps, their unreliable Breathalyzers. Seat belts became an emblem for every miserable inconvenience Massachusetts drivers had to endure. Not to mention the meter maids tagging their cars, the pols pulling down big salaries, the arrogant governor . . . Jerry was mad as hell about it all.

Why don't we make our voices heard about this stuff? he wondered on the air. The state has a public meeting hall—Gardner Auditorium—and it's at the State House, right under the noses of the legislators. Why shouldn't we take this issue right to the people who started it?

That's right, Jerry. You tell 'em, Jerry! I'm with ya, Jerry!

On a cold November day in 1985, they were hanging from the rafters at the Gardner. Jerry spoke. He introduced his people to Chip Ford, a guy from Swampscott who was getting his baptism as a political activist. He railed against the pols and the governor and those damn seat belts. The crowd ate it up. They applauded. They cheered. Jerry could smell the adrenaline rising from the crowd. He knew he was onto something.

Chip Ford needed signatures, people's names on an initiative petition to put a repeal of the seat belt law on the 1986 ballot. Jerry thought that was a terrific idea. Let the people decide whether they want this law. It was that old WMEX Town Meeting spirit alive again, just like when he'd dumped the thousands of postcards opposing Furcolo's sales tax on that table, right here in the same room, twenty-eight years ago.

When the numbers came out in mid-January 1986, Jerry knew he was going in the right direction. His show was the number one afternoon program in the city in November and December, drawing almost 10 percent of the available listeners.

Two months later, Susan gave birth to grandchild number two, William Hobson Jr. This time Jerry wasn't there. He was fighting for civil liberties, and he didn't have time to be Grampa.

It went from an occasional rant to a weekly lecture to a daily update to an obsession.

When the governor said that his 1986 New Year's resolution was "stopping Jerry Williams at a roadblock and telling him to put his seat belt on," Jerry played the tape again and again, challenging Dukakis to "slap a seatbelt over my mouth." He pledged to be civilly disobedient, daring the cops to catch him with his belt unbuckled and give him the chance to overturn the law in court. He offered to pay fines and legal fees for any listener who would volunteer as a test case. He hung the issue around the necks of the insurance companies, who stood to benefit from the higher auto rates that were inevitably coming. He attacked the big auto companies for sending one of their lobbyists to Massachusetts to lead an antirepeal campaign because they didn't want to spring for airbags in their cars—devices that really *would* save lives, by the way. He talked to authorities who claimed seat belts could be dangerous in and of themselves—suppose you were trapped in a burning car where every second counted, how would you like to have a seat belt on *then?*

Chip Ford's initiative petition began to get signatures. Jerry urged people to sign it even if they disagreed with him, so that a truly democratic referendum on the law could take place. All of a sudden, it seemed that everyone was talking about it. In April there were 40,000 signatures on the petition.

TV producers wanted Jerry to talk about the issue, so he went on the tube whenever they asked him. Arthur Miller, the Harvard law professor who hosted a weekly show on legal issues, spotlighted the law in one of his mock TV trials, and Jerry was on the jury. In May there were 56,000 signatures on the petition, and they were ready to send it to the state to claim a place on the ballot.

Traditional Massachusetts liberals were alarmed. This law was a good thing, saving lives. If Jerry succeeded in overturning it, who knew where it would lead? Some big names came out in favor of the mandatory seat belt law—Alan Dershowitz, whose civil libertarian credentials were impeccable, said that Jerry was wrong, that sometimes individual liberties had to give way to the greater good. Jerry debated Dershowitz on his own show, mixed it up with him in a TV panel discussion, and then appeared with him in May 1986 on Judy Jarvis's Channel 56 forum called *Point of View.*

That was some show. Jerry had been working the issue for six months by that time, and he had built up a whole catalog of arguments, ready for any attack. But he'd never been a great debater; he was much better, and much more comfortable, when he was running the show as well as arguing the issue. Still, the program started out fairly well. But then Dershowitz tagged him "a single-issue libertarian." Jerry was stung by the personal nature of the comment, the unfairness of it, the lack of respect. He went cold with rage. "Alan, that is a damned lie. I have been on more civil liberties issues than you have ever been . . . and I've done it in public, on the air, for over thirty years around this community, so that is a *damned lie* . . . As a matter of fact, you know how hard I've worked on the business of intruding on your body when it comes to drug testing, or urinalysis testing, or blood testing . . . I am a civil disobedient . . . I'm doing it as Dr. King did it on other issues—"

Dershowitz scoffed. "Oh, come on. Don't cheapen Dr. King's great work by saying that you're like Dr. King. This is a cheap publicity stunt . . . To compare integration in this country with a willingness of some people not to wear seat belts is insulting and preposterous."

A cheap publicity stunt! Jerry boiled as Dershowitz suddenly switched gears.

"Jerry, is gun control a freedom issue?"

"Yes, it is."

"And do you think people have the right to carry guns?"

"No, I do not."

"You do not. Why is that not a compromise of civil liberties?"

"I—because the Constitution does not prohibit that."

Uh-oh. Jerry had stepped onto Dershowitz's home turf. Big mistake.

"The Constitution says 'the right to bear arms,' specifically, and it doesn't talk about safety belts, Jerry."

Dershowitz had backed him into a corner. He felt foolish. "Alan, you're a professor at Harvard, and you know damned well that the Constitution of the United States *does* prohibit . . . the obtaining of arms for individuals."

"Jerry, there is no truth in that . . . I will pay one thousand dollars to your ridiculous anti–seat belt campaign if you can show me, show me a *word* in the Constitution that specifically, that gun laws are constitutional. You can't. You're wrong."

Dershowitz tied him in knots. He stormed off the set two minutes before the end of show, ranting off-mic as he went. Not his finest hour.

By September 1986 the campaign had been under way for ten months. The initiative petition had enough signatures to appear as Question 5 on the November ballot. An anti-repeal group was cranking up radio and TV ads attacking the referendum. Most casual listeners to the Williams show seemed to hear seat belts, seat belts, every day. They said they were getting turned off by the sameness of the show, even though Jerry had done a lot of other material—discussion of militant Islam and the *Achille Lauro* hijacking with the author Robin Wright; examination of the space program following the explosion of the *Challenger;* talking about talk radio itself with BU Professor Murray Levin, who was about to publish one of the first serious books about it (*Talk Radio and the American Dream,* which used Jerry's show and that of Avi Nelson as prime examples); and questioning what it would mean for the Supreme Court if William Rehnquist became Chief Justice and Antonin Scalia was confirmed.

Whether people were annoyed or enthralled by the seat belt crusade, they were still listening, although audience wasn't as much of a factor as some of the cynics said. In fact, the closer Jerry got to the election, the more he harped on seat belts, and the worse his numbers got; he was down to number five in his time slot just before Election Day. There were still about 150,000 people tuned in every day, but that meant that almost 100,000 *fewer* were listening at the end of the campaign than were listening when he started it. Station management urged him to give it a rest, but he only dug in harder. He always said it was principle that drove what he said on the air, not the ratings.

In the run-up to November, Jerry's show became something beyond talk radio. It was a call to the ramparts, Patrick Henry with a microphone. Nearly half of his hours on the air in October were about some aspect of the seat belt law and the upcoming vote. He hadn't given any issue so much time since May 1973, when he spent more than half of his time on Watergate.

Then it was November 4, 1986. Some very big guns had been brought out in the last weeks, and Chip Ford's group had the most meager resources, just a few thousand dollars in contributions. Essentially, it had been Jerry against the world, and, as the voters went to the polls, he figured he'd been beaten. In fact, he was comfortable with the role he was sure he was going to have to play—y' see, folks? Fought the good fight. Did the right thing. Never had a dinner.

He sat in a ballroom at the new Westin Hotel with Chip, Alan Tolz, Sandy Nagro, a couple of dozen others—political friends, people from the campaign. They watched the reports come in on TV. It looked grim.

Just before midnight, the stations had enough results to project the outcome. *The seat belt repeal had won.* It wasn't even close. Nearly 55 percent of the voters had sided with Jerry.

He raised his fists in the air when the words came out of the TV speakers. For a few moments, he didn't feel sixty-three. It was as sweet as Nixon's resignation, as sweet as the first year in Chicago, as sweet as punching Jack Molesworth, as sweet as kissing Joanne McCoy.

Oh, Mike Dukakis got reelected that night, too, but Jerry couldn't work up much concern about it. That was another battle for another day.

The glow continued, for at least a day or so. Twenty-five members of the media showed up at WRKO Wednesday for a press conference to get Jerry's reaction. UPI, the three big TV stations, the public TV station, the *Quincy Patriot-Ledger,* the *Herald,* even the *Globe,* even WBZ radio, for heaven's sake—they all sent representatives. He was all over the tube for a few hours the evening after the election.

And then, suddenly, it was old news. The crusade was over. He had won. What'll you do for an encore, Jer? And what about all those old liberals who felt you'd betrayed them?

10 TIME AND TIDE

Phone calls . . . [are] our gratification, or *not* gratification, as the case
may be. . . . It's like a guy who goes out in front of an audience and needs
applause. If he doesn't get applause, then he knows he's bombed out.
—*Jerry Williams, May 22, 1981, WNWS, Miami*

At the end of 1986 Jerry's seat belt campaign seemed to be the doorway to
Greatness. The prominence he'd attained made some long-postponed dreams
seem achievable—if he just worked a little harder, pushed himself a little
more. He wanted to have more influence on public policy and the direction of
the country. He wanted to get into the business of owning broadcast properties. He wanted recognition as a pioneer and leader in the world of talk. He
still wanted a TV show. In the next five years he would get a piece of each one
of those dreams, only to have each turn to sand in his hands.

Seat belts aside, 1986 had changed Jerry's show and his position at WRKO
significantly. For one thing, the station was relocated out of Channel 7's building, away from the Boston's Government Center, back in WMEX's old neighborhood, within walking distance of Fenway Park. One of the most important
changes inside was computer-screen technology, which provided a new and
valuable weapon for his arsenal, even though Jerry didn't like it at first. In the
past, communication between producers and hosts was limited to a few well-
chosen words on the intercom while commercials were running or even fewer
words in the host's headphones while a caller was yapping. The screens gave
the host access to much more of the producer's brain—if a VIP had been
reached and was waiting on the phone to talk, the screen in the studio would
let the host know that right away.

Tolz and Jerry used the screen to cement their working relationship. There
would be times when Jerry would know that a name was just beyond his grasp.

He'd cue Tolz with his eyes as he said something like, "I was watching that little Jewish sex doctor lady the other day," and Tolz would have "Dr. Ruth" on the screen before Jerry had said, "day," so that he could continue with "Ruth Westheimer." The screen became crucial as Jerry's memory lapses became more common. Tolz considered this just part of dealing with Jerry's age, but he had to deal with a surprising number of those senior moments in the years ahead.

Things changed operationally as well. WRKO struck a new deal with the International Brotherhood of Electrical Workers, the techs' union, that loosened their grip on the audio boards. Now producers like Alan Tolz would not only answer the phone calls and set up the commercials and mind the studio logs; they would run the audio boards as well. Tolz could now add sound effects, music, and little verbal snippets as almost instantaneous commentaries on what Jerry was saying, without directing another set of hands. This gave the show more ear interest, made it sound younger. Also, Tolz could at last get his hands on the WRKO tape machines to mix and edit little preproduced elements without scheduling time with the IBEW crews. These relatively simple changes altered WRKO's talk shows, just as they altered talk radio all over the country, giving the whole genre a looser, more improvisatory feel.

Tolz and Jerry knew that it was vital to find another horse to ride to keep the show's stature. They wrestled with the "What'll we do for an encore?" problem in actual off-the-air strategy discussions and improvisationally, as callers brought up ideas off the cuff or Jerry hit on a topic that listeners seemed to respond to.

For a time Jerry got behind the effort to resuscitate the name of Scollay Square, the city's old burlesque district, which had been buried by the New Boston boys under the stones of Government Center and made into a cause célèbre by a few who felt it was a legitimate part of the city's history. The results were satisfying: Mayor Ray Flynn sympathized with the drive and gave official recognition to the area's seedy legacy early in 1987. But that campaign just filled time entertainingly. Jerry knew—as everyone in Massachusetts knew—that there was only one abiding issue setting the agenda for the next two years: Mike Dukakis's presidential ambitions.

1987 and 1988 were the last two Reagan years. The veep, George H. W. Bush, had a good shot to be the Republican presidential nominee in 1988, but he looked vulnerable, even within his own party. Every candidate with more than an idle fantasy of becoming president was expected to make his or her move early in 1987. As soon as the rumor machine began mentioning Dukakis as a contender for the Democratic ticket, Jerry made it clear that he was not on the bus.

Why? That was the question all the old Bay State liberals kept asking themselves over the next two years. Why was Jerry Williams so exercised about the Duke? They remembered the social causes Jerry had fought for, and they knew that Dukakis was on the right side of all those issues. They all knew that a Massachusetts president would bring big political benefits to the state—a lot of those Massachusetts liberals still thought of John F. Kennedy as God's gift to their careers. Why couldn't Jerry see things their way? Why?

To Jerry, it started with the Duke's style. He hated Dukakis's way of speaking and dressing. He resented the managerial aloofness, the professorial manner, the lawyerly glibness. But he was even more galled by the thought that the Duke had betrayed his populist start in politics. After Dukakis's first term, when he was replaced by Ed King, it seemed to Jerry and many others that he'd made promises and cut deals to get back to the corner office. And once back in power in 1982, instead of fighting for the people against Senate President Billy Bulger, House boss George Keverian, and all the hundreds of state employees under their wings, he became a Go-Along-to-Get-Along guy—or worse, one of the guys on the inside where the deals were done. As Jerry saw it, the representative of the Ordinary People had taken a hike.

Jerry watched as the new Dukakis was reelected in 1986 and began presiding over the development of a third tunnel under Boston Harbor and then the marriage of that idea to the subterranean construction of a new Central Artery, all of it eventually sheltered under the verbal umbrella of the Big Dig and supported by three billion dollars in federal money from Tip O'Neill's 1987 Congress. Four years earlier, when they were still saying that the project would only cost $2.5 billion or so, Jerry began to say, "Beware," and now he was almost laughing at the cost estimates. It might be that the work would reduce the traffic congestion in town (and God knows we need *that*). It might make the city look nicer and de-isolate the North End. But think of the *money!* Anyone can see that the Duke's legacy project is gonna be a *sinkhole* of money. Listen, y' wanna depress the Central Artery? Just have Michael Dukakis *talk* to it. Your taxes are ultimately gonna pay for it. It'll be five billion, maybe as much as ten billion. (Twenty years later, the thing still isn't done and the cost is almost $15 billion and counting.)

And that was just one of the things that got under his skin. He had a persistent feeling that the state's economy wasn't as good as the Dukakis crowd kept saying. He had seen Bad Guys and Not Bad Guys as governors, and he didn't like the smell he was smelling in 1987. It wasn't that the Dukakis administration was cranking up the old-school techniques of Smile and Grease. Instead, he suspected they were inventing new high-tech ways of moving the shells in the game and making the pea disappear. He began to say it on the air: these guys are cooking the books. Dukakis is going to try to use the phony numbers to bounce himself into the White House.

This [pause] was [pause] *war.*

Just a month after the 1986 election, the Massachusetts Legislature passed the Safe Roads Act, a bill intended to combat drunk driving, and the Duke signed it a week or so later. The law said that you were presumed to be drunk if a machine testing your blood alcohol level showed a rating of .10 percent or higher, and you had no right to appeal the machine's verdict. But everyone knows Breathalyzers are unreliable—or at least the people operating them can make mistakes. And then the state began setting up jolly holiday roadblocks to conduct random checks of drivers.

It was another assault on the sanctity of his car, another Dukakis administration invasion of privacy. Jerry railed against the latitude of the law and the arbitrary power it was giving to law enforcement. The Breathalyzer-and-roadblock theme got people dancing, and Crusader Jerry put it on the playlist right away in January 1987.

He owed his WRKO colleague Moe Lauzier for Tune no. 2.

One morning in January, Jerry called Alan Tolz from home. It was one of those days that he just didn't feel he had it in him. Tolz had become accustomed to Jerry's occasional "sick" days—it was better for Jerry to recharge for a day or so than to come in and struggle through four hours without sufficient juice.

Standard procedure at RKO when a host got sick was for the program director to call in one of the weekend guys. Moe Lauzier, the young conservative host doing Saturday and Sunday mornings, was available. That afternoon, he was in the chair, with instructions to say, "Jerry has the day off," and nothing more.

Tolz had scheduled a woman named Dorothea Thomas-Vitrac, a selectwoman from New Braintree, a little town out in mid-Massachusetts. She was opposed to a prison the state wanted to build out there. Jerry was interested because he'd once thought of buying property in the area, and he liked the town. Lauzier gave Thomas-Vitrac a hard time. Whattaya fighting a new prison for? Don't we need more prison space? Aren't cons being put on the street early because there aren't enough cells?

Thomas-Vitrac was persuasive. Look, it's a tiny town—800 people, 240 families. This building they want to turn into a prison is an old boarding school. We're getting steamrolled by the Dukakis administration. The citizens would have no objection to a state school or something, but a medium-security prison? Shouldn't local people have something to say about it? And there's something fishy about the financing, she added. The guys who own it have some relationship to Dukakis. She wouldn't be surprised if this turned out to be a sweetheart deal.

So Lauzier took a drive out to New Braintree, looked over the situation and returned to Boston with his opinions reversed. This looked to him like a Dukakis boondoggle. He talked it up on his weekend shows. Jerry was listening.

A call from host to host. Hey, Moe, do you mind if I run with this? Don't wanna step on your toes or anything.

No problem, Jer. Let's work it together, like we did with the seat belt thing.

They ran with it, or to be more accurate, Jerry ran with it and Moe backed him up on the weekends. The legislature voted to build the prison in January. Jerry called for a rally against it.

"This is going to be a long, protracted struggle . . . I'm damn angry about it, and I'm going to lead the charge. I'm going to be the outside agitator that's going to come in there and rile people up against this outrage. This is an *outrage!* I'm going to take it on, even if it might destroy my audience in Boston!"

This one baffled the liberals even more than seat belts had. Who cared about this little burg? This wasn't one of those Currier and Ives towns with the little white church and the village green. It was just a small rural community with no particular character at all.

Yeah, just a bunch of Little Guys with no influence. But listen, Mr. or Ms. Columnist, that's the *point.* And if there really was some Dukakis connection, it'd be just another indication of the corruption of the administration.

Oh, and it made for great theater.

New Braintree gave Jerry a second catchy anti-Dukakis tune, and *that* one stayed on his playlist for four years, even after the Duke had lost his presidential bid in 1988, and the state's inspector general said in 1989 that the worst thing the administration had done in siting the proposed prison had been to cut a few corners, and Dukakis decided not to run for governor again in 1990, and the new governor, William Weld, finally announced in 1991 that the state would put a police training facility there instead of a prison.

Jerry could also play "Isn't There Anyone Else?" His strong ratings and incontrovertible stature (now gilded by Gene Burns's almost daily use of the phrase "the Dean of talk radio" in his honor) meant that almost every person with Oval Office ambitions was receptive to a Jerry Williams interview. Al Gore did the show on October 13, 1987. Pete DuPont was in on November 9. Jack Kemp dropped by in January 1988. Then Al Haig and Paul Simon and John Kerry. Plus, there were a host of people Jerry asked to handicap the race—Ralph Nader, Gene McCarthy, Paul Kirk (the chairman of the Democratic

National Committee), Mort Sahl, and even former President Jimmy Carter, on June 10, 1988, a month before the Democratic convention.

The zigzags of the Dukakis campaign itself, at first technocratically successful and then suddenly disastrous, provided a whole song cycle Jerry could draw upon.

Dukakis began edging toward his run as everyone else did, with 1987 meets-and-greets in Iowa, where people from New Braintree, egged on by Jerry, chased him from town to town complaining about the prison.

Jerry did a phone interview with a fellow talker in Iowa in February, poking as many holes as he could in the Duke's balloon. In May he did the same thing with a talker in Nebraska, and at the same time he mentioned his respect for the state's Senator Bob Kerrey. Now *there* was a guy who ought to think about running for president.

Then it was official, and Jerry began critiquing the debate performances, following the primary polls, tracking the ups and downs, and grinding his teeth as Dukakis pulled ahead of the competition.

In June somebody reminded George Bush about the Massachusetts prison furlough controversy a year before, a big-time embarrassment for Dukakis sparked by a rape and stabbing in Maryland. The perpetrator was a convicted murderer named Willie Horton who was on his tenth leave from the Bay State's jails. Jerry later claimed that *he'd* put that bug in Bush's ear, but there were plenty of smart guys around digging up dirt on the Duke who could take credit for it. Still, Bush's critical comments about Mike Soft-on-Crime made for more good radio that month.

Early in July Morton Downey Jr., now the host of his own noisy TV show, heard about Jerry's anti-Duke tirades. Hey, Jerry, come on down. Jerry showed up in New York with sacks of mail he'd received about Dukakis and replayed that old trick of dumping the letters all over Downey's set. Mort wasn't too pleased about it, but it made for pretty good TV.

WRKO sent Jerry to the convention in Atlanta for live broadcasts the week of July 18, 1988, where he invited the *Boston Herald*'s columnist Howie Carr to join him as color man. Jerry had been a fan of Carr's writing for years, and Carr had grown up listening to the Dean, so they were simpatico from the first word. Although Carr had done several years of TV reporting in the early 1980s, he moved into the front ranks of Massachusetts media when he returned to print, serving up an unflinchingly bitter diet of diatribes on Bay State politics, garnished with elliptical epithets and sly digs that made readers feel as though they had their own eyes and ears at the State House.

Carr discovered during that convention stint that he liked the spontaneity of radio and the fact that he could convey much more information jawing on the air than he could in a newspaper column or a canned TV spot. Jerry immediately appreciated Carr's gritty, midrange voice, and he loved Carr's daily roster of the Massachusetts political figures who were hanging on at the convention instead of doing their jobs up north—along with their salaries. This guy could be a real asset.

The events on the floor gave them lots of material. Not only was Dukakis winning, he was wowing. It looked like he'd made the right choice for veep— Lloyd Bentsen had gravitas and class and that old-fashioned Texas thing, and he looked good. Then the Duke had his big arrival, with the Neil Diamond tune playing and all the immigrant chords being struck and Kitty Dukakis looking very First Ladylike. Jerry looked around the hall during the acceptance speech and stared at the commentators on TV afterward. It was a goddamn home run. The delegates thought he was *swell*. David Brinkley was saying, "He's not a bad guy!" Even the ABC commentator Sam Donaldson thought he looked good.

Could Dukakis really fool enough of the people enough of the time to become president? Fortunately (as Jerry saw it), the legislature had written a new song for him just before the convention, voting to empower the governor to raise various fees without a legislative vote. Barbara Anderson, the head of Citizens for Limited Taxation, raised the alarm right away, and Jerry sang along. The "fees and fines" theme became a big hit on the Williams show— it played perfectly during the campaign, when the governor wouldn't want to be seen as raising taxes but might very well pump up the state's revenue with all kinds of arbitrarily raised fees.

The Duke had a nineteen-point lead over George H. W. Bush in the polls as Jerry headed to New Orleans for the Republicans' convention. While changing planes in Atlanta, he ran into Larry King and they began the usual back-and-forth about the campaign. King said that Dukakis looked good. Jerry said, "Just you wait. This lead isn't going to hold. And we don't want this guy running the country. Even Bush would be better."

King was dumbfounded. Jerry Williams, the classic liberal from Massachusetts, the guy who *owned* Boston, was dumping on his own guy? He couldn't be serious. Did he really want to see George Bush as president? What about the CIA and this guy's oil connections, all that stuff? "Jerry, you're crazy."

"Just wait."

At first, it looked as though Bush was going to combine the wisdom of Herbert Hoover with the grace of Gerald Ford. When he picked a brain-less mannequin named J. Danforth Quayle as his running mate, even Jerry couldn't resist roasting him. A plague on both their houses.

Then the knives came out and Dukakis fell on them. Bush's devastating ads, with the Duke's head popping out of a tank in one of them and a black guy in a revolving door standing in for Willie Horton in another, played to all the bad old Democratic stereotypes. Mike nose-dived, even though Bentsen eviscerated Quayle with his "You're no Jack Kennedy" line in the VP debate.

By the time November came around, Dukakis was an embarrassment to the Democrats and most folks were glad to see him leave the national stage. Massachusetts, of course, voted for him, and he was still governor.

The smart money would have said that Jerry had beaten this particular horse to death. But Jerry wasn't done with Mike Dukakis.

There was an odd sidebar in the middle of the Dukakis campaign. Jerry couldn't really hang it on the Duke, but it was good enough in itself because it provided him with another opportunity to slice away at the legislature on the air.

You had to wonder what the state's lawmakers were thinking when they voted themselves an increase in base salary from $30,000 to $40,922 and tacked on an "emergency preamble" to the bill, which allowed the raise to take effect immediately. And you had to wonder why the Duke just signed off on it on May 22, 1987, even though conservatives in the state were already screaming about it. Maybe this was a kind of devil's bargain Dukakis had to go along with to get support for his presidential run.

In any case, Jerry's reaction to this one was almost reflexive. Did anyone say, "Repeal the law"? Jerry had done that one last year, and the folks who'd worked with him then were already organizing the troops. Citizens for Limited Taxation, with Barbara Anderson and Chip Faulkner? Here. Freedom First, the organization born of the seat belt repeal, led by Chip Ford? Present. But they couldn't get the repeal on the 1987 ballot, and they had to settle for making noise about it for at least a year.

Jerry's audible opposition to the pay increase and his calls for listeners to flood their legislators' lines with complaints were effective enough to cause great annoyance on Beacon Hill. Whether that annoyance was enough to prompt payback is impossible to say . . .

You would think that William Bulger, the president of the Senate, had more important things to think about than the legislature's Science Resource Office, a research arm of the legislative branch administered by the House of Representatives. But in May 1987 Bulger moved to put the office under his direct control. He then got resignation letters from everyone who worked there and reappointed all of them except three people who had gotten their jobs through connections in the House. One of those people was Rita Frankel, who happened to be a very close friend of Jerry Williams.

Did Bulger take notice when Rita got Jerry a cup of coffee while he was testifying before the Senate Committee on Taxation in April? Did that seem to him like a little too much courtesy for one of the legislature's enemies, and did he make inquiries? William Bulger was a very busy man at the time, and it hardly seems possible that he would have had time for such petty concerns. He probably was just making room for some folks closer to the Senate.

But most observers agree that Jerry Williams was not one of Bulger's favorite people. And Jerry Williams was trying to take money out of the pockets of senators in May 1987. And Rita Frankel lost her job. And the little affair made the papers.

Generally speaking, throughout most of his career, Jerry had received pretty good treatment in the press—sometimes skeptical, mostly respectful. But after the anti-Dukakis campaign had been going on for a while, some younger writers started wondering whether he had too much power, or at least whether he was using his power wisely. Many of them had never heard the WBZ show, and nearly every journalist who could testify to Jerry's status on WMEX had already retired or died. To most of the people writing and assigning in 1987 and 1988, Jerry Williams was an exceedingly annoying example of the talk phenomenon, a guy who was cheapening public discourse and building himself up at the expense of good taste and cogent conversation.

Some veterans, such as Jack Thomas of the *Globe*, had been suspicious of the new Jerry right from the start of the WRKO years, and they'd made their distaste very clear. But the first real volley in the press backlash against Jerry began in May 1987, and the dark murmurings continued for more than a decade.

Caroline Knapp, writing for *Boston Business*, worked on a profile for two months. When it appeared, it was a remarkable contrast to almost everything that had been written about Jerry before. Knapp had no experience of Jerry's pro–civil rights and anti-Vietnam campaigns. She was repelled by him as a person and a personality, possibly because of his pre–women's lib style. She saw him as "big," probably because of his expanding waistline rather than his height. She described his voice as "born-to-be-a-deejay," which was about as wrong as it could be. She thought that "he didn't really explode into public consciousness until last year," when he'd led the seat belt campaign, ignoring his absolute dominance of the market on WMEX in the fifties and sixties, and his prominence on WBZ in the seventies.

But her opinions were far more damaging than her errors: "He's . . . mean-looking, beady-eyed. He swills Diet Coke and belches during station breaks.

He makes nasty comments about women . . . loud, relentless, incensed, driven by a self-professed commitment to civil liberties that borders on the fanatical. . . . His show is about anger. He's paid to inflame. From 2 to 6 each day, Williams leads a rage revue, an arena for mind games, an anonymous stage where people can vent, unseen and without fear of consequence. This is abuse therapy, wholesale. . . . [He] turns aggression into a spectator sport." The best compliment she mustered was that he was "terminally articulate."

Two months later John Strahinich, writing in *Boston* magazine, did one of the best features ever on Jerry, adeptly letting his friends and foes state the pros and cons. (Full disclosure: maybe we're favorably disposed because he interviewed both of us.) Strahinich had plenty of compliments on Jerry's strengths, but he also brought out substantive concerns about the actual value of his life's work, which had rarely been questioned before. When it came to speaking for himself, he gracefully and prophetically observed, "The line between populism and demagoguery can get murky, especially in the heat of battle." Unfortunately, that was the last major print piece on Jerry to show such a level of sophistication until the inevitable look-back pieces near the end of his life.

The Rita Frankel story broke in early 1988, matter-of-factly reported by the *Globe*'s Bruce Mohl in the middle of a piece on the mysterious workings of the Science Office. In September it surfaced again in a *Globe* Spotlight Team investigative report on Billy Bulger.

After Dukakis lost the election, Robert L. Turner of the *Globe* styled Jerry part of the "read-my-lips crowd" and the "government minimalists." A few months later, he was more vigorous—including Jerry as one of those he called "cynical," "venomous," "contemptuous," "silly," and "ridiculous."

By 1991 the skepticism and resentment had turned to scorn. In two pieces that year, Scot Lehigh of the *Globe* calls Jerry a "yapmaster" and a "hypocrite."

Some of the rising tide of invective simply came with the territory. In the years from 1988 through 1991, Jerry's career elevator had reached the upper story of Boston media. Because he was at the top, he was constantly heard, constantly under examination, constantly susceptible to criticism. The aspects of his work that Williams's fans had excused for decades and Jerry himself had camouflaged superbly—offhand judgments, unsupported accusations, faulty logic, volume instead of clarity—were now pointed out more frequently, and usually with justification.

But something essential in that work had changed, and the perception of that change may have subconsciously pushed buttons inside the observers of the media. Even in Jerry's bitterest tirades during the early years, there was always a sense of hope, a feeling that things could improve if America would wake up or if government would listen to the Little People. Since he had returned to WRKO, however, there had been increasing despair underlying the criticism. He had suggested that the political process was becoming bankrupt and that the American system of government—especially the variety practiced in Massachusetts—was hopelessly corrupt. Implicit was the message that the people themselves, the people he had always trusted, were now powerless dupes. Possibly this was a function of his own dissatisfaction, whatever it was that had been eating him alive for sixty years. No wonder he unsettled the people who were listening to him.

Early in 1987 Jerry began toying with the idea of reading some inspirational texts with musical accompaniment. Rod McKuen had actually had something of a hit record with stuff like that—why couldn't Jerry? So he looked around for things to read, hit on a few that might work—nothing as good as "A Child's Christmas in Wales," but what is?—and tried out a few in a studio with the help of Dan Serafini, an engineer-composer who then created original background music for them.

The experiment didn't really work that well, except for "I'd Pick More Daisies," the only one of the pieces he recorded that ever had a life outside the studio. He thought Serafini's sweet electric piano accompaniment added a nice resonance. He liked his own performance of it. So he rolled it on the air as a test-marketing exercise, and it became part of the Dean's occasional repertoire.

Anyone looking for hidden meaning in it is wasting time. Most of the sentiments and a lot of the phrasing started out in a piece written by the author-cartoonist Don Herold in *Reader's Digest* in 1953. It was retooled by a woman named Nadine Stair and the author Richard N. Bolles. Finally, it was attributed to "Brother Jeremiah," whoever he was. Jerry tinkered with the words a little so that it would speak more effectively for him:

If I had my life to live over again, I'd try to make more mistakes next time.

I would relax. I would stretch out.

I would be sillier than I have been this time around. I know of very few things I would take seriously.

I would take more trips. I would climb more mountains, swim more rivers and watch more sunsets. I would do more walking and looking.

I would eat more ice cream and less beans.

I would have more actual troubles and fewer imaginary ones.

You see, I am one of those people who lives pragmatically and sensibly, hour after hour, day after day.

Oh, I, I've had my moments; and if I had to do it over again, I'd, I'd have more of them. In fact, I'd try to have nothing else. Just moments, one after another, instead of living so many years ahead each day.

You see, I've been one of those people who never goes anywhere without my own pillow, thermometer, a gargle, raincoat, aspirin, and [he adds a chuckle here] a parachute.

If I had it to do over again, I would go places, do things, and travel lighter than I have.

If I had my life to live over, I would start barefooted earlier in the spring and stay that way later in the fall.

I would play hooky more.

I would ride on more merry-go-rounds. I'd pick more daisies.

By the time he came to be interviewed by John Strahinich for *Boston,* "I'd Pick More Daisies" had been on the air enough times to become the subject of an interview question, to which he responded, "That's my song. . . . I've been too pragmatic. I didn't take enough risks."

From late 1987 through late 1990, Jerry got his TV show and proved definitively that he wasn't right for the medium.

He had fantasized a hard-hitting approach on the tube, one that would avoid soft topics and easygoing interviews, and he talked up the idea as cable grew in importance. One of his RKO colleagues, Jack Roberts, took the bait. Roberts was producing the Ted and Janet show in the morning and hoped to take the next step up in his own career by moving to TV. When he heard Jerry's ideas, he said he'd be willing to try to pitch a Williams TV project to someone locally. Jerry said: Okay, see what you can do.

By May Roberts had the local affiliate of the new Fox network interested— Channel 25, WFXT, operating out of Needham, one of Boston's western suburbs. In 1987 there was no Fox News Channel and no FX. Rupert Murdoch's upstart little TV network was still mildly amusing to execs at NBC, CBS, and ABC—as they saw it, the "network" was just a string of rerun and infomercial stations that had agreed to clear a few hours of prime time for a few original Fox productions. But Roberts's instincts were right—these guys seemed willing to take a chance on a new concept, and, in fact, Jerry's show would be their first venture into local production.

By September he had the first pilot show in the can. On October 17 they did the official deal and signed the contracts. Jerry would be doing a weekly show airing Sunday nights from 10:00 to 11:00 P.M. Not a great slot, but at least a place to start. He'd get $750 a week, bumping up to $1,500 if the other Fox Network stations picked him up.

Roberts put together an appealing TV package, with sharp graphics, punchy music, a nice color palette, and a solid set. The program itself was relentless—all hard news and public policy, with Jerry looking tough and no-nonsense.

His trendy clothes and hip hair of the seventies and eighties (not to mention the radio attire of jeans and a casual shirt that were his usual nineties look) gave way on the tube to a suit coat and slacks (sharp, but very businesslike), close-cropped coiffure, and manicured hands. He was now silver-haired and jowly. His nose was still a beak. His eyes, which had always been heavy-lidded, now seemed recessed under his eyebrows, which made him appear hard, even sinister. One observer said he looked "ratlike." And many viewers were surprised at how little emotion showed on his face. His voice was as animated and dynamic as it had always been, but his expressions and body language seemed disconnected from it. Jerry really looked better on the radio.

There were no stars, no monologues, and no monkeyshines. Private rights and public safety, the death penalty, drug testing, credit cards, high-speed police chases—those first couple of months concentrated on the hardest of topics; they featured local guests for the most part, but they were conceived to demonstrate Jerry's ability to handle a nationally oriented show. The only relief from the political was an interview with Morton Downey Jr., whose TV show was setting new standards in Rude and Mean, and even that show was issue-oriented—should TV be going in this new direction and was it all flash and no substance?

The big coup was the show on November 22, 1987, a year before the presidential election: a candidates' debate that Fox fed to all its local stations. Jerry had all the declared Democratic candidates in the studio: Senators Albert Gore and Paul Simon, Governor Bruce Babbitt, Representative Richard Gephardt, the Reverend Jesse Jackson, and Mike Dukakis himself. On balance, though, it was the least focused show of the first year, as he had to be a ringleader rather than a provocateur.

Just after the TV show got going, there was a Washington flap over the concentration of ownership in media. It had some interesting resonance for Jerry's video employers and led to an on-air joust with Senator Ted Kennedy.

Rupert Murdoch's worldwide media empire, which included the Fox network and the Fox TV stations in New York and Boston at the time Jerry worked there, had a clear mission—a conservative, pro-business spin to counteract the perceived left leanings of most of the media. His tabloid news-papers never made much of a secret of their anti-Democratic sympathies. The *Boston Herald* (including its marquee columnist, Howie Carr) found Ted Kennedy particularly risible.

Murdoch had received a special temporary exemption from the FCC that allowed him to own newspapers and TV stations in New York and Boston. Late in 1987 Senator Ernest Hollings, chair of the Senate Appropriations Subcommittee on Commerce, tucked a provision into a spending bill that would have ended that exemption, and Kennedy supported it. The *Herald* complained, seeing the move as payback for its anti-Kennedy jibes.

Though the issue didn't appear often on his TV show, Jerry gave it regular play on the radio. He was exercised about the way the thing got passed, late at night and under wraps. Howie Carr thought that was a stand-up thing for Jerry to do, since a lot of people at the *Herald* stood to lose their jobs if Murdoch had to sell it or shut it down.

On January 7, 1988, Jerry was working the story on WRKO, quoting an Anthony Lewis *New York Times* op-ed that mirrored his own feelings. Jerry suggested that Senator Ted hadn't given perfectly forthright answers to questions about his actions to stop the FCC from ending the cross-ownership rule, and that he seemed to be pretty thin-skinned about this, unlike his brothers, who had had a witty and relaxed relationship to the press. At quarter after four, he got a call from the senator himself, who was en route to a constituent meeting in Plymouth. It wasn't exactly teatime conversation. In fact, Kennedy came out slugging: "I've been listening to some of that dribble [Kennedy meant to say *drivel*] of yours on the talk show here during the course of the afternoon, and—"

Jerry picked up the mispronunciation immediately. "Is it the dribble of mine, or the dribble of my listeners—which one?"

"No, it's yours. . . . Let's hear all these questions that I can't answer."

"Well, let's hear how it was done. I think that's what people want to know. How did you do this?"

Ted launched into his best Senatese, presenting the amendment Hollings and he had offered as a corrective to high-handed FCC activities like the decision to dump the Fairness Doctrine.

"Senator . . . you're filibustering."

"What's your question?"

"The question is [Jerry slowed his pace, trying to get control of the conversation]: How politically was this done? That's what the criticism is all about. The *New York Times,* the *Washington Post,* the *Wall Street Journal,* Mayor [Edward] Koch, Senator [Daniel Patrick] Moynihan, Governor [Mario] Cuomo,

Senator [Alphonse] D'Amato, they're all *angry* with you because of the *method* in *doing* this . . ."

"Now *you're* filibustering."

"Here's Anthony Lewis's comment today . . . 'A good end cannot justify sneaky means. It is necessary to be fair, even to those who mock the rules.'"

"We *were* fair, in the sense, to the members of the Congress and the Senate that weren't going t' wake up and find out, like we found out with the Fairness Doctrine, that the FCC had moved unilaterally. We weren't *changing* the rules, Jerry; we were *preserving* them. . . . We don't think the American people want a monopoly of communication."

And then they just went at each other for three hard minutes—not at all the way a dignified talk show host and a dignified senator ought to behave. Jerry maintained that Ted wouldn't answer his questions. Ted steamrolled over Jerry as if he were a freshman legislator who needed to be put in his place. He said he resented the things Jerry had said about JFK and RFK. The issues evaporated. Listeners, including the fledgling *Boston Globe* columnist Alex Beam, were fascinated by the spectacle.

TED: You're not interested in the substance—

JERRY: You're not answering the question. . . . You don't understand the criticism about you.

TED: You asked me about the process. You complain when I talk about the substance. . . . What, what is it that you're so outraged about?

JERRY: That it was done in the dead of night . . . by a United States senator.

TED: You're wrong. It wasn't done from a sunset point of view . . .

Finally, Ted swept Jerry aside and told him, in so many words, that the interview was over. "I'm on my way down to Plymouth. We're gonna have a meeting down here tonight on the Pilgrim reactor . . . It's always good to talk to you. I can't *wait* to get back on your program again . . . And will you put in a good word for me at the *Boston Herald*? 'Cause I've saved all their jobs."

JERRY: Well, I never said anything unkind about your brothers or anything of that nature, and that, and that—

TED: We'll, we'll let the record stand, as we say. But . . . let's go beyond that, Jerry, and look forward to our future time on your program.

JERRY: When will that be?

TED: Will you let me by there some time?

JERRY: How will I ever get a word in with you? . . . Your, your, your sarcasm is unbelievable, senator—it's, it's really incredible.

TED: Good to talk to you, Jerry, and I've got to get down to that meeting tonight. We're gonna talk to a lot of folks, we'll answer questions down there, too. Always good to be on *The Jerry Williams Show*. Thank you, Jerry Williams. Bye-bye.

Jerry took a two-second pause. "Is that an incredible interview, ladies and gentlemen? This is not a comedian doing this, by the way. Somebody might think this is a spoof, but—is that an incredible interview?"

Unfortunately, nothing on Jerry's TV show was quite that exciting.

By the spring of 1988, WFXT had seen enough to know that *The Jerry Williams Show* was not going to be the next *Geraldo*. It was scaled back to a live half hour, now including the occasional phone call, and it stayed that way for two years. Essentially, it became an adjunct to the radio show, hammering Dukakis at every turn, often featuring the same guests or the same topics—which wasn't necessarily a bad thing, considering that the radio show could be a powerful promotional vehicle.

The viewership was respectable for a locally produced half hour on an independent station—maybe Jerry had 1 percent of the available eyeballs in his time slot, but that didn't exactly make him bulletproof.

In 1990 the Boston Celtics bought WFXT and told Jerry they were canceling the show. Jack Roberts gulped hard and said he'd try to make it go as an independent production, with his own company.

On August 6 Jerry was back on TV—this time with a five-day-a-week, no-phone-calls interview show originating from Channel 27 in Worcester. Roberts had to buy the time from the station, and he couldn't sell enough ads to make it go. It lasted two months, about fifty shows, reaching maybe 65 percent of the households in the Boston area via cable, and Jack lost a ton of money. When he finally decided to pull the plug, only the *Worcester Telegram & Gazette* paid any attention.

That was it for Jerry and the tube.

While the Dukakis crusade was going strong and Jerry was trying to make the TV show go, he was also involved in trying to make a radio station in Manchester, New Hampshire, pay off. Nobody in the Boston press paid any attention to Jerry the Media Mogul, and maybe that was just as well.

Jerry had talked about owning a station or getting a piece of one for decades. He'd toyed with the idea as far back as Chicago, and he even put together consortia of investors from time to time. One thing remained constant: Jerry Williams didn't put any of his own money into the deals. He had expertise to offer, not cash.

In 1987 one of those schemes finally amounted to something. A venture capital outfit called Westin Properties tapped Jerry to look for radio stations they might buy for profit. He was supposed to get a share of the added value as the acquisitions prospered.

After talking to his old WBZ stablemate Clark Smidt, who already was a station owner, Jerry proposed WKBR in Manchester, an outfit that owned its own building and tower site. Jerry and the investors cooked up a clever deal—buy the station for a fair price, sell its building to make back part of the investment money immediately, relocate it to a new shopping mall, give it a spiffy new format, and watch the cash roll in.

Except that Jerry got rolled when he went up to look over WKBR's books. The place looked like a capitalist factory—there were plenty of salespeople on hand and the ledgers showed about $125,000 a year coming out after the expenses were paid. The truth was that the station was barely breaking even. Westin believed Jerry's rosy view and paid $1.4 million for the station, but the sell-the-building part of the plan went south with the real estate market.

They went ahead with the other part of the plan and rented new, glassed-in studios at the Center of New Hampshire, a mall connected to a Holiday Inn. As for management, Jerry wanted someone he could trust on the inside. "Hey, Alan, haven't you had it with producing my show? Don't you want to move up in the business? I've got this programming plan for WKBR, and you could be operations manager and supervise it. Whaddya say?"

"Jer, if I can do it without a decrease in pay . . ."

"Okay, you got it. And incidentally, you know my daughter Eve? Funny thing. She's decided she wants to be in the business. Studying at Connecticut School of Broadcasting in Florida. I'm sure we can use her someplace, right?"

So Alan Tolz entered the world of management that fall and Paula O'Connor, who'd been waiting in the wings at WRKO, became the new producer of the show. Jerry's concept for the station was simple—a news-talk show in the morning, followed by strong popular music jocks during the rest of the day, featuring lots of requests and audience interaction. Eve Williams was WKBR's new receptionist.

Despite Jerry's best efforts to keep his family life and Sandy Nagro separate, the streams started to converge in 1986 or so. Sandy and Jerry had been an item for four years now. He had gradually let down his guard in Boston and nearly everyone who knew him was aware of Sandy's status as his near spouse. Sandy even suspected that word of their relationship had reached Teri somehow—maybe through the grapevine of antiquers.

One morning the buzzer in his Quincy apartment rang. Jerry went downstairs and was shocked to find Eve in the vestibule. She had driven all night, up from Florida, was dog-tired, and was dropping in for a rest stop and a visit with her dad. But Sandy was upstairs. What could he do? The best he could come up with was an emergency errand: "Listen, Eve, before you come up, could you just run down to the drugstore for me? I just saw this morning that I'm out of toothpaste—get me some of that whitening kind, okay?" Eve was a grown-up, and she'd long suspected that her father might be fooling around occasionally, but this was like a scene from a soap opera. Who did he have up there, anyway?

Jerry hustled upstairs and swept Sandy out of the apartment. "You gotta leave now, now! And get all your stuff outta here! She'll be back in just a couple of minutes!" Talk about the bum's rush.

When Eve came back, Sandy was gone.

There was a constant tension in the relationship between intimacy and distance. Jerry tolerated the company of Sandy's kids, and he took something of a shine to her son, Michael, but he never really warmed to her daughter, Patty. On one occasion, when Patty had misbehaved, Jerry complained that he'd just as soon not have to deal with her kids. Sandy was unequivocal: "If you want me, you gotta take the kids."

He growled back, "I'd rather not have you at all."

There were dinners out, and more shows, and movies where Jerry fell asleep, and evenings of fun at home. And there were fights—big screaming matches, like the kind Jerry'd had with his parents. On more than one occasion, he became so angry that he pushed her—thank God, it was never more than that, but those moments, like the time he came close to pushing her down a flight of stairs, really frightened her.

Then there was the purchase of his last home, the first house he'd bought without Teri. They had looked at real estate, more for fun than for any other purpose. He preferred the southern exurbs—closer to Cape Cod—but he also explored properties as far west as the Worcester suburbs, tiny rural towns way out there like New Braintree. He wanted a property that would be an investment, of course, as all the other houses had been, but also something that would speak for him alone, the way his cars and his antique desk and his radio show spoke for him. Also, he still had a lot of furniture in the carriage house of the old property in Milton, and he thought it was about time he got those pieces out of storage. But in 1987, while Sandy was in the hospital for a minor procedure, Jerry chose to buy something that she hadn't even seen.

She came out and discovered that he'd spent a couple hundred thousand dollars on a historic 1820 farmhouse in the town of Marshfield, many miles farther south than Quincy. It seemed that he'd fallen as much in love with that house as if it had been another woman.

He had another fantasy about that house: the lot was big enough so that a full-size house could be built next door, and he proposed to Sandy that he give her half of his land so that she could build her own house there. He didn't, or wouldn't, see how much of an insult that was.

"If I'm not good enough to live in your house, I'm not going to build a house next door to you." She bought her own home in the nearby town of Norwell.

But she stayed with him, despite everything. She didn't yet know that Jerry's casual cheating had turned into something serious with a woman named Nancy Cook.

One afternoon in 1987, while Alan Tolz was still producing Jerry's WRKO show, Tolz saw a blonde woman in tears on the street outside the studios on Brookline Avenue. She had a certain style—young but dressing maturely, a bit naïve-looking, very attractive. Tolz asked her in a gentlemanly way if there was anything he could do for her. She asked him through her sobs if there was a telephone nearby she could use. Tolz brought her in to the office. Jerry Williams saw her, and something happened inside him. Speculation on the why is pointless—this is one of the oldest stories in the world, right?—but pretty soon sixty-three-year-old Jerry was involved with a woman younger than his youngest daughter and trying to keep it a secret from his regular girlfriend. By that fall, when the Democratic presidential candidates were lined up for his TV show and Sandy begged him for the chance to attend, he told her it just wasn't possible—too much security. Even so, Nancy Cook was there.

Those who saw them together in the months and years thereafter assumed they were sharing a bed, but Jerry denied it. He was just helping someone who needed help, he said. Publicly, he accepted the notoriety and the opprobrium. Maybe he enjoyed the thought that he could still be considered a Sugar Daddy.

When Eve moved north permanently to work at WKBR in Manchester, it was inevitable that her path would cross Sandy's, and Jerry invented the fiction that Sandy was someone who worked with him at WRKO. Eve got the picture pretty quickly, but she and Sandy couldn't really develop a genuine friendship because of the fictions that had to be maintained.

But how had Eve decided to follow in Dad's footsteps at last—to go into radio at twenty-eight? First, life as the CEO of an ice cream store had never been her idea of paradise. Second, she still wanted to be an actress, and, once

Sprinkles had settled into a frenetic routine, she found ways to slip out for casting calls and rehearsals. After months of pitching herself for any and all thespian opportunities with only the barest success, the light went on in Eve's head, as it had in Jerry's around thirty-five years before—if the world of acting won't have me, what about radio, where I can make my own drama every day?

And this time Dad did help out, even if it was only to get her a front desk job in Manchester, New Hampshire. Eve turned her back on ice cream and gave the business (tax troubles and all) to her sister Andrea, who had been almost a partner from day one anyway.

WKBR was a good situation for learning the business—one of those small operations like WKDN in Camden where everybody does double or triple duty. Eve saw a need for copywriting, and she talked herself into doing that. Then she asked Tolz if he'd give her a chance to read the copy on ads and promos.

Hey, she sounds all right. A nice mezzo voice with good low notes—that low stuff always helps a woman's voice on the air. A couple months after that, they gave her her own show—Jerry insisted she'd have to make it on her own, with her own identity, so she became "Eve Meredith," using her first and middle names. The first day, she blew it once—"Hi, this is Eve Williams"—and went home after her shift to tell Teri how badly she'd done. "I wanna come home!"

A long sigh from Florida. "You can't come home. You're there. You have to go through with it."

Of course, it didn't pay enough to live on. Eve moonlighted at another pair of stations in New Hampshire, B-106 and Oldies 99, owned by Clark Smidt.

Jerry's fantasy that Teri was always looking over his shoulder, suspicious of his every move, was a long way from the truth. She had a big, beautiful home near the ocean, an ivory-colored baby grand, day help, regular checks from Jerry—even if she did have to prod him sometimes—and a growing circle of friends. Now that she could choose for herself, she associated with people in the arts, musicians, show people, folks whose names didn't regularly appear in the social columns, not because they weren't just as good as Roxanne Pulitzer, but because they chose to live their lives a bit more quietly.

She became a regular at Ta-boó and the Brazilian Court, places to see and be seen at the time. Her innate sense of style, her elegant fashion sense, her ease with others—everything drew people to her. Couples and singles would gravitate back to the house on Seabreeze Avenue for post-midnight champagne and impromptu performances, cabaret songs and fun chatter around the piano. She had a companion named Arliss—just a companion, insofar as the kids knew, but she did buy him dinner quite a bit, which raised some eye-brows. Her friends from Massachusetts went down for extended stays. She set up a little appraisal business. She advised Eve, and then Andi, as co-owner of Sprinkles. Teri became very comfortable in Florida.

Meanwhile, the Dean of Talk Radio–TV personality–media mogul was trying to juggle everything in Massachusetts, and the first ball to get dropped was WKBR.

The real estate market crashed, and the building in Manchester sold for less than expected—so from the first day, the station had a debt to pay back to its investors, even though it still wasn't breaking even.

The new morning format, which Jerry considered his concept, took a long time to shake down. *Wake Up, New Hampshire*, sporting a Ken Nordine iden-tity package, certainly had potential. There were talented (if young) hosts: Jane Valliere, who was working with New Hampshire Public Radio at the time, and Roger Parmelee, who later ended up with NHPR. After a few months, they hit on the right combination of topics, the right flavor of infor-mation, and listeners seemed to be getting interested.

But the money was still not coming in as it needed to. The general manag-er, Alan Dary, went packing. Jerry nominated Chris Ryan, his second pro-ducer at RKO (now using his original surname, Cataneo) to become the new GM early in 1988. Cataneo had a mandate to economize, but there really wasn't much for him to cut—excepting necessary personnel. Alan Tolz did not bond with the new boss. He stepped into it big time when he advised a new saleswoman, "He's a good guy, but don't ever lend him any money." Since the woman and Cataneo were seeing one another at the time, Tolz moved on to other opportunities, as people in radio like to say, before George Bush beat Mike Dukakis in 1988.

A year later, Westin Properties had given up on WKBR, and Jerry was no longer a working media consultant.

But by that time, Jerry had fought and won a battle with Congress, founded a national organization, put new legs on his anti-Dukakis crusade, and become a "governor" himself.

Jerry's income from WRKO alone at the beginning of 1989 was at least $200,000, and he had more money coming in from other sources—although not as much as some people thought—the TV show, the WKBR deal, speak-ing engagements, personal appearances, and so on. Some local writers, such as Scot Lehigh at the *Globe*, felt that Jerry's criticism of people in state gov-ernment was pretty hypocritical, considering that the foot soldiers and clerks of government were making considerably less than he was. But you could hardly fault him for idleness.

Since the Democratic convention, Jerry had asked Howie Carr and Barbara Anderson to join him on the air with increasing regularity, sometimes as solo guests working on particular issues, sometimes as a triumvirate commenting on the State House soap operas. The three personalities meshed in the way that great teams do, reinforcing one another's strengths and minimizing their weaknesses. Carr was cynical, nasty, and very well informed; by now he virtually owned the word *hack* as a descriptive term for Massachusetts political figures, appointees, and government drones. Anderson was the straight voice, almost painfully sincere in her belief that government couldn't spend money wisely and the voters' primary responsibility was to keep legislators and executives from getting their cash. Jerry provided the mastery of rhetoric and outrage, crystallizing the issues into a few well-chosen words and stoking the flames of callers' anger. When he needed facts or details, he could depend on Carr or Anderson to provide them. When they drifted or drilled down too far, they could depend on him to restore the balance on the air. For some listeners, it was political burlesque in the tradition of the Marx Brothers; for others, it was collegial swashbuckling that recalled the Three Musketeers.

The first major success for the three of them came in marshaling Bay State troops to stop what came to be known as the Pay Grab in Washington.

On December 13, 1988, Ralph Nader did a guest shot on Jerry's show, in which he talked about a bill that would authorize a pay increase for U.S. senators and representatives. For some of the legislators, the new money would amount to a 50 percent pay increase. Nader thought that was a pretty arrogant grab for the brass ring. A few days later, on the anniversary of the Boston Tea Party, Nader was on Roy Fox's show on WXYT in Detroit. One of Fox's callers suggested that listeners ought to send tea bags to members of Congress with notes saying things like "Read my tea bag. No 50 percent raise."

Tea bags were cheap—and who didn't have an old tea bag in a cupboard somewhere? Pay raises were easily understood by everyone. The mode of expression was elemental: write a few words on a piece of paper, put it in an envelope with a tea bag and send it. The idea took off among talk show hosts, particularly because of the support and visibility of Mike Siegel, a highly respected talker on KING in Seattle.

Jerry hated to ride on someone else's coattails, so he soft-pedaled the tea bags and emphasized phone calls—instant action was better anyway, and radio was great at motivating it. Carr, Anderson, and Jerry made James Wright, the Speaker of the House, and the Democratic Whip, Tony Coelho, the personification of the issue. Jerry incessantly repeated the phone numbers of the local reps and the leadership. "Call your congressman! Call Jim Wright! Call Tony Coelho! Get them to vote this thing down!" And the people were heard. Hundreds of thousands of people, provoked by talk hosts with great and small reps, flooded Washington with tea bags and phone calls. Just two months after the effort started, on February 7, 1989, the pay raise came to an ignominious end; Vic Fazio, Dan Rostenkowski, and other big-deal U.S. reps commented bitterly about how talk radio had rammed it to them.

That month, Ron Doyle of the *Middlesex News* and Robert L. Turner of the *Boston Globe* both wrote columns saying that Jerry and his two sidekicks were getting mighty big for their britches. Doyle said they probably had more power than the governor himself. Turner's piece was titled "Who's Calling the Shots Here?" Jerry loved the attention, and it didn't take more than a few days before he installed Anderson, Carr, and himself as The Governors on WRKO, with a regular Tuesday afternoon spot that soon became required listening at the State House.

The success of the pay raise campaign demonstrated that talk radio was now a national phenomenon. Eric Bogosian's surreal stage monologue, *Talk Radio,* became a film at just the right time, and it excited a lot more discussion about the value (or peril) of this old idea that had suddenly become the hottest thing in radio. Jerry thought the movie was pretty good, even if it didn't reflect his kind of talk life.

Larry King began to distance himself from what talk was becoming. He drew a line in the sand—his show was about interviews, not fireworks. He even came out against the tea bag campaign and in favor of the legislative pay raise. Other veterans, including Paul Benzaquin, the guy who claimed to have invented the term *broadcast journalism,* the guy who was arguably Jerry's first protégé, looked into the future and decided they'd get out of the business for real.

But Jerry wasn't ready to go gently into that good night. The guy who'd been one of the few mighty oaks in the forest of talk was surrounded by foliage now, and there were quite a few trees stealing his sunlight. By early 1989 nearly all of the names now thought of as monsters were already famous or well on their way.

Howard Stern had not only survived but thrived as a result of his New York City competition with Don Imus. Infinity's station, WXRK, had put the two head-to-head in morning drive and Howard did so well that Infinity started syndicating the show in August 1986. All the elements of his work were in place by 1989—the meandering style, the entourage of subordinates, the naughty bits, the self-satire. It was so different from what other talkers were doing that some people didn't even consider it part of the New Talk.

Imus didn't look like an innovator any more, but any pity for his fate would have been wasted. He was doing fine as the morning lead-in to all-sports WFAN, pulling down more than a million dollars a year (and no syndication yet!) with a few hours of snappy politically oriented material, the occasional celebrity interview, and acerbic observations on life in this modern world.

Sally Jessy Raphaël had gone beyond radio and Bill O'Reilly wasn't there yet. Both were on TV—Raphaël with a sensitive guest-oriented show and O'Reilly with a tabloid news program called *Inside Edition*. And along came Rush.

August 1, 1988, marked the debut of *The Rush Limbaugh Program* in syndication, originating from WABC in New York City. Even though Rush didn't own any stations, he ran with the marketing concept of an "Excellence in Broadcasting Network" from "high atop the EIB Building," a stroke of old-time radio genius that made him sound as though he'd been doing it for a decade in the penthouse of some Gotham skyscraper. Ed McLaughlin, a former ABC Radio president who'd brought Rush to New York, wisely targeted smaller stations—those with some penetration into major markets and those that were bigger players in medium-level markets. They started with fifty-six outlets; in just three months, the show was on a hundred. After six months, Rush's combination of political satire, partisan hectoring, and produced bits, all wrapped in a personality that was so pompous and over-the-top that it seemed to be self-caricature, redefined what talk radio was supposed to do and be. The salespeople for EIB knocked on the doors of the big stations in the major markets. "Look at these numbers on this dinky little 5,000-watter in your back yard. How can you *not* have this guy on your air?" Not every manager took the bait right away, since he or she probably would have to fire a local personality to put Rush on, but that hook began to look tempting—you could save all that salary you were paying the local guy, obtain Rush's show for free by carrying his commercials, sell your own spots within it . . .

There were hundreds of other talkers, working the political angles and the issues, in large markets and small markets and tiny markets. The world of talk radio was a cacophony of conflicting opinions and approaches, but the pay raise campaign made it clear: the New Talkers had listeners.

But they still didn't have respect—at least not the kind of respect Jerry thought they deserved. Late in 1988 he sat down to dinner at Joe Tecce's with Carol Nashe, an old friend who had decades of experience as one of Boston's best-known public relations people and a prominent position at Massachusetts Blue Cross–Blue Shield. He brought with him a thick computer printout and told her to look it over.

"Jerry, what *is* this?" She saw hundreds of names of fraternal organizations, professional groups . . .

"Do you see an association for talk show hosts?"

"No."

"Well," jabbing her shoulder with his finger, "*you're* gonna do it. *You're* gonna put it together."

"No, I'm not." Jerry kept jabbing—that *hurt*. "I have a job. I make a lot of money. I'm not going to do it."

"Yes, you are."

Somehow, he got her to buy in. As the Pay Grab campaign blossomed, the National Association of Radio Talk Show Hosts became more than just one of Jerry's schemes. Nashe even talked the honchos at Blue Cross–Blue Shield into providing a little grant to set up this fraternity of talkers—they'd have a newsletter and annual gatherings, awards, the whole bit. As she developed plans for the first national conference in Boston and Jerry worked the phones to other hosts, talking it up, some of his peers around the country started saying that NARTSH wasn't such a bad idea, even if it *was* Jerry's group.

Jerry's colleague Gene Burns got it immediately, along with Mike Siegel at KING in Seattle; Tom Leykis, who was working at KFI in LA; Mary Beal, a host from Kansas; Neal Boortz from WGST in Atlanta. Some others were not so sure. Larry King was vocally against the idea. All the younger guys who had major reps going saw no reason to tie themselves to a trade group and share the limelight, and they just ignored it. And some managers were loudly opposed—John Moloney at WABC in New York (Rush's home station) forbade his talkers to attend and said this looked like an attempt to set an agenda for talk shows. Why, it might even raise First Amendment concerns. Yeah, right. A Jerry Williams–led organization was going to compromise free speech.

No one, however, ever contended that a Jerry Williams–led organization might not help the career of Jerry Williams. As the planning for the conference went into high gear, Jerry got some big-deal press, print and broadcast. Richard Zoglin of *Time* wrote a piece called "Bugle Boys of the Airwaves: Talk-Show Hosts Stir Up a Storm of Political Action" for the May 15 issue. The *Washington Post* wrote him up. Then he was on Geraldo Rivera's TV show in early June, mixing it up with Larry King about the new organization with some support from Tom Leykis. The producers also planted John Moloney in the audience to get his anti-conference management point of view on the table. Leykis unloaded on him with both barrels, suggesting that managers like him were afraid that the growing power of talk might inspire legislators to reinstate content regulations like the Fairness Doctrine.

Jerry even did a *Crossfire* show on CNN, with Larry King, Pat Buchanan, and Tom Braden. It wasn't a show for the ages, frankly; Jerry had to fight bad engineering from a remote studio in Boston that made his voice sound strident and shrill, and King was rather chummy with his CNN buddies.

As for the conference itself, it was held on June 10 at the Boston Harbor Hotel, and it didn't go exactly as planned. Ralph Nader, who was supposed to give the keynote speech, missed his plane. Morton Downey Jr. also failed to show. And the discussion about mission and strategy—well, what would you expect if you put thirty or so giant egos in one room and asked them to work together?

In the wake of the meeting, William M. Bulkeley of the *Wall Street Journal* did a front-page feature, so Jerry got his name in the paper again, even if Bulkeley was less than complimentary. And then Jerry got to do Phil Donahue's TV show, too.

A few weeks later, the National Association of Radio Talk Show Hosts was in business officially, and Jerry Williams was its president.

Mike Dukakis was not a happy guy in 1989.

For a few weeks after the 1988 election, Jerry took it easy on him. He'd had a bruising and embarrassing defeat, and he had taken it like a mensch. But by February 1989 Jerry was back on the horse about fees, fines, and taxes, and to make matters worse, the Massachusetts Miracle, which Jerry had always said was a lie, looked like it was done for.

Dukakis was making the rounds of talk shows, pitching a plan to add $604 million to the state's bottom line in new taxes, and he had the guts to accept Jerry's invitation to appear on the show—no callers, just Jerry and Mike, mano a mano. It was contentious; Jerry was hot on the budget mess, the fees and fines, the prison in New Braintree, and the mistakes of the campaign. As he had in the past, Dukakis parried Jerry's barbs, defended his record, argued that he'd done his best. But Jerry made some hard points and some listeners judged it a draw. Jerry acknowledged, as he usually did when meeting Dukakis face to face, that the governor had a good side. He could be real when he wanted to be. Maybe it was just that his handlers wouldn't let the guy be honest and direct with the people.

In June there still was no solution on the budget, and the state's finances were an escalating mess. The bond ratings had collapsed. There was going to be a huge deficit. It was a genuine fiscal crisis.

The Governors were in full cry by then, and they did not make it easier on anyone in state government. The final bill, worked out in early July, called for very bitter medicine. The income tax rate would be bumped from 5.75 to 6.25

percent. The state's gas tax would almost double. The sales tax would be broadened to include some services. There would be more than $500 million in new five-year bonds. That afternoon, and in the week after, Jerry expressed fury and disgust. He called it "the largest tax increase in the history of Massachusetts." He identified legislators who said they still hadn't made up their minds about whether to support it, and he gave out their phone numbers so that listeners could give them pieces of their minds.

A few weeks later, Mike Dukakis decided that he'd had it. He announced that he wouldn't be running in 1990. That was also the beginning of the end for Jerry Williams.

Massachusetts politicians started the scramble that usually ensues when a sitting governor takes himself out of the upcoming campaign, but nothing achieved traction on Jerry's show to compare with the seat belt campaign or Get the Duke. In fact, late 1990 rolled by in a series of snapshots.

Boston University President John Silber, a man who actually seemed to take pleasure in negative public relations, emerged as the front-runner to succeed Dukakis, and he captured the Democratic nomination. Then he suffered through a series of tough-talking gaffes that the press came to dub "Silber Shockers"; he finally tripped himself up so badly in a television interview with nice, nice Natalie Jacobson that his campaign never recovered.

Jerry found himself thinking that the genial, squash-playing, carrot-topped William Weld would be an acceptable governor. Even though he wasn't exactly a paradigm of populism, Weld was not a bad guy, which in this race was a ringing endorsement. He also liked another Republican, a fellow named Joe Malone, who was running for treasurer. At least Joe didn't look like the usual suspects angling for one of those cushy who-knows-what-they-do jobs, and he was making the right noises about fiscal responsibility.

The Governors cruised along amusingly, and Howie Carr's on-air persona became one of the chief reasons for tuning in on Tuesday afternoons. Al Giordano, a *Boston Phoenix* writer, captured a few of the epithets that made Howie such fun to listen to: Silber became Herr Doktor Silber, reflecting not only his Germanic heritage but his Ph.D. in philosophy and his study of the work of Immanuel Kant. Lust for the photo-op turned Senator John Kerry into "Liveshot." Then there were Fat Boy (Senator Edward) Kennedy, Good Time Charlie (Speaker of the House Charles) Flaherty, and the Corrupt Midget (Senate President William Bulger). Jerry picked up some of the language, but the words never seemed to be the same when he said them. Howie's shiv was sharper than Jerry's, and radio people scouting the field could hardly fail to notice talent in the raw.

The third member of the team had her doubts, however. Barbara Anderson was starting to feel that The Governors concept was becoming counterproductive. Howie's catalog of power abuses and penny-ante corruption seemed to feed the notion that Massachusetts pols would simply roll on doing what they did no matter how angry the voters were. And even though Bill Weld, Joe Malone, and quite a few other Republicans moved into executive positions in Massachusetts that November, Anderson's pet project for 1990, a referendum to cut taxes, went down to defeat.

Jerry's cynicism deepened, too. He mended fences with Larry King and appeared on his Mutual radio show in September 1990, getting a very nice intro as the president of the National Association of Radio Talk Show Hosts, along with a very big pat on the back: "One of the standouts [in talk radio] was a fella who made it happen in this town [Boston] and in Chicago, and he was one of the first, if not *the* first of what we might call the whoop-de-do talk show hosts . . . They didn't just talk, they acted. Jerry Williams was the kind of guy that went to the city council, pounded on the doors, led the people. He was on the air Tuesday night, and at City Hall Wednesday . . . At what he does, he's the best!"

By that time, there was quite a bit of tarnish on Jerry's populist image. It had come to light that he had pulled strings to help Nancy Cook get a state job.

It started in 1989, while Robert Crane was still treasurer of the commonwealth. Crane's charm and winning smile didn't keep him from being one of Howie Carr's targets, and, frankly, if you were looking for a career politician to pick on, he was a sitting duck. So why did Jerry suggest to Bob Crane that the Massachusetts State Lottery ought to look favorably upon Nancy? Did he not know how this would look if it ever came out? Perhaps she really was the right person for a courier's job that paid only $25,500 a year. Perhaps Jerry thought that lots of other people used their contacts, so why not he? Perhaps he was just a fool for love.

Gradually, Jerry became more open about his relationship with Nancy, even taking her along on a trip in a limousine with the two other Governors to a political event down on Cape Cod. That little escapade ended up in the papers, with considerable clucking about the forty-year difference in ages. If Sandy had previously suspected that another woman was in Jerry's life, she couldn't ignore seeing it in print. Hurt, angry, and yet still feeling protective, she tried to warn him that being involved with this young woman was going to come back and injure him in some way. He waved her concerns away, and they had another shouting match about it. It took more than a year for events to prove her right.

In the spring of 1991 a Lottery worker named Linda Nee was passed over for a promotion she felt she deserved. The job went to Nancy Cook instead, along with a nice pay boost up to $31,700 a year. And then, in a move by new Treasurer Joe Malone to cut the fat left by Bob Crane, the department Nancy had escaped from was eliminated.

Somebody tipped the papers that Nancy was close to Jerry Williams, and it wasn't hard for the reporters and gossip columnists connect the dots: Nancy obviously had been protected because of Jerry's influence. It was a story his enemies had been waiting for, a chance to hang the self-righteous, pompous, egocentric, garrulous, old windbag in a noose of his own making. Scot Lehigh of the *Globe* unleashed some choice language: Jerry was "the 67-year-old yap-master," and a "government-bashing pseudo-populist." Nancy was the "25-year-old girlfriend" and his "galpal." Not too nice. The day the story broke in the *Globe* and the *Herald*, Jerry avoided it by devoting the entire show to a celebration of Frank Sinatra.

And the problem simmered on, in the gossip columns and elsewhere, for almost a year, as Nee fought the state and worked her union's grievance system to get the job she wanted. In February 1992 Nancy Cook was called to testify at a hearing, which escalated things beyond mere rumor. If she were to answer questions under oath, who knew what details might emerge—and you know the union folks would have had some fun asking about her relationships with Jerry and Joe Malone. If Nancy had asked Jerry for his advice, he surely would have told her to keep quiet, resign from the Lottery, and count on him to help her out once the noise died down.

Nancy resigned. Linda Nee got her job. Then Frank Phillips of the *Globe* found out that Jerry had called Joe Malone for help finding her another state job, which started another round of ugly publicity. Malone was embarrassed by the exposure, but ultimately he shrugged it off. The answer to any question about it was simply that they had resolved the labor dispute and Nancy Cook wasn't working there any more.

But Jerry was stuck with it. The new gossip columnists for the *Herald*, Gayle Fee and Laura Raposa, put this tedious blowhard on their list of laughable old codgers. By the end of 1992 they delighted in reporting that Jerry and Nancy had been seen screaming at one another in public.

By then the romantic side of Jerry's relationship with Sandy was over. Her caring for him had morphed from love into a sort of pity. But even so, when he needed her, she would answer his calls, come to his house, listen to his troubles, hold his hand.

From 1992 through 1998, Jerry's personal and professional lives became entangled in the great corporate transformation of radio.

The old owner of WRKO had been RKO General, not exactly a traditional broadcast company, but not a new-breed outfit either. It was one of many large owners around the country dating back to the 1960s that viewed broadcasting as a long-term investment. For the most part, the execs left day-to-day operations in the hands of those crazy radio and TV guys, except when someone from corporate chose to pick up the phone and question a local GM or PD about an expenditure or policy decision.

One of those tedious FCC disputes that drag on for years forced RKO to sell its namesake AM station and its sister FM, WROR, in 1989. The folks who put up the $28 million for the two stations were named Atlantic Ventures. They were one of the first of the new-generation broadcast outfits that would eventually merge and blend and buy their way into vast holdings of radio properties—unlike anything that had been seen in American broadcasting before.

The boom atmosphere of the nineties, with its high-tech entrepreneurship and overnight millionaires, was infectious throughout the business world. Everything was supposed to go faster in the Information Age—decision making, consumer response, profit. And radio got an additional supercharge in late 1992: the FCC began making it easier for one entity to own more than a couple of properties in a market. Atlantic saw the future, and it became very successful riding the wave.

When the FCC said that it was now okay for one company to own two AMs and two FMs in each of the big markets, it started many owners thinking about how these rules could be turned to the best advantage. Atlantic saw an obvious answer for Boston: buy and diversify. On the AM side, they had the city's best talk station, WRKO. What would be the best option for another AM station? A complementary talk format—all-news or all-sports. Since WBZ virtually owned the news identity in Boston (although the public radio station WBUR was beginning to make its influence felt), the smartest thing for Atlantic to do would be to buy the market's all-sports outfit, WEEI, which at that time was owned by the Boston Celtics.

But there was a wrinkle: WRKO had competition—another talker, WHDH, and one that was just doing well enough to be an annoyance and keep ad rates down. Another factor: HDH had a very nice signal that would be convenient for Atlantic to own. So the very best option, the Machiavellian option, would be to buy WHDH, shut down its talk format so that WRKO would have that part of the market to itself, and then put the sports station at the old WHDH spot on the dial. Since Atlantic couldn't own any more than two AM stations at once, they would have to execute the plan in stages. They carried it off perfectly.

It began with the purchase of WHDH in December 1992. For more than a year, Atlantic tried out one idea after another on WRKO and WHDH to see what would work best talkwise: Give Howie Carr his own show. Try a couple of high-powered guys doing a program on business and investment. Try a newsmagazine in the morning. Bring in some of that outrageous Howard Stern kind of talent.

After they'd seen what worked and what didn't, they cozied up to Back Bay Broadcasters, a little company that had a couple of stations in Rhode Island. How would Back Bay like a Boston station? Atlantic could make it worth their while. If Back Bay bought the Celtics sports station and then sold the sports *format* to Atlantic, they could make back their investment virtually overnight. Hey, Atlantic, that's not a bad idea.

In 1994 the whole thing was consummated. Back Bay bought WEEI for a good price—only $3.8 million—and then sold the call letters and format to Atlantic. Atlantic cherry-picked the best talent from WHDH and WRKO and reformatted the Talk Station. They moved the sports station and its name— WEEI—to the 850 spot, and let Back Bay have the old WEEI spot at 590. And everyone was happy—except all those people whose jobs and programs were affected, and all the listeners who tried to keep track of where their favorites were. For a while, it was musical chairs, musical contracts, and a bit of soap opera.

The moves had begun in 1992, when Gene Burns, the stalwart WRKO libertarian who led into Jerry's show from 10:00 A.M. until 2:00 P.M., packed up his show and took it to New York to enter the world of syndication. WRKO management was kind of partial to Howie Carr to fill Burns's spot, and Carr's colleagues at the *Herald* lobbied for him, too.

Jerry thought that Howie wasn't ready for the bigs quite yet—and he suspected that Howie was one of the people who had leaked unpleasant details about his relationship with Nancy Cook. Even though Howie could legitimately be considered the latest in the long line of Jerry Williams disciples, they were barely on speaking terms.

Jerry liked the prospect of bringing Tom Leykis to Boston. Leykis was the guy from LA who'd made his reputation in the talk world by bulldozing Cat Stevens records after Stevens (now Yusuf Islam, a convert to guess what religion) said that Ayatollah Khomeini's fatwa against Salman Rushdie was okay with him. Jerry had also been impressed with Leykis when they'd appeared together on Geraldo's show in 1989. It happened that Leykis was out of a job, since he'd gotten himself into a dogfight with the police chief of Los Angeles, Daryl Gates, and in one of the most bizarre of all talk show reversals, was dumped by his station, KFI, so that they could replace him with the chief himself. Well, any enemy of a headstrong police chief was fine with Jerry. Tom had gotten a raw deal and deserved another chance—and Howie Carr couldn't possibly do the job as a solo.

WRKO management agreed on the last point, anyway. They went with Howie, but gave him a cohost, Victoria Jones, who was supposed to ease him into normal broadcast parameters during his final hour. As far as Jerry was concerned, Carr needed to do a lot more homework—let him go to Allentown or Camden and get his chops together if he really wants to do this job. What's RKO supposed to be, a broadcasting school?

There was ferment from December 1992 through May 1993. Jerry got RKO management to bring Leykis to town to do a fill-in over the holidays, and they were impressed—Tom was edgy and brash, very progressive on social issues, very skeptical on government and the pols, a lot like Jerry's formula.

When the ratings numbers for Howie's first quarter came out early in 1993, Jerry and all the other skeptics got a shock. Howie was beating the other talk stations in Boston between 9:00 and 11:00 A.M., with 7 percent of the available listeners at the time—a very respectable number, considering that Jerry had between 5 and 6 percent of the listeners in his time period. The naysayers argued, Beginner's luck. People are just curious because Jerry is so popular and Howie made his rep on Jerry's show. Besides, there are a lot fewer listeners between 9 and 11. Go with Leykis.

In the spring of 1993 Atlantic made its first moves to strengthen WRKO and redefine WHDH, and Howie got caught in the backwash. They established news-oriented talk programs in morning and afternoon drive on the weaker station, choosing a Boston TV veteran, Eileen Prose, to host mornings, and Janet Jeghelian for the afternoons. (Jeghelian had been doing morning talk on WRKO with Mike Cuthbert since Ted O'Brien left RKO to host a solo show.) Tom Leykis was hired for the 9:00 A.M.–to–noon shift, and Howie was just a well-compensated columnist again.

The mornings on WRKO were given to Marjorie Clapprood and Pat Whitley, who had been doing a left-right Ted-and-Janet-style show for about a year and a half on HDH. The team was broken up briefly early in the year, after Whitley's contract expired, and then Clapprood was bounced when the Prose show debuted, but the shifts seemed like part of the Atlantic plan to reshape their two talk stations without losing Jeghelian. Clapprood (the liberal) was a former state rep who'd held her own quite well in verbal tiffs with Jerry, on and off the air. Whitley (the conservative) was a former program director of WITS, with a nice independent income through a weekend radio program he owned outright that was built entirely on restaurant reviews and advertising. They had a five-year run on RKO, and their total time together on the air as a morning team matched that of Ted O'Brien and Jeghelian, although the tenor of their show was less genteel. Clapprood's hard, brittle voice commanded attention even though it was one of the most unpleasant sounds ever on the radio in Boston. Whitley had the chops to balance her, sometimes with his naturally soothing bass-baritone and sometimes with surprising grit.

When the smoke cleared in May 1993, it seemed that WRKO was more unified, more consistent with Jerry's eighties approach—feisty and combative. But if you shifted perspective, you could see that nearly all of the old guard who'd made WRKO into the area's first great talk success were now gone—Brudnoy, O'Brien, Jeghelian, Burns. There was one man standing, and he was sixty-nine years old.

Jerry's status was still unquestioned during this dance. From 1991 through 1993 the guest list had included the political heavies—the former presidential candidate Eugene McCarthy, Governor William Weld, the Reverend Al Sharpton, H. Ross Perot, Senator Paul Tsongas—and the entertainment figures—Angie Dickinson, Tony Bennett, Henny Youngman, Phyllis Diller, Sid Caesar, James Earl Jones—that everyone expected of the area's top-ranked show.

Politically, Jerry continued in well-worn grooves, but he changed his tone a bit. To replace Howie in The Governors, he chose Bob Katzen of Beacon Hill Roll Call, a news service, a savvy observer of state government in his own right, but the chemistry wasn't the same, and Barbara Anderson herself thought The Governors ought to retire. She later remarked, "It was the same thing over and over. We thought that if we could show people what [the political cronyism and corruption in the state] was really like, that their natural reaction would be to do something about it. Instead, the public reacted with disgust, . . . cynicism and despair."

Which Jerry shared and reflected. He briefly ran a "Mad as Hell" campaign in 1992, giving out bumper stickers to express general dissatisfaction with local and national government. He looked with distaste on both candidates for president that year—he saw Bush as feckless and Clinton as greasy and irresponsible.

Finally, as a senior figure in the world of talk, he had some national visibility as a representative of talk radio, had graduated from being president of NARTSH to chairman of the board (Carol Nashe was still doing most of the grunt work), and was riding the wave of the form's newly recognized prominence. Case in point: in February 1993, when Ted Koppel and *Nightline* did a show on the way in which talk radio hosts were inspiring their listeners to lobby legislators with onslaughts of telephone calls and mail, the producers chose two representatives of the business—Rush Limbaugh and Jerry Williams.

Say, what about Rush, anyway? Well, the big man of the Excellence in Broadcasting Network was a big deal by 1993.

WHDH had signed on two years before, fairly early in Rush's rise, airing the show live from noon to 3:00 P.M. Within a few months, Rush had established himself in Boston amid a crowded field of talkers, so much so that when HDH tried to move his show to afternoon drive in September 1991 to compete directly with Jerry, they received so many protest calls that they had to restore him to the old slot after just one day. The guy clearly had something, even if he was—maybe *because* he was—so unconventional when compared to other talkers.

Jerry had always presented himself on and off the air as his own man, politically speaking. Since the late sixties, he'd been uncomfortable with labels of all sorts. When forced to choose from conventional terms, he might opt for "liberal," even when he felt that what had come to be known as "liberalism" had moved toward something completely alien to his feelings about the role of government. Depending on what year you checked in with him, he might call himself a "radical," a "pragmatist," a "populist," or a "classic liberal." His political philosophy, such as it was, sprang from his search for the most practical solutions to the country's problems, regardless of which party put them forward.

Rush went in a different direction. He straightforwardly identified himself as a conservative, and he tied himself to the Republican Party's positions much more often than not. When he wasn't satirizing Democrats and liberals, he was evangelizing for the philosophy of the right, trying to bring new recruits into the ranks of the true believers.

He also knew how to ride the political waves. During George H. W. Bush's presidency and the First Gulf War, he was a staunch supporter of the post-Reagan approach to the world. As Bill Clinton rose and took over the presidency in 1993, Rush found an ideal foil, and Clinton's persona helped to define who Rush was by contrast.

More important, Limbaugh was primarily an entertainer, despite the anger he engendered among the humorless lefties he targeted with terms like "environmentalist wackos" and "feminazis" (a coinage worthy of good old Walter Winchell). Unlike Jerry Williams, who frequently wore one of his character hats on the air but remained a "real person" at the center of his show, Limbaugh's character was a single overblown persona, love it or hate it, and he worked it as brilliantly as anyone in broadcasting ever has.

And what was perhaps most surprising for the old broadcast hands, Rush was not a local. His show was syndicated out of New York, which, in classic broadcast thinking, was supposed to be a disadvantage. Everyone believed that audiences wanted people who spoke to them from their own community—quintessentially exemplified by Jerry Williams. As Rush began to roll up impressive numbers all over the country and even in "liberal" Boston, he proved that things were changing.

Syndication of talk radio exploded in 1993, "the Year of the Deal," according to *Billboard.*

Larry King's overnight talk show moved to afternoons in February, which gained him prime-time hearability and opened up new markets. Howard Stern was by now a sort of grandfather of syndication, having targeted stations known for music rather than talk since 1986; in March he debuted on WBCN, Boston's landmark progressive rocker, from 7:00 P.M. to midnight. The success of Don Imus's show on WFAN in NYC inspired an effort beginning in June to place him on sports talk stations, and WEEI in Boston signed up for Imus in July. And a dozen new names in talk, including that old Watergate conspirator G. Gordon Liddy, sent their new shows out via syndicators large and small beginning in 1993.

In that moment the image of the local talk show host—at least in the mind of the younger listener the advertisers and station owners coveted—went from hometown hero to glitzless has-been. Unless the local host had something new to offer—which is where Howie Carr came back into the picture.

By mid-1993 it was clear to the folks at Atlantic Radio that there was no point in trying to turn WHDH into a sort of pseudo-news station. Their afternoon drive program with Janet Jeghelian was just not working, and someone suggested bringing Howie Carr back. Maybe they were inspired by the kinds of columns Howie had written since being dumped by WRKO, columns that sometimes suggested Jerry Williams was getting a little long in the tooth for the job of opinion maker and talkmaster. Maybe folks just remembered Howie's good numbers in the morning. Maybe they realized that Howie was the perfect personality around which to build a new kind of talk show.

On October 4 WHDH introduced Carr as their new afternoon talk host, on the air from 3:00 until 7:00 P.M., directly competing with the Dean. The producers were Kevin Straley and Jim Cutler, who had a mandate to make the show sound like Imus or Stern—with regular characters, bits, imitations, produced pieces, lots of sound variety. They also took a page from sports talk and made the show nastier and coarser than political talk was supposed to be. Howie embraced all of it, along with the chance to beat Jerry at his own game.

Carr got attention right away by attacking City Councilor David Scondras. Someone provided him with tapes of calls Scondras had made to the 911 emergency line, in which the councilor tried to browbeat people in the police department into giving him the home telephone number of a captain. Howie played the tapes and worked the story primarily from the abuse-of-power angle, but Scondras's status as the city's first openly gay city councilor and a champion of progressive causes gave him some choice opportunities to make cutting personal comments as well. A month later Scondras was voted out of office.

There couldn't have been a clearer contrast over on WRKO. Incredibly, Jerry Williams was making a run at seat belts again. At just about the time Howie was punching Scondras, Representative Barbara Gray, Jerry's nemesis during the first seat belt campaign, introduced a new bill to make wearing belts mandatory in Massachusetts. The whole thing came back to life; Jerry emphasized "unwanted police entry into your car" and Chip Ford resuscitated his seat belt group under the name "No Means No."

Jerry called for listeners to lobby their reps. The legislature passed the bill.

Jerry called for the governor to veto it, and Bill Weld came on the show to nix it live. The legislature overrode the veto in January 1994.

Chip Ford started a drive for signatures to put a repeal on the November ballot.

Jerry's third grandchild, Therese, named after Teri, was born on January 19; once again, he couldn't visit Susan in the hospital, because of his seat belt campaign.

It was déjà vu all over again, with Jerry leading the charge—except that he failed to turn around and see how few people were following him.

When the ratings came out for the later part of 1993, Jerry was aghast. Howie Carr had 5.3 percent of the listening audience. He had 2.4 percent, one of his lowest shares ever on WRKO.

Jerry Williams was seventy years old. Paula O'Connor had moved on to a more responsible position at WRKO, and Eric Caldwell had taken over as his producer. Atlantic Radio merged with two other radio station owners, so he was now employed by an even bigger corporation, American Radio Systems. Other talkers were roaring by him like SUVs passing his vintage Cadillac limo. He was tired of driving the program four hours a day, five days a week. But he kept his eyes on the road and rolled on.

There were two remarkable snapshots of his state of mind at the time. Al Giordano of the *Boston Phoenix* profiled Jerry and Howie in December 1993, and he published some extensive interview excerpts. Jerry sounds angry, alone, and disappointed in the world: "I consider myself the last of the true liberals. . . . I'm very suspicious of any loss of freedom. My views on roadblocks and police entries were formed during the Warren years of the

Supreme Court. There are no civil libertarians any more, except the ACLU. And they don't want to talk about seat belts. . . . Where are the liberals today? . . . More regulation? More government? Is that what liberalism stands for? We're going to wake up someday and ask, 'Where did our freedom go?'"

A month later, he sat in the WRKO studio for a video interview designed to be cut into sound bites and used by the sales staff. Jerry was unusually frank—he knew he was speaking to people on the inside of the business:

> We have people who listen to [talk radio], who believe in us, who do what we tell them on occasion. . . . On other occasions, talk radio is a bunch of shit. . . .
>
> I have an interesting life. I mean, I keep two women and one wife. . . .
>
> I'm basically a populist. [My philosophy is:] "Whatever works." "Got a problem? Let's see how we can work on it." . . . [I'm] very conservative about fiscal matters, and liberal on some social matters. *Very* conservative on whether a policeman can enter your automobile. . . . I actually think the country is in the crapper, and I don't think either a liberal or conservative [approach] is going to solve the problems. . . . I'm "Roosevelt," y' know, politically. . . . [Franklin D. Roosevelt] was the greatest president, in my view, ever, for that particular moment in time. Harry Truman, as well. But beyond that, I have no favorites. . . . Richard Nixon—[I was] one of the early haters. Still hate him. [I] do not like the present occupant [of the White House, Bill Clinton], or any of the people we've seen recently. . . . I'm actually . . . a Zappa-ite. Frank Zappa thinks that government has to be dismantled.

He cocked his thumb towards his chest and smiled. "That's me."

A week or so after Jerry recorded the sales video, he managed to score another first—maybe his last: in one four-hour show he interviewed all ten of the sitting congressmen from the Massachusetts delegation. Shortly after that he changed offices one more time, going with all the other WRKO and WHDH folks to the new American Radio Systems headquarters on Huntington Avenue in the Back Bay—a multi-floor suite that looked more like law offices than a broadcast station.

Six months later, ARS combined WRKO and WHDH into one talk station and moved WEEI's sports format to the old HDH frequency. After thirteen years in the afternoon drive chair, Jerry Williams was replaced by Howie Carr.

They put Jerry in a two-hour slot in the later part of the morning, sandwiched between the Clapprood-Whitley morning show and Rush Limbaugh at noon. Those hours had previously been owned by Gene Burns, then Carr, and then Tom Leykis, until Tom destroyed his career in Boston by getting indicted for assaulting his wife. Jerry hadn't worked that part of the day since he'd been on WKDN in Camden in 1951.

When Dean Johnson of the *Boston Herald* got quotes for his changing-of-the-guard piece, the tone was a little frosty.

> HOWIE: I wish Jerry the best. . . . Everyone's starting over with a clean slate. I want to do the best I can, and get the best numbers I can, so I gotta be a member of the team. I have a vested interest in Jerry doing well.
> JERRY: I have no ax to grind. We'll probably rarely bump into each other, anyway. I'm trying to be the consummate professional. I've never said anything unkind about him on the air and never will.

Mark Curry was his new producer. Jerry dealt with the morning show as if it were an entirely new program—"the fastest two hours in radio," as he called it for the next two years and four months.

A month later Newt Gingrich announced the Republicans' "Contract with America," a manifesto designed to maximize support for Republican congressional candidates in the midterm elections that November. Three hundred talk show hosts across the country signed it. Jerry Williams was not among them, since he never followed anyone else's lead.

Instead, he was occupied with seat belts redux, since Chip Ford's group had successfully gotten a repeal referendum on the ballot. But this time there would be no victory party.

In March 1995 RKO sprang for a remote broadcast in Washington, where Jerry spoke with many of the new and old Republicans—Representatives Peter Torkildsen and Peter Blute of Massachusetts, Charles Bass of New Hampshire, Bob Dornan of California, and Senator Rod Grams of Minnesota.

In April he interviewed Robert McNamara, the man who had been secretary of defense during the Vietnam War. He told Mark Curry to have the tape of the Vietnam Veteran ready, and he played it for McNamara on the air. The man remained impassive—cold as ice.

In May, as a battle brewed between Republicans and Democrats over the budget, Jerry went back to Washington for another bite, speaking with Republican Senators Tom Daschle and Don Nichols, Republican Representative John Boehner, and Democratic Representatives Dick Gephardt and Joe Kennedy.

Jerry even did a remote in Las Vegas. That was where he told Mark Curry about the time his father had bought him a yo-yo, and one of the tough kids in Brooklyn stole it from him and broke it. Curry bought Jerry a yo-yo while they were there. It was just one of those things that you did because you were Jerry's producer and you cared about the guy.

There were entertainment guests—the jazz pianist George Shearing, Carl Reiner, the comedian Pat Cooper, Wally Amos of "Famous Amos" cookie fame. Things were going along okay.

Then came August 1995, and a conversation with the honchos at WRKO about his contract, in which he learned where he really stood. RKO wanted to pay him less—they were paying him upwards of $250,000 a year. For ten hours a week? They wanted adjustments in his vacation and possible severance. They wanted him to sign the new deal by September 1. It was take it or leave it. He took it.

It was as if his life were shrinking. His daughter Eve had a run at WATD, a small but respected station right around the corner in Marshfield, but that ended in late 1995 and she moved back to Florida. There was almost no relationship with Teri, Susan, and Andrea, except for the occasional phone call and holiday visits to Florida. He knew very little about his grandkids.

What passed for family in his life was a deepening friendship with Jeanine Graf, her husband, Daniel, and her kids. Jeanine was a close friend of Sandy Nagro's who'd been doing public relations and working off and on in talk radio and television, sometimes crossing paths with Jerry, sometimes not. Because she lived close by in Marshfield and could be depended on to provide a neutral ear, she became a sounding board when Jerry and Sandy argued. Jerry was invited to drop by for birthday parties or holiday gatherings, and he got into the habit of having breakfast at the local Mug 'n' Muffin with Daniel, where they'd talk about cars.

The connection between Jeanine and Jerry was cemented after she had an odd dream, in which she found herself in a deep conversation with him unlike the real ones they'd had up to that time. She dreamed that Jerry was baring his soul, confessing that he had a wall around himself, telling her that he was unable to feel love, weeping. The morning after, Jerry called to make a date for breakfast with Daniel. Jeanine decided to share her dream. He responded with long silences and what she thought was a sniffle or two. It was only later, when Jerry spoke with Daniel, that he revealed how well she'd intuited what he was feeling. "I think your wife is a witch. Did she tell you about the dream?"

Late in 1994, after the second of her kids had gone to college, Sandy Nagro was considering selling her home in Norwell and getting a smaller place. Jerry asked her to move in with him, and she agreed. Even though the romance was gone, she finally had the satisfaction of being acknowledged officially as the first of the women in Jerry Williams's life. But he still wouldn't give up seeing Nancy Cook.

Around the same time, everyone in Boston talk radio got a shock when David Brudnoy collapsed in the lobby of his apartment building. He was taken to Massachusetts General Hospital, where he lay in a coma for nine days. A couple of months later, after a very slow recuperation, he revealed publicly that he was gay and HIV-positive.

Jerry was sympathetic. When he and Jeanine Graf discussed it, he said that Brudnoy was going to have a long and difficult fight. In a minor way, he thought he could understand. For years, Jerry'd had problems with momentary blackouts—even occasionally on the air—that had been diagnosed as transient ischemic attacks. Some people thought they were related to migraines. Others compared them to tiny strokes. Alan Tolz and his other WRKO producers had seen evidence of these problems for almost ten years, but Jerry was so skilled at his work that he could cover a momentary pause without the audience knowing what had happened. Jerry thought that Brudnoy might even be a little relieved since he didn't have to hide his condition any more.

In January 1995 *Talkers* magazine, the print and online trade paper run by a broadcast veteran and publicity genius named Michael Harrison, put out a special issue naming their Top 25 Radio Talk Show Hosts of All Time. Jerry was number 13 on the list. Predictably, Rush Limbaugh was first, but the rest of the names showed some care in balancing history with success; among those mentioned were Bob Grant, Bruce Williams, Michael Jackson, and Brudnoy, alongside Gordon Liddy, Jim Bohannon, Dr. Laura Schlessinger, Alan Colmes, Dr. Joy Browne, and Armstrong Williams.

That year there was a fight among NARTSH board members about whether to give G. Gordon Liddy their Freedom of Speech award. Some of them thought Liddy ought to be singled out for his choice comments in the wake of the Ruby Ridge and Waco sieges ("Now, if the Bureau of Alcohol, Tobacco and Firearms comes to disarm you and they are bearing arms, resist them with arms. Go for a head shot; they're going to be wearing bulletproof vests."). When the Liddy supporters carried the day, several members resigned in protest. But Jerry had put a lot of distance between himself and NARTSH by then; it was too much like work. In 1997 Carol Nashe was relieved of her position as executive director after a disappointing convention. The annual NARTSH gathering was abandoned, and the group evolved into the Talk

Radio First Amendment Committee, whose sole purpose today is naming the winner of an annual Freedom of Speech Award presented at the annual *Talkers* New Media Seminar.

Jerry's last WRKO producer was Nancy Shack, who came on board in August 1995. Like every other producer, she was amazed at his resilience and creativity. She'd start by saying, "Jerry, whaddya want to do today?"

He'd reply, "I'll take care of it. Don't worry about it." And every time he'd take the chair, he'd be in control, as if the whole show were in his head already and all they had do to was let it come out of him.

She was impressed by the people who'd respond to a request for an interview without hesitation. When they went to New Hampshire to cover the primary in 1996, Mark Shields from CNN's *Capital Gang* dropped everything to reminisce about Jerry's last years on WBZ when Shields was a regular guest.

She encountered Dan Rather and told him, "Jerry Williams is down the hall." Rather responded, "I'll be down in just a second."

Like everyone else, she worked to get Bob Dole. Unlike everyone else, Jerry got a prompt return call from the senator himself. Shack later marveled to Jerry, "And what do you do? You say, 'We're a little busy. Can we call you back, or can you call back *after* the break, senator?' Which he *did.*"

Another big moment during the 1996 campaign was an interview with Pat Buchanan the day before the Massachusetts primary. Jerry got Buchanan so angry that he hung up in the middle of the interview.

There was political humor with Al Franken and George Carlin. Theodore Bikel reminisced with Jerry about being on the air with him the night JFK was shot. There was celebrity stuff with Loni Anderson, Jackie Mason, Robert Wagner, and Jill St. John.

As he had in the recent past, Jerry could rely on WRKO's production director, Bill Smith, to provide humorous original songs almost on demand. Bill and Jerry had known one another since the WBZ days, and Bill knew exactly the kinds of things that would work for Jerry. On the day that one of the Big Dig tunnels was partially opened to traffic, Bill penned and sang:

> Got a song t' sing with a message fer y'all:
> Half a tunnel's better than no tunnel at all.
> Diggin' up the city fer a long, long time,
> Spendin' all the money, down to the last dime,
> Y' know the Big Dig is a tale that's tall
> But half a tunnel's better than no tunnel at all.

In August 1996 Jerry's fourth grandchild, Katharine, was born. He wasn't there.

In September 1996 the Radio Hall of Fame announced that Jerry would be inducted at their October event. Casey Kasem was going to host it, and the other honorees would be the sportscaster Jack Brickhouse, the legendary DJ Wolfman Jack, FCC Commissioner James Quello, and the National Public Radio anchor-correspondent Susan Stamberg. Jerry looked at the dark side when he told Sandy about it: "It's the kiss of death." They put people into the Baseball Hall of Fame only when their active careers are over. This was another shove out the door.

In the following weeks his attitude changed a bit. The induction ceremony wasn't just a dinner—it would be nationally broadcast on an impromptu network; commercial stations could air it at their option, no matter what network or group owner they were affiliated with. That was at least *something.* And the organizers were giving each honoree a minute, maybe two, to say a few words. He realized that this was a chance for him to make a definitive statement about his work and the radio genre he'd helped to create. He talked about it with Jeanine Graf. He needed to start out as he usually did in public situations, with a few jokes, leaving the serious stuff for a big emotional finish. He could probably stretch his time to three minutes without causing too much trouble. Jeanine and he worked on the text. She printed it out on cards that Jerry could use to prompt himself. She tried to get him to cut it, to take out a joke or two—Jerry, it's supposed to be two minutes!—but he wanted to keep everything.

Late in October, someone conned him into going out to dinner at Joe Tecce's, his favorite Italian restaurant in the North End. When he got there, he was genuinely astonished to find a roomful of friends and colleagues, cheering him and toasting him because of the upcoming induction into the Hall of Fame. There were people from the air, including Marjorie Clapprood, Andy Moes, and even Howie Carr. Regulars from his own show—Barbara Anderson, the comedian Steve Sweeney, Bill Smith, the attorneys Albert Johnson and Larry O'Donnell Sr. The producers—Shack, Tolz, O'Connor, Caldwell, Curry. Dean Johnson from the *Herald.* Sandy Nagro and Jeanine Graf. The restaurant's owner, Sal Tecce. And John Gehron and David Pearlman, the ARS execs. They even had a prerecorded proclamation from Governor Weld naming October 27, 1996, Jerry Williams Day and gave him a crystal award commemorating his fifty years in radio.

But Bill Smith sent him a personal fax the next day that meant much more to him than the award or the proclamation. Smith compared Jerry to a wolf, a wild canine with his true nature intact, not bred away by the powerful, dangerous humans who could never appreciate his spirit. "I've witnessed from you a steady stream of the values of truth and compassion. Truth in friendship, communication, government, business. Compassion for those who suffer in their battle to vanquish the thieves of truth. I was not surprised to find that the Jerry Williams of the airwaves was the same man off the air. Even more so . . . to me, you are a hero and a great role model. I believe in you, Jerry Williams."

A few days later, it was off to Chicago for the induction at the Cultural Center. Jerry took Sandy with him, and a group of ARS managers made the trip as well. Nancy Shack and Carol Nashe were there, too.

The ceremony was just as hideous as Jerry had expected it would be. He was the second inductee, and they chose Dr. Laura Schlessinger to read remarks that the organizers had written. Schlessinger's caustic, psychologically oriented advice show was one of the newest successes in talk syndication, with more than four hundred stations. It may have made sense to have a new star introduce a pioneer in the medium, but it seemed gruesomely obvious to Jerry that she was unfamiliar with his work. To make matters worse, the words she'd been given to read were stiff and formulaic.

Then they played a montage of his work: clips from WMEX, WBZ, WRKO; the original "Do you disagree?" jingle; some Sex Survey bits, including the Washing Machine Lady. The package was wrapped with his own world-weary "I'm definitely getting out of the business." After Schlessinger came back with the official induction announcement, Jerry finally had his shot. He came to the podium in a pleasant round of applause, brought out the cards with his swan song, and began working the crowd:

Thank you very much. I can hardly wait to hear what I have to say. It's gonna be interesting. I never had a dinner, you know that? Red Buttons once said that, and I've been using that line for some time.

Why shouldn't I have a dinner? After all, I've survived 93 general managers [he paused as the audience laughed], 108 program directors [another pause for laughs], 620 producers, and that was just last year! I've dealt with 10,467 account execs, 15,000 ad buyers, who are [he darkened his tone a bit] still looking for the twenty-fives-to-fifty-fours.

As a young boy, I was addicted to talking. Talking was good for me, and I joined a group along with my family, called "On-and-On-and-On-Anon." [This got a few audience chuckles.] The meetings were very, very long.

I loved talk, because I'd listen in those days to Jack Eigen, Barry Gray, Joe Pyne, Long John Nebel—used to put my ear to the radio and listen to Dave

Garroway, late at night, *Garroway at Large*—Oh! That did it. Talk radio was
for me.
Now we couldn't—uh—broadcast in the early days—

He was suddenly distracted by someone onstage—he was trying to count
him down, and he hadn't really started yet!

—He's giving me a number, now don't cut me off, awright?

The audience laughed, a bit nervously, as Jerry suddenly became an angry
child:

I just started the stupid thing, and lemme do it. Is this old-time radio?
Come on.

He took a long pause, composing himself, trying to edit his copy on the fly.

In those days, when you had to repeat what the listener actually said, you had
to say, "Oh izzat right? You—you're calling me a dingleberry, is that what
you're calling me?" You had to repeat what they said. And you know, it wasn't
bad.
Two-way talk radio was born, and I should tell you that I invented the
whole idea of the Rube Goldberg tape that used to go 'round your body and
around, and through three tape recorders, three people holding it up, while
they're held their breath and prayed that, as the callers called in, that no one
would use that four letter word—

He took another long pause.

Heck!
Seems funny now, doesn't it? It was the first time in broadcast history that
the audience was actually part of the program.
And as my friend Professor Murray Levin points out, "It had a vibrancy
and an emotional range, a nakedness and reality that could never be measured by the public opinion pollsters. Faceless but heartfelt, a human inter-
change between real people, and not pollsters." We now could talk to John
Kennedy, Martin Luther King, Malcolm X.
You know, being a talk show host doesn't always make you popular. I've
been mugged at gunpoint, spat upon, jailed, sworn at. I remember one guest,
a stamp collector, a philatelist, who came up to wanna be on the program,

punched me right in the mouth during the show, knocked me on the floor, my
producer yelling, "What should I do now?" since I didn't get much press—

Jerry had been on for three and a half minutes. Behind the scenes, there
was distress. The broadcast would be seriously off schedule if they let him go
much longer. The stage manager cued the band, who struck up "Yakkity Yak"
at medium volume, to get Jerry to wrap it up.

"—Oh, there he goes." He struck the podium with his fist. "I knew I wasn't
gonna make it. Am I not gonna make it?" He chuckled, but it was an angry
sound.

That's it. I'm sorry about—I wanted to say—I'm gonna go right through it anyway. I want to thank the guys at WRKO who are here, currently negotiating,
my, my—uh—contract at their table. They told me I could have two minutes
out to do this. Thank you very much. Thanks to the National Association of
Radio Talk Show Hosts. And we appreciate it. *She's* shoving me off, too, as
well. I can't synthesize it into two minutes. I can't do it.

He stuffed the cards back into his pocket as Kasem strode quickly to the
mic.

There were two more paragraphs he didn't get to read, which were supposed to pay off all that jokey stuff. He'd wanted them to be his testament, his
last formal words about his own role and the role of talk radio. This is what
he would have said, if they'd just given him one minute more.

The role of the talk host is always in dispute: people expect me to be a political analyst, archivist, and sex therapist, but I am a muckraker.

Talk radio can be a catalyst for change. Critics say it only fuels cynicism. I
disagree, although I sometimes wonder what the future of talk radio will be. I
hate to see talk radio awash in four-letter words with the shock jocks. They are
encouraged by the programming jackals, hunting the X generation and fostering the junk culture. They have no idea what a privilege it has been for me to
be a talk radio show host, to be a part of unedited history, to listen and hear
the pulse of the American Dream.

Three months later, in January 1997, WRKO moved Jerry to Saturday and
Sunday, from 1:00 to 4:00 P.M., and replaced him on weekdays with Dr.
Laura's syndicated advice show. Before he left weekdays for good, he had a
looking-back show with every one of his WRKO producers, with the exception of Chris Ryan Cataneo.

The weekend show existed in a kind of twilight. Even though Jerry Williams wasn't gone, he seemed to become invisible. He still could do fine and perceptive interviews, such as the one with the movie critic Roger Ebert. He still could take something ephemeral, like a story written by Jeanine Graf's son Joshua, and build a whole show out of it.

But the man on the air was like the ghost of Jerry Williams.

In the summer of 1997 Teri Williams began to have an odd sensation—a strange, unrelievable itching all over. Her daughters pushed her to see her doctor. He saw that her eyes were yellow. She was jaundiced. Tests.

Pancreatic cancer.

In the months that followed, she went in and out of the hospital, angrier and angrier at how her body had betrayed her, and finally she went in for good. Jerry's daughters called him with periodic updates. Sandy kept telling him, "You have to go and see her. The mother of your daughters, Jerry. She's dying. You have to go."

But Jerry recoiled—the hospitals, the doctors, the awful nearness of death.

Finally, when they said Teri was near the end, he brought himself to go to Florida and say good-bye briefly, and then he escaped again. She died on January 11, 1998, leaving no will.

He came back for the funeral, to deliver the eulogy that Teri deserved. It was a vintage Jerry Williams performance. He reminisced about the courtship, how he had chased her and chased her in Philadelphia. He made people laugh and cry as he brought her back to life. There was no mention of the affairs, the separation, the lives they'd lived apart. He was the dutiful husband one last time.

It was Sandy Nagro and Jerry's daughters who had to sort through her effects in the home on Seabreeze Avenue. The kids took a few things—her piano, the portrait of the three of them with Teri. The four of them did a lot of crying and getting to know one another. When Jerry found out that Susan wanted that huge dining room table he was planning to sell, he vetoed the idea. That was an antique, and valuable. He was sure that it would bring a lot of money at auction. He wanted to see how much it had appreciated in value. Susan fought back. That was the table where they had celebrated every Thanksgiving—and because she had been born on Thanksgiving Day, it was the table where they had celebrated her birthday dinners too. Jerry was adamant, until Sandy angrily told him he was being a fool. The table went to Susan.

The house and property were sold. The money went to Jerry, and he gave each of his daughters a small settlement out of the estate. There was a big tax bite.

In the wake of Teri's death, Eve wrote a long letter to her father. She knew he'd never made a will, always thought of it as a kind of taboo—if he made a will, then he'd die. But Eve put it all down on paper—did he really want the government to decide where his money would go? Didn't he owe it to his kids to provide for them and for his grandchildren?

So finally, reluctantly, Jerry set about deciding what would happen in the event of the inevitable. His accountant recommended a respected estate attorney in Boston, Edward Jager, to draw up the will and advise him on the other stuff. Jager made suggestions. His daughters probably should share the estate equally. He could set up trusts for each of his grandchildren now and contribute money to them each year. And Jerry—is all your money in checking accounts?

Yeah, yeah. Sandy . . . what should he do about Sandy?

Well, you could give her a lump sum, maybe one of your cars.

While he was weighing his options, Nancy Cook had a pressing personal problem that got Jerry up in the middle of the night. As he had on many other occasions, he roped Sandy into helping with this "emergency," sending Jerry's credit card number to a hotel so that Nancy would have a place to stay for a few days. The next morning, Sandy delivered an ultimatum. She could be his caretaker and surrogate mother, but she wasn't going to have a good night's sleep interrupted for Jerry's chippie. She was moving out.

Jerry pled—he was in the process of making his will. What if he left her half of the land where the Marshfield house stood? That would give her enough of a lot to build her own nice big home there.

Sandy had made her decision. She was getting out of the house. But she was amenable to being nearby. If he really cared for her, he could give her that lot right now. Then she'd stay with him until she had her own house built. They'd be next-door neighbors. But no more midnight emergencies.

Jerry made all of the arrangements at the same time—the will, the trusts, the grant of land to Sandy. They drew up all the papers and he signed them. Were all these women finally satisfied?

There was one more thing: the health proxy. Who would make the decisions about his health care if he couldn't? He decided that Susan should be the one—Susan, the responsible, level-headed college girl who had made it on her own, without any help from Dad. But he never told her. She found out when they sent her forms to sign for her kids' trusts. And she and Jerry never discussed what he would want done if . . . or when . . .

On Thursday, October 8, 1998, a year after settling his estate, less than two years after he started doing weekends, seventeen years after starting on

WRKO, Jerry was given two days' notice of the end of his employment. He was told not to report for that weekend's shift, or for any scheduled shift thereafter. His services would no longer be required.

The show was over.

A week later there was a tiny mention of Jerry's departure at the bottom of Clea Simon's column in the *Globe*. He had become so invisible that she could write, "We may never know if he was fired or quit, but talk institution Jerry Williams is off WRKO-AM (680) after more than two decades of conservative chat, highlighted by his successful attack on the seatbelt law."

Barbara Anderson said good-bye on the Web site of Citizens for Limited Taxation. Scott Fybush noted the passage online at Northeast Radio Watch. There was one major piece in the press: a hail-and-farewell from Howie Carr in the *Herald*.

Howie was in good form. He credited Jerry with giving him his start in radio at the Democratic National Convention in 1988. He was philosophical (if hard-bitten) about the way radio chews up its veterans. He reminisced about Jerry's good old days but still pointed out that "the act wore thin the last few years." He obliquely referred to the Nancy Cook debacle.

And he closed with this: "What else can I say, Jerry, except that you were a great teacher, and as for all the tricks you showed me, well, I'm sure as hell not passing them on to the next generation, certainly not to some ambitious young kid, lest they come back to be thrown in my face someday, if you get my drift."

One month later, there was an unusual postscript to the career. And, as we think about Jerry sitting in his Marshfield home in 1998, trying to cope with his last bitter pink slip, we have our own post-postscript to offer.

It had been twenty-six years since the Vietnam Veteran called Jerry on WBZ and Jerry gave the tape of the call to George McGovern.

Now that Jerry was off the air, maybe for good—now that there was no way for Jerry actually to speak about this on the air—the political consultant Jim Braude chose to write about the Veteran and the guy he thought had made that call. In a piece published in the *Boston Sunday Globe*'s Focus section on November 8, 1998, Braude explained that he'd never heard the original broadcast or any of the many replays back in the seventies. He'd heard the Veteran for the first time when Jerry and George McGovern were reminiscing about the campaign on Jerry's WRKO show, fifteen or sixteen years later, in the late eighties.

He said he recognized the man's voice immediately because he knew him well—it was Domenic Bozzotto, he said, a Hotel Workers Union activist back in the early seventies who had risen in the ranks and eventually become president of his union.

Braude went to a party at Bozzotto's home shortly after he'd heard the tape, and he started asking his host some pointed questions: Had he ever heard the famous tape? The room went quiet. Did he know who the caller was? More silence.

"'That was you,' I said. Bozzotto laughed and asked me how I had found out."

Then Braude dropped his bomb: "Bozzotto . . . got no closer to Southeast Asia than an Army desk in West Germany, where he served as a clerk-typist in the mid-1960s. He left active duty in 1965."

There were the predictable follow-up articles. Bozzotto denied it. Braude's wife, Kris Rondeau, corroborated Braude's story. The *Globe* columnist Eileen McNamara said this was all going on because Braude felt Bozzotto had betrayed his past by moving to the right politically. Dan Kennedy wrote a perceptive piece for the *Phoenix.*

There were a couple of quotes from Jerry. In the *Globe:* "I never asked for names. . . . I never revealed names. The tape was everywhere. The people at the [television] networks kept asking. I don't know. How would I know?" In the *Phoenix:* "I have never known who it was. . . . What he said was more important than whether he was Joe from Framingham or Domenic from East Boston."

There were even some bizarre quotes from George McGovern himself and from Christopher Lydon, one of the guys who'd written about the Veteran in 1972 and now had his own nationally distributed public radio talk show originating at WBUR. It didn't matter, they said, whether the Veteran had actually been in Vietnam, whether he was a veteran at all. It didn't matter because what he'd said had turned out to be true.

When Steve Elman read the pieces, he thought that it did matter. Not whether it had been Bozzotto who made the call, and not even if whoever it was who made the call had been lying about his service. Crank calls came in all the time—if this was a fraud, it wouldn't have been the first one. Only one question ate away at him: If this was a put-up job, did Jerry know? Had he set it up with some guy, the way that they did the Hizzoner call on WRKO?

He thought back to 1972, to the Labor Day show and the call. He had sat there in the producer's chair and spoken to the man. "Where are you calling from?"

"East Boston."

"Hold on, sir. We'll get to you soon," or something like that. There was absolutely nothing out of the ordinary about that call. The Veteran had taken his chances and dialed in on the regular 254-5678 number, probably getting a busy signal ten or twelve times, like everyone else did. Elman hadn't given the man preference. Jerry took his call in sequence, just like everyone else's. Jerry had asked him the kinds of questions he would have asked anyone—not leading questions, not prompting questions. Yes, the man's statement did sound prepared, but it sounded prepared the way a guy would prepare something like a confession, something he wanted to get off his conscience. That's why it was so powerful. It just happened.

He didn't think Jerry knew, and that was enough. Until we came to write this book.

Elman was reviewing his own notes on those shows from 1972 and 1973, the notes that WBZ had compelled him to make and he had kept in a folder in the back of a file cabinet, God knows why, except that he had learned so much from Jerry Williams, had cared so much about the master on the other side of the glass. He didn't expect to see Domenic Bozzotto's name, but there it was, in a listing for April 23, 1973, months after the Veteran had made his call: "Tonight's show was given over to a discussion of the return of the Vietnam-era veteran—the problems he faces, and the response of government to him. Charles Sweeney, of the Veterans' Administration, spoke with Domenic Bozzotto and David Arthur, veterans from Suffolk University; Jim Mayer, the president of the National Association of Concerned Veterans; John Kerry, of VVAW; and Victor de Fazio, a psychologist who works with veterans."

He tried to remember—he thought that was a show that had been set up through VVAW, and they had selected the guys who came to the studio. There was no reason for the kid producer to doubt that they were the veterans they said they were. But if Bozzotto had really been discharged in 1965, what was he doing there? Had he been passing himself off as a Vietnam vet to others? *Did Jerry have something to do with his being there?*

And then Elman read through the Mike Barnicle column of January 21, 1974. He was struck by the distinctive way the thoughts were expressed. He wondered: Could this have been a second call from the Veteran? Alan Tolz had carefully archived the tape and had even posted it on the memorial Web site, jerrywilliams.org. Elman listened. It sure sounded like the Veteran, in phrasing, in cadence, right down to "That's all I have t' say." Could this have been a fiction? Was the Veteran's call a fiction? *Did Jerry know?*

We talked about it. In every conversation either of us had had with Jerry— right up to his last for-the-record interviews in 2002, he never said anything to indicate that the Vietnam Veteran's call was a setup. He didn't defend the authenticity of the call. That would have been presumptuous—impossible, in fact. But he said he never had reason to believe the call was a fraud and that he did not try to deceive anyone. To this day, we believe him.

But we have to ask the questions. It wouldn't be fair to Jerry Williams *not* to ask the questions. *He* would have asked the questions if it was anyone else on the hot seat.

Was Jerry overeager to promote himself and the show by making copies of the tapes and giving them out when there was no way for him to verify the identities of the callers or the truth of their stories?

Even if it were proven that these calls were frauds, if he publicized them in good faith, would that be a breach of faith with his audience?

What if it were proven that the calls were fake and he knew they were fake? And if he still used them, still promoted them, still tried to advance his reputation and the prestige of his show on a foundation that he knew to be false? Would that cast a shadow over all his other great work?

You've read this far. Now you're faced with the contradictions of personality that everyone who knew Jerry Williams faced—that he was a vain man, and a noble one; a selfish man, and a self-sacrificing one; a weak man, and a strong one; a son of a bitch, and Not a Bad Guy.

We've given you the facts, as well as we can. You make the call.

11  DOWN THE DIAL

Who is it that can tell me who I am?
—*Shakespeare*, King Lear *(Act I, Scene IV)*

After nine years of disappointments and gradually waning influence, after going from the top of the market to invisibility, after surviving his wife, making a will, settling an estate, dividing property, and having a live-in girlfriend decide to build her own home next door and move out, an ordinary person might have welcomed a little time for quiet reflection.

Jerry's protégé Paul Benzaquin, who left radio for good in 1993, had chosen that kind of idyllic pasturage—living in a tasteful condo in Duxbury, almost in Jerry's neighborhood, helped by his second wife, Grace, to deal with the inevitable consequences of age—the limited mobility, the limited hearing. When Jerry and Sandy visited the Benzaquins, it was clear that he had come to terms with the closing doors in his life.

But Jerry's nature wouldn't let him rest. He was a musician without an instrument, a sculptor without a mallet. Fighting anger and depression and fear, he called everyone—old friends and new, contacts and acquaintances. How could he get back on the air?

One of the many celebrities and near celebrities who tried talk in the wake of the great wave of syndication was Dick Cavett. He'd gotten an independent deal to do a morning radio talk show out of New York in 1999, just a few months after Jerry lost his weekends at WRKO. The show cleared in enough markets—not in New York itself, but the producers were hopeful that it would get on the air there eventually. It looked like there was at least a chance that it would make a little money. The problem was Cavett's personality. Whether it was the stress and schedule of the show itself, his own emotional instability, or personal factors in his life, Cavett crumbled. He needed to take some time off after just a few weeks, when it was crucial that the show build momentum. So Jerry Williams came to the rescue.

Jerry promised the producers that he'd move to New York and carry the ball until Cavett was ready to come back. And if Dick never came back? Well, Jerry was ready to do it permanently. He had that impressive track record, he was available, he made a deal that was mutually convenient, and he went to New York.

But his body couldn't take it. He was seventy-five years old, living in hotels during the week, commuting back to Marshfield on the weekends, getting up at an ungodly hour, feeling half dead by dinner time. Not to mention his feet, his back, the occasional mini-blackouts.

He got in touch with the ever-faithful John Rosica, the guy who had produced those Philly shows back in 1956, now a very successful figure in the world of public relations. Rosica talked the producers into paying for phone lines to New York from WATD, that little station near Jerry's home where Eve had worked for a while. After a couple of weeks, the New York guys said it was getting too expensive, new markets weren't coming on, maybe they should all take a break and think about it.

So Jerry waited. But then he found out they were trying to keep the Cavett show alive with reruns of the shows he'd done—this was a morning show dealing with controversial issues, discussing what's happening that day in the news, and the producers were running shows with Jerry Williams talking about outdated stuff as if it was just happening. Not a great idea. Besides, reruns weren't part of Jerry's deal—he wasn't getting paid for the rebroadcasts. So Jerry brought in Rosica as sergeant-at-arms. No more reruns, no more show. At least Jerry got a few bucks for the weeks he was on tape.

A few months later a radio entrepreneur named Alex Langer, who'd owned a suburban station west of Boston for more than ten years, had the idea to reconstitute this weak signal as a talk station and revive the old WMEX call letters. He signed Gene Burns, Marjorie Clapprood, Upton Bell, a veteran sports talker who had also proved he could do issue-oriented stuff, and Jerry. Maybe things were looking up again.

And something sweet happened in his family life as well—his daughter Andi found a mate. In October 1999 Jerry went to Key West for the ceremony. He was too skittish to take a small plane from Miami, so he rented a limousine and drove himself, Sandy, and Andi out along Route 1, even though he was feeling rotten. He paid for the ceremony aboard a catamaran at sunset. He paid for the dinner just before. He gave Andi away, with tears in his eyes.

On January 24, 2000, the new WMEX hit the air, just a couple of notches away from WBZ's monster signal.

Even people who really wanted to hear Jerry Williams again, fifteen months after he'd done his last WRKO show, had to *work* to tune in that weak little station. Those who did got a shock.

What had happened to Jerry Williams's voice? The man on 1060 AM sounded as if he couldn't get enough air into his lungs. That bracing bitter ale that had invigorated Boston for more than forty years had been watered down into light beer. What was worse was the obvious decay of the razor-sharp intellect, the perfect radio reflexes, the brilliant control of verbal space. People who knew his work in the great days said, "Poor Jerry." After fewer than five shows, he was gone.

What happened between the Cavett show and the new WMEX was the first serious rebellion of Jerry's aging body. His new medical condition was diagnosed as kidney disease. With the help of Dr. Winfred Williams, a nephrologist at Massachusetts General Hospital, he learned it was something he could live with and control if he took his medication.

And the mini-blackouts, those transient ischemic attacks, continued, more frequently and more severely. Jerry continued to call them migraines, but these weren't like the migraines you usually hear about. Sandy was particularly alarmed one day when they were having dinner at Pizzeria Uno. One second Jerry was talking, complaining about his pains or commenting on the Al Gore–George Bush presidential campaign or something. Then—complete blankness on his face. Nobody home in his eyes. Seconds went by. In those moments, she wondered if he was having a stroke. Then he was back, as cantankerous as ever, but not quite able to walk steadily or control his hands.

Sandy began checking in with Jerry every day. Just to make sure.

She told him she thought he shouldn't drive. As if Jerry Williams would ever give up his car or his independence or his ability to go see Nancy Cook when he wanted to. Finally, Sandy told him she wouldn't ride with him if he was driving, just as a matter of self-preservation. Of course, she was right. In the space of a few months, he totaled his Jaguar by driving it into the side of a tollbooth and then severely damaged his Mercedes. But he still kept driving.

Of his three daughters, Jerry had most contact with Eve. He was proud of her for making a go of a career in broadcasting, working now as Taylor Morgan, known for playing Today's Hits on Mix 102.3 in South Florida. But he rarely told her so directly. And Eve never shared with him her disenchantment with the corporate types who called the shots at her station. Father and daughter talked around the personal, concentrating on the mundane: "Eve, my back is killing me. I keep thinking I should come down to Florida. Whattaya think? But I love this house. I wanna die in this house."

There was an occasional call to Susan—smart, practical, with a graduate degree, a teaching career, husband, and four kids.

And there was a post-wedding set-to with Andi, who'd been pretty successful in her ice cream business until she had to shut down for a few months while she relocated it. He turned down her pleas for a loan until Sue suggested she mention Nancy Cook and Sandy acidly reminded him it was high time that he start making gifts to all three daughters. Even with that extra $10,000, Andi had to tell him a year later that it wasn't working and she had to sell Sprinkles.

He continued to speak with friends and peers in the business, still fantasizing about ways he could have an influence. When he began to understand the nature of the Internet and the sites that were making money, he called Alan Tolz. "Alan! Who owns 'tits.com'? We should try to control it! That's gonna be worth something!" When he became aware of the significance of the Indian casinos in Connecticut, he called Clark Smidt. "Clark! Think about the idea of a radio station right there in the casino! You could put a booth in the middle of the action, where everyone could see the guy on the air."

A few months into 2001, after the Supreme Court elected George W. Bush and Republicans consolidated their control of both houses of Congress, Jerry had a series of attacks that were more serious than anything he had experienced previously. Sandy had him taken to South Shore Hospital in Weymouth, a few miles north of Marshfield, where she was working in the emergency room. Doctors couldn't diagnose the attacks as strokes, but he was left disoriented and inarticulate.

As she always did when Jerry's health problems were more than routine, Sandy called Susan first, and then the other kids. When she arrived, Susan could see how much this episode had cut into her father's mental acuity. She began to be worried about his finances—and the provisions he'd made for her kids. She was accustomed to his stinginess, but he hadn't followed through on the yearly payments to those trusts he'd set up. Maybe some provisions ought to be made. She spoke with Jerry's lawyer, Ed Jager—should they arrange for a transfer of funds out of one of his accounts? To pay his bills, and to take care of things if he should take a turn for the worse?

Somehow Jerry found out. That brought him back to reality fast. He was livid, raging. "That's my money, Sue, and you keep your hands *off* it. I earned it. It's *mine*. End of story."

Sue could have said that she was just trying to look out for him, but what was the point? Since he missed the births of his second, third, fourth grandchildren—didn't even send a gift, didn't even send a *card*—she knew he was what he was and there was no point in arguing. But she sure wasn't going to stay around and nurse him through physical therapy. She had four kids to take care of and she wasn't feeling very charitable toward the old man.

Eve discussed the problem with Sue. One of the girls should really live with Jerry until he got back on his feet. Eve needed a break from the bosses at Mix 102.3 anyway, so she volunteered to get a leave of absence and move to Marshfield for a few months.

During April, May, and June that year, Eve Williams lived with her father for the first time since she'd been in high school. She got him settled, got him a wheelchair, took him to and from PT and medical appointments. She got to live with the vast quantity of stuff Jerry had accumulated over a lifetime of radio and antiques collecting. She even found his stash—can you believe it?—and wondered how many years Jerry had been toking. But there was no bonding, no intimate talk.

The time Eve had with Jerry allowed her to think about what she was doing, about the fact that she hated the management at the Mix and wasn't looking forward to going back. She rethought an old fantasy—an idea inspired by the success of Pat Whitley's restaurant program on WRKO, which she'd heard when she was working in New England almost ten years before. South Florida had a thriving restaurant scene, and it also had an active entertainment industry, with big-name stars playing the hotels and appearing in shows. Eve thought there was a way to refashion Whitley's concept for her market and her ambitions. She liked the idea of owning her own radio show and renting the time for it, so she could be her own program director. But she didn't want to do what Whitley did, taking call after call about meal after meal in restaurant after restaurant, interrupted only by ads for restaurants.

Instead, she wanted to do a real interview show, focusing on nightlife and great places to dine. In effect, she wanted to turn the one aspect of Jerry's work that had always appealed to her—schmoozing with the stars—into a business. She had carried all of her computer equipment with her to Jerry's house, and she began churning out drafts, proposals, sales packages, all the paperwork needed to get the idea going. How many restaurants and venues and concert producers were there in the area? How many of them would she need as advertisers? How much would it cost? What were reasonable spot rates? How much did stations in South Florida charge to rent time?

One of the stations she called had a three-hour block available on Saturdays—a perfect time for the concept. She ran the numbers. She had enough to float things for a short time if she could get a few advertisers to bite right away.

She talked about it with Jerry. He wasn't very excited about it—hey, is this radio or just plain shilling?—but he didn't tell her to forget about it, either. That was something like a standing ovation compared to his usual reaction.

As she worked, Jerry made progress with his mobility, and his mind cleared to the point where he was almost his old kvetchy self. Eve decided to test his strength and celebrate a bit by taking him to dinner and a Red Sox game at Fenway Park with her boyfriend and one of Jerry's buddies from Marshfield.

They started at the good old No-Name Restaurant, where the Contos family fussed over Jerry as they always had, making him feel very welcome. Then it was a cab ride to Fenway, just a few feet away from the building where he'd done his first shows in Boston forty-four years earlier. As they helped Jerry out of the cab, another man jumped in. They recognized him, as anyone in Boston would—it was Bob Lobel, one of the area's best-known sportscasters, a guy whom Jerry had known for years. But Lobel didn't know this old man hobbling along on the sidewalk, cushioned from the crowd by three others, and he sped away without a hello.

Eve couldn't know that the demand for tickets at Fenway made getting seats for games difficult at best, and what was available certainly wasn't the pick of the park. She also didn't know about the Sox's policy of providing special seating for people with handicaps. So the seats she had bought were far up in the grandstand, a very challenging trek for a man who'd had something like a stroke. And they were at the end of a row, where Jerry constantly had to maneuver himself out of the way of people on the inside making the pilgrimage to the stands for hot dogs, popcorn, and beer. By the time they got home, it was clear that Jerry Williams would never be going to a baseball game again.

As Eve's leave of absence came to an end, she and Sandy agreed that they had to have someone living in the house with Jerry. Sandy had a beautiful new home, and she wasn't about to become a full-time nurse. So the two of them interviewed medical attendants, and they hired a man from the Philippines named Francisco, who joined Jerry's household as a live-in right-hand man.

Maybe because of the damage from the attacks, and maybe because he just never wanted to try that hard, Jerry could never recall Francisco's name. He made a joke out of it, always calling him "José." Visitors didn't always understand. Sometimes it seemed that Jerry was masking his own failing faculties. Sometimes it looked as though he was parodying the way that Anglos depersonalized Latino help. Sometimes it just looked like he didn't care.

When Eve left, Sandy took over managing Jerry's household expenses, writing the checks out of a household account that the two women convinced Jerry to set up. But he still insisted that the bulk of his money remain under his sole control.

On September 11, 2001, Jerry Williams was not on the air. He had no audience with whom he could share his ideas and impressions. He watched the tube and listened to others talk about it and made phone calls to people he knew.

The attacks that day disrupted airline service around the country. It brought South Florida tourist traffic to a standstill and stopped Eve Williams's business plan dead. Without tourists in South Florida, there would be little if any restaurant traffic. Without restaurant traffic or concert sales, there would be precious little money in her advertising niche. Eve was looking at almost a thousand dollars a week in overhead and no source to offset it.

The worst of it was that she had hit on a second great idea: have restaurateurs and other businesses pay for ads on her show with gift certificates rather than cash—and then sell those gift certificates at a discount through her own Web site. She knew that the radio show and the Web site together would be a dynamite combination. All she needed was money—to tide her through the post-9/11 downturn and invest in building the site.

But no bank would fund the notion. So she turned to Dad with the full court press—the business plan, the pleading, the tears. Finally, wonder of wonders, he said he'd lend her $25,000.

It was the best investment Jerry Williams ever made. By April 2002 the Web site was launched, the radio show was thriving, and Eve Williams was a genuine businesswoman. Today the TV show that grew from her radio program, and her Web site, SouthFloridaDines.com, have made her (that is, "Taylor Morgan") a pretty important person in food and entertainment in the Palm Beach area.

Jerry's medical condition went from okay to bad to okay again in those six months. He was well enough to travel to Florida and look at condos, even to put some money down on one. But then he went downhill again—he even had to be put into a rehab facility in the Palm Beach area that appalled his daughters and frightened him. As soon as he was well enough, he went back to Marshfield.

The medical problems piled up—his fragile mobility, his pains, the mental lapses. There were speculations rather than positive diagnoses—Parkinson's disease? Fibromyalgia? Some kind of tumor?

Alan Tolz watched Jerry's decline with alarm. Although the two of them had joked about an autobiography for years, Jerry said he could never write the damn thing. From time to time, when Alan visited the barn on the Marshfield property and noted the papers and tapes and memorabilia alternately getting soaked and drying out, Jerry would allow him to cart things away "just to keep them safe." In January 2002 Tolz arranged for WBZ's overnight host, Jordan

Rich, to conduct two long interviews at Jerry's home. Tolz sketched out areas of Jerry's life in which he knew there were great stories to tell, and he asked Rich to probe for some of the hidden details.

Even though he knew this was something of a last testament, Jerry responded to the interview project with enthusiasm. Although his voice was weaker, his recall was pretty steady. There were moments when he conflated events or confused names, but the process activated the performer in him one more time. Once he got warmed up, he even took Rich to the woodshed for his interviewing technique.

They recorded two interviews and reviewed some of Jerry's airchecks and videotapes. Then Jerry fell off his bed and broke a couple vertebrae. Back to the hospital.

Of course, Susan was the first daughter to hear about the new trouble. One day while she was visiting, Jerry told her that Nancy Cook was on her way up. Wait a minute, Dad. Nancy Cook?

Susan knew about Nancy. She understood that Jerry had paid for her apartment on occasion, had bought her gifts, had given her loans to tide her over. Now this woman was here at the hospital? She wasn't trying to get more money out of Jerry, was she?

Jerry tried to be conciliatory. "Oh, she's just a needy person. She just needs some help. I do what I can for her every once in a while."

In a second, reasonable, practical Susan burst into flame. "What are you *talking* about, Dad? Where were you when *I* needed help? I can't understand why you think it's okay to help out this girl when you could be helping your children, your grandchildren. I've got $25,000 in student loans. I had trouble with my taxes, and I *asked* you for help, and you wouldn't even look at me. I wanted to buy a house and needed some help with the down payment, and you couldn't be bothered. I've got four kids, and you promised to put some of your money away for them, but you haven't done it. With you, it's always 'my money, my money.' Until someone you barely know, someone who's probably using you, taps you on the shoulder and asks for a little cash. And you think I'm supposed to *sit* here and be *nice* when this Nancy visits you? Not while I'm in here. I don't want to see her." She let it rip.

Jerry didn't say anything. He sat on the edge of the hospital bed, listening, shocked. Susan cooled off in a few minutes and left.

The word got around about Jerry Williams. Hey, the guy is on his last legs. If you're going to do one of those lion-in-winter features, now's the time to do it.

So Mark Pothier of the *Globe* went to Marshfield and interviewed Jerry for a piece that ultimately appeared in the June 16, 2002, Sunday magazine. It was very good work. Pothier covered the whole career, even if he didn't recognize where Jerry's recall was a little shaky. Again, for the last time in print, there is one of those old lies—that he supposedly started out at WMCA in New York in 1946. Jerry says he was on Nixon's enemies list, though he just *wanted* to be on it. Jerry remembers a year in Hartford—maybe those sixty days *seemed* like a year.

One thing shines through the reminiscences: Jerry's not done, he still misses radio, still wants another shot. Even though the body is crumbling, the will still burns inside him.

Pothier also talked to, and got great quotes from, Paul Benzaquin, David Brudnoy, Gene Burns, Bob Katzen, Paul Yovino, Barbara Anderson, and Dan Rea, a newsman and former talk host. He got a "Jerry who?" comment from the general counsel of Entercom, the folks who acquired WRKO just after Jerry got the boot. And he interviewed Howie Carr. Howie put it on the line when Pothier asked him how he felt about the charge that he drove Jerry from the catbird seat at WRKO: "My name's Howie Carr, not Father Time."

But Lane Turner's first photograph of Jerry was the most stunning single thing in the *Boston Globe Magazine* on that Sunday. It took up a full page, in color, with Jerry centered in the rustic clutter of the Marshfield house—dark walls of rough old wood, tufted leather couch, greenery through the window, an old ship's wheel mounted on the wall. He's seated behind one of his beautiful vintage radios, AM only (of course), one knob missing, the pointer tuned to around 1030, his old WBZ home. He's wearing a snappy blue blazer, khaki pants, a sharp striped shirt. His body is slumped a little forward, maybe to disguise the loose skin around his neck. There's no sign of the wheelchair— a brave front with an eye to the image, just like FDR. But above it all is the face of age, of decay. The hair is past steel-gray now, not quite white, but on its way. One side of the mouth is creased in a hint of the old jocular grin, some character creeping through the wrinkles. But the other side is flat, empty, shockingly free of passion or even a feeling of involvement in the moment. In the eyes, a vacant wistfulness. Thousands of people looked at him and gasped: Jesus, Jerry, what's *happened* to you?

That was the last major feature on Jerry Williams published during his lifetime.

It got Alex Canavan thinking. Alex's station, WROL, was by no means one of the monsters of the dial, but he made a good living renting out time and doing a little of his own programming. He had a solid dial position—950—and pretty good coverage. Jerry, are you strong enough to come to the Quincy studios and get back on the air? How about an hour a day—2:00 to 3:00 P.M.? On

*Jerry Williams in his Marshfield,
Massachusetts, home, 2002.*

Fridays, we might even do something live from Tecce's. You can just hear Jerry's reply: "Well, Alex, I might be able to work it in—if the money's right."

Incredibly, he did it. On Monday, December 2, 2002, he started the new show, sitting in a wheelchair, from a studio in an apartment complex called Marina Bay, not too far from his old apartment in Quincy. The voice was as thin as his hair.

Canavan knew right away that it wasn't going to last. Over the next few months, Jerry was on the air less and less. By February, the ROL experiment was done.

But even that wasn't the last hurrah. The folks at WRKO finally did the right thing and invited Jerry back for a farewell appearance on Saturday, March 1. A raft of former colleagues and producers paid tribute. No one said it, but everyone knew: it won't be long now.

In late March Sandy Nagro got a call from Francisco while she was on duty at South Shore Hospital. "He's not talking. He just won't say anything."

"Get him in here."

She went down to the emergency room when he arrived in the ambulance. "What's up?"

Nothing.

She watched as Francisco got him settled, nurses fussed. Finally, they were alone. Jerry turned over.

"I'm only faking."

Sandy said, "What?"

"I'm only faking."

Sandy was baffled. What did this mean? "Well, that's great. This is a fun thing to be doing. Are you kidding?"

Slowly, he began to respond to other people. Sandy wondered: Could he possibly be putting it on? Or was he so confused that he only *thought* he was faking? He seemed disconnected, very seriously damaged. She got on the phone to Jeanine Graf. "This is it. This is the end of it. I just know it is."

When Jerry was moved up to his own room at South Shore, Sandy kept a vigil. He *did* seem to be improving. He could carry on conversations, sort of.

After one of her updates to Jeanine, she came back to the room and was stunned to find Nancy Cook there, in a full-length animal print coat. How did she know he was here? Jerry apparently was still capable of remembering phone numbers and even making some mischief.

A few days later the hospital discharged him and he went back to Marshfield. But something had misfired in his brain. He was angry now, unpredictable. He attempted to punch Francisco. When Sandy heard that, she knew that he needed a level of care beyond what was available at South Shore Hospital. "Francisco, call an ambulance and have him taken to Mass General."

Then she called Dr. Winfred Williams, the nephrologist who had guided Jerry through his kidney problems. "Jerry's coming in. Will you have a look at him?"

When he arrived, Jerry's behavior was problematic enough for the Mass General doctors to put him on an anti-anxiety drug called Ativan, which left him nearly unconscious. When Sandy got there, she knew it was time to call Susan again.

Susan got to Boston on April 2, 2003. Soon after she got to the hospital, Jerry's blood pressure dropped so fast that the hospital staff thought he might die then and there. "Mrs. Hobson, you're the designated health care proxy. We need your guidance. We can stabilize his blood pressure with medication, but we don't know how long he will last. Or perhaps you think we should let him go?"

Susan was unprepared for this. "I can't be the one to say this on my own. I have to talk to my sisters. Can you keep him going until they get here?"

"We'll do our best."

Eve and Andi were summoned. By the time they arrived, Jerry had been moved to a semiprivate room and his medications were shifted. Morphine for the pain. He regained consciousness, but it was as if his personality had been shattered like a great pane of glass. He may not have understood where he was. He may not have recognized his daughters. He may have been terrified. But whatever the cause, he was possessed with fury when he saw his daughters or Sandy. He screamed at Susan, "Get outta my face, you bitch!" He called Sandy the Devil. He reduced them to tears.

And yet, when Jeanine Graf came to visit, she saw him interact with Dr. Williams, calling him "My buddy." And he told one of the attendants that he was faking it all.

They shifted his meds again, and he became quieter. From time to time he would show that he was in pain, and the girls let the staff know. But there were no conversations, no rational exchanges of words. The unconscious periods became longer.

The three daughters and Sandy Nagro sat through a grim briefing from one of the social workers in the hospital. "Your father has some serious problems. We're not sure of the cause. He is seriously impaired right now. He may never regain his full mental capacity. He may take a turn for the worse. You have a number of options."

The three daughters talked and thought.

A few days into April, they sat down with Sandy. Susan took the lead. They had decided that Jerry would not want to have his life prolonged like this. This is the kind of situation that he feared. He wouldn't want to be kept alive if his mind was damaged. He was obviously suffering. They had decided to withdraw food and water and let him die.

Sandy was stunned. She said she'd spoken to Dr. Williams. He thought it was possible to bring Jerry back part of the way, to give him a reasonable life even if he could never be fully himself again. "You can't do that. It's criminal."

Susan was resolute. "He wouldn't want it. We have to try to do what we think he would want. Eve and Andi agree with me on this."

Sandy couldn't accept it, but they were his daughters. She thought she might be able to turn things around if they all had some time to think.

Susan told the hospital personnel of the family's decision, and Jerry stopped receiving food and liquids.

It lasted an agonizingly long time.

Tolz and Jeanine Graf made the pilgrimage to see him. They felt that he might have recognized them, because they saw tears come from his eyes. But there were no words from the Dean.

Susan continued to talk with Dr. Williams and with Sandy and with her sisters. Susan was convinced they'd done the right thing. Not one of them had had a word of sensible dialogue with Jerry. It would be cruel to keep him alive with only a small piece of his mind still working.

Jerry was transferred to Phillips House at Mass General, a hospice for the dying. When Sandy was alone with him, she brought in a little Jell-O or applesauce and put it on his lips. She moistened a stick with a sponge on the end of it and gave him as much fluid as she could. He often bit down on the stick, which she thought showed his hunger or his thirst or his frustration. If someone came near his mouth, he'd sometimes try to bite the person's hands.

Sandy agonized when Jerry's breath rasped and rattled in his parched throat. When he would cough or gag, she would get into the bed and try to prop him up, to ease what he was going through.

It was as if everything in his mind had died but his will.

Dr. Williams consulted with them regularly. He and the other medical staff were amazed at how tough he was. After more than a week of watching and waiting, he reported that they were near the point of no return. His kidneys were failing, and if they continued to withhold fluids, the result would be inevitable.

Susan chose to go forward. The stress of being away from her family for three weeks and the weight of the decision left her desperate and tortured. One day when she was alone in the room with him, she screamed, "Just go! Just go! I gotta go home!" Jerry did not respond.

Each of them said her good-byes. Jerry did not react.

During the last several days, Jerry was comatose. Sandy had resigned herself to his death, and a kind of gallows humor set in. She tried teaching the girls to knit. They made a hat for Jerry, then a scarf. They put the things they made on his unresponsive body. They put sunglasses on him. It was horrible, and it was funny. God knows, they all needed to laugh.

On April 29, 2003, Gerald Jacoby died at Massachusetts General Hospital. Jerry Williams had died many days before.

Rod Fritz, the news director of WRKO, made the announcement to the media. The tributes and the obits appeared. Howie Carr's was among the first: "Jerry Williams invented me, at least my talk-radio persona. When Jerry started reading my columns on the air, I lived in Somerville, and now I live in Wellesley. What can I say now to Jerry except, thanks pal."

Dean Johnson in the *Herald*. Mark Pothier and Ralph Ranalli in the *Globe*. Dan Kennedy in the *Phoenix*. Barbara Anderson, in her column in the *Salem News*. Brudnoy, quoted frequently.

A cartoon by Dave Granlund in the *Metrowest Daily News* shows a carica-ture of Jerry driving a car in the clouds, with "Jerry Williams" on the driver's side door and "Mr. Radio" on the license plate. The car is passing a sign that says, "Highway to Heaven. Seatbelts Mandatory." Jerry grimaces. In a thought balloon over his head: "Figures!"

On May 1 Jerry had his wake. He had joked while he was on WRKO that he wanted his body to be laid out with bowls of chips and dip so that visitors would have something to eat while they looked at him. He said he even want-ed to have dip in his own mouth. It wasn't like that.

Susan turned to their old family friends the Thomases, who ran funeral homes in Milton and in Hyde Park. By now, the next generation had taken over operating the Hyde Park home, and Susan was assured they would do everything they could to make Jerry's send-off memorable.

Sandy and Andi assembled photos and memorabilia from his home. They asked the Thomases to display them all around the funeral parlor, so people would see memories everywhere they went. Photos of the family, Jerry's awards, reproductions of the Radio Hall of Fame program, copies of "Daisies."

The services were private, and some who read the notices in the paper thought that the wake would be private as well. Maybe that was the reason so few people came to honor the Dean.

Hyde Park is an urban neighborhood. Susan and Eve and Andi never expected the Carroll-Thomas Funeral Home to be in this lower-middle-class area, surrounded by small houses and apartment buildings that had seen much better days. It didn't fit with the suburban neighborhoods where Jerry had spent decades, the historic house in Marshfield, the mansions in Milton and Glencoe. Little People live in neighborhoods like Hyde Park. There are places like Hyde Park in Camden, and in Allentown, and in Brooklyn.

Steve Elman expected a crowd of admirers. Instead, he found an eerie calm. Tiny knots of radio folks stood around uncomfortably. The casket was closed. There were big sprays of flowers. Organ music played softly. Eve and Sue and Andi sat up front, hearing over and over: the greatest, changed my career, there's never going to be another one like him. There was something deeply strange about Jerry Williams's wake being so quiet.

Sandy Nagro and Jeanine Graf were there, and Alan Tolz, and Nancy Cook. Sandy and Jeanine were unhappy to see the crucifixes and other Christian symbols that were part of the home's regular decor. They thought Jerry would have wanted a wake with a Jewish character—or at least one that was non-sectarian.

May 2, the day after the wake, was declared Jerry Williams Day in Massachusetts. On May 3, between midnight and 2:00 A.M., the New Hampshire rock formation known as the Old Man of the Mountain crumbled into rubble, affected by days of heavy rain, high winds, and freezing temperatures. Eve Williams and her sisters thought it was a meaningful coincidence. They remembered their antiquing expeditions up north and Jerry's fondness for the Old Man.

A couple of days later, Pat Whitley hosted a four-hour tribute to Jerry on WRKO. On the same day, Boston University announced the establishment of the Jerry Williams Scholarship Fund for Communications.

And then people started to put Jerry into history, to tuck him safely away where he couldn't make any more trouble.

A year later, on April 29, 2004, the anniversary of Jerry's death, there was a memorial dinner that also kicked off fund-raising for the Williams scholarship fund. Eve Williams, Susan Williams Hobson, Andrea Williams, Sandy Nagro, Barbara Anderson, Howie Carr, Tom Ellis, Ted O'Brien, Janet Jeghelian, Steve Elman, Alan Tolz, John Rosica, Dick Syatt, even Bob Ness (Grace, Queen of the Cockamamies) were there. No mayors or governors. No figures of power. Everyone joked about Jerry finally getting his dinner. No one mentioned, or even remembered, that dinner forty-seven years before, his first anniversary as a talk host in Boston, that first taste of glory.

12  THE PERFORMANCE

It's just what you expect, the studio. A big, empty, padded room. There's no decor, unless you think of the radio station's call letters and current promotional slogan as decor. On the floor, gray carpet. Furniture, an institutional table and a few chairs. Mounted on the table, microphones. One of them has the station's name attached to it.

There's a big clock on the wall, with a red hand that jerks from second to second without a sound. There are some black audio speakers on stands, silent. There's other hardware that matters only to the tech guys. A tied-together tangle of cables and wires that flows down through a hole in the carpet and into a space under the floor.

On one side, a big window. A double pane to keep the noise out. In the distance, through the window, there's a guy just sitting down on the business side of a big audio board. He has a stack of tape cartridges and a couple of newspapers and a handful of other things on paper. He throws switches and checks things and clears away stuff, absolutely without a sound. He looks like he's in a wide-screen silent movie.

It's so padded and quiet in the studio that if you clap your hands in there, it doesn't sound like clapping at all. It's a dead-fish-on-newspaper sound. The only thing that matters here—the only thing this room is good for—is the human voice.

Right now, it's lifeless. Three minutes ago it was filled with the voice of Gene Burns, a beautifully resonant sound that microphones love. Shining mahogany for the ears. Gene's shift is over. Through two sets of doors—again, to keep the noise out—he's gone down the hall.

There's another studio where things are alive for these five minutes, where Deborah Robi is reading the hourly news.

That doesn't matter in here. It only matters that it's 2:04:15 P.M. on Tuesday, June 11, 1985, and Jerry Williams is not in this room.

Fifteen seconds later, Jerry moves in. He has a denim jacket on, and a cup of water in his hand, newspapers under his arm. He strides to the table, slides into a chair, puts a pair of headphones on. A sound finally comes out of the speakers. It's the WRKO talk radio sounder—a brass fanfare and then a vamp theme on six notes, musically saying "Double-you-R-K-O" without words.

The room is alive now. It's as if Jerry brought an oxygen tank in there with him and opened it full blast. He looks intently through the glass at Alan Tolz, the guy behind the audio board. Jerry jabs his right index finger at the microphone in front of him. A light on the wall goes on.

Jerry does not speak. He looks right at Alan and listens to the theme on the air—wordlessly repeating "Double-you-R-K-O, Double-you-R-K-O, Double-you-R-K-O" over and over. Ten seconds. An eternity in radio. Five more seconds. Alan questions Jerry with his eyebrows. *Are you ever gonna talk?* Six more seconds.

"D'ya ever wonder whether that music has any end to it?" Alan quickly brings the music down in Jerry's first words, but Jerry stops talking again, and he lets another round of "Double-you-R-K-O" go by.

"Let's see if there's an end." He waves, but even before the gesture, Alan brings the music back up. Half of the "Double-you-R-K-O" goes by, and then Jerry discards it with another motion of his hand.

"And who cares?" Alan brings the music out. Jerry launches himself: "Well, hi, hi, hi, hi, hi, hi, hi. Anybody stuck on Route 3 *south?*" His voice picks up energy. It is like a trumpet—sharp, clean, hard-edged.

Alan stares at Jerry, mouths *Who are you?* through the glass.

Jerry looks down at his shirt and mutters. "Let's see—uh—my name tag from camp on there. I'm *Gerald.*" He lets this sink in for a second. "And if you'd like to get on the *air*—" These eight words suddenly inspire him. We're off to the races.

"Hey, what an idea *that* is! Actually, did you ever hear of an idea like this? You pick up a phone, and call, and we put you on the *air!*

"*Hey!*

"What a fantastic idea! . . . I was just sitting here thinking, 'What kind of a show could this *be?*'" He looks at Alan. "D'you have a tape recorder in there?"

Alan stares at him.

"Yes? Good, *good.* What number is there?"

Alan stares at him.

"That's a good number. It coincides with our own *frequency.* Two-six-six-sixty-eight-sixty-eight. You call *me.* See? And then we put you on the *air!*

"And to keep—so that people don't, y'know, do obscene words or anything like that, why—we'll just delay the tape a little bit. . . . This could be something new in *radio!* It's—get me that book!"

Alan gets out of his chair, leaves the control booth, walks down the hall. There is no one at the controls.

Jerry vamps. "*Brecht on Theatre.* I'll tell ya how I got this idea. I was just sitting around one day, not doing anything—talking to myself, and I was saying, 'Myself, we've got to come up with some new ideas in radio.'"

He takes a long, savory pause. "Radio." He lets the word hang in the air.

Then, Alan is silently in the studio with the book and is quickly gone. Jerry's listeners hear the sound of pages turning.

Jerry lets some of the tension in his voice subside. He relaxes his pace just a bit.

"Bertolt Brecht. *On Theatre: The Development of an Aesthetic,* edited and translated by John Willett. You see, this book was written between 1918 and 1932.

"Bertolt Brecht, in an essay called "The Radio as an Apparatus of Communication"—Can you imagine? That's incredible!"

Jerry begins reading. It's obviously something he knows well. He colors Brecht's phrases with the highs and lows of his voice. He drops pauses into the text for dramatic emphasis.

"There was a moment—when technology was advanced enough to produce the radio—and society—was not yet advanced enough to accept it. The radio was then in its first phase of being—a substitute: a substitute for theatre,—opera, —concerts, —lectures, —cafe music, local newspapers and so forth. This was the patient's period of halcyon youth. I am not sure if it is finished yet, but if so then this stripling who needed no certificate of competence to be *born*—will have to start looking—retrospectively for an object in life. Just as a man will begin asking at a certain age, when his first innocence has been lost,—what he is supposed to be doing in the world.

"As for the radio's object,"—This is the important part—Brecht wrote, "I don't think it can consist merely in prettifying public *life.* Nor is radio in my view an adequate means of bringing back cosiness to the home and making family life bearable again.—But quite apart from the dubiousness of its functions, radio," he wrote, "is one-sided—when it should be two-.

"It is *purely* an apparatus for distribution,—for mere sharing out.—So here is a positive suggestion: . . . The radio would be the finest—possible communication apparatus in public life,—a vast network of *pipes*. That is to say,—it *would* be if it knew how to *receive*—as well as to transmit,—how to let the listener *speak* as well as *hear*,—how to bring him into a relationship instead of isolating him.—On this principle—the radio should step out of the supply business—and *organize* its listeners—as—suppliers. Any attempt by the radio to give a truly—public character to public occasions—is a step in the right direction."

Furthermore, in this essay he writes, "Whatever the radio sets out to do it must strive to combat—that lack of consequences which makes such asses— of almost all our public institutions. We have a literature without conse- quences, which not only itself sets out to lead *no*where, but does all it can to neutralize its readers by depicting *each* object and situation—stripped of the consequences to which they lead.—We have educational establishments with- out consequences, working frantically to hand on an education that leads nowhere and has come from nothing. . . .

"As for the technique that needs to be developed—for all such operations, it must follow the prime objective of turning the *audience*—not only into *pupils*—but into teachers. It is the radio's formal task to give these educa- tional operations an interesting turn, i.e., to ensure that these interests— interest people." etcetera, etcetera, etcetera, and he goes on to talk about other things.

Jerry reflects. "Wasn't that *insightful*."

He picks up the earlier train of thought, again becomes the Guy Who's Never Before Thought of Talk Radio: "So I just had that idea. I was just sit- ting around here, thinking about what records to play, and what I could do in my four-hour monologue today. But. If we could just organize our *listeners* to speak out. Give us the benefit of their brainpower."

He suddenly shifts and effortlessly takes the audience with him:

Years back, when I first began in talk radio, would you believe it, there weren't even such things as tape recorders.

There were *wire* recorders. Has anybody ever seen a wire recorder? If you're thirty years old, you probably don't know what I'm talking about. And you couldn't *edit* the wire. So actually, you couldn't *delay* anything on the *air*.

My first radio talk show was done with myself. It was a show called, *What's on Your Mind?* And it was done on WKDN in Camden, New Jersey, from noon to one o'clock. When somebody would call, I would repeat what they had to say, because we weren't allowed under the *rules* to put a live voice on the air.

For a few seconds, Jerry is back on the air in Camden, listening to a phone call and repeating the caller's opinion into the live mic. "Oh, is that what you think about the president? Well, I don't know about that. You, you say that the president is a good fellow. Well, I don't think that he's a good fellow at *all*."

"This went on for forty-five minutes every *day*. Me arguing with myself, and guess what, I got in *more* trouble in *those* days, particularly with my enemies on the religious right. The Reverend Carl McIntire. The American Council of Churches, whose base was in Camden, New Jersey, took a full-page ad in the *Camden Courier-Post* about remarks I had made about him being anti-Catholic."

Then it's back to the Guy Inventing Talk Radio.

Well, anyway, I was just thinking, "Wouldn't it be a wonderful concept just to have people call in. To be suppliers. Instead of just listeners. To be distributors of sound."

What a fantastic idea. This is before television, of course, when Brecht wrote *On Theatre*, and when you wanted to hear symphony or pop music, or drama, or comedy, you would listen to the radio.

Sunday night in my own house was Jack Benny, Phil Harris, Walter Winchell—my father would never miss Walter Winchell, *Manhattan Merry-Go-Round*—that was the Sunday lineup. Edgar Bergen and Charlie McCarthy. And we sat around, believe it or not, *listening* to the *radio*. *The Shadow*. *Little Orphan Annie*. *Chandu the Magician*. *Dick Tracy* was one of my great favorites. *Amos 'n' Andy*.

Amos 'n' Andy was a great program, by the way. Those two comedians were white, and they played Amos and Andy in blackface—at least that's what the publicity and promotion said they were doing—but you see, that was part of the culture at that time. It might have been racist at the time, only we didn't know it was racist at the time. And, of course, you can't go back and change the times.

You can't change Mark Twain. Mark Twain was what he is, what he was, what he did. And you can't change Booth Tarkington either. They were of that time, of that era, of that period. You can't go back and say, "Take out this line," in 1985, of Mark Twain, having to do with somebody saying, "Nigger," in *Tom Sawyer*. Because that's what Tom Sawyer might have said—Why am I explaining something so fundamental as that? Even that, probably, is controversial.

Jerry takes a moment to regroup. "Well, here we are. I've talked for twenty-three minutes. Just had that wonderful idea, of people being able to call in and give their opinions. What a fantastic idea."

Then, another inspiration:

Who were the first talkers in the United States? Jack Eigen, Barry Gray, who's still in New York, alive and well. Probably Sherm [Feller], from this town, was one of the early ones, and I hate to throw myself in that category, but I'm one of the earlier ones, too.

I first started doing talk shows in nineteen—[Jerry fills in the number with a whistle]. I'm not gonna tell. It was a little show called *Are You Kidding?* Fifteen minutes. Inspired by . . . Henry Morgan.

"Who's Henry *Morgan?*" Well, he used to be a regular on *What's My Line?*

"Who—what's *What's My Line?*" Gotta explain *that* to a lot of thirty-year-olds.

Isn't this interesting? Isn't this something you really tuned in for?

It's 2:25. WRKO. Jerry Williams. Our phone numb—Phone number! We have a *phone!* You can call and get on the air. Isn't that incredible. What an idea!

He's picking up energy. He's established the motifs of the hour. Now he has to turn them into something.

Well, then I ventured over to another restaurant in town, it was one of the biggies—Lew Tendler's. Lew Tendler in Philadelphia. Lew was a lightweight champion, or a middleweight champion at one time, and he owned a restaurant in town. And I used to sit at a little podium, sort of in the midst of the front area of the restaurant. And people used to come by me, not knowing what was going on. It was on WIBG. And people used to come right by, come about two inches away from my face, while I was talking and [he adopts a clueless voice] "Whatta ya doin'? I mean, what's goin' on?" And they had no idea why I was there.

Steve Allison—he was from Boston, Revere—was one of the early talkers in the field as well. But all the rest are all my students. They're *all* my students.

I'm going to take a very short intermission—hasn't this been interesting so far? I mean, don'tcha get a kick out of this so far? This may be a four-hour monologue. I'll see when I run out of gas.

Jerry throws his hand at Alan, and the first commercial cluster starts.

Three minutes later, coming out of a recorded commercial, without any transition or introduction, Jerry goes back to Brecht. He shifts the points of emphasis and moves a little faster than before:

"Radio is one-sided—when it should be two-.—It is *purely* an apparatus for distribution,—for mere sharing out.—So here is a positive suggestion: change this apparatus over from distribution to communication. The radio would be the finest possible—communication apparatus in public life,—a vast network of *pipes*. That is to say, it would be—if it knew how to *receive*—as well as to transmit, how to let the listener *speak* as well as hear, how to bring him into a relationship instead of *isolating* him.—On this principle the radio should step—*out* of the supply business—[Jerry taps the table for emphasis] and *organize* its listeners as suppliers.—Any attempt by the radio to give a truly public character—to public *occasions*—is a step in the right direction," Bertolt Brecht wrote, back in the thirties.

Where was I, back with some of the early talkers? Early talkers. In this city, Sherm. He was the earliest of monologists—he's a very funny monologist. 'Course, Jean Shepherd is a fine monologist. [He furrows his brow, and again the listeners can hear it.] Some people are now looking up the book, to find out what is a monologist.

Henry Morgan was early on, *very* early on. His show was called *Here's Morgan,* and it also was on WOR. And he was on at 6:30 in the evening. Just fifteen minutes—it was un*heard* of, *ab*solutely unheard of, for somebody to speak for fifteen minutes only interrupted by a couple of commercials. Henry Morgan is a very bright, satiric, witty, and caustic human being. I wish he would do more of that. He's *still* around.

One of my colleagues, Bob Grant, is in New York. He's still, he's been around for thirty-odd years, kinda right-wing, but fun and entertaining to listen to as well.

When did the two-way business begin? After the wire recordings went *out.* Tape came in in the mid-fifties. In the early days, we used to have to organize the delay by stringing one tape recorder to another tape recorder so that you could have one tape recorder recording and the other tape recorder playing back with a big *loop* in between.

I remember when the delay didn't work one time. It was right here at Fenway Park, in my first excursion into Boston talk radio. I had Daisy Bates on.

Jerry adopts the voice of a puzzled listener:

"Who's Daisy Bates?"

Daisy Bates was head of the Arkansas Little Rock NAACP. And of course, those were the days when Eisenhower was president, and a little black girl wanted to go to school in Little Rock. Daisy Bates, head of the N-double-A-C-P, was my guest. She stayed in the studio for about an hour.

And then somebody called up, and he said, "Certainly enjoyed"—really baited me into it, led me into the trap, and then said, "You had a very interesting show with Miz Bates, and you are a blankety-blank, and she is a muh-muh-mum-mum-mum-mum-mum-mum-mum-mum-mum-mum"—boom! And that tape delay didn't work.

You see, there was an engineer at the time, sitting *way* up above me—you know, they had a big theater organ in the studio—and the engineer was listening to the *delay*, seven or eight seconds later. And when he heard those words *echo through* he sorta looked down at me, an' I looked up at him—a little late, he hit the button. It was the first time that the word with the letter F, I think, was ever heard in Boston radio, and nobody said a word about it. Not a *word*. There wasn't even a re*action* to it. It's just that it was so blatant and so *cruel* that nobody said a word about it. They wanted to ignore it.

He sighs. "Twenty-three minutes before three, WRKO, Jerry Williams here."

It's time for another commercial cluster. Jerry segues into some written ad copy and cues Alan at the end. There are a couple of prerecorded commercials, and Jerry comes out of them with another short reader. Then he's back into it.

Now. Isn't this interesting, so far? This whole idea of being able to talk on the radio using your telephone as a microphone—isn't that fascinating?

Taking a review through radio. Fascinating.

For many years in this city, the *Boston Herald* would refer to it, "On radio last night . . ." And the *Globe* would do the same. I used to have Saltonstalls and the Lodges and the Kennedys on, an' every time, "On radio last night,"—it didn't mention what *station*, much less my own name. Hasn't changed much, we haven't matured. I've been here since '57, twenty-eight years. I've been in and out of the city on several occasions, but I'm back—forever, I think—it still hasn't changed.

Jerry takes a short pause. The Old Veteran of Broadcasting moves away from the mic. The Professor of Media takes a back seat. The Dean of Talk Radio steps aside. He suddenly remembers something that annoys him. The flame goes on.

Today. I met. Two very *interesting*. Well-informed *people*. Or at least I thought they were well informed. How do they remain well informed? They watch TV. And they say, "That was some story about Susan Wornick, wasn't it?"

I say, "Yes, it was." I didn't say a word, didn't give 'em a clue that the program had been involved in it at all.

And they said, "Well, it was quite a story, that he turned himself in. The source turned—"

"Now, wait a minute." (Now I got involved.) "*He* didn't turn himself in. I had Attorney Larry O'Donnell on with me, and he and I were chatting about the whole situation, about Susan Wornick going to jail, and the source *called in!* And Attorney O'Donnell convinced the source—after thirty-six hours of convincing—that he *ought* to turn himself in."

These two *very* astute people said, "*I* didn't know that."

"Well," I said, "how can you *know* it if those show-business people on the TV *news* are hung up with enter*tain*ment?"

It's no longer giving the news—it's entertainment. They all look like *Entertainment Tonight. Smiling.* Paula Zahn is the symbol of Smiling Woman. She's on the weekends, of course. And that Spanish lady—she oughta be glad she's Spanish, or she wouldn't have any work. Liz Gonzales, on the weekend, has got to take a course in just speaking the language as *good* as she can.

'Cause it's all showbiz.

Jerry cranks it up one more notch. "Has nothing to *do* with capa*bil*ity! Or *talent!* Or *truth!* Or the tenets of *jour*nalism!"

He pauses.

Then, slowly and emphatically, he lists the basic questions of journalism, with a half-second pause between each word. "WHO. WHAT. WHERE. WHEN. WHY."

Everywhere within the sound of his voice, WRKO listeners are thinking, Here he goes. Jerry turns up the volume now. His pace is measured, but it is the deliberateness of cold fury.

WHEN did the source call? [Pause] He *called* on that *day.* [Pause] At 5:34 in the *evening.*

WHO was there? [Pause] Larry O'Donnell. [Pause] Attorney. [Pause] Jerry Williams. [Pause] Happened to be hosting the talk show. [Pause] Happened to *be!*

WHERE did this all take *place?* At WRKO [Pause] AM radio, [Pause] 5:34 in the afternoon.

HOW did he get to go to the district attorney? [Pause] *He* didn't turn himself in. [Pause] O'Donnell con*vinced* him, [Pause] after a day and a half of convincing, to turn himself in.

WHY didn't Susan Wornick go to *jail?* Because *he* decided through O'Donnell, and the happenstance meeting on the *radio,* which is the drama of the *story!* How could you *leave* out the *drama* of the *story!?*

For a moment, he eases off the throttle. He muses to himself, "Why does that bug you?"

Then he turns it on full force. "It *bugs* me because it is a *prejudice* against *radio!* And particularly radio *talk* shows!" He keeps going at full volume, but a smile creeps into his voice. "And I never had a DINNER! That's why."

Everyone listening takes a breath and relaxes as he drops back to a normal pace and volume. "When I go to Atlantic City, guess who's going to be in Atlantic City? Red Buttons. And I have a choice between three or four shows in Atlantic City—I chose Red Buttons.

"Who never had a dinner. And *I* never had a dinner either. Well, that's life."

Jerry sees someone from the RKO staff walk into the control room and speak to Alan. This breaks his concentration. He's annoyed.

"What else did this smart guy wanna say when he walked in here? What, what'd he have to say?"

Jerry reads Alan's lips through the glass. "He. Loves. When. You. Do. This."

"Oh. When I just chat about the early days. You wanna bring in your wire recorder? And take this all down?"

Alan activates the studio talkback system. Listeners hear his voice as if it's coming through a Dixie cup and piece of string: "When 're y' gonna write the *book?*"

Jerry chuckles. "I can't write, so how can I write a book? I can dictate, but I can't write."

The break in the action is momentary. Jerry has an assault under way, and he has to get back to business. "But those interested—I don't think people of national *con*sequence would be interested in books by a radio *talk* show host when"—he loads more volume and intensity into each successive word—"he can't even be a *part* of a story that he was a PART OF! How I can I *be* a part of a *story* that I'm not *part* of? Y'see, that kind of thing has angered me all, ALL my professional career."

He backs off, imagining listener reaction. "Somebody'll call in and go [he gives a loud Bronx cheer] PLPLPLPLPLPB!

"Or say: 'Y' jus' tryin' t' get a li'l *press* f' y'self, huh?'

"Well, actually, I just happened to be in the right spot at the right time. All I wanna do is make sure that Chet and Nat [Chet Curtis and Natalie Jacobson, anchors of Boston's Channel 7 local news at the time] are accurate."

The heat comes on again. "When. Who. Let's go back to *school* now, girls and boys. Jeff Rosser, news director of Channel Seven." He addresses Rosser with thick scorn. "Let's go back to journalism school." He pounds the table once. He pauses. He pounds the table four times in quick succession. "Order, order, order. Now, Mr. Rosser, what are the tenets of journalism?"

He speaks very slowly, at first in a hot whisper and then more loudly:

"When.

"Who.

"Why.

"Where."

Then, nearly shouting: "WHAT!"

He pulls back just a bit. "Try, Rosser, get that through your head." He brings the volume back up. "That it didn't happen on an *RKO* talk show. It happened at 5:34 in the afternoon on THIS talk show! And THIS particular talk show is hosted by ME!" He smirks. "Gerald St. John! You might as well mention that, 'cause it—obviously nobody at Channel Seven *knew!*" He speaks very quickly: "And actually, those two people I spoke to today, who were very astute observers of the scene, didn't *know.* They didn't *know,* Jeff! You didn't INFORM them! That's because you're an AMATEUR!"

Jerry lets the word decay in the air for four seconds. It is as if smoke is settling from an explosion. He takes his volume down again. "It *wasn't* a radio talk show. It *wasn't* a WRKO—there are *many* WRKO radio talk shows."

Then, very slowly, he shouts, "WHICH ONE?! WHAT TIME?!

"WHO!

"WHEN!

"WHY.

"WHERE.

"WHAT.

"WHICH!"

Again he pulls back from full volume. "*Those* are the tenets of journalism. I don't pretend to be a journalist. I'm not. But I *know* them."

Again he turns it on: "It would be unfair if I didn't mention that a story was in the *Boston Globe!* Or that it was on Channel *Seven!*"

He pauses for breath.

Y'know who did that to me once before, couple of years back, when I was doing the Boot thing? Remember the Boot thing? We organized a *huge* crowd to go down to Faneuil Hall to march against the Boot. I think the campaign was called "Give Kevin the Boot." Because they were Booting everywhere. And guess what?

Chet came out with their little cameras and *rolled videotape!* I mean, they took yards of videotape and *never* used it, by the way, on the six o'clock news, but they used it on a subsequent *Chronicle* program about a month later, which had to do with Booting and parking in Boston. And there was *all* these people gathered together with all these *signs*, that I had organized, and on WRKO, and guess what? Not a mench—" [he interrupts himself and laughs in frustration] "not a *mention* where this crowd came from!

Or how they were gathered there. Or *why* they were there.

Jerry eases up. He begins to sound resigned to the unfairness of the situation, even though he cannot stop protesting. "*Who*, Chet. *When*, Chet. *Which*, Chet. *Why*, Chet. *Where*, Chet. I am not gonna forget. I'm gonna keep *rubbing it in.* 'Cause this is the only place it can be *rubbed.*

"Why must we have these people smiling through tragedies every weekend? Who can't speak *English.*"

Jerry and his listeners know that the climax of the hour has just passed. It is getting to be time for another cluster of commercials. Jerry takes stock with a time check. "Anyway, it's ten minutes to three. WRKO."

Alan transmits a wordless question. If they are going to take any calls before the news, he will have to speak to a few people off the air, see if anyone can add anything to this hour, and set them up.

Jerry says, "I'll—yes, I'll take some calls *eventually.* You want some calls? You want—these people wanna communicate? Wait a second. Let's see what it says here in the book. 'The radio would be the finest possible communication apparatus in public life, a vast network of pipes. That is to say, it would be if it knew how to re*ceive* as well as to transmit, how to let the listener *speak* as well as hear, how to bring him into a re*lation*ship instead of isolating him'"—he suddenly turns Brecht's words into a challenge and brings up the volume again—"TV *people!*

"Don't *i*solate *him!*

"Don't ask him a dumb question"—he jumps to a "dumb reporter" voice— "'Whadja thinka Claus von Bülow?'"

An equally dumb man-on-the-street reply: "'I t'ink he wuz guilty.'"

"'Thank you very much.' Wow.

"'Claus, how d'ya *feel?*'"

He lets out a whining moan, edging toward a stock-character complainer: "'Ahhhhh—'"

Then a choked, breathless delivery, suggesting a reporter's excitement in a crowd of media people: "'Hady'a *feel,* Claus?'"

Jerry takes a long pause. Then, in his own voice, low and scornfully, he says, "Hady'a *feel*. Hady'a feel."

He returns to his von Bülow impression, morphing him into a borscht-belt kvetcher: "Good. Have a *head*ache. Neveh had a dinneh."

He points at Alan, and another commercial cluster begins.

"Well, it's six minutes before three on Double-you-R-K-O. See, I can say that. Two-six-six-sixty-eight-sixty-eight on Double-you-R-K-O.

"'On this principle the radio should step *out* of the supply business and organize its listeners as suppliers. Any attempt by the radio to give a truly public character to public occasions is a step in the right direction.' Bertolt Brecht *On Theatre*. In the *thirties*."

He closes the book loudly. He sighs loudly. "Ohhh, *dear*. This is all, of course, in my own field. What else could I *talk* about but my own field.

"I could talk about Billy Bulger [the Speaker of the Massachusetts House of Representatives]. Naaah, we wouldn't wanna do *that*. To Billy—the character of Massachusetts politics—the people who reside in the big executive chairs in Washington"—he pauses and darkens his tone—"only a *mirror* of our*selves*."

He pauses for several seconds. Then he issues a call to action in a low, sinister voice: "*Talk back.*" He makes it sound like an act of insurrection.

Again, a breath. Again, a step back.

"I wonder if we could actually put people on the radio. Hmm. It would be an experiment.

"Well, hasn't *this* been an exciting hour. If you missed it, well, I just sorta stepped out—I won't go through the whole thing—but I will come back. And I think I will try an experiment, by putting your *actual* voice on the air, at two-six-six-sixty-eight-sixty-eight. It *can* be done. It's hard for us to do it, but we will *try*. Right here, on greater Boston's only twenty-four-hour talk station."

Alan plays the prerecorded bits that end the hour. A chorus, speaking, says, "Talk Radio Sixty-eight!" and then sings, "Double-you-R-K-O, Boston." A basso announcer's voice says, "An RKO radio station." The news booth is live. A fanfare announces the three o'clock headlines. As Deborah Robi says, "A shield law for Massachusetts now under debate," Alan looks to the next hour and Jerry walks out.

The room is quiet again.

ACKNOWLEDGMENTS & SOURCES

Isn't this all fun? All the radio buffs everywhere are listening in, saying, "Well, where'd he get all that stuff from? Izzat all true?" Sure it's all true. Are you kidding? Could I sit here and lie to you? [A pause.] Yes. I *could* sit here and lie to you. In fact, a guy wrote me a letter today, said I was the biggest liar since Hitler. So, I'm lying. Everything I just said—forget it.
    —*Jerry Williams, August 8, 1989, WRKO, Boston*

Jerry Williams left a tangled web. He may not exactly have practiced to deceive, but he definitely grew accustomed to embellishing the events of his life. Ironically, he also had a compulsive need to reveal himself, sometimes live and on the air. His faithful listeners grew accustomed to the mix of braggadocio and vulnerability. They came to appreciate the contradictions, to embrace them as part of the act, to look for the moments of honesty in the midst of the performance, finally to accept him as he was—and in many cases, love him for what he was.

Space limitations prevent us from including a complete annotation of the text of this book or a comprehensive list of the research sources. Our complete notes and sources for each chapter of the book can be found at www.jerrywilliams.org. This site also will provide updates to the research we have done and additional materials of interest to anyone who wants to know more about Jerry Williams or hear examples of his work.

The Jerry Williams papers are the source of much of the written documentation and nearly all of the aural and visual documentation that underpin our work. They consist primarily of materials collected by Alan Tolz, materials collected by Steve Elman, materials collected by Sandy Nagro, materials donated to Boston University's College of Communication by the Williams family, and the notes and research materials for this book. Steve Elman cataloged these materials and ordered them chronologically before and during the writing of *Burning Up the Air*. The Williams papers are now held by the Gotlieb Archival Research Center at Boston University. We appreciate the assistance provided to us by Professor John J. Schulz of Boston University's College of Communication and Director Vita Paladino of the Gotlieb Center.

Many individuals gave us generous insights into the personality of Jerry Williams and their firsthand knowledge of important aspects of American life in the second half of the twentieth century. We could not have told this story without their help.

Eve Williams, Susan Williams Hobson, Andrea Williams, Sandy Nagro, Jeanine Graf, and Bill Iezzi knew Jerry Williams and Teri Iezzi Williams much more intimately than we did; their memories were invaluable.

Some eminent figures in media gave us their time and courtesy, and they added to our sense of Jerry Williams's place in the business. We deeply appreciate the help provided by Jack Beatty, Paul Benzaquin, Doug Berman, Alex Canavan, Libby Collins, Phil Donahue, Harry Durning, Roger Ebert, Tom Ellis, Jack Gale, Mary Beth Garber, Larry Glick, Michael Harrison, Ben Hoberman, Janet Jeghelian, Larry King, Tom and Ray Magliozzi, Merrill Moore, Tom Moroney, Carol Nashe, Ted O'Brien, Ned Reynolds, Mark Shields, Clark Smidt, Shelley Wagner, Susan Wornick, and especially that of the most generous and gracious of all living American talk radio hosts, Gene Burns.

For their perspective on American political life and Jerry's place in it, we thank two people who knew Jerry well—personally and professionally: former Massachusetts Governor Michael Dukakis and former Massachusetts Treasurer Joseph Malone.

We also thank Jordan Rich of WBZ in Boston for conducting two very significant nonbroadcast interviews with Jerry Williams in 2002.

We hold a special fondness for our fellow producers. Only they and we know what it was like to sit across the glass, day after day or night after night, and watch the amazing performances of Jerry Williams. We remember the late Paul Fanning and the late Herb Howard, who were Jerry's producers in Chicago. We thank and salute John McDonald, Kenny Meyer (who also could tell you quite a few stories about Larry Glick), Jerry Wishnow, Network Ned Foster, Jimmy Myers, Ken Cail, Jack Kirby, Paul Yovino, Chris Ryan Cataneo, Paula O'Connor, Eric Caldwell, Mark Curry, Nancy Shack, and especially Jerry's first producer and lifelong friend, John Rosica. We regret that we were unable to speak to everyone who sat in that chair and heard Jerry yell, "Pay attention in there!"

Professor Wayne Munson, author of the seminal study *All Talk: The Talkshow in Media Culture* (Temple University Press, 1993), was kind to offer his perspective on our views of talk radio. The remarkable and indefatigable radio historian and genealogist Donna Halper, author of *Invisible Stars: A Social History of Women in American Broadcasting* (M. E. Sharpe, 2001), gave us many hours of her very valuable time and provided us with informed observations on Jewish heritage. Eric Kreitzer, a passionate devotee of New York City neighborhoods and public transportation, illuminated some of the history of that city for us. Eric Lobenfeld shared his memories of Brooklyn and of producing Barry Farber's New York radio show in the mid-seventies. Fran Schenk of Erasmus Hall looked up the attendance records of Gerald Jacoby and Herbert Jacoby for us. June Koffi of the Brooklyn Collection located the name and address of the Jacoby family store in Flatbush. Don Rose gave us insight into the Chicago Jerry Williams experienced and the struggle for civil rights in the mid-sixties.

Our first encouragement in this project came from Christopher Grattan, Mary Stohn, and Dean Johnson, and we thank them for their confidence in us.

Our agent, Sidney Kramer of Mews Books, our publisher, Webster Bull of Commonwealth Editions, and our editor, Ann Twombly, brought this project to print. We cannot sufficiently thank them and their associates for their help.

Deborah Tolz and Joanne D'Alcomo were among our first readers. We thank them for their love, support, and great suggestions.

The Internet was our constant companion through the research and writing of this book. We have tried to give credit to all substantive Internet sources on www.jerrywilliams.org. Should any others wish acknowledgment of their work, we would be pleased to provide it there, where the work of this book will continue so long as there is an interest in Jerry and his contributions. To all the obsessive compilers and anonymous authors of the Internet, and to the search masters of Google, we offer a very low bow of gratitude.

One particular Internet site allowed us to provide perspective on Jerry's earnings and the costs he had to pay for various necessities. The online computation site provided by the Minneapolis Federal Reserve Bank (http://minneapolisfed.org/Research/data/us/calc/) allowed us easily to translate prices into current dollars.

We acknowledge the following works that provided valuable background information for *Burning Up the Air*, listed alphabetically by author.

Barker, David C. *Rushed to Judgment.* New York: Columbia University Press, 2002.

Bergmann, Eugene B. *Excelsior, You Fathead! The Art and Enigma of Jean Shepherd.* New York: Applause, 2005.

Branch, Taylor. *At Canaan's Edge.* New York: Simon and Schuster, 2006.

Brudnoy, David. *Life Is Not a Rehearsal.* New York: Doubleday, 1997.

Clarke, Donald. *The Rise and Fall of Popular Music.* New York: St. Martin's Press, 1995.

Elkin, Stanley. *The Dick Gibson Show.* Normal, Ill.: Dalkey Archive, 1998.

Frommer, Myrna Katz, and Harvey Frommer. *It Happened in Brooklyn: An Oral History of Growing Up in the Borough in 1940s, 1950s, and 1960s.* New York: Harcourt Brace, 1993.

Gale, Jack. *Same Time . . . Same Station.* Palm City, Fla.: Gala Publishing, 1999.

Hilliard, Robert L., and Michael C. Keith. *Waves of Rancor: Tuning in the Radical Right.* Armonk, N.Y.: M. E. Sharpe, 1999.

Hilmes, Michele. *Radio Voices: American Broadcasting, 1922–1952.* Minneapolis: University of Minnesota Press, 1997.

Keay, John. *India: A History.* New York: Grove Press, 2001.

Laufer, Peter. *Inside Talk Radio: America's Voice or Just Hot Air?* New York: Birch Lane Press, 1995.

Levin, Murray B. *Talk Radio and the American Dream.* Lexington, Mass.: D. C. Heath, 1987.

Moos, Malcolm, ed. *H. L. Mencken on Politics: A Carnival of Buncombe.* Baltimore: Johns Hopkins University Press, 1996.

Neft, David S., and Richard M. Cohen. *Sports Encyclopedia: Baseball.* New York: St. Martin's Press, 1988.

O'Connor, Thomas H. *Building a New Boston: Politics and Urban Renewal, 1950–1970.* Boston: Northeastern University Press, 1993.

O'Donnell, Lawrence, Jr. *Deadly Force.* New York: William Morrow, 1983.

Reed, Jim. *Everything Imus.* Secaucus, N.J.: Birch Lane Press, 1999.

Salny, Stephen M., and Franz Schulze. *The Country Houses of David Adler.* New York: W. W. Norton, 2001.

Seib, Philip. *Rush Hour: Talk Radio, Politics, and the Rise of Rush Limbaugh.* Fort Worth, Tex.: Summit Group, 1993.

Singer, Arthur J. *Arthur Godfrey: The Adventures of an American Broadcaster.* Jefferson, N.C.: McFarland, 2000.

Ware, Susan. *It's One O'Clock and Here Is Mary Margaret McBride: A Radio Biography.* New York: New York University Press, 2005.

Whitburn, Joel. *Joel Whitburn Presents Daily #1 Hits.* Menomonee Falls, Wisc.: Record Research, 1989.

Wishnow, Jerry. *The Activist.* National Broadcast Association for Community Affairs (private publication), ca. 1984.

X, Malcolm (El-Hajj Malik El-Shabazz), and Alex Haley. *The Autobiography of Malcolm X.* 1966. Rept., New York: Ballantine, 1999.

The following articles, listed in the order of publication, provided major profiles of Jerry Williams or significant information about him.

"Jerry the Jock—Disc, That Is—Finds It Fun." From an unidentified Allentown, Pa., newspaper (probably the *Allentown Morning Call* or *Allentown Evening Chronicle*), ca. March or April 1948.

McMasters, William H. Title unknown (profile of Jerry Williams for unidentified Boston-area publication), ca. 1958.

Giguere, Paul. "Williams a 'Wade-in' Type." *Boston Herald,* January 1960 (specific date unknown).

Williams, Jerry. "The Truth, the Whole Truth . . ." *Brookline Chronicle-Citizen,* October 20, 1960, p. 4.

Windhager, Alice Hale. "Man of Controversy." *TV Radio Mirror,* February 1961, pp. 52–53.

"Fight Show Enlivens Hub Radio." *Boston Traveler,* May 23, 1962, pp. 1, 14.

Bibber, William. "Molesworth, Radio MC in Studio Brawl." *Boston Herald*, May 23, 1962, pp. 1, 53.

UPI. "Accounts Differ on Radio Tiff." From an unidentified Boston evening newspaper, possibly *Boston Transcript*, May 23, 1962.

"Molesworth, Williams Head for the Courts." From an unidentified Boston newspaper, probably *Boston Traveler*, May 24, 1962.

Leone, Loretta. "Sex . . . Witchcraft . . . Civil Rights: You Hear 'em All Now on Hub Radio Talk Programs." *Boston Sunday Herald*, early May 1964, p. 5.

Sullivan, Joseph T. "Radio's Word Warriors: The Talk of the Town." *Boston*, May 1964.

Benzaquin, Paul. "Who Is to Say That Jerry Wasn't Good for Boston?" *Boston Herald*, May 28, 1965.

Coughlin, Frances. "Anti-Semitic Tirade on Air Causes Furor." *Chicago Tribune*, November 9, 1965, p. B8.

Smith, Bob. "Radio's Professional Provocateur," Panorama, *Chicago Daily News*, February 12, 1966.

Gysel, Dean. "WBBM Show Causes a Furor." *Chicago Daily News*, June 20, 1966.

Storck, Dorothy. "Jerry Williams King of Talk." *Chicago Sunday American*, January 27, 1967.

Petersen, Clarence. "Talk, Talk, Talk, Talk, Talk, Talk: Radio's Latest Success Format: What Are Your Thoughts, Joe Blow?" *Chicago Sunday Tribune Magazine*, August 6, 1967, pp. 22–24.

Ebert, Roger. "Demise of Talk Radio Is Graceful, but Sad," *Chicago Sun-Times*, May 6, 1968, p. 47.

Lydon [misprinted "Lydm"], Christopher. "G.I.'s Regret Stuns a M'Govern Rally." *New York Times* (New England ed.), October 13, 1972, p. 20.

["Compiled from Wire Services."] "McGovern Rally Silenced by Taped Story of War." *Boston Herald Traveler and Record American*, October 13, 1972, pp. 1–2.

Oliphant, Thomas. "War Tape Electrifies McGovern Rally." *Boston Globe*, October 13, 1972, pp. 1, 16.

Healy, Robert. "Cry of Horror, Plaint of Shame." *Boston Globe*, October 13, 1972, op-ed.

"'Human Beings Fused Together.'" *Time*, October 23, 1972, p. 34.

Rosenswaike, Jerry. "Jerry Williams: 'What Else Can I Do?' A Few More Words with the Savior of Wilkes-Barre." *Boston Phoenix*, June 26, 1973, "Boston after Dark" section, pp. 1, 5.

Barnicle, Mike. "A Voice from the Soul of Agonized America." *Boston Globe*, January 21, 1974.

Gibbons, Michael. "Bouncing Back." *Boston Phoenix*, September 6, 1977, p. 3.

Grossman, Gary. "If Nobody Else Says It, You Know Jerry Williams Will." *Boston Herald American*, September 2, 1978, p. 9.

Henry, William A., IV. "Talk Show Host Williams, Fired by Station WITS." *Boston Globe*, October 3 or 4, 1978.

Grossman, Gary. "Williams Signs Off WITS, by Choice." *Boston Herald American*, October 5, 1978.

Thomas, Jack. "Williams' Sex Show Doesn't Go." *Boston Globe*, January 22, 1982, pp. 11–12.

O'Brian, Dave. "Raving Radio: Jerry Williams Is the Talkmaster You Love to Hate." *Boston Phoenix*, February 2, 1982, pp. 1, 6, 7, 18.

Quill, Edward. "'Send Kevin to Boot Hill,' Protesters Say." *Boston Globe*, February 24, 1982, p. 18.

McLean, Robert. "WRKO Producer Fired after White Hoax." *Boston Globe*, July 22, 1982.

McLean, Robert. "Fired after Hoax, Producer Will Sue RKO." *Boston Globe*, July 23, 1982.

Jurkowitz, Mark. "The Volatile Voice." *Boston Phoenix*, ca. February 1984.

Zorn, Eric. "Radio Host Fired for TV Antics." *Chicago Tribune*, May 23, 1985.

"Radio Host Who Pulls No Punches Is Dealt a Pair." *Chicago Sun-Times*, May 23, 1985.

Zorn, Eric. "WLS-Ch. 7 Shares Fault for Casting Freiberg as Buffoon." *Chicago Tribune*, May 30, 1985, p. D7.

"Jerry Williams." *This Week* ("A Citizen Group Supplement" to *Brookline Citizen, Allston-Brighton Item, Boston Ledger*), week of September 19, 1985, pp. 2A, 9A.

Murphy, Brian F. "When Jerry Talks, the Pols Shudder." *Lowell Sunday Sun*, March 1, 1987, pp. A1–A2.

Goldman, Martin S. "The Duke's Radio Daze." *This Week* ("A Citizen Group Supplement" to *Brookline Citizen, Allston-Brighton Item, Boston Ledger*), week of April 2, 1987, p. 3A.

Knapp, Caroline. "Born to Yell." *Boston Business*, May–June 1987, pp. 26–30.

Strahinich, John. "Hello, You're on the 'Jerry Williams Show.'" *Boston*, August 1987, pp. 157, 158, 195–207.

McLean, Robert A. "Jerry Williams Gets TV Talk Show." *Boston Globe*, September 18, 1987, p. 68.

McLean, Robert A. "Williams Returns to TV." *Boston Sunday Globe TV Week*, November 1, 1987, p. 2.

McLean, Robert A. "Democrats to Debate on Williams Show." *Boston Globe*, November 20, 1987, p. 50.

Beam, Alex. "Kennedy in Radio Shoutfest: Senator, WRKO's Williams Clash over Murdoch Bill." *Boston Globe*, January 8, 1988, Metro section, p. 1.

Mohl, Bruce. "Senate Science Office Is a Puzzler." *Boston Globe*, February 20, 1988, p. B1.

Boston Globe Spotlight Team (Gerard O'Neill, editor; Christine Chinlund, Dick Lehr, Kevin Cullen, reporters; Mary Elizabeth Knox, researcher). "Image as Dictator, Tales of Revenge Obscure Bulger's Charm" [part 4 of "The Bulger Mystique"]. *Boston Globe*, September 21, 1988.

Ciampa, Gail. "Radio Wars." *Bostonia*, January–February 1989.

Turner, Robert L. "Who's Calling the Shots Here?" *Boston Globe*, February 26, 1989, p. 81.

Parker, Andrea. "Talk Show Host Williams Declares Anti-Tax Stance." *Gloucester Daily Times,* April 13, 1989, p. A1.

Zoglin, Richard. "Bugle Boys of the Airwaves: Talk-Show Hosts Stir Up a Storm of Political Action." *Time,* May 15, 1989.

Bulkeley, William M. "Talk-Show Hosts Agree on One Point: They're the Tops." *Wall Street Journal,* June 15, 1989, pp. A1, A5.

Lehigh, Scot. "'Governors' on the Airwaves Spread Cynicism." *Boston Globe,* November 20, 1989, Metro section, p. 1.

Jesser, Edward F. "Talk-show Duende." *Boston Globe,* December 6, 1989, p. 17.

Krasner, Mike. "Roberts' Shows Hit Troubled Waters." *Worcester Telegram & Gazette,* October 19, 1990, p. C7.

Lehigh, Scot. "This Topic Doesn't Hack It on Radio." *Boston Globe,* April 25, 1991, p. 25.

Lehigh, Scot. "Dial 1-800-HYPOCRITE." *Boston Globe,* April 28, 1991, p. A29.

Wells, Jonathan. "Talk Host's Friend Subpoenaed." *Boston Herald,* February 19, 1992, p. 22.

Wells, Jonathan. "Talk-jock's Galpal Quits Lottery after Being Subpoenaed by Union." *Boston Herald,* February 21, 1992.

Phillips, Frank. "'Hack' Critic Is Said to Seek Job for Friend." *Boston Globe,* March 26, 1992, pp. 27, 32.

Fehrnstrom, Eric. "Malone Evasive on Ties to RKO's Williams." *Boston Herald,* March 27, 1992, p. 5.

Johnson, Dean. "Talk-Show Radio Hosts Convene." *Boston Herald,* June 16, 1992.

Fee, Gayle, and Laura Raposa. "'Mad' Campaign Is Just a Lot of Talk." *Boston Herald,* June 19, 1992, p. 8.

Bickelhaupt, Susan. "Changing Voices at 'RKO, 'HDH." *Boston Globe,* May 7, 1993, p. 25.

Fee, Gayle, and Laura Raposa. "Inside Track" column. *Boston Herald,* July 30, 1993.

Giordano, Al. "Air Offensive." *Boston Phoenix,* December 12, 1993, pp. 32–33, 36–46.

Giordano, Al. "Track-ing the Competition." *Boston Phoenix,* December 12, 1993, p. 36.

Siegel, Ed. "The Right Side of the Dial: The Conservative Voices of AM Radio Are Shouting Down the Opposition." *Boston Globe,* November 3, 1994, p. 63.

DeRosa, Robin. "Tuning In to High-Wattage Talk Show Hosts." *USA Today,* February 1, 1995, p. 7D.

DeRosa, Robin. "The Top 25 Radio Talk Show Hosts of All Time." *Talkers,* February 1995.

Johnson, Dean. "Jerry Williams Feted on Way to Hall of Fame." *Boston Herald,* October 25, 1996, p. 45.

Bickelhaupt, Susan, and Maureen Dezell. "A Change of Arts." *Boston Globe,* ca. January 9, 1997, p. C7.

Johnson, Dean. "'RKO Bumps Jerry Williams to Weekend Duty." *Boston Herald,* January 10, 1997, p. 43.

Carr, Howie. "Radio Legend Steps Down from Young Man's Game." *Boston Herald*, October 9, 1998, p. 16.

Anderson, Barbara. "'The Dean of Talk Radio,' Jerry Williams, Departs WRKO." *CLT&G Update*, www.cltg.org, October 9, 1998.

Braude, Jim. "An Odd Footnote in a Colorful History: In 1972, an Anonymous Call to a Radio Talk Show Made Headlines: The Story behind It Still Resonates." *Boston Sunday Globe*, November 8, 1998, Focus section, p. D1.

Abraham, Yvonne. "Bozzotto Answers Braude: 'I Didn't Make That Call': Dispute Rages over Truth behind 1972 Plea on Vietnam War." *Boston Globe*, November 10, 1998, p. B1.

Kennedy, Dan. "Caller ID: An Intriguing Talk-radio Tale about Truth, History, and Revenge." *Boston Phoenix*, November 19, 1998.

Jurkowitz, Mark. "Talk Radio's Blue Streak." *Boston Globe Magazine*, February 13, 2000.

Pothier, Mark. "Sounding Off Again." *Boston Globe Magazine*, June 16, 2002, pp. 10, 11, 29–33.

Graf, Jeanine. "Jerry Williams the 'Dean' of Talk Radio Signing Off." Unpublished manuscript, in authors' possession, April 2003.

Ray, Bipasha. "Jerry Williams, Dean of Talk Radio in Boston, Dead at 79." Associated Press, April 29, 2003.

Johnson, Dean. "Jerry Williams, Radio Personality" (obituary). *Boston Herald*, April 30, 2003, p. 52.

Pothier, Mark, and Ralph Ranalli. "Talk Radio Innovator Pushed Hard on Issues" (obituary). *Boston Globe*, April 30, 2003, pp. C1, C6.

Carr, Howie. "Jerry Williams: Not a Bad Guy, as Legends Go." *Boston Herald*, April 30, 2003.

Kennedy, Dan. "In Memoriam: Jerry Williams, 1923–2003." *Boston Phoenix*, May 2–8, 2003.

Johnson, Dean. "Tribute Set for Williams." *Boston Herald*, May 2, 2003, p. S34.

Anderson, Barbara. "Jerry Williams Was and Always Will Be 'King of Talk Radio.'" *Salem News*, May 3, 2003.

Johnson, Dean. "Boston Mourns Loss of Media Icon." *Allston-Brighton TAB*, December 17, 2004, p. 22.

Kruh, David. "WKRP in Boston," posted at www.bambinomusical.com/David/Columns.htm# WKRP.

Lauzier, Moe. "Talk Radio, You're On the Air," published at www.blogger.com/profile/06702325576036620835.

In addition, we wish to acknowledge the online resources of North East Radio Watch (and the many columns by Scott Fybush posted there, www.bostonradio.org/nerw/index.html); PoliticalGraveyard.com (http://politicalgraveyard.com/); Alex Cosper's "Boston Radio History," © 2005 Tangent Sunset, posted at www.tangentsunset.com/radioboston.htm; Station Profiles in the archives at BostonRadio.org; and the archives of the *Boston Globe*, the *Boston Herald*, and *Time*.

INDEX

In subentries, GJ refers to Gerald Jacoby, and JW refers to Jerry Williams, following his name change. Page references in *italics* refer to illustrations or material contained in their captions.